A LIFE

Brian Kellow

VIKING

VIKING
Published by the Penguin Group
Penguin Group (USA) Inc., 375 Hudson Street,
New York, New York 10014, U.S.A.
Penguin Group (Canada), 90 Eglinton Avenue East, Suite 700,
Toronto, Ontario, Canada M4P 2Y3 (a division of Pearson Penguin Canada Inc.)
Penguin Books Ltd, 80 Strand, London WC2R 0RL, England
Penguin Ireland, 25 St. Stephen's Green, Dublin 2, Ireland
(a division of Penguin Books Ltd)
Penguin Books Australia Ltd, 250 Camberwell Road, Camberwell,
Victoria 3124, Australia (a division of Pearson Australia Group Pty Ltd)
Penguin Books India Pvt Ltd, 11 Community Centre,
Panchsheel Park, New Delhi–110 017, India
Penguin Group (NZ), 67 Apollo Drive, Rosedale, North Shore 0632,
New Zealand (a division of Pearson New Zealand Ltd)
Penguin Books (South Africa) (Pty) Ltd, 24 Sturdee Avenue,
Rosebank, Johannesburg 2196, South Africa

Penguin Books Ltd, Registered Offices: 80 Strand, London WC2R 0RL, England

First published in 2007 by Viking Penguin, a member of Penguin Group (USA) Inc.

1 3 5 7 9 10 8 6 4 2

Page 316 constitutes an extension to this copyright page.

LIBRARY OF CONGRESS CATALOGING IN PUBLICATION DATA
Kellow, Brian.
Ethel Merman : a life / Brian Kellow.
p. cm.
Includes bibliographical references (p.   ) and index.
1. Merman, Ethel. 2. Singers—United States—Biography. 3. Motion picture
actors and actresses—United States—Biography. I. Title.
ML420.M39K45 2007
782.1'4092—dc22
[B]   2007014646

Printed in the United States of America
Set in Bodoni Book
Designed by Francesca Belanger

For Scott Barnes

I could spend a lifetime thanking him for his support
throughout the writing of this book—and I may.
No writer ever had a more insightful reader,
a more faithful champion, or a more loving spouse.

Too new for an empire, too big for its boots,
With cold steel cables where it might have roots,
With everything to offer and nothing to give,
It's a horrid place to visit but a fine place to live;

—Phyllis McGinley,
"A Kind of Love Letter to New York"

From the beginning of her career, Ethel Merman showed impeccable timing: she came along just when Broadway was ready to embrace her. The first half of the twentieth century was an age of electric, outsize personalities in the world of entertainment, and a great many of them were New York City born. In our era of musical theater, onstage helicopters and falling chandeliers have taken the place of eleven-o'clock numbers, and many new productions emphasize a grandiose physical production rather than the character of an individual performer. Thus, as time passes, we may have to squint a little to get a clear picture of what has come to be known as Broadway's golden age, roughly the 1920s through the 1950s. In the '30s, when Ethel Merman leaped to stardom, musicals were unashamedly star-driven. Al Jolson, Jimmy Durante, Eddie Cantor, Bert Lahr, and Victor Moore belonged to a generation of performers who dominated the productions in which they appeared. Despite the intermittent presence of what came to be known as "integrated" musicals, such as Jerome Kern and P. G. Wodehouse's polished works for the Princess Theatre in 1915 and Kern and Oscar Hammerstein's landmark *Show Boat* in 1927, what people mostly wanted to see was the new Jolson show or the new Cantor show, or the latest edition of the *Ziegfeld Follies*, which might offer several major names for the price of a single ticket.

Broadway's big personalities were the ultimate expressions of how far New York itself had come. From the beginning of the century, the town had been reinventing itself at a feverish pace, throwing off its last vestiges of gentility and becoming tougher, harder, sharper, louder, bigger. As it did so, it was embedding itself in the national consciousness in a more visceral way than it had ever done before. It was becoming for the rest of America what Joan Didion would later call "an infinitely romantic notion, the mysterious nexus of all love and money and power, the shining and perishable dream itself." Ethel Merman's lifelong love of New York stemmed from her memories of the days when the city was at its zenith, filled equally with promise and with rewards.

Major construction abounded in the early years of the twentieth century, when many of what would become New York's most famous landmarks were being born before the eyes of an amazed public. The Pierpont Morgan Library, the Knickerbocker Hotel, the Queensboro and Manhattan bridges, and Gimbel Bros. Department Store were all unveiled in its first decade. The IRT, four years in the making, had opened in 1904, with a five-cent fare. Coney Island's Dreamland amusement park, the Brooklyn Botanic Garden, and the Manhattan Opera House were new. In October 1907, a little more than three months before Merman was born, the Plaza Hotel opened, with prices for single rooms going as high as $25 a day.

Far removed from all this activity was Astoria, Long Island City, a quiet enclave of Queens just across the East River from Manhattan. Today, populated largely by Muslims and Greeks, with a smattering of Irish, Astoria still feels slightly removed from the center of things. But during Merman's childhood and youth, the atmosphere was practically countrified. Long Island City had been founded in 1870 via the pulling together of six separate settlements—Astoria, Ravenswood, Hunter's Point, Dutch Kills, Bowery Bay, and Blissville—into one large community. Even at the turn of the century, the ambience was largely rural. When the tide rolled in, Hunter's Point often became a swampy quagmire, and occasionally a fisherman who wandered out on the marshlands ran the risk of being swallowed up and never heard from again. Dropped into this setting were a few substantial mansions belonging to some select families who desired a more secluded environment. A ferry transported commuters from Manhattan to Long Island City's Front Street, but the construction of the Queensboro Bridge in 1908 soon put it out of business.

This was the peaceful, insular world into which Ethel Merman was born on January 16, 1908, to Edward and Agnes Zimmermann. According to Ethel, she was delivered at the family home, a three-story frame house at 359 Fourth Avenue, Long Island City. (There is some confusion here: her birth certificate lists her birthplace as 265 Fourth Avenue. Was she perhaps born at a neighbor's house, or was the alternate address simply a clerical error?) "Pop," as Ethel always called him, was friendly and effusive. Pop took tremendous pride in his German heritage, and his great passions included playing piano at his local lodge and with various pickup orchestras, and having an occasional glass of scotch. At the time of Ethel's birth, he made his living as a bookkeeper; later he became an accountant with James H. Dunham & Co., a Manhattan wholesale dry-goods firm, where he remained for the rest of his working life. Mom Zimmermann balanced her husband's outgoing personality with her own strong element of reserve. Her family hailed from Scotland, and throughout her life she retained a solid core of old-fashioned Scottish pragmatism. A thread of steel ran through Mom: she always exercised caution, standing back and taking the measure of a person or a situation before committing herself. Occasionally she felt it necessary to rein in her husband when he became too gregarious, but for the most part she kept a low profile, quietly and efficiently running the household while Pop commuted to Manhattan each weekday. Years later Ethel would admit that the thought of displeasing Mom terrified her. Much as she loved her mother, she seems to have regarded her as a stern authority figure, while her relationship with her father was more relaxed.

During her early years, Ethel grew up surrounded by family. The house on Fourth Avenue was owned by Agnes Zimmermann's widowed Scots-English mother, Mary Gardner. It was one of six houses on a private street with no commercial traffic, in a neighborhood peppered with families of German extraction. The Zimmermanns lived on the top floor, and the ground floor was rented out. Grandmother Gardner shared the second floor with another daughter, Agnes Pickett, along with Agnes's husband, Harry, and their son, Claude.

Since Claude was only a little more than five years older than Ethel, the two cousins spent a great deal of time together; Ethel recalled that they were "more like brother and sister than cousins." They often climbed trees in the orchard near Grandmother Gardner's house, and occasionally they went to the L. A. Thompson Amusement Park (later renamed Playland) at nearby Rockaway Beach. A few years later, Grandmother Gardner sold the house, and the Zimmermanns moved to a residence that Ethel recalled as "a beautiful fifth-floor walk-up" at the Windsor apartment building, 29-08 Thirty-first Avenue. After the move she and Claude saw less and less of each other.

Throughout Ethel's career it was widely believed that she was Jewish. In fact, Pop had grown up in the Dutch Reformed Church, while Mom's family was Scotch Presbyterian. Shortly after the Zimmermanns were married, they discovered a little Episcopal congregation at the Church of the Redeemer at 30-14 Crescent Street in Astoria. They liked it enough that they became Episcopalians, remaining so the rest of their lives. Ethel was baptized and went to services for years at the Church of the Redeemer, a modest stone building that was homey and inviting. Her parents were strict about church attendance: on Sundays she spent virtually the day there, going to morning services, followed by Sunday school, the four-thirty prayer meeting, and

Christian Endeavor, a children's study group, in the evening. Eventually, however, she fell away from the parish, for a very personal reason: she wanted to be a chorister, and the Church of the Redeemer did not accept mixed choirs. Later, perhaps as a nod to Pop Zimmermann's past, she switched to attending services at the Dutch Reformed Church, where she was guaranteed a place in the chorus.

The belief that Ethel was Jewish was a subject on which she could become downright snappish. There is no persuasive evidence that she harbored any significant degree of anti-Semitism, but it is clear that she did not like being thought of as Jewish herself. Perhaps she simply resented being taken for something and someone she was not and felt compelled to set the record straight.

The Zimmermanns were devoted to Ethel, working hard to see that she would eventually develop into their idea of a well-brought-up young lady, and she returned that devotion. Ethel was in many ways an extreme example of a certain type of only child, one who grows up with such a strong level of parental praise and support that she seldom questions herself or her motives. Indeed, one of the intriguing aspects of *Merman*, her 1978 autobiography, written with George Eells, is that she seems never to have found the slightest degree of fault with either of her parents.

That pattern is in fact typical of many of the twentieth century's great female performers. An intense parental bond, particularly with their mothers, appears in the memoirs of Katharine Hepburn, Bette Davis, Ginger Rogers, Gloria Swanson, Joan Sutherland, Helen Hayes. Ethel always—especially later in life, in the light of her own failed marriages—held up her parents' relationship as a model one, an assessment that was shared by those friends of hers who spent a good deal of time around the Zimmermanns. According to her old friend Tony Cointreau, "Ethel always felt that Pop and Mom's adoration for each other spilled over to her. Home and child. This perfect union made this thing that was the focus of their lives. And Ethel always included them. They always came first."

If Mom was the ultimate figure of authority, it was Pop who took great care to nurture Ethel's musical gifts. Her remarkable facility for singing revealed itself early on. Pop would accompany her on his upright piano at home, teaching her one song after another. Ethel's debut came at age five, when she appeared with Pop at the keyboard at Astoria's Republican Club, to which her parents had belonged for a number of years. She was invited back repeatedly, always specially presented as "Little Ethel Zimmermann." Within a couple of years, she was being invited to sing at weddings and various church functions, where her listeners were always amazed by the size and power of her voice. Supportive as they were of Ethel's talents, the Zimmermanns never thought to find her a voice teacher, probably because they had yet to envision show business as anything resembling a viable career.

By April 1917 the United States was no longer able to avoid involvement in European hostilities, and Woodrow Wilson had asked Congress for a declaration of war. As the country's involvement in World War I grew, Ethel was enough of a seasoned performer to be hired to sing at some of the local army camps used for training, embarkation, and debarkation. Her first job along these lines was probably at Long Island's Camp Mills, and offers soon followed from many other local bases, notably Camp Yaphank, also on Long Island. (Eventually it would become famous as the place where Irving Berlin wrote—and filed away for twenty years—"God Bless America.") Ethel sang mostly rousing numbers such as "Over There" and "K-K-K-Katie," and the soldiers cheered for the little girl with the big, gutsy voice. But her biggest hit at the army camps was the sentimental number "He's Me Pal," by Vincent Bryan and Gus Edwards. She dedicated her first performance of it, at Camp Yaphank, to Mom Zimmermann, and Ethel later recalled that when she had finished, many of the soldiers were in tears.

Ethel was a good, dedicated student at Astoria's P.S. 4. Mom and Pop made sure that she kept up with her schoolwork and made good marks. Even at an early age, Ethel had shown a natural inclination toward precision and order, qualities that helped to give her an academic edge. At school, her musical abilities went unnoticed. Later she would remember that she was never called upon to perform at school assemblies, adding, "I'm not even sure whether many of my classmates knew I could sing."

In 1921, Ethel's thirteenth year, life in Astoria suddenly became much more exciting when Adolph Zukor and his partner, Jesse L. Lasky, who had merged in 1916 to create the Famous Players–Lasky motion-picture company, built a large, $2.5 million film-studio complex on Thirty-fifth Avenue. Movies had by then become big business. In 1913 the United States boasted more than twenty thousand movie theaters, and the new art form was already doing significant damage to old-style theatrical road companies. Filmmaking had taken place in and around New York for years; *The Great Train Robbery*, a twelve-minute-long landmark in film narrative, was shot entirely in New Jersey. In the intervening years, filmmakers had found in Southern California a more welcoming climate, ideal for shooting westerns and other outdoor pictures. But because Famous Players–Lasky did not have a sufficiently large physical plant in Hollywood to accommodate all its movie-making ventures, in a number of years as many as 25 percent of its films were made in New York. Famous Players–Lasky would alternately produce over a hundred films at the Astoria studio. As a young teenager, Ethel got a glimpse of many of her favorite stars—the glamorous Broadway actress Alice Brady was a particular favorite—by peering through a hole that some of the neighborhood children had pounded through the fence surrounding the studio.

She got to see her share of live entertainment, too. Pop and Mom Zimmermann had a Friday-night ritual: taking their daughter into Manhattan for a vaudeville show at the Palace Theatre, on Forty-seventh Street and Seventh Avenue. In no time Ethel had developed a short list of favorite vaudeville stars. There was Harry Carroll, who appeared with his wife, Anna Wheaton, and often sang one of his own compositions, "By the Beautiful Sea" or "I'm Always Chasing Rainbows." Ethel also liked the singing-songwriting team of Gus Van and Joe Schenck, who broke up their audiences with Chinese or Yiddish dialect, and singer/comedian Bert Williams, one of vaudeville's kings. Ethel laughed especially hard when Williams did his famous pantomime of a poker game: while he was hit with a solo spotlight, he did an uncanny imitation of the entire gamut of emotions involved in playing a losing hand of poker. She also delighted in the knockabout comedy of Bob Pender's troupe, which featured an agile stilt walker, Archibald Leach, at a way station on the road to Hollywood fame as Cary Grant. Sitting in her second-balcony seat with her parents, she was thrilled by the female singers who headlined at the Palace, especially Blossom Seeley, Fanny Brice, and Sophie Tucker, and watched them carefully, studying how they breathed, how they timed their songs and comic routines, how they interacted with the audience. Often, when she came home after spending the evening at the Palace, she did her very best to imitate the singers she'd just heard. But no matter how hard she tried to emulate Belle Baker or Nora Bayes, in the end she sounded only like herself.

In the fall of 1920, Ethel entered William Cullen Bryant High School. By now she was certain that she wanted to be a singer. Much as they had encouraged her musical abilities, the Zimmermanns remained skeptical about the security of a singing career. Mom Zimmermann in particular tried to steer Ethel in the direction of teaching, since Ethel's cousin Agnes Sharkey had done well enough for herself as a schoolteacher. But Ethel hated the thought of teaching; she had a better idea. William Cullen Bryant offered what was then known as a commercial course, intended to provide apt young students with proper secretarial training. Ethel decided that this was the best path for her, and her parents gave her their full support.

From the beginning, Ethel loved the commercial course. She excelled in typing and the Isaac Pitman method of shorthand, scoring 95 percent and above. All her life she was proud of her secretarial—or, as they were then called, stenographic—skills. Long after she had become a stage star, interviewers would frequently mention that she always typed her own correspondence. Hammering out her own letters brought forth her sense of perfectionism; the recipients of those letters often noticed that there was seldom a single typographical error to be found.

Ethel enjoyed her time in high school, easily making friends and doing well in most of her courses, with the exception of history, which she hated. She wasn't much for athletics, apart from swimming, but she threw herself into a variety of other activities. For a time she was literary editor of Bryant High's news magazine, *The Owl.* She also participated in speakers' club and student government, first as a council member of the Bryant Union, later as a member of its executive committee. When she wasn't in school, she often dropped by Ross's Music Store on Steinway Street, trying out the new song sheets that came in each week. During her years at Bryant High, she made two close friends, Martha Neubert and Alice Welch, whom she met in book-keeping class. Early on, Alice had been orphaned, and the Zimmermanns welcomed her almost as one of their own.

Ethel loved movies, and often on Saturdays she and Martha and Alice would get dressed up and head into Manhattan for lunch and an afternoon double feature at one of the big movie palaces. Oddly, her interest in live entertainment was still restricted to vaudeville; she never thought about attending a Broadway show. Nor was she drawn to reading: picking up a novel, even a newspaper, just made her sleepy. Her manner of dress was a little flashy, and her outfits were typically tarted up with bows and ruffles and frills. And, like that of many other city girls in the twenties, her language often teetered on the edge of what was acceptable for young ladies. But if she chafed at conventional boundaries at school or when she was out with her friends, at home Mom and Pop's word, as always, was law.

At the end of her four years at Bryant High, Ethel completed the commercial course successfully and graduated with the class of 1924. She was only sixteen, a bit young to be a high-school graduate, and it is possible that she was one of the students who took advantage of one of the standard tests of the time that permitted exceptional students to skip one grade. Her high-school yearbook noted that she "intends to enter the business world," and her senior-year quote was "Wherever joy and laughter abound / There is Ethel to be found."

She lost no time in registering with an employment agency in Long Island City and in less than two weeks landed a job as a stenographer at the Boyc-Ite Company on Queens Boulevard. In her memoirs Ethel gives an indication of the degree of her enthusiasm for the job: "Boyc-Ite was an antifreeze for automobiles. My salary was all of twenty-three dollars a week." She was a five-day-a-week working girl now, surrounded by other five-day-a-week working girls, and it is possible that dreams of singing stardom had never seemed more remote.

Her tenure at the Boyc-Ite Company turned out to be brief. With her fellow stenographers, she frequently ate at a neighborhood restaurant patronized by people who worked at other local businesses. One day she made the acquaintance of Vic Kliesrath, a partner in the Bragg-Kliesrath Corporation. Word had gotten around that Ethel was an unusually capable stenographer, and in no time Kliesrath had offered her a job with his company. It paid five dollars more a week, but the real value that the job would hold in store for her was initially not at all apparent.

Chapter Two

• • • • • • • • • • • • • • • • • • •

Afterﾠ Ethel had become a Broadway star, the press often inti-
mated that she had spent her earlier years in complete obscurity.
This was far from the case: the six years that passed between Ethel's graduation from Bryant High and her Broadway debut are a record of a
determined young woman slowly building her name in New York music
circles.

In terms of the work she was called upon to do, Ethel's new job at the
Bragg-Kliesrath Corporation was no more exciting than the old one had
been. Bragg-Kliesrath Corporation had introduced the B-K Vacuum Booster
Brake for trucks, a kind of precursor of the power brake. (Ethel later claimed
that if you pumped the brake too hard, "you'd go right through the windshield.") Much of the technical jargon used by her bosses was lost on her;
she simply took dictation and typed up correspondence at breakneck
speed.

By this time Ethel was searching for musical work more aggressively. A
few nights each week, she took the subway to Manhattan and went from one
music-publishing house to another, picking up the newest song sheets. The
publishers knew that hungry young singers like Ethel could be of value
plugging their latest songs, in the event that they happened to pick up a few
club dates. As a result it became company policy to give many aspiring
singers sheet music free of charge.

Ethel had also signed with a couple of minor-league agents who specialized in small-time bookings, mostly weddings and parties. But Ethel wasn't
fussy. It gave her a chance to sing, after all, and at least some degree of exposure. She reasoned that you never knew who might be a guest at one of the
parties, and she grabbed as many of the five- and ten-dollar jobs as she
could round up.

Then there was radio, which did more than any other medium to send
music to the masses. A survey of the *New York Times* radio logs of the mid- to
late 1920s reveals hundreds of long-forgotten names with brief radio slots.

Shows featured dance bands, organists, string quartets, sopranos, tenors, whistlers, diction instructors who demonstrated "setting-up exercises" over the air—all of them live. During the first few months of 1927, Ethel joined their ranks with a regular fifteen-minute late-afternoon spot on radio station WPCH in Hoboken, New Jersey.

Her new job at Bragg-Kliesrath may have meant an increase of five dollars a week, but it also presented her with a problem. The company required its stenographers to punch a time clock, and when Ethel had been out late singing the night before, it was difficult for her to get to work on time. Soon she managed to con a few of her officemates into punching the clock for her while she slept in as long as she dared.

Shortly after her arrival at Bragg-Kliesrath, Ethel was made confidential secretary to the company president, Caleb Bragg. It is possible that Ethel knew Bragg by reputation before taking the job, because he was something of a celebrity sportsman. Born into a wealthy family in Cincinnati, Bragg had attended Yale, where he became entranced by the world of auto racing. From the start he had proved himself a natural at race-car driving, scoring many important victories, including the Fourth International Grand Prix in 1912. During World War I, his interest in cars gave way to a passion for flying, and in 1916 he made his first solo flight. By the following year, he had begun a string of flights that broke records for both altitude and speed. Later Bragg joined forces with Vic Kliesrath, and together they invented the vacuum booster brake. By the 1920s they had incorporated as Bragg-Kliesrath and opened their headquarters in Long Island City.

Vic Kliesrath was friendly and no-nonsense, the kind of boss who remembered the stenographers' birthdays and frequently took them to lunch or had them to dine at his home. By contrast, Bragg was, to Ethel's way of thinking, "ultra-chic." He was also chilly and remote, not the sort of person she could warm up to right away. Office decorum of the period was strictly observed: he was always "Mr. Bragg," and she was always "Miss Zimmermann."

Working for Bragg offered a few clear advantages. He was embroiled in so many business projects that he kept irregular office hours; he was frequently late, and there were many consecutive days when he didn't show up at all. Often, when Bragg telephoned to say he wouldn't be coming in until late morning, Ethel would leave her desk, run to the ladies' room, peel down to her slip, and catch a quick nap on the cot. When Bragg was on his way, one of the other stenographers would signal her, and she would be dressed and back at her desk just in time for her boss to appear.

Ethel always gave the impression that she hadn't been the most precise of stenographers, because Bragg's dictated letters were so crammed with technical minutiae that she couldn't get it all down. But decades later Mom and Pop Zimmermann clearly remembered a day when Bragg had dictated a long, multipage document full of mechanical terminology, to be sent to a patent attorney. Afraid that Bragg would become irate if she botched the job, Ethel showed a draft to Kliesrath, who looked it over and pronounced it letter perfect.

Like many other enterprising businessmen of the period, Caleb Bragg was dazzled by the world of show business and had the means to play on the fringes of it. He had made the acquaintance of a number of leading actresses on Broadway, including Gertrude Lawrence and Hope Williams. It often fell to Ethel to send flowers to one of these celebrated stars, and it was always one of the parts of her job that did not appeal to her; she thought that she was at least as talented as the quavery-voiced Gertrude Lawrence. But she was also canny enough to realize that Bragg's interest in the stage might possibly work to her advantage, and on two occasions it almost did.

The first incident took place on a pleasant Saturday afternoon on which the Kliesraths were hosting a party in a Port Washington restaurant for some of their employees. Ethel turned up in a red-and-black dotted-silk dress, a new black Milan hat, and black shoes. At some point, Bragg arrived unexpectedly, enthusing to anyone who would listen about his speedboat, the *Casey Jones.* He asked if anyone wanted to go for a spin. Several people did, and he spent an hour or so speeding small groups across Manhasset Bay to the Connecticut shoreline and back to the restaurant.

When it came Ethel's turn, she climbed into the boat, accompanied by the company's switchboard operator, Bessie Sullivan. On the return trip to Port Washington, Bragg decided to demonstrate his prowess behind the wheel and began passing, at high speed, the other boats in the harbor. Suddenly the *Casey Jones* ran into a log and overturned. Ethel lost her purse, and she and Bessie were drenched. Bragg swiftly got both the girls aboard his houseboat, the *Masquerader,* which he had anchored in the bay. Ethel remembered it as being as elegant as a lot of New York apartments, fully equipped with a complement of servants. While the girls were waiting for their clothes to dry, Bragg lent them each a pair of silk pajamas and a bathrobe and invited them to join the party he was giving on board later that day.

At dinner Ethel found herself seated next to Ruth Selwyn, wife of the stage and screen producer Edgar Selwyn. Ruth was a producer as well, with an eye toward working on Broadway. She was as pretty as she was smart, and she had a strong, independent spirit. Ruth was often quoted as saying that she found the theater "a fascinating game" that a woman could play just as easily as a man. She was just the sort of tough, determined woman that Ethel admired, and during dinner Ethel did her best to pitch herself to Ruth. She told the producer that she aimed to be a professional singer and stated frankly that she thought she was as good as a lot of the women performing at the Palace. Ruth was amused by this display of brash self-confidence and made vague promises of casting her in a show, should an appropriate part come along.

Until that point the self-absorbed, introverted Caleb Bragg had had no idea of his secretary's singing ambitions, and it seems that Ethel viewed her dunking in Manhasset Bay as an opportunity to press him to use some of his theatrical connections to help her along. Soon she had asked him to write a letter of introduction to one of the biggest names on Broadway—George White, who for years had produced a popular series of revues called *George White's Scandals*, spotlighting a wide array of comics, musical talent, and, always, a lineup of beautiful girls.

At the time some of Broadway's biggest-ticket items were revues. The lushest and most extravagant of all, the *Ziegfeld Follies,* popped up in a new edition each year from 1907 to 1925, and intermittently thereafter. There was the *Earl Carroll Vanities,* whose cycle began in 1923 and ended in 1940. *The Passing Show,* which took off mostly from the year's headlines, dated all the way back to 1912. Many big stars got their starts in these shows, even if they only danced in the chorus: Joan Crawford was discovered by a Hollywood scout while hoofing in *The Passing Show of 1924.*

A native of Manhattan's Lower East Side, George White had led a rough-and-tumble life. By age seven he was earning money as a newspaper peddler, and by fourteen he had cracked into show business as a buck-and-wing dancer in burlesque and later in vaudeville. In 1911 and again in 1915, he danced in the *Ziegfeld Follies* before breaking into producing his own shows. When his first *Scandals* opened in 1919, its initial review was headlined, GEORGE WHITE'S SCANDALS PROVES A BUCK DANCER SHOULD STICK TO HOOFING. That night White cried himself to sleep, but in the end the show proved to be such a hit that he reportedly made $400,000 from it. (Later he lost the whole amount betting on the horses; the press reported that he had dropped $100,000 on a single race.) His fortunes had continued in the same now-he's-up, now-he's-down manner ever since, but he always managed to pump more money—most of it his own—into another edition of the *Scandals,* and by the spring of 1928 he was preparing yet another version.

Ethel hand-delivered Bragg's letter to White at Forty-second Street's Apollo Theatre, where the *Scandals* were always staged and where White gave her the once-over. He had high standards of feminine beauty and was known for dismissing chorus girls who didn't make the grade as "dog faces." Ethel was far from being a stunning beauty, but she had definite sex appeal and a very good figure, with perfectly shaped legs. When White asked her if she would like a spot in the chorus line, Ethel, who had never for a moment seen herself as a chorus girl, told him she was looking for a solo singing spot. The producer coolly replied that Frances Williams was handling the songs in that year's revue. Ethel thanked him and left, determined to wait until a decent solo-singing opportunity presented itself. Until then she would stick with the nighttime club dates.

Once she began stepping up her professional appearances, it didn't take Ethel long to figure out that "Ethel Zimmermann" was too cumbersome for a marquee. She tossed around other family-tree possibilities on her mother's side, such as Gardner or Hunter, the latter being Grandmother Gardner's maiden name. Pop Zimmermann considered this a betrayal and said so, loudly. After thinking it over, Ethel excised the first syllable and the final consonant and came up with "Merman," a name she always claimed to have coined.

For months she continued her routine of working days at the office and picking up as much night work as she could manage. One place that booked her repeatedly was Keen's English Chop House, near Pennsylvania Station. She would appear in a dress made of satin or taffeta and sing her own version of one of the popular standards of the day. One of her biggest hits was Walter Donaldson's "Little White Lies," and she sang it so often that her photo wound up on the song's sheet music. (She would also be pictured on the sheet music for other popular songs, including "Side by Side" and "After My Laughter Came Tears.")

In September 1929, only a few weeks before Wall Street collapsed, Ethel got a slight career boost when she was signed to perform at Little Russia, a below-street-level club on Fifty-seventh Street off Sixth Avenue. Unlike the one-night stands she was accustomed to, this booking was for two solid weeks, every night except Sunday, for $60 a week. Little Russia was a noisy joint, and Ethel was frustrated that the clientele seemed more intent on talking, drinking, and eating than on listening to her sing. There were, of course, no microphones, and, like many of her predecessors, including Sophie Tucker and Al Jolson, she had to learn how to project over the racket.

Various showbiz types regularly tramped down the stairs to Little Russia, hoping to catch any new acts of promise. One night a theatrical agent named Lou Irwin dropped by and heard her sing. Irwin knew the club scene well: he had a reputation in the business for securing more nitery bookings, from New York to Chicago, than any other agent. He sat and listened in amazement to the girl with the big, clear voice who could be heard over the din of clanking plates and couples calling out for fresh drinks. He gave her his card and told her that he represented Helen Morgan, who only two years earlier had reached the apex of her career as Julie in *Show Boat*. To Ethel that sounded like heady company, and she asked what he had in mind for her. Irwin told her that his good friend Archie Mayo, a busy contract director at Warner Bros., was going to be in New York the following day, scouting out talent for Warners short films, and that he wanted Mayo to hear her.

This was the best opportunity Ethel had yet been given; talking pictures had recently taken the country by storm. Crude experiments at synchronizing sound effects with films stretched back to the glory days of D. W. Griffith. But in 1926, Warner Bros. joined forces with Western Electric and created the Vitaphone Company to produce background sound components for motion pictures. In a series of short subjects and one major feature, *Don Juan*, the sound was recorded on disc and matched, reel by reel, to the film. Frequent projection snafus rendered synchronization all but impossible, but in 1927, after further refinements, Warner Bros. used Vitaphone in *The Jazz Singer*, the largely silent picture that featured musical interludes and snatches of dialogue. *The Jazz Singer* broke box-office records everywhere and launched the sound era in earnest. Disc-to-screen synchronization underwent continual overhauls, and by the early 1930s it would be supplanted by the motion-picture sound track. At the time Ethel signed with Warners, Vitaphone short films had already become a successful way of introducing performers to a wider public, and many of the actors and singers in New York were shooting them during the day while appearing on Broadway at night.

The next evening after work, Ethel showed up at Mills publishing house on West Forty-seventh Street to audition for Mayo. Knowing that he was a prominent figure in Hollywood, she was terrified. But Mayo thought that this iron-lunged girl would come off well on film and offered her a six-month contract with future options, starting at $125 a week. There was no need to go to California; filming would take place in Warners' Brooklyn studio, which would allow her plenty of extra time to pursue bigger singing opportunities in New York. It sounded much better to Ethel than the pittance she was making at Bragg-Kliesrath. So she immediately gave notice to Caleb Bragg and got ready to make her first stab at films.

For Ethel it was the beginning of a lifetime of disappointment in the movie business. She had expected to begin filming right away, but weeks rolled by without a single assignment. The checks from Warners arrived regularly and were turned over to Pop and Mom, but Ethel's contract stipulated that she was not allowed to work for anyone but Warners, and she grew more and more irritable over her inactivity. After a few months, the studio finally gave her two days' work in a short film, *The Cave Club*, in which she wore a leopard skin and got chased up a tree. Then it was back to sitting around the apartment in Astoria, waiting for the phone to ring. The time weighed heavily on her, until Ethel finally called Lou Irwin and asked him to obtain a release from her Warners contract—a gutsy move, given that the country was in the throes of the Depression. Instead he cut a better deal with Warners: she would remain under contract for short films but would be permitted to do outside work in nightclubs. The first booking Irwin got her, early in 1930, was impressive, and it was even on Broadway—not in a theater but in a little club over the Winter Garden Theatre, called Les Ambassadeurs. The club's star attraction was the trio of Clayton, Jackson, and Durante—Clayton as in soft-shoe dancer Lou Clayton, Jackson as in baritone Eddie Jackson, and Durante as in Jimmy Durante.

Only a few years earlier, Clayton, Jackson, and Durante had been packing them in at the Silver Slipper on West Forty-eighth Street. At the time it was something of a risk to run any sort of club, as Prohibition had been introduced in 1920, and the only way to serve liquor was to do it on the sly. Even so, Broadway was riddled with clubs and cafés where a drink could be had. Some of them were dives, but in the elegant surroundings of the Crillon and the Lido, among others, society swells could sip martinis and champagne and—often thanks to the protection of the mob—be reasonably confident that they wouldn't be rounded up in a police raid.

All had gone well for Clayton, Jackson, and Durante until one night in the fall of 1928, when a waiter at the Silver Slipper unknowingly served a drink to a customer who was operating undercover as a Prohibition enforcement officer. The Silver Slipper was closed, and Clayton, Jackson, and Durante were briefly out of work. But when Les Ambassadeurs opened a few months later, the trio was hired, and their loyal audience from the Silver Slipper showed up in big numbers. Not long after they opened, Ethel was engaged for a limited run as their girl singer.

Jimmy Durante and Ethel were friends from the start. Jimmy's father was a barber on the Lower East Side, where Jimmy was born, the youngest of four children, in 1893. His parents insisted that he study classical piano, but he saw himself as more the ragtime type, and by his teens he was playing for dances on the Lower East Side and out at Coney Island for seventy-five cents a night. Later he played in a band at Harlem's Club Alamo. By the 1920s he had opened his own business, the Club Durant, and eventually joined forces with Clayton and Jackson to create one of the hottest acts in vaudeville. Durante was known as a soft touch who aimed to be all things to all people. Once he told George Raft, then a struggling hoofer having trouble making ends meet, "Any time you're busted, kid, go right into the register and help yourself." By contrast, Lou Clayton, who also acted as Durante's manager, was a tough businessman who provided the muscle of the organization and reined in Durante's excesses. Eventually Durante worked Clayton's shrewdness into his act. "I'm really a lucky guy to have a manager like Lou Clayton," he would say. "But tell me, folks, how much is three hundred percent?"

Ethel wasn't wild about Clayton, especially when he set her weekly salary at eighty-five dollars, a sum she considered just the right side of acceptable. But it was a high-profile booking, and she made a hit with the club's audience. Her appearances at Les Ambassadeurs marked the beginning of a lifelong friendship with Durante. Onstage he could make her laugh until she cried, with his victimized Everyman who didn't get no respect, long before the world had ever heard of Rodney Dangerfield. One writer vividly described how Durante "beat the air with his arms and cried out like a hoarse Ajax," while another observed that his hilarious malapropisms made "the pronunciation of every word of more than two syllables a suspense-filled adventure." Yet his act always displayed a certain degree of class that is typical of all great performers; it never stooped for laughs, never degenerated into blue humor. Offstage, Durante was a perfect gentleman, and Ethel immediately warmed to his sentimental, openhearted personality. Her affection was returned. "This girl was dynamite!" Durante later recalled. "Miss Merman is the world's greatest salesman of lyrics. That's for sure."

At Les Ambassadeurs, Ethel steered clear of the comedy and stuck to torch singing. Two of her numbers, "Body and Soul" and "Moanin' Low," had been big hits for Libby Holman, a remarkable singer whom Ethel admired. Ethel started getting one- and two-line mentions from Walter Winchell, Mark Hellinger, and some of the other top columnists, who often compared her style to Holman's. Ethel was grateful for the mentions, but she didn't think that she sounded like Holman, or anyone else for that matter. She wanted to sound like herself. And right from the start, she did.

Early on, Pop and Mom Zimmermann probably didn't realize what a favor they had done their daughter by neglecting to engage a voice teacher for her. The result was that she developed naturally, a step at a time. By the time she had cemented her stardom in the late 1930s, she was such a unique presence onstage that she seemed to have come out of nowhere. Strictly speaking, this wasn't true. In the earliest years of the twentieth century, most of the big female stars sang in a "legit," operetta-based style. But by the late 1920s, as orchestrations relied more and more on brass and saxophone, the soprano sound had begun to fade and a new kind of big-voiced singer was needed to cut through the bolder arrangements. Ethel listened to these women on the radio. She listened, made note of the things she liked and the things she didn't, and she learned from them.

The press had already made a case for her vocal resemblance to Libby Holman, a singer with a keen sense of phrasing and clarinet-like low tones. Holman's own role models included Ethel Waters, and she sang with a tremendous immediacy. Her numbers sounded almost conversational, as she dipped out of her sweet top register into her compelling middle range, where she used a certain amount of talk-singing. Another popular vocalist was *Show Boat*'s sad-eyed Helen Morgan, who couldn't remotely be described as a belter but whose singing had a plaintive urgency and carried a remarkable dramatic power. There was Lillian Roth, who achieved great popularity on both stage and radio. (Roth claimed decades later that Merman had copied her style, but that was probably more a reflection of the fact that her own success had been stymied by acute alcoholism; she never possessed an instrument that could compare with Merman's.) There was Ruth Etting, dubbed by Walter Winchell "Queen of All Torch Warblers." Etting had a clear, attractive voice with great forward placement. Her diction was precise, yet her manner of singing was relaxed and easy. Although she performed a lot of torch songs, there was an element of humor in her voice; at times she was reminiscent of the "Boop-Boop-a-Doop" girl, Helen Kane. When Etting sang "I'm Nobody's Baby" or her signature hit, "Ten Cents a Dance," she sounded like a good-time girl who didn't take herself too seriously.

If Ethel owed aspects of her singing style to any one performer, it was probably Sophie Tucker. Born into a poor Russian-Jewish family in Hartford, Connecticut, in 1886, Tucker shouted her way through a long, long career. While her full-barreled contralto was used to good effect in such torch numbers as her signature tune, "Some of These Days," she really owed her billing as "The Last of the Red Hot Mammas"—a title she maintained a fierce grip on until her death—to her repertoire of suggestive comic songs. Tucker was never out-and-out dirty, like Belle Barth, and as comedienne Dody Goodman, who heard Tucker several times in New York, observed, "A big fat woman like that—it's not likely that she'd be turning many people on! People would accept it from her because she was so unlikely to do it." As a singer, Tucker was a direct descendant of the old-time "coon shouters," whose job it was simply to go out and sell a song at the top of their lungs. Like Bessie Smith, she sometimes made use of a very fast vibrato, and she had tremendous lift at the top of her voice. Tucker didn't go in for nuance; with her power and style, she didn't need it, and audiences didn't miss it.

Curiously, the singers of the period whose sound Ethel's most resembled were men. There was a strong hint of Al Jolson in her stentorian delivery, and she sounded even more like the popular Harry Richman, whose whole point was to project, loud and clear; Richman's recording of Jimmy McHugh and Dorothy Fields's "On the Sunny Side of the Street," from the 1930 show *The International Revue*, sounds uncannily Mermanesque. (Ethel herself had had her eye on a part in *The International Revue* and showed up at the producer's office to audition for it. McHugh and Fields had come up with another terrific song for the show, "Exactly Like You," which she loved immediately, but the producer told her that they were looking for a Gertrude Lawrence type. In fact, Lawrence wound up playing it, but the show flopped.)

Elated to be on a regular bill with a team as famous as Clayton, Jackson, and Durante, Ethel felt that she had finally been lifted to a whole new level in show business. But her happiness didn't last long: she had to bow out of the act when she developed a recurrence of the tonsillitis that had plagued her off and on for years. This time the situation was serious, and her doctor informed her that she would have to undergo a tonsillectomy.

Ethel was frightened, for she knew about the risk that the operation had posed for other singers. The procedure turned out to be a highly delicate one, and the surgeon later told her that her tonsils had decayed so badly that they'd crumbled away to nothing when he tried to remove them. So many stitches were required in her throat that it was uncertain whether she would be able to sing again.

After two weeks of being as quiet as possible, Ethel confounded the doctors when she opened her mouth to sing and found that her voice had returned full force. If anything, she was able to produce even more volume than she had before. The suspense of waiting to see if her voice could be salvaged had taken its toll on Ethel's nerves, though, and Lou Irwin recommended that she leave town for a while. He had lined up a booking at a popular nightclub in Miami called the Roman Pools Casino, at $300 a week for a six-week guarantee. It was to be her first real time away from home unchaperoned, and Pop and Mom Zimmermann sent her with their blessing, provided that she wired home as much of her salary as possible, so Mom could bank it for her.

Ethel proved a popular attraction with the audiences at the Roman Pools Casino, once again trotting out her rendition of "Moanin' Low," which she torched while wearing a black satin dress, black fishnets, and spike heels. The engagement at the casino had advantages above and beyond the good salary, for when she wasn't performing she often made her way to the roulette and blackjack tables. In her memoirs she admitted that she "got to know the guys who hung around there," sitting next to them while they gambled the night away. After a couple of hours of keeping some of the casino's high rollers company, Ethel found that they often turned over half their winnings to her—a kind of unwritten code of the time. She spent part of these "tips," as she called them, on sprucing up her wardrobe, while the rest went home to Astoria, along with the part of her weekly salary that she had agreed to put into savings. By the end of the second week, Mom Zimmermann had called her demanding to know how she could possibly be sending home $600 when her weekly salary was half that.

At the end of the run, Ethel returned to New York, where Lou Irwin had found a pianist to work with her. Al Siegel was an arranger and a singer's coach with a good eye for talent, and Irwin thought he might be helpful in refining her singing. He was also the former husband of popular singer Bee Palmer, whom Ethel had heard on a number of occasions. Ethel would always dismiss the impact Siegel had on her style, but for years there were many in show business who believed that he'd helped her develop some of the highly individual vocal characteristics that became her trademark. (One person who rejected that theory was Roger Edens, the gifted pianist/arranger/songwriter who became Ethel's friend and collaborator for forty years. Edens felt that Ethel's style had always been her own and owed nothing to Al Siegel or anyone else. In fact, he questioned whether Ethel really had any particular style at all, or simply a natural ability to project that was frequently *confused* with style.)

More likely, Siegel's principal contribution was as a top-notch arranger. It didn't take long for him to observe that Ethel had an uncanny sense of rhythm, and he tried to make maximum use of it in the jazzy arrangements that he began writing for her. She likewise had an astonishing ability to project the lyrics loud and clear, and there were other little quirks and characteristics that seemed unique to her. Chief among them was her ability to sustain the decibel level of a climactic phrase. Many singers with substantial voices—Ethel Waters, for example—would slowly diminish the volume as they reached the end of a key line. But the Merman style was to keep the volume consistent, and even raise it a little, delivering a wonderful final kick. Most of all, she had her phenomenal breath support. There was no mystery in how she achieved this, as she merely filled her lungs with air when she needed to breathe. Around the time Ethel started working with Siegel, she did finally consult a voice teacher, but the results were discouraging: he told her that she would not make much progress unless she learned to breathe from her diaphragm. However, Ethel found that when she concentrated on her diaphragm, she wasn't able to sing naturally. She thanked the teacher and never returned, then went back to her usual way of breathing.

Together Ethel and Siegel worked out an act, and Lou Irwin got them booked on the renowned Keith vaudeville circuit, opening in Elizabeth, New Jersey, in June 1930. As their tour wound down, Irwin informed them that their next appearance would be a high-profile one: they were to play seven weeks at the Brooklyn Paramount, where they would perform several shows a day, in between screenings of the latest Paramount feature films. Ethel was thrilled to have a job that would last practically the entire summer and later recalled that she and Siegel "broke up the place" for the entire run at the Paramount.

Around the same time, Paramount signed her to make her first feature film, *Follow the Leader,* based on a popular musical comedy, *Manhattan Mary.* Heading the cast was Ed Wynn, the stage's beloved "Perfect Fool," in his first talkie, while newcomer Ginger Rogers had the female lead. Ethel, a last-minute replacement for Ruth Etting, played a musical-comedy star, the intended victim of a kidnap plot that goes awry. Although she did have one song—"Satan's Holiday," by Sammy Fain and Irving Kahal—she doesn't seem to have had much affection for the movie, which is scarcely mentioned in her memoirs.

One engagement that Ethel had been lusting after was the Pavilion Royale, a tony club in Valley Stream, Long Island, where many big names went to try out—for no salary—new acts before facing the more demanding audiences in Manhattan. Irwin secured them a booking there, and Ethel scored a hit with Siegel's uptempo arrangements of "Singin' in the Rain" and the lusty "Sing You Sinners"—such a hit that they were put on salary for regular Saturday- and Sunday-night engagements, which they performed after appearing all day at the Brooklyn Paramount. For Ethel this turned out to be another big step up in class: one night she got a chance to sing with one of the most popular bands around, Guy Lombardo and His Royal Canadians.

Ethel and Siegel's notices at the Paramount were so good that Irwin soon was able to get them booked at the Valhalla of vaudeville houses—the Palace. Ethel could hardly believe that she was about to land on the stage of the theater where only a few years earlier she had first seen the Marx Brothers, Nora Bayes, and many other great performers. It would bring her the biggest salary she had earned yet—five hundred dollars a week—and she couldn't wait for the engagement to begin. And then, one night toward the end of the run, Broadway producer Vinton Freedley came to the Paramount and heard her sing.

By the time he heard Ethel at the Brooklyn Paramount, Vinton Freedley had become established as one of Broadway's most successful musical-comedy producers. Nothing in his background indicated that he might carve out a career in the theater: he was born in 1891 into a prominent Main Line Philadelphia family, and it was expected that he would become a lawyer. He buckled to family pressure up to the point of studying law at the University of Pennsylvania's Wharton School, but once he graduated, he immediately started scrambling for acting jobs. In those days of honey-toned matinee idols, his squeaky voice proved a major handicap, and early on, he flubbed an audition with the great stage actress Mrs. Minnie Maddern Fiske. By Freedley's own admission, he was never much of an actor, but during the five years that he spent touring the United States, he picked up an enormous amount of knowledge about stage direction, lighting, script doctoring, and all other aspects of production. In 1923 he joined forces with the successful Broadway producer Alex A. Aarons. For Freedley the partnership came with a built-in advantage: Aarons had an association with George Gershwin that stretched back to his production of Gershwin's 1919 musical *La, La, Lucille*. In 1924, one year after they formed their partnership, Aarons and Freedley produced Gershwin's new *Lady, Be Good!*, the show in which Gershwin truly found his jazz-based voice. It ran for 330 performances, and the Aarons-Freedley team stuck together, producing many more Gershwin works—*Tip Toes* (1925), *Oh, Kay!* (1926), and *Funny Face* (1927)—in addition to other musical hits. Aarons and Freedley were smart producers: most of their shows came in at around $60,000 and earned their investments back in fourteen weeks or less. The partners were so successful that by 1927 it felt natural enough for them to open their own Broadway theater at 250 West Fifty-second Street. They dubbed it the Alvin—a conflation of the first syllables of both their first names.

The Aarons-Freedley-Gershwin team did much more than make money; it helped establish American musical comedy as a viable and popular genre.

Prior to the 1920s, operetta had been the favored musical style on Broadway. Audiences loved the lavishly upholstered productions, the reassuringly old-fashioned plots that dealt with romantic intrigues among European royalty, the thundering choruses of soldiers and peasants. Best of all, there were the lovely, lyrical melodies—easy to listen to and easy to remember but just "legit" enough to satisfy people's cravings for something on the highbrow side.

There was something inevitable about George Gershwin's breakthrough into popular culture. The 1920s gave him the perfect climate in which to launch his new sound, because the United States was caught up in the dizzying process of reinventing itself. The nation had finally stepped out of the long shadow cast by European culture and asserted itself as never before. It was the age of a frantic new consumerism, of the explosion of advertising, an industry that had previously been relatively genteel in its scope and ambitions. Everything was suddenly being pitched to the youth market. (As F. Scott Fitzgerald observed, "After all, life hasn't much to offer except youth.") Prohibition was going strong, and with it came the growth of speakeasies. Literature was dominated by a new breed of writers—among them Fitzgerald, Theodore Dreiser, and John Dos Passos, whose daring and provocative works made the florid bestsellers of only a few years earlier seem laughably quaint. A new sexual candor was spreading by the day; all anyone had to do was to see how many women had shortened their skirts, rolled their stockings below the knees, and thrown away their corsets, or how they openly smoked and drank. That candor was evident in the movies, too. In 1921 audiences poured into movie theaters to see Rudolph Valentino and Agnes Ayres play out a glorified rape fantasy in *The Sheik*. By 1928 flapper ideal Joan Crawford was raising a toast in *Our Dancing Daughters*: "To myself! I have to live with myself until I die—so may I always like—myself!" Fitzgerald summed it all up nicely: "The whole golden boom was in the air, its splendid generosities, its outrageous corruptions, and the torturous death struggle of the old America."

Gershwin's early years had coincided with New York City's rebirth as the great American melting pot. As children, George and his brother Ira had run rampant through their various neighborhoods with the children of Italian and Irish families. The city was growing up fast; with street traffic increasing and life being lived at an ever-quickening pace. It only made sense that the new music was ragtime; its infectious syncopated rhythms seemed the ideal match for the pace of the times. Songs like "Fascinating Rhythm," "Sweet and Low-Down," and "Lady, Be Good!" expressed the reckless youth of New York in the 1920s.

At first the new sound of Gershwin coexisted amiably enough with operetta. The two grand masters of the form, Rudolf Friml and Sigmund Romberg, scored some of their biggest successes during the 1920s, but by 1930 they were in eclipse. Both composers had shows open that year: Romberg's *Nina Rosa* was a disappointment, and Friml's *Luana* was an outright flop. Depression-era economics helped put the entire genre out of business, as producers simply could not afford to back such elaborate productions and enormous companies. All of this happened just as Gershwin was about to enter his most fertile period of writing for the theater.

But it took more than music for the Gershwin shows to succeed; they needed bright, sparkling words to match their jazzy, spiky rhythms. George found his ideal lyricist in his brother Ira, who brought a startling syncopation to the English language. While George had always been outgoing and confident, Ira had been an introverted, bookish child. George and Ira's parents had undertaken a long string of failed businesses over a period of many years, one of them a Turkish bath on Harlem's Lenox Avenue. Ira, pressed into service as an attendant there, passively delighted in the failure of the whole enterprise, because it allowed him more time to read. With his endlessly imaginative wordplay, Ira turned lyric writing on its head, breaking up lines in unorthodox ways to create startling rhymes and using slang in American song in a way that was fresh, everyday, and elegant all at the same time. Master lyricist Sheldon Harnick perhaps summed up Ira's gifts by saying that his entire career was an "unremitting battle against clichés." Once audiences had fallen under his spell, they might be forgiven for wondering why it had taken so long for anyone to figure out how to write this way.

Since the words had now become so important, so much wittier and more specific than much of what had been written during the glory days of operetta, different types of singers were needed. A big, legit voice and perfect, pear-shaped tones were less critical than an ability to put the words across in such a way that everyone in the audience could easily understand them. For this reason many of the top composers wanted to write for Fred Astaire, whose singing voice might not have taken any prizes but who had a beguiling way with a lyric.

If what the Gershwins were bringing to the Broadway musical was new and exciting, the book of *Girl Crazy*, by Guy Bolton and Jack McGowan, was anything but. Its plot was really nothing more than a gals-and-gags show centering on Danny Churchill (played by Allen Kearns), a spoiled rich kid from New York whose father sends him out to Custerville, Arizona, to oversee the family's ranch. Much of the humor of the piece stemmed from the conflict

of East versus West. Danny gets to Custerville by cab—it costs him $742.30—
and soon he decides to transform the family property into a dude ranch.
Meanwhile his cabdriver, Gieber Goldfarb (comedian Willie Howard), runs
for sheriff of Custerville—a tough job to hold on to, since all the previous
sheriffs have had a way of getting themselves shot about every two weeks.

Danny's love interest, Molly, was played by Ginger Rogers, only a few
years before she would emerge as a major Hollywood star. She had two wonderful songs, "Embraceable You" and "But Not for Me," that she managed
well enough. But Rogers, despite her charming stage presence, was no more
a first-class singer than Kearns and Howard were. The Gershwins needed at
least *one* strong voice in *Girl Crazy*, which made the casting of the part of
Kate Fothergill—a San Francisco café singer who comes with her husband,
Slick, to run Danny's gambling room—critical. It wasn't so much a part as a
glorified singing spot, but it offered the kinds of songs that demanded a
gutsy delivery. In the beginning Kate was to have been performed by someone listed only as "Miss Barry." Just exactly who Miss Barry was remains
something of a mystery, but it may have been Vivian Barry, who appeared in
the later Gershwin shows *Of Thee I Sing* and *Let 'Em Eat Cake*. Vinton
Freedley's trip to the Brooklyn Paramount to catch Ethel's act, however, ef-
fectively eliminated Miss Barry from *Girl Crazy*'s history.

As Ethel began to sing, Freedley watched and listened in amazement.
She was far from pretty, and she was wearing an unflattering black dress, all
tricked up with bows and ribbons. But with her big, bold sound, she knocked
every lyric out over the orchestra, articulating every syllable perfectly. There
was a tremendous electricity to her singing, and she seemed to have barrels
of confidence. Freedley thought she was exactly the sort of singer likely to
appeal to the Gershwins.

That day as Ethel came offstage, Freedley was waiting for her in the
wings. Of course she knew him by reputation. He told her that he was producing *Girl Crazy* and that he wanted to arrange an audition with George
and Ira Gershwin.

Only a few days later, Ethel was nervously riding up in the elevator at
33 Riverside Drive, where George occupied the penthouse on one half of the
floor and Ira had the other half. The very scale of the building intimidated
her, but the brothers greeted her warmly and tried to put her at ease. She
sang two of her old standby numbers, "Little White Lies" and "Exactly Like
You." The Gershwins liked what they heard and began describing *Girl Crazy*
to her. The character of Kate was to have three songs in the show: "Sam and
Delilah," "I Got Rhythm," and "Boy! What Love Has Done to Me." George

played while Ira sang, and Ethel listened attentively. Each one was a gem, and, oddly enough, they all could almost have been written with her voice in mind.

What happened next was to become a central part of the Merman legend. She always told the story exactly the same way, as if she were reciting Scripture, and to alter one word would have been blasphemy.

George Gershwin took his hands off the keyboard and said, "Miss Merman, if there's anything about these songs you don't like, I'll be most happy to change it."

Ethel was dumbfounded. Here was the greatest composer on Broadway offering to make concessions to a little-known girl from Queens. All she managed to get out was, "No, Mr. Gershwin, they'll do very nicely." Years later, when she was performing her act in nightclubs and with symphony orchestras around the world, she always recalled the exchange with Gershwin, and took pains to remind the audience, "And you know, ladies and gentlemen, you never change one note of a Gershwin tune."

Ethel was signed at a salary of $375 a week, and rehearsals started immediately at the Alvin Theatre. It was a hectic time, because of the two-show-a-day run at the Palace that she and Al Siegel were playing. When they opened in mid-September, the *New York Times* called Ethel "a comely ballad singer" whose Palace debut "promises well for her debut later in the season on the musical comedy stage." Ethel and Siegel rehearsed at the Alvin in the morning, dashed to the Palace for a matinee, came back to the Alvin to rehearse the rest of the afternoon, then went back to the Palace for the evening show. Usually there was one more late-night stint at the Alvin, where she was making a strong impression on her coworkers. She had a snappy way with her few lines, which she delivered simply and naturally, because she really believed them. She had crack comic timing, and there was nothing actressy about her. She instinctively knew the most important rule of comedy: when you try to make it funny, you usually fall flat; just play it straight, and if the scene is any good at all, it *will* be funny. It wasn't long before Freedley was instructing the book writers to beef up the role of Kate.

In the script Kate was originally described as being something of a Diamond Lil type, but in the end the role shaped up to be the kind of part that Eve Arden would later make a career of in the movies. When Kate catches her husband, Slick, on the make, she berates him, "You promised me a divorce two years ago. And if you can ever make enough money for me to hire a lawyer, I'm gonna sue you." Kate reassures the lovelorn Molly with some

sage sisterly advice: "Men are like buses. There's always another one coming along. . . . And if you wait long enough, there'll be the same one coming
back." As the show finished rehearsals and moved on to Philadelphia for its
out-of-town tryout, the word around Broadway's bars and coffee shops was
that the Gershwins had an exciting new star in the making.

Ethel was so excited she could barely contain herself—excited, but not
actually nervous. Always a quick study, she had her lines down cold and felt
thoroughly prepared by the Gershwins, who were completely captivated by
her diligent, working-girl manner and no-nonsense attitude. Both the brothers dined out for years on one particular story: Ira had come up with some
extra lines for "Sam and Delilah," and Ethel asked him to dictate them to
her over the telephone while she calmly took them down in shorthand. It was
typical of her levelheaded approach to solving problems, and not the kind of
thing, Ira pointed out, that just any Broadway singer would have been able
to pull off.

The only thing that worried Ethel as she prepared to open in Philadelphia was Al Siegel's condition. He had not been well for some years; by now
his chronic, rattling cough was getting much worse, and he was spitting up
blood. The diagnosis appears to have been tuberculosis. His doctors tried to
persuade him to enter the hospital, but there was too much at stake with
Ethel for Siegel to drop out now. His energy steadily plummeting, he packed
to go to Philadelphia with the rest of the company.

Few Broadway-bound debutantes have ever been as lucky as Ethel. The
part of Kate was cleverly designed to catch the audience by surprise, for
though she first appeared in the play's second scene, she had only a few
snatches of dialogue until the first act was about to come to a close. Just as
the audience had accepted Ethel as a straight comedienne with book scenes
only, she suddenly sauntered onstage, leaned against the piano where Al
Siegel was seated, and launched into "Sam and Delilah." She toyed with a
cigarette, and her provocative costume—a black satin skirt slit daringly
high, red silk blouse, garter, and ankle straps—caused a stir on its own. But
when she opened her mouth and shot out the song's first line, "De-li-
laaaaaaaaaah was a *floozy*!"—the audience was both delighted and riveted.
It was a sexy, funny blues song, and Ethel's precise delivery guaranteed that
every single joke came through. She finished the song to a big ovation. Then,
immediately afterward, came "I Got Rhythm."

One of the first things that must have struck Ethel about the song when
Gershwin first played it for her was how simple it was—just a quick trip up
and down the pentatonic scale. The words were equally simple. For weeks Ira

had wandered around fiddling with a dummy lyric for the song (at one time it was "Roly-poly / Eating solely / Ravioli / Better watch your diet or bust!"), and at last he hit on the idea of abandoning a rhyme scheme and simply repeating the words "I got" at the beginning of each line. The Philadelphia audience loved it and applauded it even more than they had "Sam and Delilah."

Ethel also made a hit in the book scenes; she seemed a natural comedienne, and the audience roared at her lines. After the first show in Philadelphia, Jack McGowan wrote even more dialogue for her—none of which sat too well with Ginger Rogers, who was starting to get the feeling that Ethel was taking over the entire show. But Rogers wasn't in a position to argue. Although she'd made a good impression in a few Hollywood films, she was still some distance from major stardom, and she had little clout. She watched helplessly as Ethel's part grew and grew.

On October 14, 1930, *Girl Crazy* opened on Broadway. Al Siegel, still very sick, managed by sheer will to be on hand for opening night. The orchestra, which would go on to become part of musical legend, included several members of Red Nichols and His Five Pennies: Benny Goodman on clarinet, Jimmy Dorsey on saxophone, Glenn Miller and Jack Teagarden on trombone, and Gene Krupa on drums. Further luster was added by having George Gershwin himself conduct the premiere performance. The first-nighters included Gertrude Lawrence and George White. Ethel later recalled, with wicked delight, that "all the big shots I'd sent notes and flowers to when I worked for Bragg were out front."

From the time Gershwin gave the downbeat, *Girl Crazy* sailed through with the confidence that belongs only to a sure hit. The audience liked the first number, the easygoing "Bidin' My Time," sung by a quartet of ranch hands. The songs that followed in act 1, including the jaunty "Could You Use Me?" and the wistful "Embraceable You," all got a warm response. Then Ethel came out in her black satin dress and tore into "Sam and Delilah." All through the number, the audience loudly registered its pleasure, so much so that Ethel would remember, "I thought my garter had snapped or I'd lost something." By the time she reached its end, she knew she had landed safely, and she braced herself for "I Got Rhythm."

The Gershwins must have been certain all along that the song would be a hit: it was the first tune heard in the overture and the last the orchestra played at the end of the show. (Perhaps it helped the audience forget "Cactus Time in Arizona," the clunker that was the final melody of the evening.) For "I Got Rhythm," the brothers had taken advantage of Ethel's lung power and included a stunt in the second chorus that they hoped would stop the show: on the word "I," she was to hold the C above middle C for sixteen bars. It was a daring trick that few singers could have pulled off with such panache, and it had an electrifying effect on the audience, which responded with cheering and clapping and more cheering. Lyricist Dorothy Fields was in the audience that night and recalled that Ethel seemed slightly stunned by the reaction, as if she didn't quite believe what was happening. There was a time when encores were the audience's seal of approval on a Broadway musical. That night "I Got Rhythm" took more encores than anyone would later be able to remember.

At intermission everyone out front crowded into the lobby, chattering in exclamation points about the new discovery. There was excitement backstage, too: at the end of the first act, Al Siegel collapsed and had to be carried away on a stretcher, and Roger Edens, another member of the Red Nichols orchestra, was preparing to take over for him in the second act. In Ethel's dressing room at the top of the theater, the mood was calmer. Mom and Pop Zimmermann had come backstage, trying not to show that they were bursting with pride while Ethel sat at her dressing table, methodically adjusting her eye makeup. Suddenly there was a knock on the door, and George Gershwin himself exploded into the room.

"Ethel," he gasped, "do you know what's happened? Do you know what you've done?"

Ethel didn't quite understand. "You've just been made a star!" George shouted. She still seemed nonplussed. Exasperated by Ethel's inability to grasp what had happened, George turned to Mrs. Zimmermann and said, "Did you ever see a person so unconcerned as Ethel?"

Before he dashed out to congratulate the other cast members, George made her promise that she would never go near a singing teacher. Then he added, "And never forget your shorthand."

Chapter Four

Perhaps the famed Yiddish theater actress Molly Picon described
Gershwin's music best, after seeing *Girl Crazy:* "Your music does
funny things to me. I feel like I'd just had a Swedish massage, sort of
all a-tingle." Some of the critics didn't quite share Picon's enthusiasm, but
the press generally liked *Girl Crazy,* despite their reservations about the
quality of the book. The *New York Times* set the tone: "One song, 'Sam and
Delilah,' sung by Miss Ethel Merman, as a tough girl from the Barbary Coast,
was specially interesting." The review went on to note that Ethel sang "with
dash, authority, good voice and just the right knowing style." The *New Yorker*
found Ethel "imitative of no one. . . . She approaches sex in song with something of the cold fury of the philosopher. She rhapsodizes, but she analyzes.
She seems to aim at a point slightly above the entrails, but she knocks
you out just the same. She shouts; she ravishes the words, and her 'Oh's go
sailing out over the orchestra like balloons."

It wasn't until noon on the day after *Girl Crazy* opened that Ethel became aware she'd made such a hit with the press. After the curtain came
down, she had taken her parents to the Central Park Casino, where she was
suddenly given the star treatment by the staff and shown to one of the best
tables in the house. She later went to the company party at the Gershwins'
but left before the newspapers were delivered. She grabbed a few hours'
sleep, then showed up at George Gershwin's apartment for lunch the next
day. A jubilant George had spread the reviews out everywhere, proof that he
and Ira had another hit on their hands.

He could scarcely believe it when Ethel told him that she hadn't thought
to pick up any of the newspapers. It wasn't false modesty; she'd always considered herself a singer, not an actress, and although she'd gone avidly to
vaudeville, she'd seen very few Broadway musicals. She simply had no idea
at all about the traditions of the theater.

Girl Crazy settled in for a long run at the Alvin. Ethel's coworkers marveled at how little all the attention seemed to have affected her. She showed

up punctually at the theater eight times a week, stepped out onstage, knocked the audience dead, then went back home to her parents in Astoria. This was the beginning of a pattern that was to mark her entire career. Much as she loved singing, she approached it simply and matter-of-factly as a job.

Although the Gershwins left New York shortly after *Girl Crazy*'s opening for a sojourn in Hollywood, George and Ethel stayed in close touch. George wrote her warm and affectionate letters, once addressing her as "my favorite singer of songs," and it looked as though their working relationship would continue in the future. "I want you to be in a big success next season," he wrote to her in November 1930, "because I think it is very important to your career. And whatever book they bring me, I will always look for your part very carefully." Ethel had, as she would always admit, come along at just the right time. Seldom had a composer and a singer fused their talents so successfully.

For now, Ethel hardly had time to think of future shows. A few weeks after *Girl Crazy* opened, she began a limited run at the Central Park Casino, an engagement that cemented her arrival. With its circular hardwood dance floor, elaborate floral displays, and high-octane celebrity clientele, the Casino was one of Manhattan's most elegant night spots. Her accompanist was now Roger Edens, leading many to wonder what had happened to Al Siegel. After Siegel had been taken to the hospital on the opening night of *Girl Crazy* and Edens had substituted for him in the pit, Ethel found herself immediately charmed by Edens's deep voice, Texas drawl, and kindly manner. Best of all, he was a musician par excellence. Later in the 1930s, he would go to Metro-Goldwyn-Mayer, where he would stay for years as a crucial member of Arthur Freed's production unit. There he helped to create the style and sound of another big-voiced singing phenomenon, Judy Garland.

Shortly after her opening in *Girl Crazy*, Ethel, accompanied by Lou Irwin, went to visit Siegel in Bethel, Connecticut, where he was recuperating. With an important booking coming up at the Casino, Ethel wanted some new song arrangements, and she and Irwin had it in mind to extend the deal she had previously had with Siegel: 25 percent of her club fees for use of the arrangements. But Siegel had read the reviews of *Girl Crazy*, too, and knew an opportunity when he saw one. He countered that he would be happy to write the new arrangements in exchange for 33 percent of all Ethel's earnings *in perpetuity.*

Ethel was livid. Now that she was launched on a career as a musical-comedy actress, she could see no reason that Siegel was entitled to *any* cut of her salary on projects that didn't involve him. Irwin backed her up 100 percent, and in a heartbeat Al Siegel was erased from her life.

This was to become one of the dominant cycles of Ethel's life. If some-one used her, or if she felt that someone was trying to use her, she could make him vanish instantly. It played into the vulnerable side of her person-ality, a side she took great pains to hide from everyone except her closest circle, and it helped establish her enduring reputation for toughness. Her longtime friend Tony Cointreau remembered that she had no ability to edit her thoughts or reactions, no matter how strong they were. "We all have that little policeman in our heads," said Cointreau. "She didn't have that little policeman. If you were faking it, you wouldn't get away with it for one sec-ond. And it could be trivial. She couldn't let it go. She had to make it an issue. Black or white. She couldn't go to the gray area." Ethel's reaction was always strongest when she felt that someone had lied to her or taken advan-tage of her, even slightly. No matter how long the friendship or association, it could end in a matter of seconds. She even had a word that she used to describe her abrupt cutting-off of people: "Fing!" Finished.

At first it seemed that her "Fing!" was not going to have much effect on Al Siegel. He talked to many people about what he considered Ethel's be-trayal of him, one of whom happened to be the powerful columnist Walter Winchell. Winchell then ran an item about Siegel's claim to be the master-mind of her singing style. Ethel fired back a sharp telegram to Winchell that concluded with, I'M TELLING YOU THE ONLY THING THAT AL SIEGEL EVER DID WAS WRITE ARRANGEMENTS. HE NEVER TAUGHT ME ANYTHING. Winchell printed her remarks, which Ethel considered "as close to a retraction as you could get from him in his prime."

The next several months were among the busiest of Ethel's life. Para-mount released *Follow the Leader* in early December, to generally positive notices, although most critics concentrated on the performance of its star, Ed Wynn. After Ethel's Casino engagement ended, she signed a contract with Paramount to make a series of ten musical short subjects. What these reveal today is that the Merman persona was already well on its way to being fully formed. In *Roaming*, Ethel plays the daughter of a traveling medicine-show peddler who is tired of her vagabond life. In *Ireno*, she is a woman on the brink of breaking up with her husband after a silly argument. In both she has a big, rousing number, the type that would come to be associated with her. In both she also has a ballad that she delivers in a beautifully shimmering tone, showing a decided soprano mix that she would eventually abandon.

By March of 1931, the Central Park Casino had reengaged her, along with Edens, who was now providing arrangements that she liked every bit as much as she had Siegel's. A particular hit was his treatment of the popular tune "Just a Gigolo." The *New York Evening Post* noted, "Never before has Ethel Merman been more charming or stimulating. She keeps her audience spellbound with her group of individual songs and her 'Gigolo' is something to be remembered."

All this success and the attendant publicity still had little effect on Ethel's personal life. She continued to live with Mom and Pop Zimmermann at the Windsor Apartments. When she could, she helped Mom with the housework, although she showed no interest whatsoever in cooking.

After the engagement at the Casino, she and Edens played the New York Paramount, and by July they were back at the Palace. They were still there when *Girl Crazy* closed, on June 6, 1931, with an impressive total of 272 performances. The show had been the most thrilling event of Ethel's life, but she didn't mind its coming to an end. She was sure that someday soon she would work with the Gershwins again.

"Nothing lasts forever in the theater," says the playwright's wife, played by Celeste Holm in Joseph L. Mankiewicz's 1950 movie classic *All About Eve*. People in show business have always been famous for their short memories, and it's impossible to tell when yesterday's rejection is going to turn into tomorrow's job offer. Only a few years earlier, George White had no time for Ethel; now he found himself in desperate need of her. The newest edition of his *Scandals*—his eleventh—was in big trouble, and to save it he wanted the girl singer who had just made such a hit in *Girl Crazy*. What Ethel wanted was a vacation. After her run at the Palace ended, she had booked herself, along with Pop and Mom, into a quiet resort at Lake George. Eager to see her parents travel in style, with some of her earnings from the Palace she purchased a Chrysler and engaged a chauffeur to drive them all upstate.

Ethel's vacation lasted a single day. At the end of the first afternoon at Lake George, she came back to the hotel and was handed a fistful of increasingly frantic messages to get in touch with George White. Once she telephoned him, the producer wasted no time sugarcoating the situation: the *Scandals* was in its Atlantic City tryout, and it was in trouble. White not only produced his shows, he staged them, as well. Each time he had mounted a new edition of the *Scandals,* friends advised him to throw the whole thing away. He never listened and always brought in a hit. This time, however, things really were not gelling, and he was growing frantic.

Ethel didn't bother reminding him that he had passed on her years earlier. This was another job, in one of Broadway's most high-profile revues. There was one minor problem: she was still contractually bound to Vinton Freedley, who wasn't about to do White any favors. Freedley made the terms of buying up Ethel's contract tough—the *New York Times* reported that the amount was $10,000—but White had seen *Girl Crazy,* and he was sure that Ethel was the one performer who could save his ailing show. He handed over the buyout money to Freedley and signed Ethel at a weekly salary of $1,500.

The 1931 version of the *Scandals* was a lot like its predecessors: loud and fast, a little bit vulgar, and heavy on topical satire. It starred crooner Rudy Vallee, then at the apex of his popularity, who had stiff competition from the rest of the talented cast. First and foremost were Willie Howard, fresh from *Girl Crazy,* and his brother Eugene, who together appeared in most of the comic sketches, including the famous "Pay the Two Dollars" routine. Also on board were dancer Ray Bolger, who played former New York State governor Al Smith in the tart-tongued "Empire State" spoof that opened the show, and power-mad columnist Walter Windshield in "The Daily Reflector," one of the comic highlights of the second act. Metropolitan Opera comprimario Everett Marshall closed the first act with a social-message song, "That's Why Darkies Were Born." There was major talent even in the chorus—namely, Alice Faye, a pretty, cow-eyed girl whose mellow contralto would later be heard in some of 20th Century Fox's biggest musical films. (She was only sixteen, but, as was the custom of the time, she had lied about her age to land a chorus job.)

On arriving in Atlantic City, Ethel studied the rehearsals. The physical production was undeniably first class, with sets by Joseph Urban, the brilliant designer whose style combined elements of the Viennese Jungendstil painters with a bold American showmanship. Urban's work had ranged from *Parsifal* and *Les Contes d'Hoffmann* for the Metropolitan Opera to the *Ziegfeld Follies.* The superb costumes were by Charles LeMaire, who would go on to become an Academy Award–winning designer for the 20th Century Fox studio. The comedy sketches were in pretty good shape and were getting their laughs. Ethel felt that the trouble lay in the songs, by Lew Brown and Ray Henderson. With their ex-partner Buddy DeSylva, they had been one of the most successful songwriting teams of the 1920s. (The 1926 edition of the *Scandals* had included their hits "Birth of the Blues" and "Black Bottom.") But DeSylva left his partners in 1930, after they wrote the Bert

Lahr vehicle *Flying High,* and without him Brown and Henderson had come up with a score for the new *Scandals* that fell far short of the team's old standard.

Initially several of the show's songs had been entrusted to another Ethel: Ethel Barrymore Colt, of Broadway's royal family. Her taking her millionaire father Russell Colt's last name showed her streak of independence, for she had worked hard to distance herself from the overpowering legacy of the Barrymores. Another way to do this was to distinguish herself as a singer. She had a legit voice, and would eventually achieve a marked degree of success as a nightclub chanteuse, but somehow she wasn't coming across in the songs that Brown and Henderson had given her. It was decided that Colt would remain in a few sketches but that the songs would be handed over to Merman. Years later Merman recalled that this turn of events devastated Colt, who considered leaving the show. In the end she swallowed hard and stood back while a different Ethel took center stage.

Ethel's instincts about material once again proved unerring. She listened to "Hosanna," her solo number in the first act, tried it out, and didn't think it was right for her. Her other solo in act 1, "(Ladies and Gentlemen), That's Love," was much more her style and worked reasonably well. Then she had "My Song," a duet with Rudy Vallee in the second act. Brown and Henderson agreed with her about "Hosanna," went back to work, and came up with "Life Is Just a Bowl of Cherries." In Ethel's exuberant performance, it provided the musical high spot that the first act was desperately missing, and the production team knew that at last their show had a fighting chance.

Despite his former dismissal of her, Ethel admired White's professional style. As an ex-performer himself, he had developed an astute eye for what was wrong with a scene and how to fix it, and Ethel happily took direction from him. His hands-on management style impressed her; on some days he even sold tickets himself at the box-office window. In the end White was so delighted with Ethel that he gave her the coveted eleven-o'clock spot: she simply came out and sang a batch of her favorite songs. They weren't by Brown and Henderson, but it didn't matter, as the rules of revue were anything but strict.

Although the *Scandals* didn't give Ethel a book part, like Kate in *Girl Crazy,* she scarcely minded: despite the enormous boost that the Gershwin show had given her, she still thought of herself as a singer more than an actress. She was thrilled to be part of such an important Broadway institution

as the *Scandals,* which went to Newark, and then to Brooklyn for additional
fine-tuning, before reaching Broadway's Apollo Theatre on September 14,
1931. John Mason Brown in the *New York Post* called the new *Scandals* "by
all odds the best musical show that has struck this town since *The Band
Wagon.*" The *New York Herald Tribune* stated that White "finds himself the
proprietor of the brightest and richest revue he ever owned." The presence of
opera baritone Everett Marshall seemed to add a certain legitimacy to the
show. His big number, "That's Why Darkies Are Born," was singled out for
particular praise, although some reviewers felt that the latter was compro-
mised by the excessive staging, which included showgirls dressed up as angels. (One critic felt that this effect "had no particular bearing on the song,
but raised the uneasy suspicion that the taste elsewhere evinced was the result of a happy accident.") Again Ethel received plenty of enthusiastic praise.
The *New York American* found that "Ethel Merman has been called in to
croon things in her lusty way, whereby she seems to take all Newark and
Nebraska into her confidence in one fell whoop [*sic*]."

Despite the show's success, it was to be the sole partnership of White
and Ethel. There would be only two more editions of the *Scandals,* in 1935
and 1939, after which White settled into quiet retirement in California,
emerging only occasionally to produce an old-fashioned girlie show.

Shortly after the 1931 *Scandals* opened, Ethel's old, staid life and her
new, exciting one came together: the Secretary Club of America presented
her with a miniature solid-gold typewriter and named her America's Most
Successful Secretary.

There was no question that Ethel enjoyed every minute of her success. One
night during the *Scandals* run, she and some friends ducked into Les Ambassadeurs, where only a short time earlier she had appeared with Clayton,
Jackson, and Durante. On this particular evening, Helen Morgan was the
headliner. At some point in her program, Morgan announced that she was
going to sing two numbers made famous by Miss Ethel Merman in *George
White's Scandals.* It was, as Ethel pointed out, "a gratifying moment for an
ex-secretary from Astoria." Still, Ethel didn't lose her head, having already
seen enough to know that fame didn't usually last long, no matter how
much talent you might have. Money-conscious as ever, she wanted to set
aside as big a nest egg as possible. She calculated that in her first twenty-
two months in show business—coinciding with some of the worst days of the
Depression—she had earned a total of $100,000. Since she worried that her

luck might not last indefinitely, she continued to double at the Central Park Casino during the *Scandals* run, still watching every penny, still commuting to and from Astoria.

The *Scandals* closed in March 1932, after a 202-performance run. Beginning on April 24 Ethel was back at the Palace. In vaudeville, as in radio, there wasn't the great gulf between "high" and "low" culture that would eventually blight the American entertainment scene; at the Palace, Ethel's co-players ranged from comic Jack Haley and comedienne Patsy Kelly to Metropolitan Opera soprano Frances Alda. Many offers of Broadway shows soon followed, including one by the Gershwins that never materialized. Ethel sifted through the possibilities but didn't say yes until she was approached by Buddy DeSylva and Laurence Schwab.

Their show was called *Humpty Dumpty,* and it was another revue—sort of. *Humpty Dumpty* could not have been more self-referential: its plot hinged on the pitfalls of putting on a revue. The main backer was played by dialect comic Lou Holtz, and its various numbers aimed to spoof famous figures in American history, including Betsy Ross, Miles Standish, and Abraham Lincoln. Initially no one seems to have thought that a spoof of Lincoln sounded like a particularly bad idea, and DeSylva had high hopes for the show. To write the score, he had hired Nacio Herb Brown and Richard Whiting, both of whom had left Broadway for Hollywood, where the sound revolution had kept them busy turning out movie musicals.

In the 1930s, when the financial stakes were so much lower than they were to become in future decades, musicals were often thrown together quickly. In many cases the book and score didn't exist in any kind of reasonable form when the stars signed their contracts, and sometimes the show was still being written while rehearsals were under way. Work was fast, frenetic, and often trial-and-error.

Humpty Dumpty was a prime example of such a show, and Ethel recalled that "no word has been invented to describe" the condition of the original book. Rehearsals began in August 1932, and on September 12, *Humpty Dumpty* opened in Pittsburgh—and promptly closed. Ethel was furious. She hadn't had a failure yet, and now it looked as if her perfect record had crumbled. Assembling the dispirited company for a passionate pep talk, DeSylva told them, "Ladies and gentlemen, I know this show is going to be a hit. We just have to work it over again. We've got great songs, great performers, but there's something wrong. We've got to keep working. We've got to take a chance." In a split second, he knew he had the title for his beleaguered production. *Humpty Dumpty* was rechristened *Take a Chance,* and the determined company headed back to New York.

For several weeks frantic rewriting went on. A number of cast members were dropped, including Lou Holtz, who stayed on to help rework the piece. Most of the historical episodes were scrapped. The book, still extremely loose, now focused on a pair of tinhorn gamblers (Jack Haley, Sid Silvers) who leave the small-time carnival circuit behind in hopes of finding bigger pickings in the legitimate theater. Their lady friend aspires to be a singer, and her love interest, a Harvard man (baritone Jack Whiting), having distinguished himself in productions of the Hasty Pudding Club, decides to try his luck as a show-business professional. As in *Girl Crazy*, Ethel was cast as a tough nightclub singer. It was a secondary role, but she had the best songs: "You're an Old Smoothie," a duet for Ethel and Jack Haley, and "Eadie Was a Lady," a blowsy comic saga of a loose woman that owed a little to "Sam and Delilah" and a little to "Frankie and Johnny."

The only one not participating in the show's overhaul was Richard Whiting, who had lost heart, despite his admiration for Ethel. His daughter, the distinguished pop singer Margaret Whiting, remembered, "My father told me later she was a shining star. She could be tough, but she could be magical. She came out on the stage and took a bow and then she went on with it. She was like a royal lady." Already Richard Whiting was plagued by a worrisome heart condition and high blood pressure—he would die in 1938 at forty-six—and he missed his wife and daughter in Hollywood. "I've never gone through a thing like that, where everything was falling apart," he said later. "I'm writing for pictures now, and it's much easier." He begged DeSylva to let him return to California. DeSylva and Ethel both demanded that he stay, but Whiting held firm. "I've given you three or four good songs" he said. "Let me go." When DeSylva refused to take no for an answer, Whiting countered that there was only one composer who could finish the show: Vincent Youmans. With that, he said good-bye to New York and to *Take a Chance*.

Youmans was brought in and provided five new songs, including a raise-the-rafters number for Ethel called "Rise and Shine." Roger Edens, meanwhile, had gone to work on "Eadie Was a Lady," preparing a hilarious middle section that gave the number even more sardonic bite. In tone it resembled some of Mae West's risqué songs from the movies. From the first performance, audiences were stunned when Ethel, wearing a red dress and black boa, sashayed onto the set of a New Orleans supper club and began to sing about Eadie, her "sister in sin."

By November 5 the still-wobbly production opened in Wilmington, Delaware. The reviews were much better than anyone had expected, with the *Wilmington News* noting that Ethel "just about walked away with the show." Then came more reworking in Philadelphia and Newark. But *Take a Chance* had to face New York sometime, and when it did, at the Apollo Theatre on November 26, the reviews gave no indication of its troubled history. Percy Hammond in the *New York Herald Tribune* headlined his review "Here Are Happy Days Again" and called *Take a Chance* "fast on its feet, quick-witted, insolent, and full of pleasing sounds. It contains everything that Broadway craves, from smut to sentiment." Brooks Atkinson in the *New York Times* found it "fast, loud and funny. . . . Ethel Merman has never loosed herself with quite so much abandon into ballads and pagan revival numbers."

Take a Chance was a hit, and "Eadie Was a Lady" became the latest song sensation around Broadway. The *Times* even took the trouble to reprint its lyrics in their entirety.

Although she didn't fully grasp it, Ethel had, in just three shows, completely rewritten the rules for girl singers on Broadway. With her cocky, hip-swinging walk, her shoulders rolling from side to side, her hands thrust out as if to grab the audience or, alternatively, thrown up over her head, she was unlike any Broadway star anyone had experienced before. She had a raw energy that up to now had been found only in a handful of male performers. Like Al Jolson, she possessed a genius for selling a song, an infallible instinct for what made a number work. There had been other brassy female singers before, but never one with such a cold-eyed command of the stage, such a powerful vocal apparatus, such a knack for making a song sound like ordinary conversation—admittedly, conversation at earsplitting volume.

Ethel stayed with *Take a Chance* until it closed, on July 1, 1933, after 243 performances. That made her record three hits in a row, and for the first time she decided to take a show on the road. A few weeks later, *Take a Chance* opened in Chicago with the comedy team of Olsen and Johnson standing in for Jack Haley and Sid Silvers. Ethel brought Pop and Mom with her and set them up in an apartment. At the time the city was playing host to the World's Fair, which had taken for its theme "A Century of Progress."

Ethel's stay in Chicago was short, and she later claimed that the chlorine in the city's water supply irritated her throat and forced her withdrawal.

But she can hardly have been happy about playing opposite Olsen and Johnson—especially Johnson, who, as one critic noted, would take a gag and practically choke the life out of it in his trademark manic style. After two weeks Ethel was happy to head back to New York, where she hoped to sign on to another show. But not long after arriving, she decided to branch out in another direction—west, to Hollywood.

E thel took her first stab at Hollywood in the fall of 1933. Lou Irwin, whose business interests were increasingly focused on the West Coast, had arranged a contract for her with Paramount Publix. Once the studio had been known as Famous Players–Lasky, the same company at which Ethel had once caught a glimpse of Alice Brady and other stars in Astoria. Earlier on, it had developed a major distribution wing by acquiring Paramount Pictures Corporation, and now it was one of the biggest film factories in Hollywood, with a roster of stars that included Claudette Colbert, Miriam Hopkins, Sylvia Sidney, and W. C. Fields. Ethel was uneasy about being so far away from home on her own, so it was decided that Mom Zimmermann would accompany her. Mom had never been separated from Pop for any length of time in their entire marriage, but she felt the need to support Ethel in this exciting and somewhat intimidating new venture. They traveled west by train and, like most newcomers to California, were stunned by the miles and miles of orange groves that paved the way to the Pasadena station. Once in Los Angeles, they moved into a Hancock Park apartment building called the Ravenswood, where Paramount's number-one female star, Mae West, also resided.

At the time the recommended road to success for a Hollywood novice was to sign a standard seven-year contract with a major film studio. These contracts were loaded down with options, almost all of them on the studio's side; an unlucky actor might find himself unceremoniously dropped at any moment. For the independent-minded stage actor, long-term Hollywood employment could seem a kind of human bondage, and some of them did their best to negotiate time off to return to the theater. This didn't always work out to their benefit. "I had a stupid contract," recalled Jane Wyatt of her early days in Hollywood. "I was supposed to come out in the summer and then go back to New York in the winter to do plays. But of course it didn't work, because they wouldn't have the picture ready, and then you'd miss the play."

But the seven-year contract did have its advantages: in general, the studios worked overtime promoting their contract players, gradually building their names before the public. Most actors found that such benefits outweighed the annoyances. If the scripts were not always what they hoped for, they were well paid, got to live in luxurious surroundings, and acquired an avid army of fans that they might never have dreamed of during their Broadway days.

Ethel, however, wasn't offered a seven-year contract. Instead Paramount handed her a one-picture deal, which she enthusiastically accepted. She figured if Hollywood wasn't to her liking, the relationship would be over within one picture. If she did like it and managed to make good, the studio would ask her to stay on longer.

The one picture was called *We're Not Dressing*, based on a 1903 J. M. Barrie play, *The Admirable Crichton*. The director was Norman Taurog, under contract to Paramount, who had also directed Ethel's feature debut, *Follow the Leader*. (In the interim he had won an Academy Award for his direction of the 1931 Jackie Cooper hit *Skippy*.) The cast was impressive: Paramount's hot singing star Bing Crosby had the lead, up-and-coming comedienne Carole Lombard was cast opposite him, and George Burns and Gracie Allen had the second leads. The songs were by Harry Revel and Mack Gordon. The problem was that *We're Not Dressing*, a knockabout farce centering on a gang of eccentrics marooned on an island, wasn't very good basic material. Ethel might have been surrounded by some of the studio's top talent, but she couldn't quite see how *We're Not Dressing* was going to give her much of an opportunity to shine.

On top of everything else, she didn't like the treatment she was getting at the studio. They were blunt in their assessment of her looks, and first they cut her hair short, then only to insist that she wear a long, dark wig. Every choice they made was further indication that they didn't know what to do with her. Because she wasn't under a long-term contract, as most of her co-players were, she later commented that having a one-picture deal at Paramount "was like being in on a pass."

In *We're Not Dressing*, she was given two comic solos. One, "It's a New Spanish Custom," wasn't much, but the other, "It's the Animal in Me," was a big production number with camels, kangaroos, monkeys, and elephants, all trained to execute some rather complicated choreography. "It's the Animal in Me" was a catchy, lively tune, and Ethel's one chance of emerging from the picture with any credit.

Shooting dragged on through the Christmas holidays. It was the first Christmas that Ethel had been away from Pop, and she grew even more miserable. She was seldom invited to parties and spent most of her evenings at the Ravenswood having dinner with Mom. It hadn't taken her long to figure out that her Broadway success counted for very little in the film capital. She was hardly the first stage star to have her eyes so abruptly opened to the ways of Hollywood. Helen Hayes, whose reputation in the theater had already been established when she came to California on an MGM contract in 1931, remembered that early in her stay she was invited to a grand-scale Hollywood party at the home of decorator Billy Haines. "It was so extravagant and wonderful," Hayes recalled, "and yet everyone had a hunted expression. They told me, 'Oh, you're so lucky to be in the theater.' They were all complaining. And I finally said to Billy, 'It surprised me. I thought everyone would be so happy out here. You're secure, you have this great money coming in. These beautiful contracts with the big companies promoting you. I don't understand why nobody is happy about it.' And Billy said, 'Out here, you're only as good as your last picture. And everybody is scared to death of what the next picture will bring.' "

Tired of having her achievements overlooked, Ethel got a little testy with the Hollywood press when it was suggested that her performing style owed something to Mae West's. Although they occupied different floors of the Ravenswood, West had not been particularly friendly, and Ethel got even by telling reporters that it was she who had started the Mae West vogue, not the other way around. "I was singing 'Eadie Was a Lady' all dressed up with the wiggly hips an' everything before Mae West's first picture, *Night After Night*, came out," Ethel said, ". . . so I shall always claim Mae sailed to glory on my vogue." In fact, West's style was fully evolved by the time of her big stage successes of the 1920s, long before she hit Hollywood. But Ethel's rewriting of history was a good indication of her defensiveness over her treatment in Hollywood.

After her first true vacation—several weeks' rest in Cuba—Ethel returned to New York. The question of whether to continue living in Queens had been on her mind for some time. For one thing, Astoria had lost much of its peaceful ambience; during the 1920s the borough of Queens had grown 130 percent. For Ethel the commute from Astoria to Broadway had also become impractical, so she set up her first Manhattan residence, a large apartment in an elegant art deco building, the Century, at 25 Central Park West. She needed the space, since Pop and Mom, along with the pet terrier, Scrapsie, were all moving in with her.

.   .   .   .   .

As Ethel's fame grew, columnists began to hound her for details about the men in her life. She was discreet to the point of being closemouthed, especially in Hollywood, where the press machine was so intrusive and overpowering. Her stock answer to such personal questions was that her professional commitments kept her too busy to consider a serious romance. In fact, she had dated several men since achieving stardom. Her most serious beau was Al Goetz, a Wall Street whiz kid with the firm of Ungergleider and Goetz, whom she had met while appearing in *Girl Crazy*. He was upfront about his situation: he was married, but he and his wife were legally separated. This wasn't good enough for Mom Zimmermann, who viewed him with suspicion from the start, though Ethel did her best to quell her mother's fears. After all, she could do much worse: Goetz was an attractive enough man about town with important connections. Pop, for his part, believed that the romance with Goetz had distinct benefits. From the time she hit stardom, Pop had urged Ethel to make sure she got what was coming to her financially and warned her not to let anyone take advantage of her. Pop thought Goetz had done a remarkable job of investing Ethel's money, and even Mom had to agree. Even though the nation was suffering an intense economic crisis, Ethel was able to keep it all at a safe distance, thanks to Al's wise counsel. As her fortunes grew, so did her feelings for Goetz. In time she was confiding to Josie Traeger, Alice Welch, and her other closest friends that she had fallen in love for the first time. But as the romance intensified, months, then years rolled by, and Mom became ever more skeptical, since Goetz still showed no sign of divorcing his estranged wife.

By the spring of 1934, Ethel was casting around for a new Broadway show. She still had not shaken off the difficult time she'd had in Hollywood, and the pain of the whole experience was driven home when *We're Not Dressing* was released in late April. Her own notices were positive: the *New York Daily News* thought she had mastered "all the tricks of the clever comedienne," while the *Daily Mirror* found her "an unusual and very effective roughhouse comedienne." But to Ethel's dismay, "It's the Animal in Me" had been eliminated from the final print. No one from Paramount had bothered to notify her; she found out at the New York opening, in the company of her family and closest friends. Since she had told them all that the number was her best spot in the picture, she was doubly devastated. Norman Taurog later told her it had been cut because it detracted from the main story line, which was probably an evasive way of saying that it detracted from Bing

Crosby—no matter that it had been a costly and complicated number to film. For Ethel it was Hollywood's first real slap in her face. There would be others, far more painful and far more wrongheaded.

For now she was determined to try again, and very soon there was another Hollywood offer—this time from an unusual source. In 1930 independent mogul Samuel Goldwyn, in the process of scouting major stage talents, had signed comedian Eddie Cantor to a contract. Prior to coming to Hollywood, Cantor had been one of the great stage clowns: a skinny, eye-rolling nitwit always getting into scrapes. He was a kind of precursor to both Bob Hope and Jerry Lewis, and for much of the 1920s and 1930s there were few bigger names in show business. When he pranced around in blackface or launched into one of his signature tunes, "If You Knew Susie" or "Makin' Whoopee," audiences went wild.

The first film Cantor made for Goldwyn was *Whoopee*, the screen version of his 1928 stage show. The movie was a big hit and led to a whole string of Goldwyn-produced Cantor vehicles. In mid-1934, Cantor was having a meeting in Goldwyn's office when a call was put through from his teenage daughter, Marilyn. As it turned out, Marilyn was president of the first official Ethel Merman Fan Club and had kept up a steady correspondence with her favorite star. When Cantor mentioned that he and Goldwyn were discussing the next film they were going to make together—it was due to start shooting that summer— Marilyn told her father that Goldwyn should use Ethel in it. "Why don't *you* tell him?" responded Cantor, handing the telephone over to Goldwyn.

Cantor's precocious daughter wasn't intimidated in the least by talking to one of Hollywood's biggest producers. "This woman is terrific," she enthused, "and if you don't test her, you'll be losing a big bet." Goldwyn took the girl's advice and cast Ethel in *Kid Millions*. The film was a variation on the standard Cantor formula that had worked well for Goldwyn in the past. In this one, Cantor played a simpleton who inherits over $70 million and becomes the target of money-hungry villains, including a shady song plugger (Ethel) who passes herself off as Cantor's long-lost mother. The plot wasn't much, but the humor was hearty and genuine, and Ethel was pleased to be cast in such a big-budget film.

Shooting on *Kid Millions* began on July 16, 1934. The best song in the movie was Irving Berlin's "Mandy," recycled from the 1919 *Ziegfeld Follies* as a production number centered on Cantor. Again Ethel's part was definitely secondary, but early in the film she got a good song, Walter Donaldson and Gus Kahn's "An Earful of Music," which she delivered with panache. Cantor was fond of Ethel and took the time to coach her on some of the camera and lighting nuances that could make such a difference in how she appeared on-screen. In joking reference to *Kid Millions'* plot, Cantor and Ethel always called each other "Junior" and "Mama." Marilyn Cantor recalled that in 1941, when Cantor was acting on Broadway in *Banjo Eyes*, Ethel came backstage and yelled, "Junior! Junior! It's Mama!"

Kid Millions wrapped on September 22, and the film was released two months later. Cantor's box-office power, plus a spectacular finale set in an ice-cream factory and shot in early three-strip Technicolor at a cost of $210,000, combined to help make *Kid Millions* another hit for Goldwyn. The *New York Times* praised it as a "superior screen comedy" and judged Ethel's performance of "An Earful of Music" to be "joyous and healthy." In *Vanity Fair* she got what amounted to a rave: "The most important thing about the picture, however, is not Mr. Cantor this time, but the introduction of Ethel Merman as a bona fide screen comedienne and a swell gal for putting over a song—as nobody needs to be told."

Ethel does come off very well in the film—in all her scenes she shows superb comic timing, and her personality never seems too large for the screen, a criticism that would haunt her throughout her career. But the success of *Kid Millions* was ultimately of little value to her personally. Once again it was a case of no contract, no momentum.

Chapter Six

• • • • • • • • • • • • • • • • • • •

W hile it is often argued that Ethel Merman was launched into superstardom by Cole Porter's 1934 musical *Anything Goes*, it would be more accurate to say that it was that show that cemented the Merman image of the softhearted tough girl in a way her previous shows had not. What is indisputable is that the production that proved to be a crucial turning point in her career had a difficult birth.

The idea for *Anything Goes* came from Vinton Freedley. It had been only four years since he'd featured Ethel in *Girl Crazy*, but in that time his position had slipped considerably. This was partly due to the conditions that existed on Broadway in 1934, as the Depression had severely undercut producers' potential for commercial success. As recently as the 1928–29 season, Broadway had been in terrific shape, with a total of 224 productions opening. Many of them closed quickly, but performers weren't necessarily in a cold panic about finding their next job; usually they were certain that another show would come along soon enough to take its place.

But by 1930–31, the season of *Girl Crazy*, the total number of Broadway shows had dropped to 187, and by 1933–34 it had declined further, to 125. Actors, directors, composers, and writers had fled to Hollywood, with its lure of big money and security, like people in a crowded theater trying to find the fire exit. In the meantime Freedley's lucrative association with the Gershwins had run aground. Sam H. Harris had produced the brothers' 1931 Pulitzer Prize winner *Of Thee I Sing*. The following year the producing reins were handed back to Freedley with *Pardon My English*, but it was a dismal flop, and he never again worked with either the Gershwins or with his partner, Alex Aarons. Battling illness and dispirited by the turn in his fortunes, Freedley took an ocean cruise, which gave him the inspiration for a new show, a musical to be set on a luxury liner.

To a precision worker like Ethel, it must have been disconcerting to stand by and watch the haphazard way in which a show's book was often assembled. Since the musicals of the time were primarily lightweight,

song-driven star vehicles, it was not unusual for the book to be the last component to be pulled together. A substantial story was not deemed essential
or sometimes even desirable, as it might detract from the score and the
stars. Ethel may have thought that the writing of the book for *Take a Chance*
set a new standard of chaos, but *Anything Goes* threatened to surpass it.
Freedley believed in hiring his stars first and only then building the piece
around them, so not a comma had been committed to paper when he pitched
the show to Ethel and to the two men who would be her costars, William
Gaxton and Victor Moore. The brash, dynamic Gaxton and the timid, fey
Moore were already a team in the public's mind, having starred as President
Wintergreen and Vice President Throttlebottom in the Gershwins' *Of Thee I
Sing* and *Let 'Em Eat Cake.* All three stars gave Freedley a tentative yes,
especially after he had dropped the possibility of Cole Porter's composing
the music. Now all Freedley had to do was find someone to write the book,
and he settled on Guy Bolton and P. G. Wodehouse, two seasoned pros whose
successful track record ranged from Kern's *Leave It to Jane* (1917) to *Girl
Crazy.*

Bolton and Wodehouse undertook *Anything Goes* in far-from-ideal circumstances. By now tax troubles prevented Bolton from leaving England for
the United States, and Wodehouse was disinclined to abandon his haven in
France, so Bolton cobbled out a treatment after consulting with Wodehouse
by telephone. What they submitted wasn't a finished script at all, but a
lengthy, unfocused outline of scenes with a few passages of dialogue—a
framework that could give Cole Porter a rough idea of where to hang his
tunes. It featured some nonsense involving a low-ranking public enemy on
board a ship and a lot of chases and disguises, but there was practically
nothing to Ethel's part.

Freedley was horrified when he saw how little Bolton and Wodehouse
had come up with. But as they were distinguished theater writers, and since
Freedley didn't want to undercut his long association with them, he decided
to keep their names on the project and get someone else to do an overhaul
of the book. His first choice was the show's director, Howard Lindsay, who
didn't see how he could manage to direct and write the entire project himself. Lindsay told Freedley that he would agree to rework the book only if he
could have a collaborator.

Out of this mess, one of the most successful writing partnerships in the
history of the American theater was formed. By this time Lindsay was a
twenty-five-year veteran of the stage, having started out as an actor, segued
into directing, and written one play, a 1933 hit called *She Loves Me Not.*

Russel Crouse was then working as a press agent for the Theatre Guild and burning to write. The Ohio-born Crouse had started in journalism while still in his teens, and it was during a stint as a sportswriter for the *Kansas City Star* that he picked up the nickname "Buck," after the prizefighter Buck Crouse, by which he was thereafter known throughout his three-decade career in the theater. Before *Anything Goes* entered his life, his stage experience had consisted of providing the books for two flop musicals. But he was warm and funny and affable and well liked by everyone who worked with him. Among his admirers was Neysa McMein, a noted magazine illustrator who happened to be a close friend of Cole Porter's. The story became part of Broadway legend, though Ethel was never quite sure it was true: supposedly Porter asked McMein to help him come up with a collaborator, and that night she had a dream about Crouse. Lindsay grew frantic to find him, and as it turned out, he didn't have to look far: the Theatre Guild's offices were on the north side of Fifty-second Street, directly across from Freedley's headquarters. Lindsay popped the question simply by raising the window and hollering to Crouse across the street.

That night, Crouse showed up at the Greenwich Village apartment where Lindsay lived with his wife, the actress Dorothy Stickney. Cole Porter was there and played through several songs that he'd written with no real book to guide him. After hearing the score, Crouse accepted the offer, though Freedley's terms were far from princely. He had already paid out so much to Bolton and Wodehouse that he could pay only half of 1 percent of the royalties—what amounted to about fifty dollars a week—to both Lindsay and Crouse. But since the project was so prestigious, they agreed to the paltry terms and began writing that same night. They would have to move quickly, since rehearsals started in ten days.

Within twenty-four hours, they had devised what Crouse remembered as "a beautiful story." They went to Porter's, and Lindsay outlined the plot while Porter, as always, served cocktails. Lindsay's capacity, if he wanted to remain on top of his game, was two martinis, but he risked a third. The next morning neither he nor Crouse could remember the story, so they started from scratch. What they eventually came up with was a very funny script about a stockbroker, Billy Crocker (played by William Gaxton), who runs around town with a nightclub singer named Reno Sweeney (Ethel), who is sailing to London with her bevy of chorus girls. Reno is crazy about Billy, but he is really in love with the beautiful Hope Harcourt (Bettina Hall), who has plans to marry an English lord and is traveling abroad with him on the very same ship Reno is taking. When Billy realizes this, he decides to make one last try for Hope and sneaks onto the ship without a ticket or passport. Once on board he crosses paths with a minister, the Reverend Dr. Moon (Victor Moore), who is really Moonface Martin, Public Enemy Number 13, on the lam and hoping to elevate his status and climb to the top of J. Edgar Hoover's Most Wanted list. Moonface takes a shine to Billy and offers him a ticket and the passport of his cohort Snake Eyes Johnson, who has failed to reach the ship in time to sail. But two federal agents are also on board, and they wind up in hot pursuit of Billy, who tries to dodge them by disguising himself as a chef, a Spaniard— even the wife of the president of Columbia University.

In order to help Bolton and Wodehouse save face, the story was concocted that their original script had been abandoned because it involved a shipwreck. Shortly before rehearsals were to start, an explosion had occurred on the USS *Morro Castle*, just off the coast of New Jersey; the ship had sunk, taking with it 134 lives, and it had become clear to all concerned that a musical about a shipwreck would be the height of tastelessness. This ruse worked so well that, as Ethan Mordden later admitted, it had "taken in three generations of theater historians."

The Lindsay and Crouse script was sharp and sassy and contemporary, a perfect match for the score Cole Porter had devised. Unlike Ethel, Porter had not been a smash from the beginning. Born to comfortable circumstances in out-of-the-way Peru, Indiana, in 1891, he entered Yale in 1909. There he ran with a sophisticated crowd that included actor Monty Woolley, while writing a great number of football songs and shows for the Yale Dramatic Club. His first attempt at a Broadway musical, *See America First*, came in 1916, and closed after fifteen performances. With World War I still raging and the United States now fighting in it, Porter went to Europe, eventually enlisting in the French Foreign Legion. In 1918, while serving with the American embassy in Paris, he met the beautiful and wealthy socialite Linda Lee Thomas, whom he married the following year. The Porters lived abroad for several years, becoming part of the rapidly expanding café society. Porter continued to write, occasionally turning out a popular tune, but he didn't fully hit his stride until 1928, when his fourth Broadway musical, *Paris*, became a success. One of its songs, "Let's Do It," gave Broadway its first real taste of Porter's diamond-hard wit. In a line that began with Kern and moved through Irving Berlin, Rodgers and Hart, and the Gershwins, Porter worked to scrub away the layers of starch that had built up in the years when operetta was king. And nothing, not even the casual, democratic charms of the Gershwins, had prepared audiences for the man who wrote:

Old sloths who hang down from twigs do it,
Though the effort is great,
Sweet guinea pigs do it,
Buy a couple and wait.

Porter punctured Americans' puritanical attitudes toward sex in a way that neither enraged nor alienated his audiences. Instead it disarmed and delighted them. There was something else daringly new about Porter: he wrote about desire with a white-hot intensity that had never before been imagined. In *Gay Divorce* (1932), the Broadway show he composed just before *Anything Goes,* he expressed that desire with amazing directness:

Night and day, under the hide of me
There's an, oh, such a hungry yearning burning inside of me,
And its torment won't be through
Till you let me spend my life making love to you
Day and night, night and day.

Soon after they began working together, it became a commonplace for people to remark that Porter and Ethel seemed an unlikely combination. The Yale man steeped in art and classical verse, and the girl who hardly ever opened a book; the soigné man whose friends described his life as one long "frantic flight from boredom," and the upbeat girl who doted on simple pleasures; the man who prized elegant food and wine, and the girl who thrived on hamburgers and frankfurters; the man who had frequent relationships with other men yet remained devoted to his wife, and the girl whose sexuality was thoroughly uncomplicated; the impeccably tailored man, and the girl who loved loud hats and flashy jewels; the man who had seen much of the world, and the girl who had scarcely been out of New York—they did seem on the surface to be an odd pair. What mattered was what lay beneath the surface: a determination to share their talents with the world, a consummate professionalism, and most of all a clear understanding of themselves, with no apology for what they weren't. (Given Ethel's deep attachment to her own past, she must have loved it when Porter served fudge from Peru, Indiana, at his most elegant dinner parties.) The admiration that Ethel and Cole had for each other never flagged. Porter often said that Ethel sounded "like a band going by," and Ethel loved singing his songs, both the soulful and the risqué ones.

At first, however, Ethel wasn't entirely sure that Porter's musical style was quite right for her. She had no reason to worry, since Porter had seen *Girl Crazy* and her other shows and made a careful study of her voice. He determined that A-flat, B-flat, and C above middle C were the best notes in her roughly octave-and-a-half range, and many of the songs he would write for her would hover around one of those central notes, often ending on it. He loved to flat a sustained note for her, because of the exciting sound she made. And noting her ability to toss off the end of a song with great abandon, he grew fond of writing extended "tag" endings that allowed her to show off a little. But Ethel was wary enough of Porter's new style to insist that Freedley give her contractual approval of every single number. Throughout his career Porter was famous for never wanting to rewrite a song. Usually, if a performer objected to a particular piece, Porter threw it out altogether and started from scratch, as he felt that rewriting drained the life from it. But his admiration for Ethel was so great that he swallowed his pride and agreed to her demands. Even more surprisingly, he bowed to her second stipulation: that he go to the Century and play all her songs for Mom and Pop Zimmermann's approval. Porter, no doubt amused by Ethel's parental devotion, showed up at the apartment, where the Zimmermanns gave thumbs-down to only one song, "Blow, Gabriel, Blow," a big, brassy revival-type number in the second act. It was Ethel's least favorite as well: she found the melody too rigid, not fluid enough. After studying it, Porter realized she was right and rewrote the melody, and the song stayed in the show.

Porter had written a remarkable score that would go down in history as one of his best. Ethel's first number was a witty lament, "I Get a Kick Out of You," with its tricky, restless beguine rhythms. She also had "Kate the Great," which showed off Porter at his bawdiest. Then there was a duet for Gaxton and Ethel, a dizzying list song called "You're the Top," which Porter had composed in Paris after he and a socialite friend had amused themselves one day by devising a list of rhyming superlatives. He decided to turn the trick into a song that played on his love of topical references. Among the names he dropped: Greta Garbo ("You're Garbo's sal'ry"), Mahatma Gandhi, George Jean Nathan, even Mickey Mouse, while the sites included the National Gallery, the Louvre Museum, the Whitney Stable, the dam at Boulder. It was a laughably simple idea for a song, and Porter dashed off several refrains, figuring that it would probably come and go quickly.

For the close of the first act, Porter gave Ethel "Anything Goes," his merry tribute to hedonism that seemed more a backward glance to the reckless twenties than an anthem for the crippled thirties. In the second act, she had one of the few numbers that could be called so-so, "Buddie, Beware," but finished with the red-hot revival number "Blow, Gabriel, Blow," which exploited her trumpeting high notes better than any other song in the show. Ethel learned them all quickly, and at the first day of rehearsal in New York she performed "I Get a Kick Out of You" so movingly that the entire company broke into cheers and applause.

By the time rehearsals began, Lindsay and Crouse had hurriedly met their ten-day deadline and turned in a first act, which the cast quickly set about learning. It was pandemonium, with lots of daily changes being thrown at the actors. Ethel kept her head down and worked harder than anyone, noting everything on her shorthand pad. "Kate the Great" was dropped because Ethel thought the lyrics were too dirty. Billy's sweet romantic ballad, "Easy to Love," had to be put aside, because it proved too rangy for Gaxton, who also lost his original duet with Bettina Hall, "Waltz Down the Aisle." Porter knew that the show needed a tender moment amid all the comedy and came up with the haunting "All Through the Night," a descending chromatic tune that Gaxton sang with Hall. There were also some fixes in the lyrics for "I Get a Kick Out of You." Initially Porter had written a stanza that read:

> *I wouldn't care*
> *For those nights in the air*
> *That the fair Mrs. Lindbergh went through. . . .*

But the song had been written a few years earlier, and in light of the kidnapping and murder of the Lindbergh baby in 1932, it was thought best to replace the lyrics with:

> *Flying too high*
> *With some guy in the sky*
> *Is my idea of nothing to do,*
> *Yet I get a kick out of you!*

It was a musical-comedy score of astonishing depth and breadth and variety. One critic later amused himself by imagining what Victor Herbert might have made of it: "He would say, 'What sort of musician does this fellow Porter want to be? I had my style, the Victor Herbert style, which anybody could recognize. . . . What is the Porter style which he wants people to recognize as his?'"

Lindsay and Crouse, both suffering from sleep deprivation, drafted the second act of *Anything Goes* while the first one was being rehearsed. By the time the company had to leave New York for opening night of the out-of-town tryout at Boston's Colonial Theater on November 5, the writers were still trying to figure out the last scene. When the scenic designer, Donald Oenslager, asked them whether it would take place indoors or outdoors, they replied that he should play it safe and design something that could pass for either.

The Boston reviews gave little indication that *Anything Goes* had been such a rush job. The *Boston Evening American* called it "the best musical show in years," and the *Boston Post* found that "in liveliness and beauty, wit and humor, it weaved a spell of genuine enjoyment that far exceeds anything the stage has given us in many a season." On opening night Ethel was rapturously received by the audience. During rehearsals she had fretted over "You're the Top," wondering whether the audience would take to it, since it was so unlike anything that had ever been done. She could have saved herself the worry: "You're the Top" was a smash, and she and Gaxton wound up singing all seven refrains. After "Blow, Gabriel, Blow," she was called back for three encores. The *Boston Daily Record* didn't overstate things when it reported that "hers was a genuine triumph, . . . the most rousing Boston debut in a long time."

As further tinkering went on in Boston, Crouse was amazed to find Ethel such a quick study. His widow, Anna Crouse, remembered, "She could pick up anything really fast and play it, so that you really saw whether it worked or not. . . . They could walk in at five in the afternoon with a new scene and she would do it."

In Boston, Freedley's mean-spirited side revealed itself. Although Ethel always remained grateful to the producer for discovering her at the Brooklyn Paramount, she was starting to understand why many people in the theater disliked him. "He had the air of commander in chief," recalled Nanette Fabray, who later appeared in the Freedley shows *Let's Face It* (1941) and *Jackpot* (1943). "He was the big boss—it emanated from him." He seldom interfered with the creative process, but he could be appallingly cheap. While the show was still at the Colonial, Crouse as a matter of course came in every night to see it and make the necessary adjustments. Freedley's way of saying thank you was to send him a bill for his nightly ticket. When Crouse blew up at him, Freedley said, "Oh, all right, I'll give you a check." Crouse told him not to bother. "Vinton," he said, "I'd rather tell people what you did."

On November 21, *Anything Goes* opened on Broadway at the Alvin Theatre. The audience, already primed for a hit by the advance word from Boston, loved the show from its very first moment. "I Get a Kick Out of You" received a huge ovation, and Porter went wild over one particular touch that Ethel brought to it. As written, the second verse read:

> *Some get a kick from cocaine.*
> *I'm sure that if I took even one sniff*
> *That would bore me terrific'ly too*
> *Yet I get a kick out of you.*

Ethel put a fermata over the *r*'s on "terrrrrrrrrrrrrrific'ly," one of those inspired, instinctively "right" moments that she would create throughout her career. During "You're the Top," the audience could barely contain its excitement. The reviews were excellent. While allowing that the show was "not suitable to the ears of bashful theater-lovers," the *New York Herald Tribune* found some of its songs and scenes "almost breathtaking in their splendor." The *New York Post* raved over Ethel: "She is vivacious and ingratiating in her comedy moments, and the embodiment of poise as well as technical adroitness when she is called upon to 'put over' a song as only she knows how to do. Even if there were nothing else to recommend *Anything Goes* to your attention . . . it would be decidedly worth your while to journey to the Alvin for the sheer joy of listening to her as she projects such a profane spiritual as 'Blow, Gabriel, Blow' or as she sings the amusing lyrics of such admirable melodies as 'You're the Top,' 'Anything Goes,' or, even more especially, 'I Get a Kick Out of You.' "

Ethel reveled in the success of *Anything Goes*. It enhanced her status in a number of ways, and she knew it. Not only was Porter the most exciting composer on the scene, but he had written songs that allowed her to show off a new dimension of her talent. Just when Broadway thought it had her pigeonholed as a torchy blues singer, Porter had come along and, as she told an interviewer, "I have a chance to show that I don't have to sound like the Sandy Hook foghorn."

Anything Goes settled in at the Alvin for 420 performances, one of the longest runs ever recorded for a musical comedy at the time. As far as Broadway audiences were concerned, Ethel had unquestionably arrived some time ago. Now she seemed destined to stay for a long time. She was part of the good life—just like Garbo's sal'ry.

During the run of *Anything Goes*, Ethel became close friends with William Gaxton and his wife, Madeline. They shared many interests, including dancing and professional football, and they often rode together to Yankee Stadium in the Gaxtons' baby Rolls-Royce, singing every mile of the way. Through the Gaxtons, Ethel met socialite Winthrop Rockefeller, grandson of John D. Rockefeller, founder of the Standard Oil Company. Madeline Gaxton had cautioned Ethel that Rockefeller wasn't accustomed to being around showbiz types and that she might want to tone down her language. Madeline needn't have worried: Rockefeller was charmed and intrigued by Ethel, and the two began going out steadily. They both loved to drink and dance and often wound up at El Morocco until all hours, worrying Mom Zimmermann no end. Ultimately it was a not-too-serious romance that ran its course; Rockefeller seems mainly to have perceived Ethel as having novelty value, and he soon returned to his own social set.

Ethel played happily in *Anything Goes* until the midsummer of 1935. Normally she stayed with a show until its last performance, but she withdrew from *Anything Goes* for what appeared to be a good reason: Goldwyn wanted her for another picture with Eddie Cantor. This one, *Strike Me Pink*, was based on a story by Clarence Dudington Kelland, "Dreamland," about an amusement park that is being threatened by mobsters. Cantor played a meek college dry cleaner. For Ethel it was essentially a retread of *Kid Millions*—a tough-girl comedy part with songs thrown in—but she was determined to conquer Hollywood as she had Broadway, and she told Lou Irwin to accept the offer.

She was replaced in *Anything Goes* by Benay Venuta, an unknown singer/actress four years her junior. A native of San Francisco, Benay had started her career as a dancer and toured in vaudeville for a time, but *Anything Goes* marked her Broadway debut. She sang in a brassy, all-out style that showed more than a little Merman influence. She very much fancied herself a Merman type and hoped that one day she might have a career that rivaled Ethel's. She learned the part of Reno in only three weeks, taking

over for Ethel on July 22, 1935. She did a competent job, and the show continued until November 16. At first Benay seemed content to follow in Ethel's
footsteps, also replacing her on her Sunday-night CBS radio show, *Rhythm
at Eight*. Benay never achieved her ambition to be another Merman, but in
the years ahead she would become a member of Ethel's inner circle. Ethel
appreciated her tough, no-nonsense manner and her sharp, catty wit. For
much of the time, Benay seemed able to play the role of supportive friend
and second-tier actress. Eventually, however, the two women's friendship
would go through increasingly complicated and stormy patches.

When Ethel arrived in Hollywood, she learned that *Strike Me Pink* was
not yet ready to go into production. She was making plans to return to New
York when she received an urgent call from Lou Irwin. Paramount had purchased the screen rights to *Anything Goes* and was about to go into prepro-
duction. Initially they had passed over Ethel; her *We're Not Dressing* costar,
Bing Crosby, was playing the part of Billy Crocker and had persuaded the
studio to cast his wife, singer Dixie Lee, as Reno Sweeney. Lee had been
signed for seven weeks' work at $10,500, but for reasons unknown (possibly
the alcoholism that would cut short her career), she was suddenly out.
Paramount had been happy enough with the way Ethel had performed in
We're Not Dressing, and now, backed into a corner, they asked her to repeat
her stage triumph. Delighted to have such an opportunity dropped in her lap,
Ethel signed on at a salary of $30,333 for a forty-day shooting schedule.

Filming began on September 4. The studio was buzzing with activity:
Marlene Dietrich and Gary Cooper were starring in *Desire*, and Ethel's old
nemesis Mae West was making *Klondike Annie* on a nearby soundstage.
From the beginning, however, it was clear to Ethel that *Anything Goes* was
not going to turn out as she'd hoped. Again the spotlight was on Crosby, and
again she was confined to the sidelines. The emphasis was on screwball
comedy scenes and Billy's romance with Hope Harcourt, played by a very
young, very blond Ida Lupino. Ethel was stuck with one witless line after
another—"What's the idea?" and "What is this, a gag?" and "What are you
doing over here?"—as straight woman to Crosby.

Worst of all was what the studio had done to Porter's score. The year
before, the Motion Picture Producers and Distributors of America had insti-
tuted the Production Code, to ensure that material deemed morally objec-
tionable got a thorough cleansing before it reached the screen. Producers
and directors grumbled and protested, but every single film script had to be
vetted by the MPPDA's director, Will H. Hays, and his colleague Joseph I.
Breen. Porter's lyrics would routinely prove too suggestive for the comfort of

the code's officers, and his references to the denizens of Broadway and café society were considered by movie producers to be too sophisticated to be appreciated by Middle America. In the end, many of the songs he wrote for a particular show would be jettisoned for the screen and replaced with clunky "novelty" numbers by considerably lesser talents.

For the film version of *Anything Goes*, "You're the Top," "I Get a Kick Out of You," and the title tune all managed to survive the cut, but not without changes. Still, jabbing references to Hollywood's censorship policies did manage to slide by:

> *When New York scenes of fun and folly*
> *Would shock all the gals in Holly-*
> *Wood Studios—Anything goes!*

"Blow, Gabriel, Blow" was deemed unnecessary and dropped. In its place, Ethel got a ridiculous number, "Shanghai-dee-ho," written by Leo Robin, in which she cavorted in a silver frock and a headdress made of peacock feathers, surrounded by fifty LeRoy Prinz dancers, all costumed as Chinese slave girls.

Shooting proceeded at a deadly pace. The director, Lewis Milestone, was more at home with sensitive dramas such as his Academy Award–winning *All Quiet on the Western Front* and seemed completely at sea in the world of musical comedy. He frequently showed up late on the set, and on one particular morning not a single shot had been completed by eleven o'clock.

During filming, Ethel had a pleasant surprise: "It's the Animal in Me," her big number from *We're Not Dressing*, was resurrected from the cutting-room floor and thrown into Paramount's all-star musical extravaganza *The Big Broadcast of 1936*. Most reviewers deemed it the high point of the picture, and Ethel was delighted to be paid for it all over again.

Anything Goes finally finished $201,000 over budget and seventeen days behind schedule. All told, Ethel worked for twenty-two days, and when she wasn't needed, she hurried over to Goldwyn to attend rehearsals for *Strike Me Pink*.

She began filming the Goldwyn picture on October 19, one day after *Anything Goes* wrapped. By now she was sick of California and aching to get back to New York, and if she had any hopes of succeeding at the Hollywood game, she didn't do herself any favors with an interview she gave to the Associated Press that month. She complained about Hollywood's absence of after-dark life; it was a nine-o'clock town, and she missed the nightclubs and great restaurants of New York. "The things that make life worth living just aren't here," she said. "It isn't the people, it's the place. If you don't exist in, for and through the movies—well, you don't exist at all." The reporter wanted to know how she felt about Southern California's lovely climate and scenery. "My idea of real scenery is the farm belt of the Middle West. . . . I get a thrill out of the country around Des Moines." It was Ethel in full sail, refusing to edit herself, and newspapers all over the country picked up her sharp comments.

To top it all off, *Strike Me Pink* was another dud. Eddie Cantor was disgruntled throughout filming, and complained about being typed as the same dim-witted character. Ethel had one decent Harold Arlen song, "First You Have Me High, Then You Have Me Low," imaginatively filmed by the brilliant cinematographer Merritt B. Gerstad. In this one number, she came across more strongly than she ever had on screen. She sang it with a soprano mix, hitting meltingly beautiful high D-flats throughout. The picture wrapped in mid-December, and Ethel was happy to return to New York to spend the Christmas holidays with Mom and Pop.

Both films were released in the first part of 1936, to generally undistinguished notices. Reviewing *Anything Goes*, the *New York Herald Tribune*'s Richard Watts Jr. thought that a sharp Broadway show had been turned into a "dull and commonplace musical comedy" and that Ethel did "as well as possible, but it cannot be said that she registers on the screen as magnificently as she does on the stage. I think it is the screen's fault."

In the spring of 1936, the press reported that Ethel might reteam with William Gaxton in Broadway's *White Horse Inn*, but Kitty Carlisle was cast instead. In April, Ethel returned to the New York Paramount, headlining a revue with Little Jack Little and his orchestra. She was billed as "The First Lady of Rhythm," and in eighteen days grosses came to more than $105,000.

Hollywood loves sequels, but Broadway has usually been less kindly disposed toward them. From *Let 'Em Eat Cake*, the Gershwins' unsuccessful follow-up to *Of Thee I Sing*, and on through *Life with Mother* to *The Best Little Whorehouse Goes Public*, stage sequels have typically had a rough ride. But Vinton Freedley was eager to rekindle the magic of *Anything Goes*, and his 1936 show, *Red, Hot and Blue!*, might well have been subtitled *Anything Goes 2*, even if it sported different characters. Seeking to reunite the show's winning team, Freedley corralled Lindsay and Crouse to come up with a story line, but the writers misstepped in their pitch to their three prospective stars. They got a yes from William Gaxton by telling him that he would take center stage and that Ethel would have only a glorified singing spot. Backstage at the New York Paramount, they proceeded to pitch to Ethel a show built around her, with Gaxton and Victor Moore in support. Unfortunately for the writers, Gaxton unexpectedly dropped by to see Ethel, overheard the deception afoot, and refused to have anything further to do with the show. Moore, probably out of loyalty to Gaxton, quickly followed suit.

Lindsay and Crouse spent a lot of time kidding their own image. They called themselves "the poor man's Beaumont and Fletcher" and told the press that they got their inspiration by receiving psychic messages from Neville W. Mudge, a bartender at London's Mermaid Tavern who claimed to have written all of Shakespeare's plays. But they took comedy writing very seriously. Unfortunately, with *Red, Hot and Blue!* they came up with an idea more appropriate for an extended vaudeville sketch than for a full-length musical comedy.

Ethel's part was Madam "Nails" O'Reilly Duquesne, an ex-manicurist–turned–wealthy young society matron. "Nails" is in love with her lawyer, but he is still searching for his lost love, whom he hasn't seen since she was six years old. He'll know her when he finds her: As a child, she sat on a hot waffle iron and was branded for life. "Nails" agrees to fund a lottery designed to locate the lawyer's missing girlfriend. She is helped in this enterprise by "Policy" Pinkle, a convict whom she gets sprung from Larks Nest Prison, where he has a bachelor suite—"three cells and a dungeon."

Eddie Cantor desperately wanted to get back to New York to play "Policy," but his film commitments kept him stranded in Hollywood. Eventually Freedley signed Jimmy Durante for the part, giving Ethel a chance to reunite with her old pal from Les Ambassadeurs. For the part of the lawyer, Freedley cast comedian Bob Hope, who had appeared in hits such as Jerome Kern's *Roberta* and the revue *Ziegfeld Follies of 1936*, in which he introduced Vernon Duke and Ira Gershwin's "I Can't Get Started." The supporting cast sounded like Damon Runyon knockoffs: Billi Benner as "Ratface" Dugan, Leo Shippers as "Flap-Ears" Metelli, Bernard Jannsen as "Louie the Louse," and Polly Walters as Peaches LaFleur. Doubling in two walk-ons was Vivian Vance, who was also assigned to be Ethel's understudy.

Production was delayed because Porter spent the first part of 1936 in Hollywood working on the score for an Eleanor Powell musical for MGM, *Born to Dance.* When he came east, he brought with him two songs that had been dropped from the picture, "Goodbye, Little Dream, Goodbye" and "It's De-Lovely," which he figured he could plug into *Red, Hot and Blue!* As

Lindsay and Crouse continued to struggle with the book, word must have gotten out to the principals that the story was having trouble taking shape. On June 20, Freedley and Crouse turned up at Pennsylvania Station to meet Ethel, who'd been in Hollywood to discuss future picture deals. She was wearing a strong perfume, and once inside the limousine, Crouse, trying to be funny, said, "What smells in here?"

"Probably that part you're writing for me," snapped Ethel.

With *Red, Hot and Blue!* stalled, Ethel decided that this was a good time to make her first Atlantic crossing. She had been feeling restless and ill at ease, mostly because her romance with Al Goetz showed no signs of moving in any particular direction. She booked passage for Mom, Pop, and herself to sail on the SS *Normandie*, the plan being to visit London and Paris, then come back to begin rehearsals for the new show in the fall.

On August 7 a smiling Ethel, decked out in a fur coat despite the summer heat, waved to photographers as the *Normandie* set sail for London. It was a starry crossing: also on board were Fred Astaire, Peggy Hopkins Joyce, and silent-film star Laura LaPlante. Unfortunately, during the voyage Pop became gravely ill—with what, it has never been clear, since Ethel didn't see fit to provide the press with details. When the ship docked in Southampton, Pop had to be carried off the boat on a stretcher and immediately moved to the hospital. Ethel and Mom checked in to the Savoy, but they spent most of their time at Pop's bedside. For the next few weeks, they monitored his condition constantly, doing practically no sightseeing at all, but Pop was slow to rally. September arrived, and the start date for *Red, Hot and Blue!* loomed. Heartbroken at having to leave her ailing father, Ethel sailed for New York aboard the *Queen Mary* on September 7, leaving Mom behind to manage things.

Once Ethel showed up for rehearsals, she wondered why she had hurried home. She had entered into *Red, Hot and Blue!* with the understanding that it was her show. Much as she had loved being part of *Anything Goes*, Reno Sweeney was not the star spot by any means; both Gaxton and Moore had had much more stage time than she had, and occasionally she had felt that she'd been hired to keep the audience in its seats with a song while Moore and Gaxton got ready for the next scene change. Now she discovered that Lou Irwin had failed to specify in her contract that she got top billing in *Red, Hot and Blue!* She didn't want to yield the number-one spot, but neither, as it turned out, did Jimmy Durante. Finally someone—it appears that it was Linda Porter—suggested crisscross billing, with the names to be switched from left to right every two weeks. It was a democratic decision that mollified everyone, and at last rehearsals could begin.

Porter had come up with some top-notch material for her. "It's De-Lovely," a duet with Bob Hope, was a lightning-paced alliterative patter number that traced a romance from courtship to middle-aged parenthood. The birth of the couple's son is especially memorable:

> *Those eyes of yours are filled with joy*
> *When Nurse appears and cries, "It's a boy!"*
> *"He's appalling, he's appealing,*
> *He's a pollywog, he's a paragon,*
> *He's a Popeye, he's a panic, he's a pip,*
> *He's de-lovely!"*

There was also "Ours," a list number in which two lovers gently clash over where exactly their romance should continue to be played out. He imagines them on "the white Riviera under the moon" or in a Venetian gondola, but she wants to stay closer to home:

> *Ours, the glitter of Broadway, Saturday night,*
> *Ours, a box at the Garden, watching a fight,*
> *Ours, the mad brouhaha of the Plaza's Persian Room,*
> *Or, if this fills you with gloom,*
> *We can go and admire Grant's Tomb.*

And Ethel's big first-act closing number, "Ridin' High," was a finger-snapping ode to joy, with lots of sustained high notes and one of Porter's famous name-dropping patter devices:

> *What do I care*
> *If fair Tallulah possesses tons and tons*
> *Of jewels from gents?*
> *Or, if someone observes*
> *That I haven't the curves*
> *That Simone Simon presents?*
> *I'm doin' fine,*
> *My life's divine,*
> *I'm living in the sun*
> *'Cause I've a big date*

With my fate,
So I rate
A-1.

On *Red, Hot and Blue!*, Ethel worked for the first time with a young pianist named Lew Kesler. Porter had great faith in Kesler's judgment and talent, using him in one show after another for many years, and Ethel soon grew to like him, too. Kesler was young and brash, with kinky red hair and a smart mouth. Because he had Porter squarely behind him, he often made loud, critical comments in rehearsal about one or another performer. Ethel thought he was funny, and in time Kesler became her musical right arm, rehearsing with her in the theater lobby while the dancing chorus went through its paces on the stage. Their friendship got off to a rocky start, however. From the beginning Ethel was very strict about the keys for her songs. Cole Porter believed that she could sing much higher than she did, but she reasoned that she would be onstage knocking her brains out for months—why should she be forced to sing anything higher than C above middle C? At this particular rehearsal for *Red, Hot and Blue!*, she was about to go through "It's De-Lovely" with Kesler, and she asked that it be transposed to the key of B, which would make it easier for her to sing. The key of B is a tricky one for transposition, as it contains five sharps, and Kesler struggled along, banging out wrong notes and not getting the right harmonies. When Ethel finished the song, she turned to him and said, "For Christ's sake, will you take the Vienna rolls off your fingers?" Kesler thought he was about to be fired, but instead it marked the beginning of a long professional association; Ethel liked people who could take her harshest jabs without dissolving in tears.

Red, Hot and Blue! had its premiere at Boston's Colonial Theatre on October 7, 1936. Even though it was much too long—the final curtain didn't fall until after midnight—the audience loved it. Durante scored the comic high point with a hilarious routine in which, as both a criminal on trial and a prosecuting attorney, he cross-examined himself. The book was still sketchy—in fact, the entire show, with its wild comic interludes and specialty dances, was really little more than a dressed-up revue. Ethel found herself "stuck" onstage a good deal of the time, and she said, "What are we gonna do?" so many times that the audience must have stopped paying attention. But her songs went over in a big way. While "It's De-Lovely" was the hit of the evening, the audience also responded warmly to "Goodbye, Little Dream, Goodbye," although Freedley, who had never liked it, began making noises about having it cut.

Red, Hot and Blue! moved on to New Haven, where Porter finally gave in to Freedley's harangues and wrote a song to replace "Goodbye, Little Dream, Goodbye." In doing so he gave credence to the adage that all the best songs are written out of town. The new number was "Down in the Depths," a torch song for "Nails" that ranked with the best work Porter had ever done. After taking the verse to outline her shaky position—a socialite with lots of money and swell surroundings but no man to share it with— "Nails" launched into the funny and moving refrain, which showed Porter's matchless gift for inner rhymes and unforced alliteration:

> *While the crowds at El Morocco punish the parquet*
> *And at '21' the couples clamor for more,*
> *I'm deserted and depressed*
> *In my regal eagle nest*
> *Down in the depths on the ninetieth floor.*

While the show was still out of town, Ethel ran into trouble with Bob Hope. It was a scenario that would recur with many performers—stars, bit players, and chorus girls—during her career. Being a quick study, Ethel had no trepidation about having new material thrown at her, and she never failed to astonish her coworkers with the speed with which she could pick things up. She had one hard-and-fast rule, however: once the show was a week away from opening night in New York, she refused to learn anything new. Composers, book writers, and directors, so often unable to keep them-selves from fiddling with the show right up to opening, could do their best to talk her into trying a new scene or tune, but she never budged. One week before New York, there was no more fooling around. If it wasn't right by then, it was *their* fault, not hers.

Ethel's insistence that things fall into a fixed pattern extended to the stage deportment of her costars. Nothing could make her flash with anger more quickly than an actor who suddenly decided one night, without a word to any-one else, to change a line or deliver it from a different spot on the stage. In "It's De-Lovely," Bob Hope had a habit of deviating from the staging and ad-libbing to the audience. One night Ethel turned in mid-refrain to find him lying on the floor, grinning up at her—definitely not part of the staging. Once offstage she didn't lower herself to confronting Hope; instead she went directly to Freedley and told him to be sure that it never happened again.

Red, Hot and Blue! opened on October 29, 1936, at the Alvin Theatre. Many of the reviewers found Porter's score below his usual high standard (although Porter claimed that they said this about nearly every score he composed, with the exception of *Anything Goes*) and Lindsay and Crouse's book far less funny than the one they'd whipped up for *Anything Goes*. The *New York Herald Tribune*, referring to the plot about the waffle-iron brand, found that "the anatomical jokes grow a trifle feeble upon occasion." For the stars, however, there was nothing but praise. John Mason Brown found Ethel "Broadway made vocal; Broadway given a melody of its own, and having found a perfect way of putting it across." The *Brooklyn Citizen* wrote, "Of all performers, from Cornell on down, there is none more poised, more sure of registering with audiences, whether she is handling dialogue or projecting songs in the low-down and blue style which is her own." Perhaps Bob Hope's stage etiquette hadn't improved after all: the *Brooklyn Eagle* wrote that in his scenes with Ethel, he seemed "never to care about anything but a couple of little jokes he has in mind."

During the show's run, a new man came into Ethel's life: Walter Annenberg, scion of one of the most prominent families from the Philadelphia Main Line. The family business was publishing, specifically Triangle Publications, which was responsible for the *Philadelphia Inquirer* and the immensely successful *Daily Racing Form*, among other titles. Educated at the exclusive Peddie School in New Jersey and the University of Pennsylvania's Wharton School, Annenberg had started at Triangle in a minor post in the company's bookkeeping office.

If his background wasn't quite what Ethel was accustomed to—she remembered that when he took her to meet his family, it was the first time she'd eaten off a gold service—she was attracted to Walter, and she admired the way he constantly sought creative ways to improve Triangle's standing in the business world. Annenberg shared the conservative political leanings that Ethel had inherited from Mom and Pop, and she delighted in the way he loved to play the man about town. They were seen so often around New York's hottest night spots that the columnists began tagging them as a couple to watch. In the end it turned out to be a fairly short-lived romance, the kind Jerome Kern and Oscar Hammerstein had in mind when they wrote "All in Fun." Annenberg would go on to found *Seventeen* magazine in 1944. In 1952 he determined that the fledgling television industry needed a national publication and, against great opposition, launched *TV Guide*. It became his biggest success, and he eventually built its paid circulation up to 20 million. Later still, he became President Richard Nixon's ambassador to Great Britain. Ethel saw him now and then socially for years and never regretted that she had broken it off with him.

For the first several weeks, *Red, Hot and Blue!* played to sold-out houses, and it looked as if it might run beyond the season. But early in 1937, the box office began to drop off, and within a few months Freedley decided to close the show and send the company to Chicago, where a long run was anticipated. It was booked to open at the Grand Opera House, Chicago's home to many of the top touring shows, but the theater wasn't prepared for some of the show's technical challenges, and the opening had to be postponed. The delay gave rise to gossip that all was not right with the show, and Ethel recalled that once it opened, "the public acted as if we were under quarantine." *Red, Hot and Blue!* closed in two and a half weeks. It was a disappointment to the entire company, perhaps most of all to Ethel. It must have crossed her mind that she had yet to set the world of show business on fire outside New York City. But if her failure on the road unnerved her, she reacted with typical shortsightedness: if the road didn't like her, to hell with the road.

This was one of the few major mistakes of her career. In those days it was standard practice for the top theater stars to play out the season in New York, then take the play on tour, for they understood the importance of developing a national following. Almost always the strategy was beneficial: the Broadway theater still had a high national profile, thanks to the extensive coverage it received in newspapers, magazines, and on the radio. In most of the major U.S. cities, and even in many of the not-so-major ones, there was a healthy ticket-buying market that jumped at the chance to see Katharine Cornell, Alfred Lunt and Lynn Fontanne, or Helen Hayes, live. But it would be fifteen years before Ethel would again consent to take a show out of town, even briefly.

Maybe *Red, Hot and Blue!* simply got off on the wrong foot and stayed there. *Anything Goes* had been created out of such chaos that everyone seemed to have viewed success as a necessity and pulled together to make the show a hit. *Red, Hot and Blue!* was marred by infighting from the start. There is no question that the whole experience left Ethel feeling frustrated and fatigued. She knew that she didn't want to start another Broadway show immediately, and once again her thoughts drifted to Hollywood.

In the summer of 1937, Ethel was distressed to learn of her friend George Gershwin's illness. For some time he had complained of headaches and dizziness, and his behavior had grown increasingly erratic, to the point that his sister-in-law, Ira's wife, Leonore, often had to cut up his food for him. On July 9, while staying at the Los Angeles home of songwriter E. Y. "Yip" Harburg, Gershwin passed into a coma. He underwent a five-hour surgery at Cedars of Lebanon Hospital to remove a brain tumor, but the operation was a failure, and he died on the morning of July 11.

Ethel was devastated by this loss. The man who had so generously handed her her first big opportunity had been silenced, and it was agonizing for her to imagine what great accomplishments might have been ahead of him. On August 9 a memorial concert was held at Lewisohn Stadium in upper Manhattan. It was an appropriately democratic site for this most democratic of composers, as Lewisohn had a long and admirable history of offering low-priced concerts to the general public. It was also sentimentally fitting: Lewisohn was where George had made his conducting debut in 1929, leading the New York Philharmonic in performances of *An American in Paris* and *Rhapsody in Blue*. The memorial was a distinguished gathering before a crowd of twenty thousand musicians: Harry Kaufman played the Concerto in F, while Anne Brown, Todd Duncan, Ruby Elzy, and the chorus of *Porgy and Bess* sang selections from Gershwin's folk opera. Ethel, conducted by Ferde Grofé, performed "I Got Rhythm," "The Man I Love," and, perhaps most appropriately, "They Can't Take That Away from Me."

At this point Ethel's attention was yet again turning toward the movies, and it was Lou Irwin who was responsible. More and more, Irwin had been working on West Coast projects, and by mid-1937 he had decided to relocate there, in hopes of cutting himself in on some of the big Hollywood money. Ethel let him know that she would be willing to try the movies one more time, despite the fact that they mostly had proven inhospitable to her, and Irwin went to work trying to find her a picture deal. While she waited for him to get results, Ethel did another stage show on the Keith circuit, supporting showings of a Gene Raymond picture, *The Life of the Party*. She sang several of her famous hits, plus Gershwin's "They All Laughed" and "They Can't Take That Away from Me." An eight-day run at Boston's RKO Theatre pulled in $32,000.

Irwin finally reported an offer from Warner Bros. to costar in *Fools for Scandal*, a comedy with Carole Lombard. The picture had already been announced in the trade papers when Irwin came up with a much better offer. Only three years earlier, Darryl F. Zanuck had merged his fledgling company, 20th Century Pictures with the artistically bankrupt Fox Studios. The new company, 20th Century Fox, had gotten off to a strong start, with a roster that included Shirley Temple, Alice Faye, Tyrone Power, and ice-skating star Sonja Henie, whom Zanuck had signed up the previous year and put into a musical called *One in a Million*. It made a fortune, and Zanuck had instructed his staff of writers and producers to work overtime developing more Henie vehicles. It was one of these that Irwin had lined up for Ethel. She wasn't wild about the film's title, *Bread, Butter, and Rhythm*. But it was a big-budget production, and at $210,000 a year Henie was Hollywood's highest-paid star, so Ethel eagerly signed on—especially after Irwin worked out a deal with 20th Century Fox for future picture options. In early October, Ethel, accompanied once more by Mom, took the Superchief to Los Angeles, where they moved into the Beverly Wilshire Hotel.

In its brief existence, 20th Century Fox had already made remarkable strides and was well on its way to becoming one of Hollywood's most important studios. In the 1930s each studio had an individual thumbprint, personified by its top stars. MGM meant plush, soft-focus glamour (Greta Garbo, Norma Shearer, Joan Crawford); RKO stood for streamlined art deco sophistication (Katharine Hepburn, Constance Bennett, Fred Astaire and Ginger Rogers), Warner Bros. specialized in starkly lit crime dramas (James Cagney, Humphrey Bogart, Bette Davis). At 20th Century Fox, Darryl F. Zanuck would eventually delve into social-problem pictures such as *The Grapes of Wrath* (1940) and *Gentleman's Agreement* (1947), but during his company's early years he settled for making sunny musicals and historical dramas, often with a homespun, rural setting.

The studio's films were filled with bright, affable, uncomplicated performers like Henie, Don Ameche, Cesar Romero. (Sometimes the relentlessly chipper atmosphere could be a little irritating; reviewing the 1941 musical *Weekend in Havana*, Pauline Kael found everyone on the Fox lot "beaming with fatuous good will.")

Happy Landing (the new title for *Bread, Butter, and Rhythm*) was cast in this genial mode. It was a fluffy bit of nonsense about a madcap playboy flier (Romero) and his manager (Ameche) who make an emergency landing in a Norwegian village. The playboy dallies with a local maid (Henie), who takes him seriously and follows him back to the United States, where he deputizes his manager to give her the brush. Ethel was cast as Romero's on-again, off-again girlfriend, given to throwing chairs and lamps when she doesn't get her way. She got a couple of middling songs, "You Appeal to Me" (which called on her to imitate Garbo at one point) and "I'm Hot and Happy in Love," in which she pulled out the old "I Got Rhythm" trick of holding a note for several bars. She was fit and trim, and she had gotten the Hollywood treatment—penciled eyebrows and gowns by Royer. Aside from a foot injury she suffered when she took a fall during a skating sequence, she enjoyed the filming. She got some extra publicity through her studio-arranged dates with Cesar Romero. It must have amused Ethel, coming from the world of Broadway, to watch Hollywood pretend that Romero wasn't gay.

The movie wrapped on December 11, 1937, and Ethel returned to New York in time for Christmas. *Happy Landing* was edited quickly and put into release in January 1938. The *New York Times* thought it had "pace, humor, spectacle, and a pleasant, if minor, score." Most of the critics concentrated on the stars and gave Ethel short shrift, but Louella O. Parsons did allow that "the Broadway torch singer gives a good account of herself as the jealous fiancée."

By the time *Happy Landing* was playing to enthusiastic audiences, 20th Century Fox had already exercised its option and put Ethel into another picture. On this one she got lucky: her new assignment was the studio's number-one prestige production for 1938, the musical extravaganza *Alexander's Ragtime Band*. The picture had been a pet project of Zanuck's for some time. Knowing that he could never compete with a powerhouse like MGM when it came to building stars, Zanuck decided to concentrate on developing the best stories. Here he showed that he was, after so many years, still a writer at heart. A studio like MGM might put a high quotient of inferior scripts into production, confident that their stars could get the public to buy them. Zanuck, on the other hand, sweated over his properties. In endless story and script conferences, he hammered away at his writers to polish, refine, fix up credibility gaps, do anything they could to make audiences *believe* what they were seeing.

Initially Zanuck envisioned *Alexander's Ragtime Band* as a biography of Irving Berlin, but the composer shied away from the idea. Instead it was decided to use the Berlin song catalog to tell a fictional story that had close parallels to Berlin's own life. In addition to Berlin himself, many screenwriters worked on the project, although in the end only two, Kathryn Scola and Lamar Trotti, were credited. For months nothing in the development of the story was to Zanuck's liking. He saw it as "a story of an imaginary character, 'Mr. Alexander,' who could start humbly with an idea about music and who could finally end up after a number of years in the highest musical temples." What finally emerged was a plot about "legit" violinist Roger Grant (Tyrone Power), who finds his real musical voice in ragtime. With his best friend, composer Charlie Dwyer (Don Ameche), he puts together a band. They attract attention with the tune "Alexander's Ragtime Band" and take it for the name of their group. The two friends fall in love with Stella Kirby (Alice Faye), the band's saucy singer, who leaves them behind when she gets a crack at Broadway stardom. The band dissolves, World War I intervenes, and eventually everyone is reunited when Alexander's Ragtime Band gets a chance to play Carnegie Hall.

Although the plot was essentially simple, it had great sweep, moving from the Barbary Coast in 1911 to New York in the late 1930s. The intrusion of war and Stella's desolation after she leaves the band and marries Charlie, even though she doesn't love him, gave the film a touch of darkness unusual in movie musicals of the time.

Ethel was cast as Gerry Allen, the peppy singer who takes Stella's place in the band. She doesn't show up until the last third of the picture, but she is given plenty of screen time, with lots of Berlin tunes to sing: "A Pretty Girl Is Like a Melody," "Say It with Music," "Blue Skies," "Pack Up Your Sins and Go to the Devil," "Heat Wave," and two new numbers Berlin had written for the film, "My Walking Stick" and "Marching Along with Time," the latter of which was cut before the film's release. Berlin was knocked out by Ethel's renditions of his songs and immediately began talking about writing a show for her.

Alexander's Ragtime Band was in production for sixty days and was a happy experience for Ethel. Jack Haley, who had appeared with her in *Take a Chance*, was in the supporting cast, and she enjoyed working with him again. The studio saw to it that she was presented to good advantage, putting her on a strict diet and lightening her dark brown hair to auburn, a change she liked so much that she kept it that color for years. Unfortunately, she seemed curiously muted in her dialogue scenes, the result of Henry King's constant efforts to tone her down. In "Say It with Music," she was coached to abandon her natural diction and use "pretty" vowel sounds instead. Elsewhere she performed with the expected Merman magic.

In later years, those who attempted to explain why Ethel never quite took off in Hollywood often argued that she was just too big for the screen. This was a misdiagnosis. What really held her back in films was that she failed to grasp one of the cornerstones of screen acting: the camera has to move in on the performer, picking up on her unspoken thoughts and feelings. Alice Faye, for example, wasn't really an actress, but she understood film technique, and the hardest heart in the audience would melt when she sang a sentimental ballad and cast her limpid eyes upward. In most of her movies, Ethel didn't show many signs of inner life. She spit out her lines and threw herself at the camera, instead of letting it come to her.

Nevertheless, *Alexander's Ragtime Band* was a high spot in her movie career. Thanks to the performances, the great care taken in presenting the musical numbers, and the adroit and sensitive editing of Barbara McLean, it had the feel of an important picture. In overall quality and scope, no MGM musical of 1938 could touch it. When it was released in August of that year, the critics cheered it. The *New York Times* said that it "demands recognition as the best musical show of the year." The *Hollywood Reporter* called it "a turning point of the industry and a new trend in the utilization of music in story telling." Merman fan Louella Parsons thought it featured Ethel's "best acting part." The press preview in Hollywood was a major event, with Claudette Colbert, Joan Crawford, Paul Muni, Constance Bennett, Janet Gaynor, Jack Benny, and Irene Dunne all in attendance. That night Ethel received a congratulatory note from 20th Century Fox executive Sol Wurtzel: "I think your performance in *Alexander's Ragtime Band* is the first real step toward success in motion pictures which you so well deserve."

If that was indeed the attitude of the studio bosses, they should have come up with a better project for Ethel's next movie. *Straight, Place and Show*, filmed in the summer of 1938, was a half-witted comedy featuring the Ritz Brothers; Ethel had a couple of forgettable songs and pined after the leading man. For years she tried to forget that she had ever made it. *Alexander's Ragtime Band*, meanwhile, was setting box-office records: it took in $3,848 in its opening day at Loews State, New York, and would eventually gross over $3 million. But *Straight, Place and Show* was a loser.

"I liked to be in control. You couldn't be, in films." Ethel's explanation for her decision to quit trying to make it in Hollywood was only shorthand for the real problem: she had been typed as the sharp-tongued girl who doesn't get the guy, and she knew that in Hollywood you never reached the top playing that kind of role.

By the fall of 1938, with *Alexander's Ragtime Band* pulling them in at the box office, Ethel had lined up her next Broadway vehicle. Its source was actually another show, Harold Rome's 1937 hit *Pins and Needles*, a

left-leaning spoof of international politics created by members of the International Ladies Garment Workers' Union. Arthur Schwartz, the brilliant
composer of immortal songs such as "By Myself," "Dancing in the Dark,"
and "You and the Night and the Music," was casting about for a new project.
In discussions with the producer Dwight Deere Wiman, Schwartz began bat-
ting around the idea of having a leftist composer like Harold Rome go to
Hollywood on a movie contract; the comedy would grow out of the situation
of a flaming liberal trapped inside Hollywood's capitalist machinery. Wiman
liked the concept and began developing it. Along the way, novelist and
screenwriter J. P. McEvoy was signed to create the book. For the lyrics
Wiman and Schwartz turned to the talented Dorothy Fields, whose collo-
quial stylishness had matched up beautifully with the music of Jimmy
McHugh and Jerome Kern.

Dorothy Fields had been born into the business—her father was Joseph
Fields, of the famed comedy team Weber and Fields. For years she had
worked in Hollywood, and in 1936 she became the first female songwriter
ever to win an Academy Award, for her lyrics to Kern's "The Way You Look
Tonight" from the Astaire-Rogers film *Swing Time*. She was taking a health
retreat at the Arrowhead Springs Hotel when Schwartz reached her; the telephone was brought to her while she was having a mud bath, and she instantly said yes. The team went to work and in a short time had come up with
a loosely structured spoof of the labor-union movement in Hollywood.

To direct, Wiman engaged Joshua Logan, who earlier that year had
leaped to the forefront of Broadway directors with three hits, *On Borrowed
Time, Knickerbocker Holiday*, and *I Married an Angel*. The troubles that
were to haunt the new show cropped up almost immediately, when Logan
took a look at the script. Ignoring the runaway success of *Pins and Needles*,
he decided that a musical comedy about the left wing—"the red side," as he
called it—sounded like box-office poison. He insisted that the union angle
be omitted almost entirely, and he began to work with McEvoy to retool the
book as a general Hollywood satire. It was eventually called *Stars in Your
Eyes*, and Ethel and Jimmy Durante were signed on for the leads. There was
some concern that the thorny question of billing that had delayed *Red, Hot
and Blue!* would recur, but Schwartz appealed to Durante by reminding him
that Noël Coward had allowed Gertrude Lawrence to be billed before him in
Private Lives. Durante figured that if Coward, as both actor *and* playwright,
could be that magnanimous, he could, too.

The book was in terrible shape when Ethel signed on, but eventually
Logan and McEvoy pulled together a story about a young intellectual (Rich-

ard Carlson) who arrived in Hollywood with dreams of making a movie about the labor problems among sharecroppers and coal miners. But his ambitions to create serious art are trampled by a variety of Hollywood types, including Jeanette Adair (Ethel), the temperamental number-one star at Monotone Pictures, who sets her sights on the writer. Logan had taken the idea from his old friend James Stewart: several years earlier, Stewart had arrived at MGM, a young, green contract player, and had immediately fallen under the gaze of Norma Shearer, queen of the MGM lot. Shearer was so taken with Stewart that she insisted he travel around town in her yellow limousine. Not wanting to offend the wife of MGM production chief Irving Thalberg, Stewart complied, but he hid on the limousine floor so his friends couldn't see him. Durante was to play the comedy lead of Monotone Pictures' "idea man"; the supporting cast included Mildred Natwick, a distinguished stage actress making her musical debut, and the talented young comedienne Mary Wickes. The show was heavy on dance, and the corps de ballet included future notables Alicia Alonso, Nora Kaye, Maria Karniloff (Karnilova), and Jerome Robbins. Dwight Deere Wiman seemed unworried about the changes in the book; he was more concerned that the show provide a good showcase for his new protégée, the beautiful Ballets Russes star Tamara Toumanova. And Arthur Schwartz had written successful revues but had yet to compose a book show that found an audience.

In rehearsal Ethel once again amazed her colleagues by how hard she worked. To Dorothy Fields, her first line readings were almost perfect. She never overplayed her hand in the comedy scenes, making every connection absolutely right. Ethel was no towering intellect, Dorothy observed—she didn't read much, and she didn't keep up too closely with current events; most of her conversation was gossip about people in show business. That was fine with Dorothy, who loved Ethel's bawdy, raucous wit. The two women admired each other's professionalism and work ethic. When she was younger, Dorothy had taken Jerome Kern's advice that to be a successful songwriter it was necessary to rise early, around 6:30 A.M., and be ready to sit down at the piano by 8:00. She wrote daily from early morning through to 3:00 in the afternoon—as she put it, until her wastebasket was filled up. To her friends she was a warm, refined, hospitable woman who loved her craft. Ethel took to her right away, and Dorothy returned the feeling, becoming close enough to get away with calling Ethel "Mermsey." Later on she would say that Ethel had the greatest discipline of any woman she ever met.

To Logan, Ethel seemed a consummate actress who moved easily from the comedy scenes to the tender moments. In the Schwartz-Fields song "I'll

Pay the Check," in which Jeanette Adair realizes that she can never make the young writer fall in love with her, Ethel was achingly poignant. Logan would demonstrate a piece of business that he had concocted for her, and Ethel would write it on her steno pad. "She took everything down in shorthand," said Anna Crouse, who worked as Logan's assistant on *Stars in Your Eyes*. "That was supposed to be *my* job, but she was so much faster!"

Ethel also again demonstrated her unerring instincts about whether new material was going to work. One of the political numbers left over from the show's original conception was "My New Kentucky Home," a satirical ditty in which the sun, the moon, and the stars functioned only during union hours. It was a clever song—so clever, Ethel thought, that it was dragging the show down, but Schwartz was mad to have it in. Anna Crouse later recalled the first hearing of "My New Kentucky Home" at the New Haven tryout. "Ethel said she would try it in New Haven," said Crouse. "And she didn't dog it or try to do anything to say to the audience, 'I'm not enjoying this.' But it had little to do with the rest of the show, and it just lay there. She was a good sport to do it, although she herself knew, better than Arthur did, that it wasn't going to work." Schwartz and Fields saw her point, sat down to work, and came up with a replacement number, "A Lady Needs a Change," which was a hit from the instant it went in.

In New Haven, *Stars in Your Eyes* ran much too long, and Logan made nearly a half hour's worth of cuts. The show moved on to Boston, where many of the cuts were gradually reinstated. By the time it opened at Boston's Shubert Theatre on January 17, 1939, the curtain didn't come down until midnight. Still, the *Boston Herald* thought the show gave "every indication of proving a big, popular success" and was "a field day" for Ethel. Logan made more drastic cuts, but this time his hacking seemed to inflict significant damage on the show's delicate balance of humor and pathos, and it never quite recovered.

Stars in Your Eyes opened at Broadway's Majestic Theatre on February 9. Several of the big scenes scored strongly with the audience, in particular one in which Jeanette tries to seduce the young writer in her studio dressing room, where he gets progressively drunker on champagne. Just as he is about to move in for the big kiss, he spots a copy of his favorite book, *Alice in Wonderland*, and asks Jeanette to read it aloud to him. When Ethel opened the book, she took a perfectly timed pause, then boomed the title of the opening chapter: "DOWN THE RABBIT HOLE." There was a great rolling laugh in the audience. Fade-out. Then the lights came back up to indicate the passing of time. "CHAPTER TEN," blasted Ethel. "WHO STOLE THE

TARTS?" Logan recalled that she gave the line such a shot of electricity that the audience was screaming with laughter. By the time she slammed the book shut and tossed it across the room, they were wildly applauding.

Another audience favorite was Jimmy Durante's duet with Mildred Natwick, "Terribly Attractive," which they performed in a prop auto in front of a screen with a running film. As they raced through traffic, nearly driving off the cliff roads, members of the audience in the front row shrieked in terror; it was almost like an early example of Cinerama. The big eleven-o'clock number, "It's All Yours," with Durante and Ethel trotting out one hoary vaudeville joke after another, was also a smash. From the wings someone would throw out a telephone, which Durante would answer, saying, "Hello, is this the *meat* market? Well, tell my wife to *meet* me at five o'clock!" They do a buck-and-wing exit, then come back to do another refrain. Logan would recall it as one of the most thrilling numbers he ever saw on any stage.

The reviews were mixed for the show but excellent for the cast. "As for Miss Merman," offered the *New York Herald Tribune*, "she sings as fascinatingly as ever and plays with a comedy skill far greater than she has shown us before." Burns Mantle, in the *New York Daily News*, thought the show "gives Merman a chance to be something more than a response to song cues, and she, with Joshua Logan's help as a director, takes complete advantage of her chance."

It looked as if *Stars in Your Eyes* would run through the season, but, unfortunately, no one had reckoned on the impact of the 1939 New York World's Fair, which offered a staggering array of good reasons not to attend a Broadway musical. Tourists were more interested in taking in the Heinz Food Pavilion, Eleanor Holm in Billy Rose's *Aquacade*, or other family-oriented fare, than they were in plunking down their money for a musical spoof of Hollywood. Ethel always claimed that she never appeared in a Broadway flop, but on May 27, *Stars in Your Eyes* closed with a disappointing run of 127 performances and $1,300 owing in refunds.

Fig rom the time she was very young, Ethel had a strong attraction to tough guys. Few of the men in her life were tougher than Sherman Billingsley, the proudly self-made man from Oklahoma who became a major celebrity as owner of the Stork Club, for years one of the most famous nightspots in the world. Ever since she played in *Red, Hot and Blue!*, Ethel had been an occasional drop-in at the Stork after her Saturday-night shows. When she returned from Hollywood in 1938, she began going oftener, and by 1939 she was a regular. Her constant attendance at the Stork Club was not entirely due to the royal treatment she received as the Queen of Broadway Musicals—though that was certainly part of it. More to the point, she and Sherman Billingsley had fallen deeply in love.

To her closest friends, it made perfect sense, for Billingsley was her ideal type. Born on a farm in the Oklahoma Territory, he had been fiercely ambitious from the start. When he was a kid, he spent hours scrounging around the streets of his hometown, Enid, looking for empty whiskey bottles to resell to the local saloonkeepers. He picked plums, washed dishes in a Mexican chili restaurant—any kind of job he could find, he took. Before he was twenty, he had acquired a half interest in a pair of drugstores, and he later got his hands on a chain of grocery stores. Many of these businesses were a front for his bootlegging activities, which ultimately landed him a short stint in Leavenworth Prison. Following his release he moved to New York, where, after investing in real-estate ventures in the Bronx, he decided it was time to move up the social scale. First Billingsley opened an earlier incarnation of the Stork Club on West Fifty-eighth Street, then plotted a move to a tonier location, where, he hoped, his clientele would be "strictly carriage trade or nothing." His revamped Stork Club opened in 1934 at 3 East Fifty-third Street, and quickly it became the favorite gathering spot of Broadway and Hollywood celebrities, café society, and stargazing out-of-towners.

Billingsley's place figured prominently in innumerable magazine layouts and a number of radio shows, and eventually it became so famous that it was used for the name of a 1945 movie starring Betty Hutton. It was, for much of America, the epitome of New York elegance. For Ethel it was a place where she made some lasting friendships, including J. Edgar Hoover and his boyfriend Clyde Tolson, and Bea Lillie, who could toss back beers as fast as Ethel downed champagne.

At the Stork, Billingsley insisted on a strict code of behavior, and he wasn't afraid to enforce it. Drunken rowdiness or even the mildest form of tasteless behavior—table-hopping was a no-no—was not tolerated and could result in at least temporary banishment. Billingsley unapologetically catered only to what he considered the best sort of people, which could include tourists, so long as they knew how to behave. He reserved the right to keep anyone on the other side of the velvet ropes. (This especially applied to blacks, whom he despised.) He went out of his way to welcome the cream of New York's young set, especially many of the city's most famous debutantes, notably Brenda Frazier. The father of several children himself, Billingsley kept a close watch over his young patrons, making sure that they never fell in with the wrong crowd, and often cutting their dinner checks in half.

Most of all Billingsley loved celebrities, and by showering them with gifts he guaranteed that a steady stream of them flowed into his establishment. Favorite regulars received gold and silver cigarette cases, expensive ties, cases of champagne, and bottles of Sortilège, a chic perfume whose distributorship he had acquired. "I started giving things to people because I felt so happy about their patronizing my place," he once told a journalist, and the gambit worked with most of the celebrities he courted, including Ethel, who was soon such a fixture at the Stork Club that Billingsley assigned a waiter just to stand by to light her cigarettes.

Ethel had an intense physical attraction to Billingsley. He was a good-looking man, extremely masculine, with a low-key, soft-spoken manner and icy blue eyes. His tentative smile had a sexy charm, but there was the hint of enormous strength behind it.

What cemented his appeal for her was his uncompromising, single-minded approach to the way he ran his business. He seldom took a vacation or even a day off, and he monitored every detail of running the Stork himself: he made sure the food was fresh, hired the chefs, inspected the waiters' uniforms to see that they were clean and well pressed. He managed his career in exactly the same way Ethel managed hers, and she thought that at last she had found her soul mate.

There was one difficulty, and it was a major one: Billingsley was married, with children. He was also a devout Catholic, for whom deserting his family seemed unthinkable. Mom Zimmermann was sure that Ethel was making a terrible mistake and gently remonstrated with her; Ethel's romances with Al Goetz and Billingsley caused Mom to worry that her daughter was developing a pattern of going after married men. Dorothy Fields, by now one of Ethel's closest girlfriends, warned her repeatedly that Billingsley would never leave his wife. But Ethel turned a deaf ear to all this well-intentioned advice. Billingsley had told her, over and over, how much he loved her, how much he wanted to be with her and her alone. She couldn't believe that it wouldn't all come to pass, if she just bided her time.

Ethel's romance with Billingsley was a welcome distraction from the bumps in the road that her career had suffered over the past two years. The abrupt closing of *Red, Hot and Blue!* in Chicago, her failure to secure Hollywood stardom, and the relatively brief run of *Stars in Your Eyes* all had made her feel somewhat restless and uneasy, and she began casting around for another show.

After the success of *Take a Chance*, its producer, Buddy DeSylva, had gone out to Hollywood to helm the film version and had stayed to make several more pictures. But when his 1939 hit *Bachelor Mother*, starring Ginger Rogers, had covered all concerned with glory except DeSylva himself, he decided to head back to Broadway to produce the kind of success that would make Hollywood take him seriously. At the suggestion of the agent Louis Shurr, DeSylva began casting around for a property to star Bert Lahr, the brilliant stage clown who had just made a splash as the Cowardly Lion in MGM's *Wizard of Oz*—not a big enough splash to please Lahr, however, since MGM had declined to keep him under long-term contract. DeSylva dug out an old story he'd written with Herbert Fields, brother of Dorothy, that Paramount had planned for Mae West but never produced. He and Fields went to work, refashioning it into a musical-comedy book, and Louis Shurr talked Cole Porter into composing the score.

Porter was eager to work with Ethel again, especially given the misery that had blighted his life over the past two years. In October 1937, during a riding party on Long Island, his horse had shied and rolled on top of him, shattering both his legs. He developed osteomyelitis and underwent several operations, which left him in chronic and often agonizing pain, but he bravely bore his affliction and continued to write. In November of 1938, his new show, *Leave It to Me!*, opened on Broadway and became a big hit. When the unknown ingenue Mary Martin stepped out to sing Porter's "My Heart Belongs to Daddy," the audience responded with a roar of approval: Dorothy Fields recalled that the only reception she'd ever heard to equal it was the one that greeted Ethel after she introduced "I Got Rhythm" in *Girl Crazy*.

Ethel was thrilled to be reunited with Porter, and she loved the script for the new show, which had the Mae Westian title *Du Barry Was a Lady*. In it she played May Daly, a nightclub singer at the Club Petite, and the (unrequited) love object of the club's washroom attendant, Louis Blore (Lahr). After Louis wins $75,000 in the Irish Sweepstakes, he works up enough confidence to try to get rid of May's boyfriend, Alex, by slipping him a Mickey Finn. But the drinks get mixed up, and Louis gets the Mickey Finn, whereupon he passes out and dreams that he is Louis XV and May is the courtesan Madame Du Barry. The jokes ranged from the topical (Louis: "I saw a picture the other day without Don Ameche in it") to the ribald (Louis: "Every time I look at her, I feel like I'm sliding down a banister covered with peach fuzz.").

Du Barry was the most visually opulent show in which Ethel had yet starred. To design the scenes and costumes, DeSylva had engaged Raoul Pène du Bois, the Staten Island–born banker's son who had dazzled Broadway four years earlier with his spectacular sets and costumes for Billy Rose's *Jumbo*. For *Du Barry*, du Bois designed and oversaw the creation of seven scenes and 360 costumes, all completed in a dizzying three weeks' time.

"The company for *Du Barry Was a Lady* was wacko—*completely* wacko," recalled Lewis Turner, a member of the show's dancing chorus. Leading the pack was Bert Lahr, whose inspired, euphoric clowning onstage masked a gloomy, pessimistic personality offstage. Lahr was a nervous performer, never quite sure, even after a show had opened successfully, whether the audience was on his side. His anxieties had not been helped by the fact that MGM had dumped him, and on top of everything else he was in physical discomfort: a condition diagnosed as spastic colon was plaguing him during rehearsals. Lahr also had doubts about the new show's chances for success. By Broadway standards Porter's lyrics pushed "sophisticated" about as far as possible. "When Cole got dirty," Lahr later said, "it was dirt, without subtlety. Nothing I sang in burlesque was as risqué as his lyrics." He was especially concerned about "But in the Morning, No," a comic duet for Ethel and himself, in which Du Barry and Louis catalog all the things they love to do at night but avoid like the plague when the dawn comes:

> HE: *D'you like Old Point Comfort, dear?*
> *Kindly tell me, if so.*
> SHE: *I like Old Point Comfort, dear,*
> *But in the morning, no.*

There were further mentions, over the course of ten refrains, of "shooting," "poker," "Pike's Peak," "double entry," and other bold double entendres. Ethel had no qualms about the lyrics. Since the days of *Anything Goes*, when she objected to the smuttiness of "Kate the Great," she'd gained a more relaxed attitude about what was appropriate to sing onstage. She delighted in her opening number, "Come On In," in which the ensemble sings:

> *If you go for pie, sweetheart,*
> *Why don't you try my cherry tart?*

She was less pleased, however, with her costar. She had great respect for Lahr's talent, and the two of them performed brilliantly together from the start: her sharp, streetwise dame made for a magnificent contrast with his addled buffoon. But she remained slightly wary of him, rankled, perhaps, by the fact that he commanded first billing. What is more likely is that she could never fathom his brooding personality. Because Ethel approached life as a black-and-white proposition, with little room for gray area, she remained allergic to complicated personalities. Lahr was in a Cole Porter show that looked like a sure thing, and he himself had funny lines, great songs. But in rehearsal he read his scenes almost tentatively, constantly stopping to make suggestions for honing a line or a piece of business. He never gave an all-out performance; that he was saving for the audience. Who could tell what his trouble was? Certainly not Ethel.

Lahr was also uneasy around Ethel. "She's an individual with a special way of working," he said. "There was nothing vicious in what she did, she is a great performer. But she's tough. *She never looks at you on stage*." This, in fact was a charge that Ethel's costars would level at her throughout her career. Her method of planting herself stage center and throwing her lines straight out to the audience could be disconcerting to her colleagues, who craved *some* degree of onstage rapport with her. Lahr considered it a trick, but Ethel would have insisted that it was the style that worked best for her. It had evolved during her revue days, when she was often alone onstage, and now that she was appearing exclusively in book shows, she saw no reason to change it. Audiences loved it, so why should she?

In *Du Barry*, Porter gave Ethel a number of terrific melodies, from the heartfelt "Do I Love You?" and "When Love Beckoned" to the rousing final duet with Lahr, "Friendship," which could be seen as an extension of their slightly edgy relationship onstage. She continued to suffer Lahr's anxieties right up to the New Haven opening. During the second act, Louis was supposed to chase Du Barry around and over the bed. On opening night in New Haven, as they were running in circles, Lahr was so lumbering and slow that Ethel passed him. The theater shook with laughter, and the "accident" became a regular piece of business in the show. In no time Lahr was worrying about whether the audience was laughing at him or at Ethel.

But if she was not sure about Lahr, onstage she exuded greater magic than ever. Chorus member Don Liberto recalled an early rehearsal in which Ethel turned up wearing a black dress and a black cape with a little diamond necklace. "I saw this lady coming from one side of the stage to the other," Liberto remembered, "and I said, 'My God—*there* is a star.' There was just something about her that was different from everybody else. Nobody could bring the joie de vivre that Merman brought on that stage. It was like every spotlight in the theater went on. You could see the sparks just coming out of her eyes. Nobody, not even Mary Martin, was like that." Ethel's approach to her work was simple: "Always give them the old fire, even when you feel like a squashed cake of ice."

The "wacko" group of players also included Betty Grable, the vivacious blond dancer making her Broadway debut after a discouraging nine-year stint in Hollywood. Grable was funny and unpretentious, always cracking jokes with the stage crew and chorus members, and her foul mouth could give Ethel's a run for its money. Also on board was Charles Walters, a dancer who had been kicking around Broadway for years and would soon go to MGM, where he would enjoy great success as a choreographer and director. The chorus was full of ravishing women, including Helen Bennett—a top photographer's model who, according to Cecil Beaton, had the world's most perfect bone structure—sugar heiress Geraldine Spreckles, Adele Jergens ("She was screwing around all over the place," said Lewis Turner), and Janice (later Janis) Carter, who, like Walters, would soon head for Hollywood.

Du Barry Was a Lady moved on to Boston, where the show had a good run, although the content proved a challenge to Back Bay sensibilities. The *Boston Transcript* warned, "It is scarcely an entertainment for children" while the *Boston Globe* observed that "But in the Morning, No" was sung "to the accompaniment of raised eyebrows here and there in the audience." The songs and jokes were all in solid shape, however. The audience loved "Friendship" so much that they wouldn't let the stars off the stage, and Porter had to come up with additional refrains overnight.

When *Du Barry* opened at Broadway's 46th Street Theatre, on December 6, 1939, it was disappointing to the cast to face a somewhat tepid audience reaction and mixed notices. In the *New York Times*, Brooks Atkinson found that the material "comes a little short of expectations, having only one idea in its comedy and that a disconcerting one. Fortunately, Miss Merman and Mr. Lahr are the people to make vulgarity honestly exuberant." But word of mouth made the show a sellout by week's end, and the principals could all relax, confident that they had a hit—all except Lahr, that is. On opening night Louis Shurr popped by Lahr's dressing room to congratulate him on what looked to be a long run. "Yeah," Lahr responded glumly. "But what do I do next year?"

The New York run of *Du Barry Was a Lady* was one of the highest times in Ethel's life. Her romance with Billingsley was still raging. Night after night, elegant presents, all courtesy of Sherman, arrived at her dressing room at the 46th Street Theatre. At one point he presented her with a ruby-and-diamond bracelet with FROM SHERM engraved on one side, TO MERM on the other. Friends continued to caution her, but as far as Ethel was concerned, the bracelet was proof of his devotion. Surely the next turn of events would be his separation from his wife, Hazel.

Ethel felt even more confident when Billingsley gave her his most extravagant gift yet—a yacht. Mom and Pop Zimmermann were uneasy with such ostentation, but Ethel was delighted. Frequently she would tell Dorothy Fields to meet her at the Seventy-ninth Street Marina, and the two of them would take off for an afternoon of sailing up and down the Hudson, with a superb champagne lunch provided by Billingsley.

Sometimes, though, his generosity jeopardized the show. Frequently he would send over cases of champagne and trays of hors d'oeuvres for the cast to consume during intermission. The result, as the weeks went by, was an increasingly chaotic and sloppy second act, until DeSylva stepped in and put an end to the intermission festivities.

When it came to holding the show together, Ethel functioned as the company's chief policeman. During a long run, a play's ensemble effort always deteriorates, and *Du Barry* was no exception. One cast member whom Ethel observed from a somewhat critical distance was Betty Grable. Over the years Ethel would acquire a reputation for being tough on the beautiful girls in her shows. But it wasn't Grable's looks or popularity with the rest of the cast that unnerved her; it was her fondness for cutting up onstage. "Grable was happy to have a job," remembered Lewis Turner. "But she hated doing the same thing every night. It was just so boring to her. She would try to make everyone screw up somehow." One night, in the middle of a scene, Grable whispered in Lahr's ear, "How would you like to stick your cock up my ass and make some fudge?" Turner recalled that Lahr "couldn't remember the next line. The audience didn't know what was going on. He was hysterical."

Geraldine Spreckles committed a more serious infraction. One night she conned several of the showgirls into blowing up a few packages of condoms, writing their names on them, and sticking them underneath their hoopskirts. When the transition from the Club Petite to the court of Louis XV took place, all the girls came out singing, "*Mesdames and Messieurs, écoutez-vous*," and lifted their skirts to reveal the bouncing balloons. "After the curtain came down," said Turner, "they pulled everybody together. And then Ethel Merman came out and said, 'I don't know what the hell you're doing. This is a job like any other job you go to. It's like being a plumber or carpenter or anything else. You come to this theater and you come to work. And you don't pull this kind of shit.' "

Midway through *Du Barry*, Ethel did something unusual for her—she missed a number of performances. She was out on more than one occasion. The exact nature of her illness is not clear. Ethel normally enjoyed robust health even during the longest of runs, and in some circles it was rumored that she had become pregnant by Billingsley and had to have an abortion. Her part was taken by her understudy, Betty Allen, whom she thanked with a gift of a big yellow-topaz ring set in gold, and later by Gypsy Rose Lee.

By the summer of 1940, Ethel was preparing for her new show, *Panama Hattie*. The winning team from *Du Barry Was a Lady* took an encore: producer Buddy DeSylva, book writers DeSylva and Herbert Fields, director Edgar McGregor, choreographer Robert Alton, designer Raoul Pène du Bois. *Panama Hattie* was a departure for Ethel in one respect only, but it was a crucial one: This time she wouldn't be sharing the spotlight with a star comic like Durante or Lahr. *Stars in Your Eyes* had been a step forward for her as an actress and comedienne, but in a way *Du Barry* had been a step back: she had handled the songs while the real meat of the comic situations was given to Lahr. DeSylva had noticed that she'd been chafing a bit in *Du Barry* and decided that this time he would build the whole show around her. As plans for the project got under way, Ethel grew more and more excited: she seemed to sense that *Panama Hattie* was the start of a whole new phase in her career—as a solo star who had no need of a strong male lead.

Panama Hattie was in no way revolutionary; it was just another of Porter's well-crafted musical comedies. Its heroine was Hattie Maloney, the tough but goodhearted operator of a popular cabaret in Panama City, the Tropical Shore. Whether intentionally or not, DeSylva and Fields seemed to have used Ethel's own life as the basis for the character: Hattie was a flip, raucous gal with bows on her shoes; the script indicated that "she'd wear two hats at a time, if she could, and she usually rattles from inexpensive jewelry." Hattie has plans to marry the Philadelphia blueblood Nick Bullett (a stand-in for Walter Annenberg?), but their romance is sabotaged by a jealous admiral's daughter who wants Nick for herself. There was also a comic subplot about three sailors who discover a stockpile of explosives, part of an espionage plan that Hattie helps foil.

Panama Hattie was fully cast by midsummer. James Dunn, an all-purpose leading man from the movies, was signed to play Nick. Dunn was amiable enough, but a fairly nondescript actor—the better not to detract from Ethel. The rest of the cast was anything but anonymous: Arthur Treacher, the screen's perfect butler, was brought out to play Nick's perfect butler, Vivien Budd. Phyllis Brooks, in the throes of a much-publicized romance with Cary Grant, played Leila, the admiral's daughter. A frenzied, manic young nightclub entertainer named Betty Hutton was signed for the comic part of Florrie, who develops a mad crush on Vivien.

The real heart of the show, however, was Hattie's relationship with Nick's worldly eight-year-old daughter, Gerry, played by Joan Carroll. Porter had written a duet for Hattie and Gerry that was quite different from anything he'd done before. Porter wrote primarily with passion and wit, and often with a combination of the two, though seldom with openhearted sentiment. But DeSylva and Fields had come up with a lovely scene that required a sentimental number. It came in the first act, when Gerry coaxes Hattie to tone down her appearance by cutting the bows off her shoes and removing her jangly bracelets, to "walk plain . . . without the bouncing." Porter provided a beautiful song, almost in the style of Irving Berlin, about the unlikely pair's burgeoning friendship, and everyone had to hear "Let's Be Buddies" only once to know it would be the hit of the show.

Although Ethel was always at her most vulnerable with men, it seems to have taken an unusually long time for the scales to drop from her eyes where Sherman Billingsley was concerned. Eventually, however, the realist in her had to surface and take over. One illuminating moment came when Dorothy Fields confronted Billingsley about the affair and told him that she knew he would never leave Hazel and the children. Billingsley's response was to ban Fields from the Stork Club. Ethel, always a loyal friend, was angry that Dorothy had been treated this way in what she thought of as "her" establishment. At the same time, gossip columnists, including Billingsley's close pal

Walter Winchell, were dropping broader and broader hints in the newspaper about her relationship with Billingsley. The capper came when Hazel Billingsley became pregnant again and Ethel began to comprehend what being cast in the role of home-wrecker might do to her career. Hazel had many friends in theater circles, and Ethel worried that public sympathy might well be with Hazel and against her. (Years later the public's reaction to the Ingrid Bergman–Roberto Rossellini affair and the Elizabeth Taylor–Eddie Fisher–Debbie Reynolds triangle would show that she'd had reason for concern.) Ethel finally confronted Billingsley angrily, telling him in no uncertain terms that she was not about to spend the rest of her life as a married man's mistress. To friends she confided, "I'm not gonna be somebody's sweetheart!" With deep regret, and after many nights of crying into her champagne, she called off the affair.

Sherman Billingsley didn't rate a "Fing!" from Ethel, but the experience had left her deeply wounded, and she thought it best to take a hiatus from the Stork Club. Had she possessed much talent for introspection, she might have taken a close look at the pattern she had been repeating thus far and made some vital connections that would have benefited her in the future. She was, in certain crucial ways, a case of arrested development: the adored only child whose profound emotional connection to her parents had created in her a kind of childlike view of the world around her. It was admirable that Mom and Pop Zimmermann had brought her up to be honest, straightforward, hardworking, thrifty. But her simplistic approach to life and its problems did not always work to her advantage in the sophisticated and often treacherous world of show business. Life was filled with ambiguity, but Ethel could not or would not bring herself to acknowledge it. "She was on the up-and-up every second," observed Lewis Turner. "This lady didn't know anything else." An honorable trait, certainly—but also one that would lead her down the blind alleys of intractability, rage, and loneliness. If her refusal to bend, to answer in anything but the strongest yeses and nos, would help her forge one of the greatest careers the theater has ever known, it would also bring her tremendous disappointment and pain.

After her breakup with Billingsley, it might have been wise for her to sit back and take stock before jumping into another romance. Instead she promptly took her first fling at marriage.

From the start of rehearsals, Arthur Treacher and his wife, Virginia, always called Ethel "Hattie," and she began seeing a good deal of them after rehearsals. One evening she was invited to their apartment for cocktails, and there she met Treacher's agent, William Smith, who worked for the Feldman-Blum Agency in Hollywood. Publicist Julian Myers, who later worked with Smith at 20th Century Fox, recalled him as "a New York character in the best sense. He didn't have a subdued voice. He was bigger than life. He was part of the international radio scene, and anything promotion-wise he could deliver with a snap of his fingers. He had his little empire consisting of Bill Smith. . . . He was intelligent and well-connected, but he didn't have a lot of time for other people."

Bill Smith was tall, with broad shoulders and dark hair and a tough demeanor. He was reasonably good-looking, although he gave the impression that he could easily run to fat. Much of the time, he chomped on a big cigar, and he had a salty vocabulary to match Ethel's. She liked him well enough, though she did not feel any great sparks. She reminded herself that she had felt nothing *but* sparks with Billingsley, and that had not turned out favorably. She also reminded herself that she was thirty-two—well along, at the time, for a woman still to be unmarried. Smith had several things going for him: he was respected in the agency business, he had an independent income from his family in Brookline, Massachusetts, and best of all he was single. Ethel and Bill and the Treachers quickly became a steady foursome around town.

Panama Hattie had its out-of-town opening at New Haven's Shubert Theatre on October 3, 1940. One of the show's attractions was an unusually talented collection of chorus girls: Janice Carter, from *Du Barry Was a Lady*, was back this time, with a step-out number, "Who Would Have Dreamed?," and the dancing chorus included future Hollywood notables June Allyson, Lucille Bremer, Doris Dowling, Vera-Ellen, and Betsy Blair. Often the girls stood in the wings listening to Ethel sing "Let's Be Buddies" with Joan Carroll, or her big second-act solo, "Make It Another Old-Fashioned, Please," a number that Porter had set to a beguiling beguine melody:

> *Once I owned a treasure, so rare, so pure,*
> *The greatest of treasures, happiness safe and secure,*
> *But like ev'ry hope too rash,*
> *My treasure, I find, is trash,*
> *So make it another old-fashioned, please.*
> *Leave out the cherry,*
> *Leave out the orange,*
> *Leave out the bitters,*
> *Just make it a straight rye!*

"I thought 'Make It Another Old-Fashioned, Please' was the most so-phisticated song I had ever heard," recalled Betsy Blair. "My impression of Ethel Merman was of this tornado on the stage. She was very tough with her equals and her bosses." At the same time, Ethel was remarkably patient with Betty Hutton's brash antics backstage. (Hutton had a habit of addressing her fellow players with a loud "HIYA, DOLLFACE!") Blair remembered Ethel's treatment of the chorus girls as "perfectly democratic. She didn't snub us. She knew we were working hard—they had us dancing like crazy."

Panama Hattie played four performances in New Haven to rave notices and a box-office take of $13,400, which outdistanced the Shubert's previous record holder, another DeSylva show—Irving Berlin's *Louisiana Purchase*. Arthur Treacher's comedy solo, "Americans All Drink Coffee," judged by *Variety* to be "a weak sister," was dropped. The show moved on to Boston on October 7, where several critics found it superior to *Du Barry*. It was too long, with the curtain coming down at eleven forty-five, but the *Boston Herald* predicted, "It isn't going to be easy to cut. Not when each number meets with so hearty a welcome."

At *Panama Hattie*'s sold-out Broadway opening night on October 30, Ethel's dressing room was flooded with telegrams from Joan Crawford, Al Jolson, Helen Hayes, Victor Moore, and many others. The show ran like a well-oiled machine, and the audience received it rapturously, as did the critics: the *New York Journal* ranked it "among the best in her long list of hits. . . . Miss Merman has never been better, never surer or glossier." *Theatre Arts Monthly* thought that "her humor displays a new warmth, her attack on the part a new assurance, especially in certain scenes with the small Geraldine, played very capably by a youngster named Joan Carroll." Only Betty Hutton got hit with a few critical arrows: The *New York Herald Tribune* said, "Miss Hutton should be given one number, if that, in the course of an evening and then be permitted to work off her surplus energies elsewhere."

Bill Smith was still Ethel's constant companion, and shortly after *Panama Hattie*'s opening night, with the immediate future looking wonderful, the couple decided to make it legal. (According to Sherman Billingsley's biographer, Ralph Blumenthal, Ethel informed her ex-lover of her wedding plans by leaving him a curt telephone message.) On November 15, Ethel and Bill were married by J. Warren Albinson, rector of the Trinity Church in Elkton, Maryland. Also in attendance were Mom and Pop Zimmermann and Arthur and Virginia Treacher. A few hours later, Ethel was playing Hattie Maloney on the stage of the 46th Street Theatre.

Ethel's marriage to Bill Smith marked her first real attempt to break away from Mom and Pop and strike out on her own. For their new home the Smiths had settled on the Hotel Pierre, at 2 East Sixty-third Street. Dorothy Fields supervised the redecorating of a suite to Ethel's specifications. The only thing Ethel moved from the Century was the display counter—it looked big enough for the first floor of Saks Fifth Avenue—that held her rapidly growing collection of toilet waters. The Smiths moved in and spent their first night together in their new home, before Bill had to return to his job in California the following evening. The plan was for him to wind up his affairs on the West Coast and come east to establish a New York office of Feldman-Blum. To the press, the couple dropped hints that Ethel would retire from the stage when *Panama Hattie* ended its run.

In her autobiography Ethel admits that the tears she shed on her wedding day were not tears of happiness but ones of regret: she already knew that she had made a dreadful mistake. What exactly happened on the morning after that first night at the Pierre is not entirely clear; tight-lipped as ever about her personal life, Ethel never spoke about it to reporters. Her memoirs say only, "Tempers flared. Some ugly things were said." What is clear is that she was looking for any excuse to get out of a marriage that she already recognized was ill conceived. According to Lew Kesler, it was as simple as this: she and Smith spent the night together, and the next morning he disappeared into the bathroom with his newspaper and cigar. Over an hour later, he was still there, reading and smoking. Ethel, incensed that her bridegroom would indulge in such selfish, insensitive behavior, blew her top. Smith did indeed return to Los Angeles that evening. Fing! Once again she put a decisive period at the end of a major episode in her life.

Or at least an ellipsis. Knowing that the resulting publicity was not likely to be flattering, Ethel agreed to give the marriage half a chance more. She and Smith decided to have a summit meeting in Chicago. Ethel boarded the train at Grand Central Station, dreading the meeting, certain it would accomplish nothing. She soothed her raw nerves by adjourning to the club car for a few drinks before retiring to her compartment. While she was sleeping, the air-conditioning in the compartment was turned on high. Like many singers, Ethel had little tolerance for a sustained blast of cold air, and when she awoke the next morning, her throat was sore and closed up tight, and her muscles ached all over. Feeling miserable, she took a taxi to the hotel, where Smith was waiting in the room with a tray of fruit, champagne on ice, and the bed turned down. When Ethel walked through the door, Smith found himself on the receiving end of her accumulated anger: it was all *his* fault, because if he hadn't insisted on meeting her in Chicago, she wouldn't be in such terrible shape. An unholy quarrel ensued, and Ethel took the next train back to New York. Two months later it was announced in the press that Ethel would seek a divorce from Smith, on grounds of desertion.

In the years to come, Ethel said little about this first, abortive marriage. On the rare occasions that she did refer to it, it was only as the first of her four mistakes. But in 1941 she was angry, confused, and embarrassed that things between her and Smith had imploded so quickly. She had always put her career before her personal life. Now, alone again, she was beginning to wonder if that had been such a wise move.

D uring the run of *Panama Hattie*, an incident took place that would fuel Ethel's reputation as the toughest, most ruthless star on Broadway. Initially Betty Hutton had three numbers, "Fresh as a Daisy" and "They Ain't Done Right by Our Nell" in the first act and "All I've Got to Get Now Is My Man" in the second. During the out-of-town tryout, more than one critic complained that Hutton's unique performing style—she was in constant overdrive—wore out its welcome over the course of an evening. The result was that "Nell" was cut before the New York opening. No doubt it was a sensible decision made by DeSylva and the rest of the creative team, but Hutton later complained to anyone who would listen that it had all been Ethel's doing. In years to come, many in the Broadway community— most of them people who had never worked with her—gossiped that Ethel was one star not to be crossed if you happened to be a member of her supporting cast. If an attractive young actress was cast in a Merman show, her agent was apt to warn her to give Ethel a wide berth and not call attention to herself; otherwise her part was likely to be cut to shreds. These rumors compounded over the years, to the point that many of the girls in the chorus feared they would be fired just because they were prettier than Ethel.

One actress whose experience refuted such tales was another member of *Panama Hattie*'s cast, June Allyson. An energetic young dancer, Allyson was eager to get ahead, and everyone in the company knew it. "June had that ambition, that drive," remembered Betsy Blair. "Being the smallest one in the chorus, she was last onstage. I remember Tyrone Power and all the movie stars being in the audience, and June always managed to trip and fall down and get up and be embarrassed and adorable as the whole line went off. In my book [*The Memory of All That*] I said, 'Good for her,' but at the time we all thought it was pretty crummy." Ethel, however, seems to have admired Allyson's go-getter spirit. At one point in the middle of the run, Betty Hutton got the measles and was out of the show for ten days or so, and Allyson took over her part. Normally she dressed on the third floor with the other chorus girls, but Ethel didn't think this was appropriate for a girl getting her first big break, so she insisted that Allyson share her star dressing room. She even had a large bouquet of spring flowers delivered, which Allyson remembered "made me feel like a star."

Happy as she was with *Panama Hattie*'s success, Ethel often felt lonely and dispirited. The sense of utter perfectionism that had already made Ethel a legend in the theater extended to her personal life as well. To Ethel a perfect existence was one of order and balance. She didn't like messes, and when she helped to create them, as in the case of both Sherman Billingsley and Bill Smith, she seemed unwilling to share the responsibility. *Panama Hattie* was still playing to packed houses nightly. It was her eighth Broadway show and her seventh major hit—a remarkable record matched by few if any performers. But when it came to developing a genuine, deep adult emotional life, she had made no progress at all. Ethel approached the dilemma with her usual black-and-white reasoning. She was far from cynical about men and was certain that she would find her Mr. Right in due time, if only she looked hard enough. And in mid-1941 she believed that had finally happened.

It was a Saturday night early in April, and New York was caught in what would be the final snowstorm of the year. Hearst Publications was sponsoring a benefit dinner and art auction that evening at the Plaza Hotel, and Ethel, along with Danny Kaye, currently appearing in Kurt Weill and Ira Gershwin's *Lady in the Dark*, had agreed to entertain. Once the curtain for *Panama Hattie* had come down, Ethel, as was her habit after the Saturday-night performance, had friends to her dressing room for drinks. By the time she and Lew Kesler, who was to accompany her on the piano at the benefit, reached the Plaza, only Danny Kaye and his wife, Sylvia Fine, were left—with the exception of one lone representative of the Hearst empire, a dark-haired, strikingly handsome man with strong shoulders and a charming smile.

"Where the hell are all the people?" asked Ethel.

The man from Hearst introduced himself as Robert Levitt, promotion director for the *New York Journal-American*, one of Hearst's biggest newspapers. Both Ethel and Danny Kaye had been under the impression that the affair started around nine and would go until all hours. "I'm terribly sorry I'm late," Ethel said. Levitt seemed less than conciliatory. "Well," he said peevishly, "the party's over."

Ethel's temper started to rise as she reminded Levitt that she'd taken the trouble to get dressed up and slog over to the Plaza in the middle of a snowstorm; the least he could do was to take her out somewhere. With a noticeable lack of enthusiasm, Levitt agreed, and the party of five adjourned to the Monkey Bar, a popular spot in the Elysée Hotel. The Kayes left shortly, followed by Lew Kesler. By now Levitt was intrigued enough to ask Ethel if she wanted to go to an after-hours spot, and they wound up drinking late into the night at the Club Carr.

On the way home, Ethel asked Levitt if he had any chewing gum. He said no and didn't bother to stop at an all-night drugstore to buy her a pack. Instead he dropped her at the Century—she had returned there to live after giving up the short-lived honeymoon suite at the Pierre—and let her walk through a snowdrift to get to the curb. As romances went, this one looked like a dead end, but the next day Levitt had a big carton of chewing gum delivered to the Century. Shortly after that he began asking her out to dinner. On one of their dates, troubled by the fact that he'd never mentioned having seen her onstage, Ethel asked him how he liked her current show. Levitt replied that he hadn't been to *Panama Hattie.* A little more digging on Ethel's part revealed that he'd never seen any of her shows, because he didn't think much of musicals. Ethel immediately arranged for tickets for him for the following night. Bob went out drinking with a friend beforehand, had a few too many, and slept through much of the show. But he and Ethel continued seeing each other.

In many ways they were a strange pair. Bob was born in Brooklyn to a Jewish family that stressed education and career advancement. (His brother Arthur would eventually become the comptroller of the State of New York.) Early on, Bob was interested in writing and literature, and he developed a profound love of poetry in general and Middle English in particular. He began his journalism career as a reporter on the *New York Journal,* covering Brooklyn politics and community affairs, and he soon advanced to the promotion department when the paper merged with the *New York American.* As did many newspapermen of the period, he liked to drink, and he became known for his sharp, even cutting, wit—whether drunk or sober. "He was a very funny, acerbically funny man," recalled veteran publishing executive David Brown. "He was able to crack wise, and didn't respect anyone too much, and was rather liked because of that. Nice personality—but hardly a warm personality."

Bob's deep streak of cynicism didn't always mesh well with Ethel's flat-out sincerity and earnestness. Another significant gulf between them was the fact that Bob didn't care much for the company of show-business types and wasn't afraid to say so. Show business was Ethel's whole life; she was not terribly interested in the world beyond Broadway and Hollywood, and a social evening with her usually meant lots of gossip about people in the business. Yet she was somehow drawn to Bob's blasé attitude about her profession, which she considered an indication of his strong character. To her he was another tough guy, albeit a very polished and intelligent one. Bob saw in Ethel a driven, opinionated woman with a lot of raw sex appeal. In no time they developed a passionate attraction to each other, and soon Bob was picking her up every night after *Panama Hattie*'s final curtain. Since Bob had to report to the Hearst offices early in the morning, he would come home after work, sleep for a few hours, then head to the 46th Street Theatre to collect Ethel and take her out on the town until the early-morning hours.

By the fall it was clear to everyone close to Ethel and Bob that theirs was not a fleeting romance. Despite the great difference in their personalities, their interests, their friends, they had fallen deeply in love. Around November, Ethel discovered that she was pregnant. Since rumors had spread throughout the theater community that she had missed performances of *Du Barry Was a Lady* because she had terminated a pregnancy by Sherman Billingsley, she did not want to have an abortion. She and Bob Levitt looked hard at the situation, and things were going so well between them that they decided to get married.

This was a task that required careful maneuvering, since her marriage to Bill Smith had not yet been legally terminated. In mid-1941, Smith had applied for an interlocutory divorce in California, a protracted process that might take up to a year. Eager to have the whole thing behind her as quickly as possible, Ethel had rashly applied for a Mexican divorce. According to Levitt, she hadn't even bothered to go south of the border to attend to it; the whole process had been completed by mail. Now that she wanted to marry Bob, she was told that her divorce from Smith was not legally valid in the United States. But she and Bob went ahead with their plans anyway and were married quietly by Justice of the Peace Herbert MacDonald in North Haven, Connecticut, on December 18, 1941. Three days later the *New York Times* reported that Ethel had "confirmed reports of her marriage to Robert D. Levitt." Ethel never specified exactly where the wedding took place and only vaguely maintained that she and Bob had been married in the late fall, for fear that the tabloids would print the truth.

Marriage did nothing to weaken Ethel's bond with her parents. She couldn't bear being far away from the Zimmermanns, so she and Bob took another apartment in the Century, a ten-room duplex with a roof-garden terrace. Within a matter of weeks, Ethel's pregnancy was showing, making it

impossible for her to continue in *Panama Hattie* without a complete overhaul of costumes. The show closed on January 31, 1942, after an impressive
run of 501 performances.

Not long after the Japanese attacked Pearl Harbor, on December 7,
1941, Bob decided to enlist in the U.S. Army. He went through officers'
training and quickly took up a post as a captain in the Quartermaster Corps
for the army's Port of Embarkation in Brooklyn. Before long he had been
promoted to the rank of lieutenant colonel in charge of the port's public relations. In his new post, he reported to General Homer Groninger, a longtime
military man who played by the hard-and-fast rules of officers' behavior.
Part of official protocol dictated that the officers' wives entertain at social
functions. This was a task that Ethel didn't relish, no matter how important
it was to her new husband, and she informed Bob that she was not about to
be caught pouring out tea at the officers' club or fawning over General
Groninger's wife. The fact that Bob's spouse was Ethel Merman was deemed
irrelevant by the top brass, some of whom had been living far from New York
and weren't even entirely sure who she was.

The situation finally came to a head when General Groninger gave a
cocktail party for the officers at Fort Hamilton in Brooklyn. Tired of Bob's
list of excuses for Ethel's absence from official functions, Groninger all but
ordered him to make sure his wife attended the party. Ethel was mostly a
champagne drinker, but there was none in sight that day, and what was being offered was manhattans—warm ones. While Bob was trailing after Groninger, Ethel tossed back several of them, all the while giving a cold shoulder
to the officers' wives who attempted to make small talk with her. After cocktails a sit-down dinner was served, with a band playing. While Ethel was
eating, General Groninger's wife approached her and asked her if she would
like to sing a few numbers.

"Get out of my way, Cuddles," said Ethel, "before I spit in your eye."

Fortunately, Mrs. Groninger appears to have had a sense of humor, because another invitation soon arrived, this one for a party aboard the general's yacht. It was a balmy Sunday afternoon, and the officers' party sailed up
the Hudson River to Camp Shanks in New Jersey. To pass the time, the
general had arranged a marathon of his favorite game, old-fashioned rummy.
As he shuffled the cards, he announced to his opponents, "I never lose at
this game." For Ethel this was too much of a challenge to resist, and she proceeded to clobber him in every single hand, picking up fistfuls of cards and
playing out every last one. The general, not amused, retired belowdecks.

If she wasn't an ideal officer's wife in the realm of social obligations, Ethel did plenty for the war effort as an entertainer. She gave numerous concerts at two of the camps under General Groninger's command, Camp Shanks and Camp Kilmer. Bob Levitt recalled that as her pregnancy advanced, she was given a smaller and smaller spotlight; by the time she was in her seventh or eighth month, the spot hit only her face. Ethel also spent many evenings singing at the Stage Door Canteen, the nightclub launched by the American Theatre Wing and the United Service Organization to provide entertainment, free of charge, for soldiers.

During this time, she saw a great deal of Josie Traeger and Alice Welch; although they had nothing to do with show business, they were still Ethel's closest friends.

By the last month of her pregnancy, Ethel had ballooned to an enormous size and grown increasingly irritable. Bob, by all appearances, was a devoted father-to-be and tried to divert her with endless card games and gossip from the outside world. Finally, on July 20, Ethel gave birth by cesarean section to a seven-pound, one-ounce baby girl. She was named Ethel Merman Levitt, but soon the nickname Bob had given her, "Little Bit," stuck.

While she was pregnant, Ethel had insisted that once the baby arrived, she would take a year off from performing. It was time for her to put her home life first, she maintained, and she sounded serious. But the reality of being at home, steeped in one domestic crisis after another, riding herd on Little Bit's nurse and the rest of the household help—most of whom had a way of coming and going very quickly—took its toll. With the exception of her appearances singing for the troops, Ethel had been idle for more than six months—by far the longest stretch of unemployment in her professional career. She and Bob had barely had any time at all to have a romantic life together before they were saddled with the immense responsibilities of parenthood, and frequently their tempers flared. They had at least made peace over the subject of income. Although Bob's salary of $200 weekly was considered good money in the publishing business, it paled next to Ethel's earning power. Bob claimed not to be bothered by this, and they had worked out an arrangement by which his salary would go toward basic family and household needs; if Ethel required the luxury items that living like a star always requires, she would pay for them herself.

When it became obvious to all that Ethel's confinement was causing discord at home, she and Bob talked it over and agreed that she should begin to shop around for another show. There was no lack of offers, including one that had been floating around for some time, *Birds of a Feather*, with unpublished songs by the Gershwins. Ethel was delighted at the prospect of doing another show by the man who had launched her career, but the book, by Bella and Samuel Spewack, never pulled itself into shape, and the project languished.

Then there was *Jenny Get Your Gun*, a property that had first been brought to Ethel's attention while she was still pregnant with Little Bit. It had a fancy pedigree: songs by Cole Porter, book by Dorothy and Herbert Fields. Vinton Freedley was supposed to produce it, but when he listened to the songs Porter had written and the idea the Fieldses had for a script, he told them bluntly that he thought they were all off on the wrong foot. Hurt and angry, the threesome decided to look for another producer. Porter's suggestion was Mike Todd.

Born in dirt-poor circumstances in Minneapolis, Todd had been a hustler from childhood. He'd always been obsessed with making money and had worked at a variety of colorful enterprises—from hawking potato peelers at a carnival to promoting a floating crap game that netted him ten cents a pot. His first venture into show business was hardly auspicious: at the 1933 Chicago World's Fair, he produced a number known as the Flame Dance, in which a beautiful girl clad only in a moth costume danced closer and closer to a flame until it burned off her clothes and she ran stark naked into the wings. But by 1939, Todd had hit the big time, producing *The Hot Mikado* on Broadway, with an all-black cast headed by Bill Robinson. Most of his subsequent stage ventures weren't as high-toned. "I believe in giving the customers a meat and potatoes show," he said. "Dames and comedy. High dames and low comedy—that's my message." In 1942 he demonstrated this credo with the big, splashy Broadway hit *Star and Garter*, starring Gypsy Rose Lee and lots of gorgeous girls. It made a mint, but by now he had won and lost so many fortunes it all seemed familiar. "I've never been poor," he said, "only broke. Being poor is a frame of mind. Being broke is a temporary situation."

Todd had none of Freedley's reservations about *Jenny Get Your Gun:* the team of Porter, Dorothy and Herbert Fields, and Merman was good enough for him. A key part of Todd's style was investing a great deal of energy into putting the gaudiest, most exhilarating show possible on the stage, but he did not interfere with the creative process. He handed the directorial reins to his friend and collaborator Hassard Short, who had staged both *The Hot Mikado* and *Star and Garter*.

Ethel immediately took to Todd's high-octane personality and loved his common streak—he said "tink" for "think" and "dem" for "them." But he was shrewd and, in his own way, quite sophisticated; the critic George Jean Nathan once characterized him as "an Oxford man posing as a mugg." Best of all he was a whiz at coping with the shortages imposed by wartime conditions. Time and time again, Todd wangled a way of getting substitutes for elaborate set and costume elements that looked good onstage but could be had on the cheap.

Dorothy and Herbert Fields spent the next few months working on the book. One day they read in the newspaper that Lucille Ball had discovered she was picking up radio signals in her dental fillings. It sounded crazy enough to belong in musical comedy, so they added it to their plot about three distant cousins named Hart—Harry, a street vendor; Chiquita, a burlesque artiste; and Blossom, a Rosie the Riveter type—all of whom inherit a ranch in Texas near an air force base. They turn it into a hotel for military wives, but their enterprise runs into trouble when the authorities suspect them of running a bordello.

During World War II, topicality was highly prized in both movies and the theater; audiences wanted their entertainment to comment, one way or another, on the challenges and heartaches of wartime. *Something for the Boys*, as the show was now called, gave them their money's worth, as a sampling of its dialogue demonstrates:

SOLDIER (admiring Blossom's legs): Boy, look at those drumsticks!
BLOSSOM: How would you like a kick in the teeth from one of those drumsticks?
SOLDIER: How do you like that? And this is the womanhood I'm fighting to protect!
BLOSSOM: And this is the womanhood *I'm* fighting to protect!

Something for the Boys went into rehearsal in the fall of 1942, a period when Broadway was experiencing a drought of splashy musicals. A few shows that had opened at the end of the previous season—notably Todd's own *Star and Garter* and *By Jupiter*, featuring Benay Venuta as Hippolyta, Queen of the Amazons—were doing well, but wartime economics dictated that many of the more recent musicals be rather downscale revues, such as *Keep 'Em Laughing* with William Gaxton and Victor Moore and *Laugh, Town, Laugh!* starring Ed Wynn. With *Something for the Boys*, Todd was determined to bring razzmatazz back to Broadway. He spent the princely sum of $158,000 on the production, which was extremely complex. It featured twelve sets, so elaborate that they would have to be shipped in five freight cars from New York to the out-of-town tryout in Boston. There was even a spectacular final bit involving an onstage bomber, aimed right at the audience, that got tossed around in a thunderstorm.

Ethel pronounced Porter's score the best he'd ever written. It wasn't, in fact, top-drawer Porter, but it did give her a generous helping of catchy numbers, including "He's a Right Guy," "Hey, Good-Lookin'" and a song that showed off Porter's passion for poking fun at current trends: "The Leader of a Big-Time Band" spoofed American women's newest heartthrobs—the Benny Goodmans and Harry Jameses:

> *When, in Venice, Georgia Sand with Chopin romped,*
> *Her libido had the Lido simply swamped,*
> *But today who would be buried in the sand?*
> *Why, the leader of a big-time band.*
> *When Dorsey starts to tilt*
> *That horn about,*
> *Dear Missus Vanderbilt*
> *Bumps herself out,*
> *So, if, say, you still can play a one-night stand,*
> *Be the leader of a big-time band.*

Something for the Boys was cast from strength. Allen Jenkins, the Brooklyn-accented cabdriver of dozens of Hollywood movies, played Harry the vendor. In the role of Chiquita the striptease artist was a dry, sharp, horse-faced comedienne named Paula Laurence, who had earned acclaim in nightclubs and in the Broadway comedy *Junior Miss*. The tricky production was beautifully paced by Hassard Short. A gentle, soft-spoken Englishman, Short had begun his career as an actor—his high-water mark had been playing opposite Laurette Taylor in her great hit *Peg O' My Heart*—and his keen understanding of actors and their problems ensured a smooth rehearsal process.

For the out-of-town opening of *Something for the Boys*, Ethel was back at the Shubert Theatre in Boston. The first night, December 18, 1942, played to a packed house and enthusiastic notices. "Undoubtedly the season's first smash musical hit," proclaimed the *Boston Herald*, adding, "Ethel Merman has never looked better, nor sung with more verve and bounce." The show took in $9,000 during its first three performances at the Shubert, then moved on to New York, where it was to open at the Alvin Theatre. The occasion was a satisfying one for Ethel, as she moved into the star dressing room, recalling the days during *Girl Crazy* when she had to dress on the fourth floor. Her relationship with Porter remained as affable as ever. The composer would go over a song with her, then inevitably throw up his hands and say, "Oh, just do whatever you want, darling."

Something for the Boys opened on January 7, 1943, to the sort of notices that were by now standard for a Merman-Porter show. "One of the song and dance delights of the season," reported the *New York Herald Tribune,* while the *New Yorker* stated, "There is nobody quite like this Merman, or even a reasonable facsimile of her." Ethel's belief in the show was vindicated when the first five performances pulled in $20,655 at the box office. Despite the fact that not one of the score's songs became a breakaway hit, the company played to standing-room-only audiences for weeks.

It was only after *Something for the Boys* had opened successfully that some of the most interesting events connected with it took place. Ethel was no less given to extremes than she'd ever been: even now, at the peak of her fame, she tended to regard people as being either with her or against her. During rehearsals for *Something for the Boys,* she became extremely fond of two young actresses in the show. Betty Bruce, a tough, funny tap dancer, made Ethel break up with the pornographic lyrics she invented for the symphonic hit "Holiday for Strings," and in time would become one of her closest female friends. Betty Garrett, who played the supporting part of Mary Frances and also served as Ethel's understudy, was warm and unpretentious and outgoing, one of the most popular members of the company. She had a solo at the start of the second act, "I'm in Love with a Soldier Boy," written for the New York opening when Garrett's other number, "So Long, San Antonio," proved unworkable. "I'm in Love with a Soldier Boy" was a sweet, tender ballad about wartime romance, and it provided the audience with a respite from the general rambunctiousness of the rest of the show. Although in no way outstanding as a song, it stopped the show night after night. Chorus dancer Lou Wills Jr. felt that it went over "because so many in the audience had men overseas." Ethel was to make an entrance immediately after the number, but the applause was so great that she often called Garrett back to take a bow.

Friends assured Garrett that no understudy for Merman ever got the chance to go on, but midway through the run, Ethel came down with a bad cold, complicated by laryngitis. Garrett took over as Blossom for a week and gave a wonderful performance, one that paved her way to Broadway stardom in *Call Me Mister* a few years later. "I was so frightened," recalled Garrett, "and Ethel called me. And she said, 'How ya doin', kid?' I told her how nervous I was. And she said, 'Listen, kid, if they could do it better than you, *they'd* be on the stage and *you'd* be in the audience.' "

But if Ethel looked on Betty Garrett and Betty Bruce as angels, there was another woman in the company she chose to cast in the role of demon. Initially, Ethel had gotten on well with Paula Laurence. It was clear to many in the company that Laurence was fiercely ambitious, but she performed wonderfully, and her second-act duet with Merman, "By the Mississinewah," was a bona fide showstopper. Clad in fringed dresses, pigtails, and beaded, fur-trimmed moccasins, Ethel and Laurence played a pair of Indian squaws who share a man and dream of the day they will both be reunited with him and be able to plan a life together—all three of them:

> BOTH: By the Miss-iss-iss-iss-inewah,
> CHIQUITA: There's a husband who me adore,
> BLOSSOM: Me more.
> BOTH: By the Miss-iss-iss-iss-iss-inewah,
> CHIQUITA: There he waits in a wigwam built for four,
> BLOSSOM [spoken]: Are you expectin' too?

Its suggestive lyrics unfolded over Porter's many refrains; the published version would have to be cleaned up considerably. During rehearsals, Hassard Short, busy with the big dance numbers onstage, had asked Lew Kesler to rehearse it with the two women upstairs in the theater, and together they had all worked out some hilarious pieces of business that never failed to land with the audience. The invention didn't stop once the show had opened. Ethel accidentally dropped a moccasin onstage one night, and the audience roared; soon Laurence was picking up the moccasin bit and using it to milk applause. Another night Ethel got a huge laugh by swinging her braids back and forth; soon Laurence was copying her.

It was upstaging, pure and simple, and Ethel would have none of it. Tensions built, and Ethel complained to the stage manager, Sammy Lambert, on more than one occasion. "Paula didn't stop doing it," said Lou Wills Jr., "so she was fired. Everybody was talking about it." Laurence, for her part, steadfastly maintained that she was never fired but that she gave her notice on May 31, 1943. She went on to appear in Kurt Weill's *One Touch of Venus* that fall, and she appeared in many other productions over her long career. But true stardom was elusive, and in theater circles she remained perhaps best known as the woman who crossed Ethel Merman. "It was very traumatic for Paula," recalled Betty Garrett. "But it was very foolish of her to do that." At Ethel's insistence, Betty Bruce was promoted to be Laurence's replacement.

Something for the Boys continued to play to sold-out houses, and columnists constantly cited it as a perfect example of wartime entertainment. The run of the show was a happy period for Ethel. She loved being a mother, and although like most stars she employed a nurse to look after Little Bit, she wound up supervising nearly every move the woman made and spent a good deal of time with her baby daughter. Late afternoons in particular were sacrosanct: that was when Little Bit rose from her nap and had a solid hour of playtime with Ethel before Ethel had to leave for the theater. Although it was Bob who read all the books on child rearing, Ethel took raising her daughter as seriously as she did preparing for a new show. Eventually Bob would feel that she didn't make any great distinction between the two things; she approached them both with equal diligence.

It had now been five years since Ethel had set foot in Hollywood. Perhaps she had not expected the interval between films to last this long, especially as she racked up one Broadway success after another and was now viewed as the undisputed queen of musical comedy. But the movie studios could not have been less interested in acquiring her services, even when the films they made of her stage hits with other actresses in her roles didn't pan out particularly well. In October 1942, MGM released its version of *Panama Hattie,* starring Ann Sothern, who was at least an acceptable replacement for Ethel. The *New York World-Telegram* didn't agree, calling Sothern "a little china doll making an amusing attempt to be as tough as Ethel Merman was in the stage version," while the *New York Herald Tribune* called the film "a sorry job of switching a show from the stage to the screen. . . . There is only one Ethel Merman." These comments were echoed ten months later when MGM brought out the movie of *Du Barry Was a Lady.* This time Lucille Ball, with her newly dyed "strawberry pink" hair in glaring Technicolor, took Ethel's role. While many reviewers hardly bothered to comment on Ball's presence, the *New York Telegraph* took a tougher stand: "One sure does miss Ethel Merman in a show like this. There ought to be a law or something." Outwardly Ethel paid little attention to Hollywood's repeated snubs, claiming that she had never liked working there and was perfectly happy playing to enthusiastic audiences on Broadway. Then, in 1943, she did get paged for a movie, and she didn't have to leave New York for it: it was *Stage Door Canteen,* an all-star extravaganza in which she sang one song, "Marching Through Berlin."

When *Something for the Boys* closed, on January 8, 1944, Ethel decided to do something she'd done only once before: go on tour with it. As it turned out, her time away from New York was short: she played Philadelphia only, where the show was a big hit, grossing an astonishing $35,000 in its second week. She had declined to continue for a good reason: she was pregnant. It was a cause for rejoicing, but she lost the baby in April. Joan Blondell—the future Mrs. Mike Todd—took over the part of Blossom in Chicago and played the rest of the tour.

While Ethel always looked back on her experience in the show with great fondness, *Something for the Boys* does seem in retrospect a kind of swan song. Only two months after the show reached Broadway, *Oklahoma!* opened at the St. James Theatre. The "integrated" musical, a concept that had fleetingly appeared over the years, was now pronounced the path of the future. Musical numbers, it was thought, had to flow organically out of the plot and action, rather than being stuck in as all-purpose tunes. That this turn of events was inevitable seems clear if one looks closely at the reviews for *Something for the Boys*. The *New York Herald Tribune* thought the show was "bright, but it shares the structural weakness of many large-scale musicals in that its dance numbers are not convincingly integrated in [*sic*] the plot."

Something for the Boys was to be Ethel's final collaboration with Cole Porter. Perhaps the changing atmosphere in the theater threw the composer slightly off his game; certainly, his next several shows were not up to the quality of the ones he had written for Ethel. He wouldn't return to form until *Kiss Me, Kate* in 1948, when he surpassed himself, brilliantly.

Nineteen fifty brought Porter's *Out of This World*, starring Charlotte Greenwood as the goddess Juno, a role that sounds as if it might have been composed with Ethel in mind. But for the next several years, the girls, comics, and topical gags of the Porter-Merman shows would begin to seem increasingly quaint. It had been a great and glorious era, and Ethel would remain forever nostalgic for it. But she could not afford to ignore the advances that the American musical was making as it prepared to enter a new kind of golden age. And she could have no way of knowing that her greatest professional triumphs were still to come.

The January closing of *Something for the Boys* wasn't especially well timed, as it left Ethel to spend much of the year at home, with not much to do except look after Little Bit and meet friends for lunch. For many women it would have seemed an enviable existence, but Ethel tended to grow irritable if too long a period elapsed between projects. By now Bob had been promoted to the rank of major, and his officer's duty occupied an increasing amount of his time. Following the miscarriage she suffered in April, Ethel grew more and more anxious. It represented a failure to her—a thought that she found difficult to bear in any dimension of her life. Although by no means a hypochondriac, Ethel could be somewhat nervous about her state of health, and she began to worry that she might not be able to have another child.

It has often been said of women in show business that they are far too self-absorbed and career-obsessed to make good mothers. But in the 1940s that criticism did nothing to stifle their desire to have children. No matter what the level of their professional accomplishments, most women were socialized to think of themselves as incomplete without a husband and children. Ethel was no exception. She believed that having children would help complete the picture of a solid, well-ordered life that she wanted to present to the rest of the world. Most of all, she wanted to give her own children the same experience that she had had growing up with Mom and Pop: that of feeling completely loved and supported. She reasoned that to achieve it would require hard work—the same kind of hard work that she put into her performing career—and with her customary all-or-nothing determination, she set out to become the best wife and mother she knew how to be. But the subtleties and intricacies of the role escaped her. Onstage, she could give precisely the same performance night after night, but at home, she had to be sensitive to the changes that came, unpredictably, minute by minute. Often she didn't succeed, and when she didn't, she searched for somewhere to place the blame. More and more, Bob became the object of her wrath, as she fumed that he didn't take his family duties as seriously as she took hers.

Perhaps Ethel felt that Bob's military duties occupied him too much and made him insufficiently supportive when she needed him most. Whatever the case, the tensions between them escalated, and by June of 1944 they had embarked on a trial separation. It was of short duration: within a month they were back together, and Ethel let it be known that she was ready to do another show in the fall.

On September 18 she began rehearsals for *Sadie Thompson,* a musical version of the Somerset Maugham short story "Rain." It had already enjoyed one highly successful Broadway adaptation, a drama by John Colton and Clemence Randolph that opened in 1922 and ran for 648 performances, providing Jeanne Eagels with her greatest triumph. Set in a hotel in Pago Pago during the rainy season, it told of the conflict between Sadie Thompson, an American hooker on the lam, and the puritanical but hypocritical Reverend Davidson, who sets out to save her soul at any cost. It seemed to producer A. P. Waxman a terrific basis for a musical, and he hired Vernon Duke, who had written standards such as "April in Paris" and "I Can't Get Started," plus the groundbreaking black musical drama *Cabin in the Sky,* to write the score. For the lyrics Waxman chose Howard Dietz, an old theater hand who had provided the words for the great songs from *The Band Wagon* (1931), including "Dancing in the Dark" and "I Love Louisa." A few months earlier, Duke and Dietz had collaborated on a flop show for Vinton Freedley called *Jackpot,* but under the direction of Rouben Mamoulian, who had helmed the brilliantly successful *Oklahoma!* the year before, *Sadie Thompson* seemed to be an all-but-guaranteed hit.

And then rehearsals began. The role of the blowsy Sadie, who thumbed her nose at conventional morality, seemed a natural for Ethel, but this was unlike any musical she had attempted before. It wasn't a girls-and-gags show; the second act featured a big montage sequence involving young Sadie and a chorus of inner voices, and there was a ballet called "The Mountains of Nebraska." To Ethel it all seemed a little high-toned. And there was another major problem. She found she couldn't retain the lyrics; to her, they just didn't scan. Since she had throughout her career been letter-perfect in rehearsal, she was sure it was all Dietz's fault.

Ethel took the lyrics home. Having great respect for Bob's literary efforts—he had written her reams of poetry during their courtship—she asked him to give them a once-over. He did, and Ethel gleefully showed up for rehearsals with his "improvements" in hand and pronounced that *these* were the lyrics she would be singing. Dietz objected strenuously, but Ethel wouldn't budge. One lyric in particular had vexed her by making mention of something called "Malmaison."

"What the fuck is Malmaison?" Ethel demanded, not about to sing something she didn't understand. When Dietz assured her it was a kind of lipstick popular in Paris, Ethel went out and randomly questioned over twenty women, none of whom had heard of Malmaison. She continued singing Bob's lyrics in rehearsal, until Dietz told her that if she couldn't sing the songs as written, she'd have to go. She resigned on September 30, to be replaced by the rising actress June Havoc. *Sadie Thompson* opened on November 16, 1944, and quickly closed. In his memoirs Dietz did express some regret: "The show would have been a perfect vehicle for Merman and there is little doubt that had she played Sadie it would have been a hit, but my pride which went before the fall couldn't take it."

Walking out on *Sadie Thompson* was not something Ethel did lightly, and it appears that her decision caused her some anxiety. After all, she was thirty-six and had been a star for fourteen years, a long reign by Broadway standards. She was fully aware of the impact of musicals such as *Pal Joey,* *Lady in the Dark,* and *Oklahoma!,* shows that explored more serious themes. Then there was *On the Town,* which opened in December 1944. With music by Leonard Bernstein and book and lyrics by Betty Comden and Adolph Green, *On the Town* presented the freshest view of New York life since the Gershwins had burst onto the scene. Everything about it seemed to point in a blazing new direction for the musical, especially the dances, which were choreographed by Jerome Robbins, who had been in the chorus of *Stars in Your Eyes.* Privately Ethel may have worried that her kind of show, with its basic plot, raucous comedy, and splashy, belt-'em-out numbers, was in danger of going out of style.

Although Ethel may have professed otherwise, Hollywood's continued lack of interest in her was a sore subject. Adding to her frustration was the fact that so many supporting players in her shows had gone out west with great success. Mary Wickes, from *Stars in Your Eyes,* was a popular character actress in films such as *The Man Who Came to Dinner* and *Now, Voyager.* Lucille Bremer and June Allyson, from the chorus of *Panama Hattie,* were playing leads in big-budget MGM musicals. Betty Hutton was now one of Paramount's biggest attractions in pictures such as *And the Angels Sing* and *The Miracle of Morgan's Creek.* And Betty Grable was the queen of the 20th Century Fox musical and Hollywood's number-one female box-office draw.

After Ethel pulled out of *Sadie Thompson,* no other show of quality was offered. In early 1945 she discovered that she was pregnant again. After her miscarriage a year before, she didn't want to take any chances and forced herself to lead as quiet a life as possible. Bob was delighted—at last she seemed able to settle into a comfortable domestic routine, and he enjoyed the many evenings they spent together, playing with Little Bit and having endless card games. Ethel's professional activity was confined to radio appearances and continuing to entertain the troops at Camp Shanks.

On August 11, 1945, Ethel and Bob's second child was born at Doctors Hospital. This time it was a boy, and they named him Robert Daniels Levitt Jr. That made a namesake for each of them. Since Bobby was a cesarean birth, as Little Bit had been, Ethel anticipated a lengthy, uninterrupted recovery period.

As it happened, though, she was being pestered to do a new show before she was even released from the hospital. In those long-gone days, ideas for shows often came from odd and quite unexpected places. A case in point: One evening Dorothy Fields and her husband were having dinner at '21.' Sitting next to Dorothy was a woman who worked at Pennsylvania Station's Traveler's Aid bureau. The woman was talking about the many soldiers who came through very late on their way back to the camp after a night on the town. In particular she was describing one young soldier who had come in recently, quite drunk after being out at Coney Island, where, at one of the arcades, he had won everything he could possibly win in the shooting galleries. As the women rattled on about the sharpshooter, something suddenly sprang into Dorothy's mind: Merman as Annie Oakley. A few days later, at a meeting with Richard Rodgers and Oscar Hammerstein, Dorothy asked them what they thought of the idea. They weren't interested in composing the show, but they agreed on the spot to produce it.

This presented Dorothy with a slight problem: she and Herbert had just done *Up in Central Park* for Mike Todd, and he had right of first refusal on their next project. They didn't need to worry; when they approached Todd with the idea, he dismissed it out of hand. Oddly, his main reason was that he thought Ethel was washed up, and he assured Dorothy that she would never do another show. Was his reaction the result of her motherhood or a response to the fact that she had quit *Sadie Thompson*? It seems a strange judgment, given that she had drawn very well for him in *Something for the Boys,* but it may have been an indication of how Broadway in general had come to view her in the post-*Oklahoma!* era.

With Mike Todd decisively out of the way, Rodgers and Hammerstein and the Fieldses began discussing composers. The logical choice for such an all-American subject as Annie Oakley seemed to be Jerome Kern, but he had been happily settled in Hollywood for years, performing the comparatively simple task of turning out movie scores for films such as *You Were Never Lovelier* (1942) and *Cover Girl* (1944). His last Broadway musical had been *Very Warm for May* in 1939, and despite the fact that it introduced "All the Things You Are," it had a disappointing run. Kern insisted that he had no desire to face Broadway again and that, in any case, at sixty he was too old to take on such a taxing project. But through an endless series of long-distance phone calls, Rodgers and Hammerstein prevailed, even offering to mount a revival of Kern's *Show Boat*, and soon the composer was on board.

The Fieldses had practically nothing on paper—just the opening, in which Annie Oakley makes her entrance by shooting the bird off a woman's hat, plus the finish of the first act. But Dorothy insisted that they waste no time in pitching the idea to Ethel and went to Doctors Hospital to visit her on what was only the second day of her recovery. Ethel was propped up in bed, green with nausea and plagued by gas pains. Amazed that Dorothy couldn't wait until she was at home to sell her on the idea, she weakly answered that it sounded all right to her. Her enthusiasm got a big boost weeks later when the terms of her salary were set: $4,500 a week, plus 10 percent of the gross.

Dorothy and Herbert set to work on the book and finished the first act by midautumn of 1945. Kern and his wife, Eva, had left California and journeyed east so he could work on the score. Then, on November 11, while walking down the street in New York, Kern suffered a cerebral hemorrhage, and died six days later. Saddened and shocked as they were by Kern's sudden death, none of the parties involved in creating the Annie Oakley musical wanted to see the project fade away. Over lunch at Louis XV on Forty-ninth Street, the Fieldses and Rodgers and Hammerstein hesitantly suggested that Irving Berlin come aboard—hesitantly because Berlin, whose last Broadway show had been *This Is the Army* in 1942, always wrote both music and lyrics, which obviously meant Dorothy would be out as lyricist. But Dorothy felt that Berlin was far and away the best man for the job and agreed to step aside as lyricist if Rodgers and Hammerstein could sign him. Berlin, who always exerted absolute authority over the projects with which he was involved, was chary about taking on a show that had originated with Dorothy and Herbert. After days of pondering, he said yes.

The Fieldses sped through the rest of the book at a quicksilver pace. For a title they switched *Jenny Get Your Gun*, the original title of *Something for the Boys*, to *Annie Get Your Gun*. From the beginning it was a hot project. Joshua Logan, eager to be reunited with Ethel after his admiration for her talent in *Stars in Your Eyes*, jumped at the chance to direct. The brilliant scenic designer Jo Mielziner, whose credits ranged from *Pal Joey* to *The Glass Menagerie,* also signed on, as did Lucinda Ballard, the inventive costumer of *I Remember Mama.* Helen Tamiris, who had earned glowing notices for her clever "Currier and Ives" ballet in *Up in Central Park,* was engaged as choreographer. She came up with a showstopping Native American dance for a song Berlin had written called "I'm an Indian Too," and her passion for modern dance was felt at various points in the show.

On April 19, 1945, Rodgers and Hammerstein's *Carousel* had opened on Broadway, and it quickly became another runaway success for the composing team. *Carousel* was adapted from an unusual source, Ferenc Molnár's *Liliom,* and its dark-hued story of death and redemption had distinctly operatic overtones. The main character, the hot-tempered, violent carousel barker Billy Bigelow (played by John Raitt), was the kind of antihero the musical stage had never seen before—not even in *Pal Joey.* Billy's "Soliloquy" near the end of the first act was essentially a dramatic scena. *Carousel* barreled through the door opened by *Oklahoma!,* and critics and other observers were abuzz about the possibilities presented by this new kind of musical drama and where it all might lead.

Not only was *Annie Get Your Gun* being created against a backdrop of tremendous change, but several of the show's principal talents were experiencing a kind of homecoming after a significant absence. Ethel was returning to the stage after having been away for nearly two and a half years, the longest hiatus she'd ever had on Broadway. *Annie* was Joshua Logan's first show after several years of army service. Irving Berlin, too, had been immersed in the service, producing his phenomenally successful revue *This Is the Army* and supervising productions of it all over the world. Because the bulk of his stage career had been spent working in the revue format, and because *Annie*'s Wild West setting felt alien to him, Berlin was not entirely sure he was the right man for the job. His last Broadway book show had been *Louisiana Purchase,* but Rodgers and Hammerstein had subsequently proven themselves unmatched masters of that form. Berlin was, even in the best of times, nervous and fussy about his songs, constantly worrying whether they were of good enough quality, and *Annie Get Your Gun* found him at his most self-critical.

It was clear to Rodgers and Hammerstein and to Logan that Berlin was turning out a superb score at record speed, but the composer needed constant reassurance. He had written one number, a show-business anthem called "There's No Business Like Show Business," that was a simple tune—so simple that his secretary turned up her nose at it—but when coupled with his bouncy, jubilant lyrics, it sounded like an instant classic. The first time

Berlin played it for Rodgers and Hammerstein and Logan, they were all (they thought) properly enthusiastic. Later, when he played an extra verse he'd written, he felt that their response was cool, and he promptly went home and tossed the song aside. When Logan and the producers found out what he'd done and protested, the music was recovered only with some difficulty by Berlin's judgmental secretary.

As they constructed the book, Dorothy and Herbert followed the life of the historical Annie Oakley only in the loosest sense. Born in Darke County, Ohio, in 1866, Annie had been fascinated by guns from an early age. As a child she had picked up a forty-inch cap-and-ball rifle and fired it; the kick was so great that the butt of the gun broke her nose, but in the years that followed, she kept on shooting. At fifteen she met Frank Butler and squared off against him in a match that required them both to shoot live birds out of a trap. Annie won the hundred-dollar prize, and her fame quickly spread. She had remarkable skill: she could hit two-inch flying balls over her shoulder by sighting them in the gleaming surface of a bowie blade. Annie became a star whose celebrity spanned the nineteenth and twentieth centuries; she even gave two private performances for Queen Victoria. In 1901 Annie was seriously injured in a horrible train wreck and underwent a series of operations, but she continued to shoot well, living until 1926.

The Fieldses' book for *Annie Get Your Gun* was funny and tart but strictly conventional: its Annie Oakley is a rough and rowdy, fun-loving country girl who gets a job performing stunts in Buffalo Bill's Wild West Show, where she falls in love with the show's star marksman, Frank Butler (the rich-voiced Ray Middleton). Frank's idea of a wife is someone soft and yielding (Berlin provided the lovely tune "The Girl That I Marry" to show the audience what Frank means), and the raucous Annie doesn't seem to qualify. But she becomes the show's star attraction and is soon being billed as "The Greatest Rifle Shot in the World." Business is so good that Buffalo Bill's company finally reclaims the ground it has lost to the rival show, run by Pawnee Bill. As Annie's fame grows, Frank, enraged to think that she has played him for a sucker, decamps to Pawnee Bill's company. The ending is anything but progressive: counseled by Chief Sitting Bull (Harry Bellaver), Annie purposely loses to Frank in a sharpshooting contest, thus ensuring that she will become his wife.

If the book wasn't exactly the last word in sophistication, it did the job and delivered the laughs, and any weakness it did have was lessened by Berlin's superb score. In addition to his rigorous artistic standards, Berlin set great store by a song's commercial success. As critic John Lahr has suggested, he may have observed how enthusiastically audiences had embraced folk musicals such as *Oklahoma!* and *Bloomer Girl,* but whatever the source of his inspiration, Berlin surpassed himself with the score for *Annie Get Your Gun.* He freely admitted that he hadn't a clue about how to compose backwoods music, and, to his credit, he didn't try, although "Doin' What Comes Naturally" and "You Can't Get a Man with a Gun," both establishing songs for Annie, have a jaunty, country feel. Berlin had long been associated with songs that were sweetly sentimental ("Always"), patriotic ("God Bless America"), or jaunty ("Puttin' on the Ritz"), but never had he come up with anything so downright hilarious as "You Can't Get a Man with a Gun."

Berlin never lays Annie's backwoods manner on too thick: it's country filtered through a Broadway showstopper sensibility. In the marvelous "Moonshine Lullaby," sung by Annie to her little brothers and sisters on a train, she ends on a gentle, sweet note, then picks up her rifle and shoots out the overhead light.

There was something new for Ethel in this score, too: in addition to her usual uptempo numbers, Berlin decided to expand her range and gave her two stunning, wistful ballads, "They Say It's Wonderful" and "I Got Lost in His Arms." These weren't torch songs—Ethel had sung plenty of those in the thirties—but plaintive expressions of a yearning human heart, without a trace of Cole Porter's dry-eyed wit. Not that Ethel sang them in a plaintive way, exactly. For the most part, she would not return to the sweeter style, with its occasional dip into soprano mix, that she had used in numbers such as "Make It Another Old-Fashioned, Please" and "I'll Pay the Check." From this point on, no matter what the emotional temperature of the songs, she generally sang one way: the big, stentorian Merman way, if with great precision and depth of feeling. As she aged, it seemed to be what nature dictated. It felt comfortable, and audiences were thrilled by it. Her brassy delivery led critics and fans alike to describe her as Broadway's biggest belter, but "belting" isn't really an accurate description of her style. True belting takes many forms. At one time it was most commonly a pushing up of the chest voice to the highest part of the range; most often it is simply an aggressively forward, speech-based singing in which the breath isn't so much lofted as it is hurled forth. Ethel's vocal production was so even throughout her range that she didn't need to resort to any technical trick. Her naturally forward placement, strong resonators, superb command of breath support, and solid physique helped her to sing like an operatic tenor: the sound moved up through her chest and resonated in her head, with true tenorlike ping on the high notes. As Karen Morrow, the big-voiced Broadway singer of the 1960s, observed,

"Ethel's sound was hers. I don't think she ever strove to achieve it. She never made any adjustments—she just never got in the way of it."

Rehearsals for *Annie Get Your Gun* started on February 25, 1946. On the first day, Joshua Logan came up with a wonderful piece of business for Ethel that would provide her with one of the indelible moments of her career. They were rehearsing the scene in which Annie lays eyes on Frank Butler for the first time. The Fieldses' script indicated, "She looks at him and in a second falls in love with him forever." This was tricky, and not much help, as stage directions go. Logan solved the problem brilliantly: he thought Ethel should let her entire body deflate, like a puppet whose strings have been snipped, while keeping her eyes fixed on Ray Middleton. "Her mouth dropped open, her shoulders sank, her legs opened wide at the knees, her diaphragm caved in," wrote Logan. Miraculously, Ethel captured exactly what he wanted on her very first try. "Later," said Logan, "we dubbed it 'the goon look,' and it won for me the eternal devotion of everyone, including myself. It seemed to be the catalytic moment—the moment at which the play became a hit."

On April 2, *Annie Get Your Gun* began a three-week engagement at the Shubert in Boston. The show was in remarkable shape early on, and the critics found little to carp about, although the *Boston Globe* reviewer did point out that the second act could use a comedy number to balance the preponderance of love songs. At the first seven performances in Boston, the box office took in $32,000, and the remainder of the run quickly sold out. Annie moved on to New Haven's Shubert, where the response was equally ecstatic. Everyone was certain that they had a hit on their hands as they prepared for the New York opening at the Imperial Theatre on April 25. But while the scenery was being hung, it proved too heavy for the Imperial's walls. A girder buckled, and the scenery had to be moved out while the walls were repaired and reinforced, which meant a lag of two weeks—a potentially devastating amount of time, financially, for the producers. Management scrambled to find an available theater out of town and quickly came up with the Philadelphia Shubert, where *Annie* played during the interim—again to wild audience response and great notices.

Finally, on May 16, the show opened in New York. Rodgers and Hammerstein, Logan, and Berlin were all nearly giddy with excitement; the only one remaining cool and concentrated was Ethel. And then the unexpected happened. From the time the curtain rose, the opening-night audience seemed frozen. Nothing—not the hilarious "You Can't Get a Man with a Gun," not the ravishing "They Say It's Wonderful," not the surefire "goon look"—registered.

Laughs were stifled and applause polite. Logan was in a panic. Backstage at intermission he ran up to Ethel wringing his hands and demanded to know how she'd been able to get through a near-hostile first-act audience.

"Easy," she snapped, echoing almost exactly the advice she'd given Betty Garrett in *Something for the Boys.* "You may think I'm playing the part, but inside I'm saying, 'Screw you! You jerks! If you were as good as I am, you'd be up here!' "

Ethel's no-fuss attitude was apparently the right one to have. As Logan remembered, "The second act went roaringly." Oddly, the reviews the next morning seemed to reflect the cautiousness on the audience's part. While Ethel's personal notices could not have been improved upon, many reviewers were curiously ambivalent about the show. The *New Yorker* carped that *Annie* was "burdened with a book that makes it appear, contrary to legend, that the celebrated Miss Oakley led a rather monotonous life—just love, love, love, diluted now and then with a little rifle practice." *Time* dismissed it as "a great big, follow-the-formula, fetch-the-crowd musical. It bothers with nothing artistic or bizarre. . . . Irving Berlin has written more tuneful music in his time; the dances are lively but not spectacular; the book is much like April weather." Brooks Atkinson, in the *New York Times,* called Berlin's score "routine" and "undistinguished," noting that "I Got the Sun in the Morning" was "as close as he comes to imaginative music writing."

It seems inconceivable today that Berlin's magnificent score should have elicited such a tepid response. In fact, he was being judged not on the quality of his songs, which was stunningly high, but on his participation in a show that looked backward, not ahead. He had hefty consolation, however, in the fact that every single one of Ethel's songs became a hit—a much higher than average yield for a Broadway show; *Annie* added overwhelmingly to Berlin's personal wealth.

Meanwhile the notices for Ethel were up to her usual standard. "By the time she is finished with either a song or a part she possesses it completely," wrote Atkinson, "and very nearly possesses all the other performers and has, at least, a lien on the scenery." The *New Yorker*'s critic admitted that Ethel could make him laugh "just by coming out on the stage." And the *Saturday Review* offered perhaps the warmest words of all: "Miss Merman *is* Broadway. She is Broadway with its flash in the flesh; Broadway making noon of darkness and ready to turn each night into New Year's Eve."

The morning after *Annie* opened, Bob Levitt was lounging in the apartment at the Century with all the reviews spread out in front of him. It seemed to him that he'd never read such ecstatic praise for any Broadway star. But

Ethel didn't have time to look over the notices carefully, for she was on the telephone with the manager of their local grocery store, demanding to know why she'd been charged for a can of peaches that hadn't been delivered the day before. As much as Bob tried to distract her with the reviews, she wouldn't be put off her mission, and she spent some time haggling until the manager finally relented and agreed to send over an extra can of peaches.

"If anybody," Bob complained, "asked you how you spent the morning after this great triumph, they just wouldn't believe it."

"Well," said Ethel, "I guess that's right. But that goddamned guy isn't going to cheat me out of those goddamned peaches."

With *Annie Get Your Gun* having generated a huge advance sale, Ethel knew she was going to be committed to the show for many months—just how many, she could never hope to guess. She settled into her familiar routine of waking up late and answering mail and returning telephone calls with the efficiency of the Wall Street secretary she easily might have become. She oversaw the household (which sometimes involved getting down on her hands and knees and scrubbing the kitchen and bathroom floors herself, since she never hung on to a housekeeping staff for long). Much of her clothes shopping she did at Wilma's, on Fifty-seventh Street. It was a place known for somewhat flashy fashions and had a reputation for catering to the mistresses of wealthy men, but Ethel's own wardrobe was fairly conservative: blue and black dresses off the rack, or specially made evening gowns running as high as $500. She spent time with the children and had an early supper of lamb chops and green salad on a tray before leaving for the theater in the early-evening rush-hour traffic. She expended so much energy onstage every night that she saw no reason to take up any other form of rigorous exercise, although she was always fond of walking in the city and did a great deal of it. She smoked a moderate amount, tried never to drink except after a show and then often only after the Saturday-night performance, when she was known to toss down one glass of champagne on the rocks after another. She took great care to stay away from air conditioners, people with colds, and all other occupational hazards familiar to singers. Her health was excellent; she took such good care of herself that she seldom picked up a virus, and when she did, it was usually of the one-day, in-and-out variety.

Backstage she concentrated on her work, and although she was never hostile to her coworkers, she didn't mix with them much. "She did her job, she did it perfectly, and she expected the same of everyone else," remembered Helene Whitney, a chorus member in *Annie Get Your Gun*. To some actors in the supporting cast, Ethel appeared to have the cold-blooded, methodical detachment of a factory foreman, and she never grew so comfortable during the course of the run that she stopped policing company activity. Once, when featured player Danny Nagrin announced that he was going to march in the Communist Parade with his wife, choreographer Helen Tamiris, Ethel exploded:

"You march in that parade, and you'll never get a job anywhere else I work. I don't care what you do anywhere else. But not in my show. I'm an American citizen, and I'm proud of it. And if you don't like working here for a very good salary, Mr. Nagrin . . ."

Nagrin didn't march in the parade, and Ethel's strong feelings on the subject never changed. On April 29, 1950, she would serve as Queen of the Loyalty Day Parade down Fifth Avenue, which she did as a way of undermining the Communist Parade.

Ethel held everyone in the company to the same high standard, even the children. One of the juvenile actors in the show, Warren Berlinger, was already an autograph hound at the age of eight. With so many big-time stage and film stars coming to see the new hot-ticket Broadway musical, Warren's autograph book was getting filled up quickly. One night he spotted Walter Pidgeon, the suave leading man of *Mrs. Miniver* and *Madame Curie*, sitting up front and decided to sneak out through the stage door to get his autograph. Pidgeon obliged. Unfortunately for Warren, Ethel had seen him slip out into the audience. As the curtain was about to rise for the second act, Ethel beckoned to him to come over to her.

"We never, ever do that," she said firmly as Warren froze in abject terror.

"*We* never, ever do that," Ethel repeated.

"I'm sorry," stammered Warren.

"All right," said Ethel. "But *remember*." And she took her place for the second act.

At other times she moved even more swiftly. One night a chorus girl with the unlikely name of Truly Barbara turned to talk to one of the chorus boys while Ethel was in the middle of singing "I Got the Sun in the Morning." Nothing in the theater ever escaped Ethel's hawk-eyed attention: if a chorister's hem was half an inch too long, if a pink gel wasn't in place, if a clarinetist was playing flat, she would make note of it. That night, as Ethel came offstage, she cornered Charles Atkins, the stage manager, and said, "Get rid of her." That was the end of Truly Barbara. As Warren Berlinger recalled, "That story went right through the entire company. We all knew that when Miss Merman was onstage, you'd better focus or you were out of there."

In her autobiography Ethel praised her leading man, Ray Middleton, and said that she enjoyed working with him. He was a fine performer with a stunning voice, but others in the company remember a certain coolness between the two stars. "He was full of himself," said Berlinger. "Miss Merman and Ray Middleton had no camaraderie that I could notice. There was no 'You were wonderful, no, *you* were wonderful.' Nothing like that at all." Helene Whitney remembered that Ethel, old-fashioned as always, had taken great offense when Middleton struck up an affair with a chorus girl who was a romantic interest of Richard Rodgers's. "The scuttlebutt," said Whitney, "was that she eventually got him fired for that."

But Ethel could be kind and thoughtful, too. One night at an onstage party after a performance, someone asked if she would mind singing a few numbers from some of her other shows. Many stars are prickly about being asked to perform when they aren't being paid to do so, but Ethel seldom had such qualms. "This was after she'd had two shows," remembered Don Liberto, "and she said, 'Okay! LEW!'" Lew Kesler sat down at the piano, and Ethel proceeded to sing several of her hits, including "I Got Rhythm," with all the famous gestures. "The whole thing was for us," said Liberto. "I thought that was great of her."

Annie Get Your Gun was the kind of smash that the theater seldom saw. It was still a runaway hit in the summer of 1947, but by then its star was feeling less than her best. For some time she'd been suffering from hemorrhoids, and the pain and discomfort were increasing by the week. She wasn't missing any performances, but getting through the show each night was becoming more and more of a challenge. Finally, in September of that year, her condition worsened to the point that she had to drop out of the show. Her doctors told her that the problem was aggravated by her fondness for champagne and recommended immediate surgery. Ethel agreed, and her understudy, the talented Mary Jane Walsh, who had introduced "I Didn't Know What Time It Was" in Rodgers and Hart's *Too Many Girls*, took over as Annie. Although Walsh was getting $750 a week, a huge salary for an understudy, she wasn't a box-office name, and Rodgers and Hammerstein fretted while the show fell into a slump during Ethel's two-week absence. (A few weeks later, *Annie* went on a cross-country tour, starring Mary Martin, and cleaned up wherever it went.)

While Ethel was recuperating at Doctors Hospital, columnist Dorothy Kilgallen came to interview her for her radio program. William Weslow, a dancer from the *Annie* company, was visiting when Kilgallen turned up with a recording crew. "Dorothy said, 'What are you in here for?'" recalled Weslow. " 'I hear you're in here for appendicitis.' And Ethel said, 'No, you dumb ass! I'm in here for hemorrhoids!' That part of the tape didn't go out."

By the end of March 1948, Annie had grossed over $4.5 million, and ticket sales showed little sign of tapering off. Rodgers and Hammerstein pleaded with her to stay with the show for another season, but Ethel had no interest in doing so. It was the most physically demanding musical she had yet done, and she was feeling drained. But the producers were ruthless businessmen and kept hammering away at her, stressing how important a continued run was to the welfare of the company members. This touched Ethel's soft spot, and reluctantly she agreed to an added season, with the proviso that she be allowed a six-week vacation beginning July 5, 1948. It was only the second vacation she had taken, and Rodgers and Hammerstein balked a bit before finally giving in.

Mary Jane Walsh again took over, and this time receipts sank precipitously, from $36,000 a week to $22,000. During Ethel's six-week rest at the Colorado Hotel, a mountain resort in Glenwood Springs, Colorado, Rodgers and Hammerstein persuaded cast members to take a salary cut in order to compensate for the losses at the box office. When she came back in August, Ethel was furious about this turn of events and resented that the producers' penny-pinching ways had made her feel personally responsible for the sacrifices inflicted on the rest of the company. The upshot was that the cuts were instantly reversed, but she never forgot or forgave Rodgers and Hammerstein for their niggardly behavior. Like Berlin they were making a fortune—far more than she was—from a show that she was responsible for putting over to the public. In later years she had only to hear mention of their names to cut loose with a stream of profanity.

By Christmas of 1948, it was announced that *Annie Get Your Gun* would close, but an upsurge in the box office over the holidays kept the show hanging on for a few more weeks. The run finally ended on February 12, with a staggering total of 1,147 performances. "I felt as if I had been freed," Ethel later wrote. In terms of stamina alone, her record was impressive: for the entire run of nearly three years, she had taken only two vacations and missed two performances on account of illness.

Tired and feeling the need of a good long rest, she looked forward to spending some time with the children and with Bob. She told her new agent, Sonny Werblin, to cast around for something reasonably nontaxing. Werblin got her a guest spot on Milton Berle's hit variety television series, *Texaco Star Theater*. It had premiered on NBC in 1948 and had quickly become one of the top-rated programs in the industry. Ethel, looking smashing in a shoulder-length bob, sang terrific renditions of "I Got Rhythm" and "I Get a Kick Out of You." She joined Berle for "Friendship," from *Du Barry Was a Lady*, fluffing the lyrics when Berle purposely broke her up, and she also did a tribute to Tin Pan Alley, in which she appeared as a high-stepping flapper, complete with cloche, singing DeSylva, Brown, and Henderson's "Varsity Drag." Also for NBC she did a half-hour radio series, *The Ethel Merman Show*, a comedy, with songs dropped in around the weekly plot. It bowed on July 31, 1949, but received poor notices and limped along for only a few months before going off the air. Again Ethel seemed unable to conquer any entertainment field other than Broadway.

Ethel wasn't overly concerned about the failure of the radio project, but she was becoming extremely uneasy about her home life. Since *Annie Get Your Gun* had closed, she and Bob were having increasingly frequent arguments. Part of the trouble was that he was spending more evenings away from home. He had always been able to put away a good share of alcohol, but his drinking had recently grown out of control.

Alcoholics do not become alcoholics overnight. It is a disease of encroachment: a once-a-month night out can turn into a twice-a-month, then once-a-week, bender. All too soon liquor can dominate nearly every night of the week. Such was the case with Bob. By now he was working for the *American Weekly*, the *Journal-American*'s Sunday supplement, and socializing a great deal with his cronies, who included the hard-drinking restaurateur Toots Shor, William Hearst Jr., and Herb Mays, an executive at *Good Housekeeping*. The postwar era was all too conducive to late nights out. It was a time, according to David Brown, "when many people were on the town because we were all cooped up during the war, and the town was alive with, not the sound of music, but the sound of testosterone. Hearst was a crony kind of company in those days. Bob was a night person to some degree, and very funny. There was a bar across the street from the Hearst Building called the Parisienne, and everyone gathered there, and lots of booze was taken there by the Hearst employees."

With Bob out carousing, Ethel grew increasingly suspicious that he might be enjoying the company of other women. One night when she had an engagement of her own and knew that Bob would be out with newspaperman Jack O'Connell, she grumbled about it to David Brown, who assured her that O'Connell was a good friend and that she shouldn't worry—everything would be fine.

"Fine?" snapped Ethel. "Levitt would fuck a snake!"

Nanette Fabray had by this time moved into the Century, and she later recalled that in the summer of 1949 many people in the building were aware of the Levitts' marital spats. "Because there was no air-conditioning," recalled Fabray, "everyone's windows were open to the courtyard. We could hear them going at it for hours. Finally people would scream, 'SHUT UP!' You could hear her in Long Beach. She never listened to what he had to say. He would come back with something that was a reasonable explanation or question of his own, and she absolutely wouldn't listen to him."

Perhaps Ethel was also disappointed in Bob professionally. His ambitions, part of the reason she had initially been attracted to him, seemed to have waned. "He never really amounted to a great deal," said David Brown. "Yes, he was at Hearst as a marketing guy, but he wasn't a star in the publishing business. He wasn't a big shot, although he could trade on the name of Hearst, and did. And Ethel was the star of stars."

Bob and Ethel's marriage had probably been destined to fail, for the simple fact of the great intellectual gulf that existed between them. Although Ethel was now keeping up with current events, she paid closer attention to the gossip columns and industry news than she did to the world of international politics. Her favorite topics were show business and her husband and children. Many of her close friends, Dorothy Fields among them, believed that these shortcomings became tiresome and all too predictable for Bob and that, in turn, Bob's keen intellect and wit became an irritant to Ethel.

It was true: Bob was getting fed up with Ethel's blunt, uniform approach to handling all her problems. He felt oppressed by the strictness with which his wife managed her life and hemmed in by her inability to change her opinion of anything or anyone. Although she wanted to present the image of a successful, happy woman to the rest of the world, she failed to make much distinction among the components of a successful woman's life: a responsible and attractive husband, well-behaved children, a nice home and wardrobe, a thriving career—all were pursued with the same dogged determination. She loved Bob and the children deeply, and if one of them got sick, no more attentive wife or mother could be found. While she was anything but cold or selfish, she had little talent for genuine empathy. It was very difficult for her to get inside the minds and hearts of her family and intuit what they might be thinking or feeling. Ethel lived her life moment to moment; she had never taken much in the way of a broader view. She was, in many respects, the embodiment of the Greatest Generation—all common sense and work ethic and full speed ahead, never looking to the side.

Being between jobs on Broadway only amplified these tendencies, and with the situation at home rapidly deteriorating, Ethel began to look forward to the day when she could go back to work.

B y the time her next show, *Call Me Madam,* opened, Ethel had made one of the most important transitions of her working life. A superficial look at her career might lead to the conclusion that she had started at the top and stayed there. This was true in a sense, when her swift rise is compared with the decades-long struggle that most performers endure. But Ethel's life on Broadway had actually been a series of segues, most of them too subtle for the general public to notice.

In *Girl Crazy* she had gone from unknown to sensational young discovery; in *Anything Goes* from revue artist to crack singing comedienne in a book show; in *Panama Hattie* from a star comic's leading lady to a star who carried the show; in *Annie Get Your Gun* to a character star capable of greater dramatic dimension. Now, with *Call Me Madam,* she would cross over from Broadway star to Broadway institution—from Ethel Merman to "The Merm." Her nearly three-year run in *Annie Get Your Gun* had clinched her status as one of Broadway's legends. From this point on, as far as Broadway was concerned, she was nothing less than a national treasure.

Not that everyone in America got Ethel's message. Many in the West, the Midwest, and the South—people who had never experienced her live, thanks to her dislike of touring—regarded her from her records and TV appearances as crass, vulgar, and loud—the vocal equivalent of a rusty saw. Those who had not seen her perform onstage were, of course, less likely to accept her as a recording artist. In the words of cabaret entertainer Klea Blackhurst, her singing was anything but "make-out music." Ethel had made a few recordings that had done well, namely her 1940 Decca disc of selected songs from *Panama Hattie* and the original cast album of *Annie Get Your Gun.* In 1950 she was put under exclusive contract to Decca, where over the next few years she cut a number of singles, mostly novelty numbers and knockoffs of other people's Broadway hits, such as "Diamonds Are a Girl's Best Friend," from *Gentlemen Prefer Blondes,* and "Love Is the Reason," from *A Tree Grows in Brooklyn,* with lyrics by her pal Dorothy Fields.

But she and Ray Bolger had a hit with Bob Hilliard and Dave Martin's nostalgic comic ditty "Dearie," paired with another novelty tune by George Wyle and Eddie Pola called "I Said My Pajamas (and Put On My Prayers)." This single, recorded on January 4, 1950, and released one month later, sold two hundred thousand copies in its opening weeks. Later singles, with Bolger and on her own, were disappointments. At a time when the recording industry was dominated by smooth-voiced female vocalists such as Jo Stafford, Dinah Shore, Helen O'Connell, and Margaret Whiting, Ethel seemed destined to remain an acquired taste to the record-buying public.

Nor did Hollywood regard her as anything but unmarketable, the latest evidence being MGM's screen version of *Annie Get Your Gun,* which was released in May 1950 and became one of the studio's biggest successes, grossing over $8 million. The film had a strife-ridden production: Judy Garland had been assigned the part of Annie, but her personal difficulties had built to a peak during filming. When the project fell seriously behind schedule, in no small part due to Garland's inability to function properly on the set, MGM fired her and replaced her with a supporting player from the Broadway production of *Panama Hattie*—none other than Betty Hutton. At no point does anyone at the studio appear to have considered asking Ethel to repeat her stage triumph on film, and the picture's overwhelming success must have stung. To the press, however, she always denied that she cared about missing these Hollywood opportunities.

She remained a puzzlement even to some people in show business. Shortly after moving to New York from California in 1940, dancer Marge Champion saw Ethel for the first time, in *Panama Hattie.* "I didn't have a clue to what Ethel Merman really was," said Champion, "because I was not a New Yorker. I couldn't look through New York eyes. I didn't have a New York perspective until after I moved here, and then it took me a while. Even when I saw her in *Annie Get Your Gun,* and she leaned back and sang, 'I GOT LOST IN HIS AAAAAAAAAAAAAHMS!'—*lost in his arms?* I thought, 'Well, he wouldn't put his arms around that!' "

One factor that kept Ethel from being widely accepted outside of New York was the ongoing perception of many that she was Jewish. "She seemed like the darling of the Bronx, Brooklyn, whatever," Champion recalled. "And, for me, coming from another part of the country, that said 'Jewish.' That's wrong. It can be Irish, Italian, anything. And who cares what it is anyway?" But many people in rural areas and small cities perceived Ethel to be the essence of Jewish New York show business—and for them, unfortunately, that was a negative.

But if much of the rest of the country had reservations about Ethel, New York audiences loved her more than ever. And when it was announced that she and Irving Berlin would reteam for another Broadway show, the excitement around town was palpable.

The genesis of *Call Me Madam* came in the summer of 1949, when Ethel, Bob, and the children were once again vacationing at the Colorado Hotel. Also staying there were Howard Lindsay and Dorothy Stickney—Ethel had recommended the hotel to them as an ideal quiet getaway. One day, while looking out the window of his room, Lindsay spotted Ethel poolside. He watched the way she walked, the way she plopped herself down in a deck chair, and found himself thinking that this had to be the most American American woman he'd ever seen. He happened to have been reading a magazine article about Perle Mesta, the freewheeling society hostess whose down-to-earth charm and bottomless reserves of cash had been of enormous aid to the Washington political scene.

Lindsay called down to Ethel that he'd just had an idea for her next show: it would be about Perle Mesta.

Ethel, who was never much interested in following society news, and certainly not society news from Washington, shot back, "Who's Perle Mesta?"

Quickly the writers gave Ethel some of the background for what would become her next role. Mesta started life as the daughter of a rich Oklahoma oilman. She married well, to Pittsburgh manufacturer George Mesta, who left her a widow at age thirty-six. She moved to Newport, Rhode Island, where she became actively involved in women's rights and was an early champion of the Equal Rights Amendment. Her loyalty at this time was strictly to the Republican Party, but after moving to Washington, D.C., in 1940, she allied herself with the Democrats. Mesta became one of the capital's most enchanting hostesses, in part because of the unpretentious spirit of the parties she gave. She could make even the stuffiest, most reticent politicians and diplomats feel instantly comfortable. One of her favorite figures was the equally no-nonsense Harry S. Truman, and she threw her support behind him wholeheartedly. In 1949 he rewarded her with an appointment as the first-ever U.S. ambassador to Luxembourg, a distinction that landed her on the cover of *Time* magazine.

Fourteen years had passed since Ethel had last worked with Lindsay and Russel Crouse in *Red, Hot and Blue!*, and in that time they had achieved undreamed-of success: their *Life with Father* opened in 1939 and ran for 3,224 performances, becoming the longest-running dramatic play in the history of the American stage. In 1941 they had switched to producing and scored another massive hit with *Arsenic and Old Lace*. Returning to play-writing, they came up with *State of the Union*, a biting comedy-drama about political infighting and corruption that earned them the 1945 Pulitzer Prize for drama. But their 1948 sequel to *Life with Father*, naturally enough called *Life with Mother*, had failed, and they were looking for another hit. A vehicle for Ethel seemed a sure bet.

In the years that followed the chaotic creation of *Anything Goes* and *Red, Hot and Blue!*, Lindsay and Crouse had developed a highly methodical way of working. In the case of *Life with Father*, they spent two years discuss-ing and planning the play's architecture before they committed one word to paper. Once they sat down to write, they finished the dialogue in only seventeen days. For the script of *Call Me Madam*, they did not allow themselves such a generous amount of time. The two worked at fever pitch, Lindsay with his sure theatrical savvy and Crouse with his keen sense of comedy, but they found that the book was not easy to assemble. Early on, they had approached Irving Berlin, their first and only choice to write the songs, and as the project moved forward, all three creators expressed some concern that the plot be carefully handled, in case Perle Mesta should take offense and pursue legal action. Then there was Ethel, who threw them a curveball by announcing that she wasn't looking for another musi-cal but a meaty dramatic role. As work on the book progressed, Ethel conceded that she would sing a little—maybe two or three songs. Eventu-ally she came around to accepting the idea of *Call Me Madam* as a full-scale musical comedy, but her resistance didn't make the playwrights' work any easier.

Berlin, ever anxious where his own work was concerned, was particu-larly fretful about the general climate on Broadway. The musical theater showed no sign of slowing its journey into seriousness: witness the 1949 premiere of Rodgers and Hammerstein's *South Pacific*, a tale of racism and interracial love that earned the Pulitzer Prize for drama, the first musical to be so honored since *Of Thee I Sing* in 1931. As a nod to Broadway's prevail-ing mood, Berlin had followed up his "old-fashioned smash" *Annie Get Your Gun* with *Miss Liberty*. Weighed down by a shapeless, spiritless book by Robert Sherwood, it closed without recouping its investment. Now Berlin was frantic to return to what he knew best, the old-fashioned musical com-edy, but equally unsure that audiences would accept it.

By May 1950, Lindsay and Crouse were still trying to iron out a few of the book's problem patches. While they were in the home stretch, Ethel and

Bob took the children back to Colorado for a six-week rest before rehearsals began on August 14.

The cost of producing a show had escalated since the war years, and *Call Me Madam* was budgeted at a hefty $250,000. The producer was Leland Hayward, the former agent who in the preceding few years had emerged as one of the most successful producers on Broadway, with hits such as *State of the Union, Mister Roberts,* and *South Pacific.* Slightly high-strung, with a neatly trimmed crew cut and crevasselike lines in his face, Hayward was something of an enigma: he was the definition of the peripatetic producer and could carry on as many as six telephone conversations at once. He eagerly signed up clients about whom he knew little, but the passing of time didn't necessarily mean that he got to know them better. Lindsay and Crouse, who referred to themselves as Hayward's "common-law clients" because they had always declined to sign a contract with him, once threw a party for Hayward, inviting many of the illustrious writers and stars in his stable. When Hayward got to the party, he asked Lindsay and Crouse, in all sincerity, who these people were.

Hayward possessed a nose for what would make a good show: he had purchased James Michener's collection of stories, *Tales of the South Pacific,* only a few days before it won the Pulitzer Prize for fiction, and persuaded Rodgers and Hammerstein to set it to music. He had come across a series of sketches about World War II naval life in the *Atlantic Monthly*; it eventually became the long-running *Mister Roberts.* A producer, Hayward believed, could easily run aground if he sought only commercial success. "You have to stage it with love," he once said. "Then, you have to get the best people you can. I'm considered an extravagant producer. There's no such thing as economy in the theater. Only quality counts."

Unlike Vinton Freedley and other producers of an earlier era, Hayward didn't necessarily put his own money into his shows. For *Call Me Madam,* he arranged to get 100 percent of the financing from RCA and NBC, with the idea that the former would record the original cast album and the latter would have the television rights if *Call Me Madam* should be transferred to the small screen. It was customary for a show's management to split profits fifty-fifty with the backers, but in the case of *Call Me Madam,* RCA/NBC would receive only 35 percent of the net earnings, as Hayward had assured them that the difference of 15 percent would be made up by an increase in operating profits: orchestra seats were to be set at an all-time high of $7.20.

If Hayward was a force to be reckoned with, so was *Call Me Madam*'s director, George Abbott, who was working with Ethel for the first time. A former actor, Abbott had switched to writing and directing in the 1920s and had made a name for himself as the expert director of both melodrama (*Broadway, Chicago*) and farce (*Twentieth Century, Three Men on a Horse, Room Service*) before moving into musicals. He had directed many of the great Rodgers and Hart successes, including the groundbreaking *Pal Joey.* Abbott was something of a pragmatist in his approach to the theater, which he regarded as more a craft than an art. He was extremely shrewd at assessing what would make a show a hit, and even after the rise of Method acting, with its emphasis on sense memory as a means of communicating emotion, he was not afraid to hand actors their line readings. He believed in economy onstage and worked very hard to make his productions as simple and pared down as possible. He could be dictatorial in rehearsal: everyone referred to him as "Mr. Abbott," as nothing else was acceptable. He loved women and liked to be around the beautiful girls in his shows when he wasn't working; frequently he gave big Sunday parties to which all the showgirls were invited. (He was much less comfortable around gay men, who normally were not invited to the Sunday get-togethers.) And he could be shockingly tight-fisted. Helene Whitney, who sang in the chorus of *Call Me Madam,* said, "He was the cheapest man this side of the Mississippi. I remember going out to a bagel place in Philadelphia, and he asked all the girls to go. We did, and we all had bagels, and he put down a dollar and said, 'Here's my share,' and got up and left."

Leland Hayward had gone all out for the *Call Me Madam* production. Thousands of actors were auditioned for the twenty speaking parts and the thirty-nine spots in the singing and dancing choruses. (Assisting in this task was Abbott's twenty-one-year-old casting director, Harold Prince.) Raoul Pène du Bois, who had not worked with Ethel since *Panama Hattie,* was engaged to design the sets and costumes. To create Ethel's costumes, Hayward pulled off a major coup when he signed up the famed clothing designer Mainbocher. Born in Chicago, Mainbocher was once described by teacher/director John Murray Anderson as resembling a "poor famished faun." He longed to become an opera singer and studied voice off and on with the famous Madame Schoen-Rene, teacher of Risë Stevens, among others. His art studies led him to open a salon on the avenue George V, one of Paris's great fashion centers. Having become the first American to break successfully into the world of French high fashion, he opened his own business in New York. His *maison de couture* occupied a three-story space on Fifty-seventh Street, just around the corner from Tiffany's. In the 1940s he began to branch out into the theater. Ruth Gordon, whose clothes he designed for her hit *Over Twenty-One,* claimed, "Next to Lee Shubert, Main's the most stage-struck man I've ever known." Having been credited with dreaming up the cocktail suit and the tailored evening coat, he brought his clean, sharp, simple lines to Broadway. In 1943's *One Touch of Venus,* Mary Martin created a sensation when she walked out onstage in Mainbocher's low-cut black satin gown. He always took care that his designs didn't fade into the background. "I believe in the exact opposite of realism on the stage," he once said. "The theater is bowed down by realism. The movies do realism so much better, and the theater should stand on its own legs. It should produce a sort of unreal brilliance."

Since Ethel was cast as social butterfly Perle Mesta, Mainbocher thought it only logical for her to be presented as a clotheshorse for the first time onstage, and he created a stunning array of costumes, including an elegant black-and-white suit, a chic black tulle dress with flame-red lace, and a point d'esprit negligee sparkling with gold. Ethel, whose diamond-in-the-rough roles had never really allowed for ultraglamorous presentation (with the exception of *Du Barry Was a Lady*), was delighted by the deluxe treatment Mainbocher gave her. A fast, inventive, and precise worker, Mainbocher earned her respect immediately.

When the script of *Call Me Madam* was finally finished everyone on the creative team recognized that it was in no way an outstanding book. As a musical that dealt with current events and current figures, it fell into the trap of many "topical" shows: it was a bit too self-consciously bright, ribbing the Truman administration and the postwar situation with hearty verve rather than satiric deftness. But as a vehicle for Ethel, it got the job done pleasantly and, for the most part, efficiently. It was a show that set out to have a good time, not to inspire. Lindsay and Crouse had painted a colorful central character for the Perle Mesta figure, a rich American hostess named Sally Adams, whom President Truman appoints as ambassador to the tiny duchy of Lichtenburg. Mrs. Adams reports for her new post with a canned speech she has learned by rote ("I am happy that my duties take me to a country it has long been my dream to know and love—the glorious grand duchy of Lichtenburg") but a complete ignorance of the specifics of the country. Her brash American manner immediately puts her in conflict with Pemberton Maxwell, the U.S. embassy's prissy chargé d'affaires. When Maxwell rebukes her for the lateness of her arrival in Lichtenburg, she unfolds a large map of Europe:

SALLY: This is supposed to be Rand McNally's latest map of Europe. Take a look at this. Now there's Lichtenburg. It's green, isn't it? And there's Italy. That's yellow. Well, let me tell you something Rand McNally doesn't seem to know. Italy isn't yellow. It's green.

Later on, as Sally insists on being addressed as "Madam," she tells Maxwell:

SALLY: Okay, now we understand each other. I'm the madam and you're just one of the girls.

Sally's unpretentious style succeeds in disarming most of the Old World Europeans who surround her. She kicks off her shoes, complaining, "My dogs hurt." She serves franks and baked beans at an embassy soiree. While curtsying before the grand duke and duchess, she loses her balance and falls on her behind. There were frequent references to President Truman's policies, and to his daughter Margaret's unsuccessful attempts to launch a singing career, and a plot thread about America's eagerness to lend huge sums to a struggling postwar Europe—all timely jokes that the audience was expected to get. Most of *Call Me Madam*'s book scenes failed to rise above the level of middling situation comedy, but luckily there was something else besides the endless culture-clash jokes. Lindsay and Crouse had provided two love stories, one between Sally and the suave Lichtenburg prime minister Cosmo Constantine (played by Academy Award–winning screen actor Paul Lukas, who had retreated to the stage after his Hollywood career had run out of steam), and another between Sally's likable press attaché Kenneth Gibson (rising young actor Russell Nype) and the Princess Maria (dancer Galina Talva).

And there were the songs. It would have been all but impossible for Berlin to surpass his stunning achievement with the score of *Annie Get Your Gun*, and in *Call Me Madam* he didn't come close. But he turned out a good score nonetheless, one that was merry and tuneful and instantly memorable. Among the high points were Sally's establishing number, "The Hostess with the Mostes' on the Ball," in which she lays out the qualities that have made her indispensable on the Washington scene. There was a charming trio of romantic numbers, "Marrying for Love," "It's a Lovely Day Today," and "The Best Thing for You," all showing Berlin in solid if not inspired form. There was "Lichtenburg," a wistful paean to the duchy's simple, old-fashioned qualities of life. And there were two comic songs: "Mr. Monotony," which Berlin strongly believed in despite (or because of) the fact that it had been dropped from both the Fred Astaire–Judy Garland film *Easter Parade* and his Broadway failure *Miss Liberty,* and "Can You Use Any Money Today?," which kidded America's generous lending policies.

And there was the song that, over time, would receive the most widespread play: "They Like Ike," a comic tune predicting that the popular war hero Dwight D. Eisenhower would run for the presidency in 1952. Although *Call Me Madam* had a Democratic spirit, with its constant references to Harry Truman, Berlin was a rock-ribbed Republican. "They Like Ike" gave him a chance to get his point of view across, and he was delighted with the success the number eventually achieved when it was used in Eisenhower's real-life presidential campaign. So was Ethel, whose politics had always leaned toward the conservative, although, like many actors, she declined to take extreme sides in public and once told the *New York Times,* "In politics, I'm noncommittal."

Rehearsals for *Call Me Madam* began on August 14 at the Golden Theatre. (It was scheduled to open at the Imperial, the same theater where *Annie Get Your Gun* had made history.) To choreograph the show, Hayward had signed Jerome Robbins, who had become one of Broadway's most sought-after talents following his creation of the dances for *On the Town* and *High Button Shoes.* There was no denying that Robbins had one of the keenest imaginations in the business. He also had one of its most blistering tempers. He could be unthinkably brutal to the dancers in the chorus if he found them at all lacking—as he often did. He would berate them in the most humiliating ways, railing at them for being stupid or fat, until they were reduced to tears; the sadist in him loved to single out one particular girl as his object of abuse. He might unleash his fury on anyone, including the producer or director, or on the star—unless the star happened to be Ethel. She had not worked with Robbins since he'd danced in the chorus of *Stars in Your Eyes,* and although she acknowledged his subsequent success in the business by her respectful treatment of him, there was an unspoken understanding that he wasn't to try any of his temperamental stunts with her.

Ethel had absolute approval of everything Robbins worked out for her, and when something wasn't to her liking, she was perfectly clear about it. Choreographer/dancer Donald Saddler observed rehearsals of Ethel's first number in the show, "The Hostess with the Mostes' on the Ball," and as he recalled, "Jerry said to me, 'This morning I have to stage this song for Ethel.'

And he was always in awe of her. I could tell he was apprehensive and nervous about it. He showed her something, and she tried to do it. And she said, 'Nope. Jer—what else have you got?' " Robbins did a slow burn but swallowed his anger and went off to work on a new bit of business. "When he gave her something she liked," said Saddler, "she took it and locked it in solid."

All of Ethel's shows over the past decade-plus, from *Du Barry Was a Lady* through *Annie Get Your Gun*, had been smoothly assembled; everyone connected with them felt from the outset that they were bound to be hits. So she was understandably troubled when rehearsals of *Call Me Madam* got off to a slow start. Berlin, in his series of neatly tailored suits with the jacket thrown over one arm, nervously paced back and forth as he watched what was happening on the stage of the Golden Theatre. Early on there was tension between Lindsay and Crouse and George Abbott, particularly after Lindsay complained that too many of their lines were being changed. Abbott called them aside and coolly informed them that a great many changes were necessary and that he would brook no interference. Paul Lukas was exceptionally nervous about singing Berlin's songs, and no amount of encouragement from Ethel would quell his fears. Like Bert Lahr, Lukas suffered from a kind of performer's paranoia, and Ethel grew irritated with it fairly quickly, going so far as to make fun of him behind his back for the benefit of the chorus girls.

Ethel had worked harmoniously with Berlin during *Annie Get Your Gun*'s development, but this time she was underwhelmed by parts of the score, in particular two numbers, the repeatedly orphaned "Mr. Monotony" and "Free," a heavy-handed windbag of a song, intended to shine a light on good old-fashioned American principles. Ethel knew a dog when she heard one, but out of respect for the composer she kept her head down and went to work, trying her best to make something powerful out of it.

At this point the performer who was shining brightest was Russell Nype. A native of Zion, Illinois, Nype had become a radio actor while still a teenager and the previous year had received some attention in the Broadway presentation of *Regina*, Marc Blitzstein's operatic adaptation of Lillian Hellman's *The Little Foxes*. There he had played Leo, the slimy nephew who commits theft to finance the family's shady business venture. Nype jumped at the part of Kenneth because it would prevent him from being typecast as a villain. When he auditioned, Harold Prince remembered thinking, "I hope this guy can sing and act, because he's the only actor in New York that looks like a Harvard graduate." Later on, *Mademoiselle* magazine would decree that he had "A.S. (Academic Sexiness)."

At some point the acutely nearsighted Nype was allowed to wear the horn-rimmed glasses he'd been trying to do without, and his mop of hair was trimmed to a crew cut, giving him an attractive/brainy look. Nype handled his big number, "It's a Lovely Day Today," so well that all concerned agreed his part should be built up. Ethel liked him as much as she loathed Galina Talva; she told the show's apprentice press agent, Bob Ullman, that Talva "always looked as if she sniffed bicycle seats."

As was now standard practice for a Merman show, *Call Me Madam* had its world premiere at the Shubert Theatre in New Haven, on September 11, 1950. Ethel must have had misgivings about the opening, since she went to a local Episcopal church to take communion beforehand. There were congratulatory telegrams from many of Ethel's show-business friends and colleagues—DEAR ETHEL: I KNOW YOU WILL BE BRILLIANT TONIGHT IN OTHER WORDS FOR MERMAN YOU'LL BE DOIN' WHAT COMES NATURALLY—LOVE JUDY GARLAND. And: THEY MAY CALL YOU MADAME [*sic*] BUT I THINK YOU'RE VERY GREAT AND VERY WONDERFUL—MARY MARTIN.

The first act was in good shape: "The Hostess with the Mostes'" got things off to a rousing start, and all of Ethel's other songs landed with the audience. Russell Nype stopped the show with "It's a Lovely Day Today." The second act was something of a desert. Neither "Free" nor "Mr. Monotony" worked. The latter wasn't a bad number; in fact, with its dark, jazz-inflected undercurrents, it was rather interesting, and a departure for Berlin. But it wasn't a song for Ethel, and when she announced that it was out, she met with little resistance from anyone. The bombastic "Free" was also cut. When Ethel informed Berlin, "We gotta have something to lift the second act," she wasn't telling him anything he didn't know, and he proceeded to barricade himself in his room at New Haven's Taft Hotel to come up with a new number.

Ethel wasn't surprised when the reviews turned out to be mixed. "Will probably not go down in the record as a great musical production. As of now, show inspires warm applause rather than cheer," *Variety* offered. The *New Haven Evening Register* found it "no *South Pacific*" but thought that Ethel "again displays all the vocal brass and personal brashness which are her particular charms."

The result of Berlin's seclusion at the Taft was "Something to Dance About," a swingy tune for Ethel and the ensemble. It was pleasant and likable, but not the second-act showstopper so desperately needed. Having admired Russell Nype's style and professionalism, Ethel said, "What I'd like to do is a number with the kid." Berlin went back once more to his hotel suite. Buck Crouse, who had the room above Berlin's, heard him working all night on an infectious melody. Crouse hoped for the best, and he wasn't disappointed when, a day and a half after his self-imposed seclusion, Berlin turned up with "You're Just in Love." Like his old 1914 hit "Play a Simple Melody," it was a counterpoint tune—sedate and melancholy for Russell Nype, brassy and bold for Ethel. After she heard it, Ethel predicted, "We'll never get off the stage." She was right. When *Call Me Madam* opened in Boston on September 19, the song received seven encores. At some performances Paul Lukas, who appeared in the scene that followed, had to step out onstage and wait while the number was still going, just to cue the audience that the show had to keep moving.

Call Me Madam played to standing-room-only audiences for its entire Boston run. *Variety* reported that the show grossed $37,300 for its first seven performances, and though reviews were better than they'd been in New Haven, they were still decidedly qualified. The *Boston Record* found that for all the money spent on it, the show offered "only an occasional flash of inspirational fire." For the New York run, the $7.20 price tag for the best seats didn't cause any lull at the box office: by the time it came into New York, *Call Me Madam* had earned a record advance sale of $1 million. As much as $200 was being offered for some tickets, and the *New York Daily Mirror* reported that scalpers were asking $400 for opening night.

A few days before the opening Ethel uttered a remark that quickly became part of Broadway legend. Lindsay and Crouse, realizing that the book did not show them at their best, were continuing to refine and polish their lines. They stopped only when Ethel said, "Boys, as of right now I am Miss Birdseye of 1950. I am frozen. Not a comma!" Always willing to do whatever it took during the rehearsal and out-of-town tryout periods, she knew that sooner or later the show had to be fixed—otherwise how could she be expected to do her best work? Forever after, when a show was in its final stages of previews, "Miss Birdseye" became Broadway code for no more tinkering allowed.

Call Me Madam opened at the Imperial on October 12, 1950. In the audience that night were Joan Blondell and Mike Todd (who only a few years earlier had pronounced Ethel a has-been), Sylvia Fine and Danny Kaye, Dorothy and Richard Rodgers, Nedda and Joshua Logan, and Linda and Cole Porter. The show was ecstatically received by the audience, and, predictably, "You're Just in Love" was the hit of the evening. Years later Russell Nype stated that he felt it was probably "the greatest musical comedy duet that's ever been written."

Brooks Atkinson, in the *New York Times*, found that *Call Me Madam* was one of Berlin's "most enchanting scores: fresh, light, and beguiling, and fitted to lyrics that fall out of it with grace and humor." The *New York Post* called Ethel "indescribably soul-satisfying. In addition, she is a comedienne of rare skill, who combines richness and warmth with her humor. Miss Merman, the illustrious American institution, is one of the joys of the world."

The critics, justifiably, complained about the book, but these reservations were not enough to prevent *Call Me Madam* from becoming an enormous success. The only real canker in the rose was the loud and long objection to the high ticket prices and the avalanche of publicity over the huge advance sale. Nearly every reviewer mentioned the drum beating that had preceded *Call Me Madam*'s arrival in town; Ward Morehouse, writing in the *New York World-Telegram and Sun*, felt that "there hasn't been anything with more of a ballyhoo since Sarah Bernhardt trouped the land in tents."

With colossal hits like *Oklahoma!*, *Annie Get Your Gun*, *South Pacific*, and now *Call Me Madam*, there was no longer the standard expectation that a show would come in at the start of the season and play through only to its end. Suddenly the possibilities of success had rapidly expanded. Now there was serious money to be made on Broadway, and the industry's marketing and publicity machine beefed itself up accordingly. Many in the theater who were in a position to call the shots found themselves getting a little greedier. In the future, the core members of a show's creative team would begin to ask for a bigger cut; in terms of how business was done, the Broadway musical was beginning to suffer a kind of loss of innocence. Ethel all too willingly adapted to this turn of events: she knew how much Irving Berlin and Rodgers and Hammerstein had made from *Annie Get Your Gun* while she was the one out there onstage carrying an extremely strenuous show on her back and keeping it running for nearly three years. Now, with *Call Me Madam*, she had insisted on receiving 10 percent of all profits from the show, including road companies, film sale, and all subsidiary rights. In time, *Call Me Madam* would make her richer than ever.

Ethel settled in, assured of yet another very long run. *Call Me Madam* had opened twenty years, almost to the day, after her spectacular debut at the Alvin in *Girl Crazy*. No other stage performer had ever come close to matching her remarkable record of hit shows. It seemed impossible for her to fail professionally.

At home, however, Bob's drinking episodes and his absences became more and more frequent, and the marriage she had initially been so sure of was rapidly dissolving. Nothing, not even a new hit show, could prevent her from facing up to that fact.

Chapter Thirteen

● ●

*C*all Me Madam* helped usher in a glorious season on Broadway: that
year's dramas included Tennessee Williams's *Rose Tattoo*, Clifford
Odets's *Country Girl*, and Lillian Hellman's *Autumn Garden*. Leading
the way for musicals were *Guys and Dolls*, which opened only a few weeks
after *Call Me Madam*, and *The King and I*, which opened in March. In terms
of artistic achievement both of these shows easily overshadowed *Call Me
Madam*, and it came as no surprise when *Guys and Dolls*, with all its brilliant
exuberance and evocative lyric writing, swept the fifth annual Tony Awards,
winning for Best Musical, Best Score and Lyrics, Best Book, Best Choreography, Best Actor in a Musical (Robert Alda), and Best Featured Actress in a
Musical (Isabel Bigley). *Call Me Madam*, however, was not entirely left out
of the Tonys: Russell Nype was voted Best Featured Actor in a Musical, and
Ethel had the honor of being named the season's Best Actress in a Musical.
It was the first time she'd been in the running, as the awards had been in
existence only since 1947, one year too late for her greatest triumph, *Annie
Get Your Gun*, to be considered. But awards did not mean as much to her as
they did to many other performers. For Ethel the old cliché was a truism: her
work, and the best possible execution of it, was her greatest reward.

Guys and Dolls would run for 1,200 performances, *The King and I*
for 1,246. The public's taste in musicals continued to grow in sophistication: each year musical innovation and the underpinning of a strong story
seemed to become a little more important. While the old-fashioned gags-
and-girls shows that had so proliferated when Ethel started would largely
disappear in the next decade, in the early 1950s they were still in evidence—witness *As the Girls Go*, with Bobby Clark, and *Ankles Aweigh*, with
Betty and Jane Kean. They opened, played the better part of a season,
amused a lot of tourists and businessmen entertaining out-of-town clients,
and closed forever.

The 1950s were not kind years, professionally, to many of Ethel's closest
colleagues. Howard Lindsay and Russel Crouse would never have another

blue-ribbon hit again, as they turned their attention to middling star vehicles such as *The Prescott Proposals*, starring Katharine Cornell, and *The
Great Sebastians*, with Alfred Lunt and Lynn Fontanne. After the hit revue
Two on the Aisle in 1951, Bert Lahr would not appear in another musical
until *Foxy* in 1964. Jimmy Durante had not played Broadway in years, preferring the lucrative worlds of radio and television. Although Cole Porter
had several more hits in the 1950s, such as *Can-Can* and *Silk Stockings*,
they were not up to the quality of his earlier shows, and his worsening physical condition led him to give up writing altogether in 1958. And, most
surprising of all, *Call Me Madam* would be Irving Berlin's last Broadway
show until the ill-advised *Mister President* in 1962.

But in 1951 the wolf was not yet at the door where old-fashioned Broadway entertainment was concerned, and to the general public the musicals
still represented a world of glamour and excitement and prestige. Many of
the top tunes on *Your Hit Parade* continued to come from Broadway shows,
and Broadway stars frequently appeared as guests on the nation's top variety
programs on both radio and television. Americans knew who they were and
what kind of shows they had appeared in, and they welcomed them into their
homes. The great divide created by the rise of rock and roll, which would
grow wider and wider in the decades that followed, as "high" and "low"
cultures became increasingly alien to each other, had not yet struck the
American entertainment scene.

It was in this environment that Tallulah Bankhead's famous radio
program, *The Big Show*, was launched, in November 1950. Airing on
NBC Sunday evenings from six to seven-thirty, *The Big Show* aimed,
through quality writing, music, and production values, to recapture some of
the audience that had been lost to television, which had become a national
obsession far beyond the wildest imaginings of most. By the beginning of
1950, there were 4 million television sets in use across the United States, a
number that would mushroom to 21 million in the next two years. Rather
than ignore the phenomenon, as the big movie studios had attempted to do
in the beginning, the producers of *The Big Show* set out to offer the new
medium some stiff competition. On the first show, Bankhead's guests included Jimmy Durante, Jose Ferrer, Danny Thomas, Fred Allen, Frankie
Laine, and, on a night off from *Call Me Madam*, Ethel, Russell Nype, and
Paul Lukas. A key ingredient of the show's format was having Bankhead swap barbs and insults with her guests. Take the following exchange
with Ethel:

BANKHEAD: Ethel, I suppose you must have been bothered by hundreds of friends calling up to get tickets for themselves. Of course, I wouldn't dream of bothering you about the two I've been trying to get . . .
MERMAN: Oh, it's no bother at all. I happen to have two tickets with me. But they're way back in the fourth row, and knowing your eyes . . .

Ethel proved so adept at this sort of banter that Bankhead invited her back again and again during the run of *Call Me Madam*. At a staggering weekly production cost reported to be around $50,000, *The Big Show* would last only until 1952, but while it endured, it made a big noise in the dying days of radio.

As the months rolled by, the audience's love affair with *Call Me Madam* and its star continued to swell. Sheldon Harnick, then a young lyricist who had recently moved to New York, recalled sitting in the last row of the Imperial's second balcony—all he could afford—for one performance. Ethel came out for "The Hostess with the Mostes'," planted her feet, and began to sing. "She opened her mouth and that trombone came out, and I thought, 'Now I understand the legend of Merman,' Harnick remembered. "Even that far up, it just engulfed me."

The Broadway musical was in full, spectacular flower, and Ethel must have wondered if it could go on forever. If Hollywood continued to ignore her, New York provided her with more love and acclaim than she could possibly hope to absorb.

Ethel's standby in *Call Me Madam* was again the reliable Mary Jane Walsh, but when Walsh decided to get married and move upstate, her job was taken over by twenty-five-year-old Elaine Stritch. A brilliant young comedienne who had been making a name for herself in New York revues, Stritch had yet to click with the public. She had certain things in common with Ethel: shrewd comic timing, a tough way of delivering her lines, and a highly individual singing style (though the raspy-voiced Stritch could never hope to compete with Ethel's clarion tones). Stritch also had fierce ambition, which did not go unnoticed by Ethel. "I've always suspected that Stritch's glands worked overtime," Ethel wrote in her memoirs, and throughout her life she maintained a somewhat guarded, tongue-in-cheek attitude toward this brash actress seventeen years her junior. Privately she wrote off Stritch as a mean drunk. Certainly she acknowledged Stritch's fearsome talents, but she wasn't about to let her get near the part of Sally Adams if she could help it. "A role is a very personal thing to an actress," Ethel wrote. "You don't want someone else fooling around with it any more than you do with your toothbrush." Each night, Stritch popped by Ethel's dressing room at the Imperial at half hour with a wry, "I gather you're well."

In her dazzling one-woman show, *Elaine Stritch at Liberty*, created with John Lahr, Stritch told a story about standing by for Ethel in *Call Me Madam* that drew one of the show's biggest laughs. Stritch recalled a particular performance when Ethel was onstage singing "Can You Use Any Money Today?" while being heckled by a loud, drunken man in the orchestra section. She tried to continue with the number but found it next to impossible with the constant, earsplitting interruptions of "ATTA GIRL, ETHEL, LAY IT ON ME, SWEETIE POOPS!" Finally, when she could stand it no longer, she left the stage in the middle of a lyric. While all the chorus girls remained frozen in place, Ethel went into the wings, down the stairs to the front of the house, back down the aisle, over to where the heckler was seated, and proceeded to force him bodily out of the theater before hurrying back for the end of the number.

Funny as this story is, it has been questioned by several of the players from *Call Me Madam*, who tell a different version. They do recall that one night, when a drunk in the orchestra section disrupted the performance, Ethel did leave the stage in mid-number to deal with the situation. But according to Dody Goodman, she simply went out the side door, confronted the house manager, and told him, "Get him out of here, and give him his money back—and tell him we never want to see him in this theater again." This is an infinitely more plausible version of the incident. Ethel, with her highly developed sense of professionalism, would surely never have laid hands on a paying customer (let alone a drunk who easily could have overpowered her). And, as Dody Goodman pointed out, "Elaine wouldn't have known anyway. She left every night at half hour."

Bob's drinking and erratic behavior were now taking their toll at the office as well as at home. Ethel felt frustrated, helpless, and finally angry. Once again her lack of tolerance for weakness overcame the very deep love she had felt for her husband; she simply could not see how Bob could yield to his sense of inadequacy in such a self-destructive way. She was, of course, supported by Mom and Pop Zimmermann in her feelings of betrayal. Bob seemed intent on failure, on succumbing to his own diminishing view of himself. In time he lost his position with Hearst and was forced to scramble for work elsewhere. This only exacerbated the tension between husband and wife, and by May 1951 their disagreements had become so frequent and so wounding that Bob left the apartment and found a place of his own. Exactly whose idea the separation was has never been entirely clear. Ethel was fairly tight-lipped about the details, but in show-business circles it soon became received wisdom that she had thrown him out. "In later years," said Alex Birnbaum, "I would hear how she left him. The hell she did. He walked out on her—which was devastating."

Ethel was soon keeping company with a new clutch of friends, chief among whom were the Duke and Duchess of Windsor. They were, of course, one of the most discussed couples in the public eye. Back in 1936, Ethel had followed the news accounts of the duke's ascension to the British throne, as Edward VIII, and his subsequent abdication when his family did not approve of his relationship with the twice-married American socialite Bessie Wallis Warfield Simpson. Ethel had no interest whatever in cultivating the aristocracy; she simply enjoyed the duke and duchess's company and appreciated them for who they were—particularly the duchess, whose belligerent, domineering personality and sense of outrageous fun appealed to her. The Windsors were in turn huge admirers of Ethel, and soon they were seeing a great deal of each other on the town after theater, often with Russell Nype along to make it a quartet.

The duchess took a special interest in Nype and introduced him to many friends in her social circle. For the ex-minister's son from Illinois, it was exhilarating to be in such company. "Life was so exciting and you were doing so many things, so many activities, and you were out socially so much," he later said. Ethel was with him every step of the way. In the past, both before and during her marriage to Bob Levitt, she had been a bit cautious about how much socializing she did after a show. Now, whether she was relieved that the tension of Bob's presence had been removed or she simply wanted to give the impression of reveling in her independence, she was out night after night. There were post-dinner invitations to the homes of many in the duke and duchess's lives, and there were all of New York's toniest night spots to choose from: '21,' El Morocco, the St. Regis Maisonette, and the Stork Club, where Ethel and Nype found themselves going most often. The chill between Ethel and Sherman Billingsley had thawed some time ago, and now she was happy to be a regular at the club once more. During the war, after his rift with Ethel, Billingsley added what had become the restaurant's elite attraction, the Cub Room. It was set apart from the rest of the club, and reserved only for A-list celebrities: Spencer Tracy, Ernest Hemingway, Alfred Hitchcock, Bing

Crosby, Leland and Pamela Hayward, Helen Hayes, Hedy Lamarr, Gene Tunney, Dorothy Lamour, Rebecca West, and countless others dined and drank there regularly. Walter Winchell posted himself nightly at Table Number 50 and day after day mentioned the Stork Club in his widely read column; this ritual was immortalized in the 1957 film *Sweet Smell of Success*, with Burt Lancaster as the Winchell prototype. Ethel loved holding court there, loved the jewelry and designer scarves and Sortilège perfume and ice-cold bottles of Dom Pérignon that once again came her way.

With her new single-girl status there also came a variety of interesting men to squire her around town. Wealthy investment banker Charles Cushing became one frequent escort. Through Cushing, Ethel met many members of the social set on Long Island and in Fairfield, Connecticut, and soon she was ducking out of town after the Saturday-night performance to spend the weekend at one fashionable country estate or another. One of her most frequent hostesses was the duke and duchess's good friend Edith Baker, whose home in Glen Cove was one of the most magnificent mansions on Long Island's Gold Coast.

Although Ethel had dated wealthy men before, such as Walter Annenberg and Al Goetz, she had never really circulated with members of society, as she was now doing. If she was simply showing off a bit—proving to herself and the world that there could be an exciting new chapter in life after Bob Levitt—she didn't take any of it too seriously, and the acquisition of a few upper-crust friends certainly brought about no change in her demeanor, her language, her love of sharing a good dirty joke. She remained resolutely herself, and her new set seemed to delight in her rambunctious, bawdy style. And no one, no matter how socially influential he might be, could make her do something she didn't feel like doing. Around this time columnist Leonard Lyons reported that the social arbiter Elsa Maxwell had approached Ethel with a hefty commission to perform at the society debut of the daughter of one of New York's most prominent families. Ethel found the whole thing distasteful and turned Maxwell down flat. Shortly afterward the Duchess of Windsor threw a party at the recently opened restaurant Gogi's LaRue. When the duchess asked her if she'd mind singing, Ethel got up and trumpeted "I Get a Kick Out of You," along with several of her other hits. (Her reward was a letter from the American Guild of Variety Artists reprimanding her for performing in public at no charge. Ethel dismissed this nonsense: if a friend as good as the duchess wanted her to do something, of course she would do it—as long as the friend responded in kind when it was Ethel's turn to ask a favor.)

Another popular companion of Ethel's during this period was Jimmy Donahue. The grandson of retail magnate F. W. Woolworth, Donahue had exhibited a spoiled, willful nature from childhood. His father, Jim Donahue, was a compulsive gambler who once lost $900,000 during the Palm Beach season of 1931 and who later committed suicide. Ethel admired Jimmy's devotion to his mother, Jessie, and to his first cousin, Barbara Hutton, to whom he was "shield, sounding-board, escort, and confidant." Gay at a time when such matters were seldom discussed openly, Donahue allied himself with many top society ladies, but his relationship with the Duchess of Windsor was much more complicated: she was passionately in love with him. Once, during a row, the duchess reportedly screamed at him, "And to think I gave up a king for a queen!" Gaunt and sunken-faced, Donahue had the appearance of an "epicene gigolo" and drank far too much, often becoming hostile and argumentative when inebriated. Still, Ethel adored him, and when he was sober, she found him one of the most kindly and cultivated men she'd ever known.

Charlie Cushing and Jimmy Donahue might have been good company, but what Ethel really longed for was another all-consuming, serious love affair, like the one she'd initially enjoyed with Bob Levitt. At forty-three she felt in perfect health, and she had kept her figure. She considered herself an excellent catch, and for all her professional success she did not feel complete without a man in her life. She still had enormous faith that another great romance, possibly even a great marriage, lay ahead.

On October 20, 1951, *Call Me Madam* celebrated its one-year anniversary on Broadway with an elegant party at the chic restaurant L'Aiglon. There she was introduced to a roughly handsome, broad-shouldered, six-foot-four man named Robert Six. He had an easy, pleasant, unpretentious manner, and he behaved like a thorough gentleman, paying proper attention to Ethel but never fawning over her. She was attracted to him immediately, and it appeared that he felt the same way about her. Ethel had been too busy socializing and speaking with reporters to eat much at the party, and after the festivities broke up, she and Six headed to a nearby Hamburger Heaven, where she spent the next several hours finding out all about him and his background.

It turned out that Six was nothing less than the president of Continental Airlines. Their attraction made complete sense: they had in common tremendous ambition and a will to succeed. Like Ethel, Six was entirely self-made. A high-school dropout, he had led a rather hardscrabble existence in his early years, working as a seaman, a bill collector, and at other odd jobs.

But his great passion was flying, and at a fairly young age he had run a charter service in California that soon went bust. Other flying enterprises included a few years in the Far East as a pilot for China National and part ownership of an airmail route from Texas to Colorado; in between times he'd put in a stint as district circulation manager of the *San Francisco Chronicle* before he got his hands on enough money to found Continental. It was a rather patchy background for a major airline executive, but Ethel was pleased with the idea that Six seemed to have done it the hard way. Unlike Bob Levitt, he'd seen many of her shows and professed great admiration for her as a performer.

There was something else about Six that Ethel responded to, something that may have been more important than any of his other qualities: he was tough. "She loved tough, masculine guys," said her longtime friend Bob Schear. "That was very important to her. She told me that she liked it when gay men didn't *seem* gay." In many ways Bob Six came much closer to fulfilling Ethel's dreams of ultimate masculinity than anyone else ever had. In the early stages of their acquaintanceship, she continued to date Charlie Cushing and a few others, but soon she and Six were seeing each other so regularly that their names frequently popped up in the gossip columns.

In the meantime she kept playing *Call Me Madam* to full houses. The press items on her romance with Six only helped fuel the box office, as did a stunt that Leland Hayward had dreamed up. At her solo curtain call, Ethel brought an actor onto the stage who bore a stunning likeness to Harry Truman and insisted that he take a bow with her. No mention was made of the actor's identity, but it was in fact Irving Fisher, a Broadway veteran who had, only four years earlier, played Truman in Moss Hart's play *Christopher Blake*. Although some in the audience may have been duped into thinking that Fisher was really the president, most understood that it was a joke and relished it. It was an audacious public-relations stunt, and it paid off, as many ticket buyers came back again and again, hoping to catch another glimpse of "the president."

One aspect of the show proved to be a major disappointment for Ethel. In those days a musical's original-cast album was always recorded on the Sunday following opening night. As backer of the show, RCA was eager to record *Call Me Madam* and although Ethel had signed an exclusive contract with Decca, it was assumed that some sort of deal would be worked out, permitting RCA to borrow her for its recording. But negotiations bogged down, and RCA issued its album with the entire original cast *except* for Ethel, who was replaced by the rather pallid Dinah Shore. Decca, not to be outdone, went ahead and recorded its own version of the show with Ethel and a faceless group of supporting players (including crooner Dick Haymes). As an ensemble it had none of the zing of the original company. The result, *Ethel Merman: Twelve Songs from Call Me Madam*, did well enough, but the simultaneous presence of two albums obviously undercut sales for both.

For most actors, keeping a performance fresh and alive throughout a long run at some point becomes a challenge. It was less of an issue for Ethel than for most performers, thanks to her way of locking in her reading and never varying it. Audience members who went back again to see her in both *Annie Get Your Gun* and *Call Me Madam* were amazed by how utterly consistent she remained—too consistent, some complained. For several years many of Ethel's fellow actors had felt that she always gave a brilliant performance in the opening weeks of a show, then tended to go on automatic pilot for the rest of the run. "We all do it," said her understudy, Helene Whitney. "It becomes very mechanical. There's no way that doing a show for eighteen months or two years does *not* become mechanical, because you cannot expend that emotional energy every single night." It was often said of Ethel that she tended to walk through the matinee performances, partly because she found matinee audiences inattentive and unresponsive. If they weren't going to show their respect by giving her their full concentration, why should she beat her brains out for them?

In the early weeks of 1952, *Call Me Madam*'s box office began to taper off a bit, and on May 3 the show closed, with an impressive tally of 644 performances and a box-office gross of over $4 million. Ethel was relieved to be out of the show, since it meant that she would have more time to spend with Bob Six, who had been turning up in New York more and more frequently. First, however, she had to head the *Call Me Madam* company for an engagement at the National Theatre in Washington, D.C. Ethel had made it very clear that she was not about to break her no-touring rule—Elaine Stritch would play Sally Adams in the national company, and Joan Blondell would take on the role at the Dallas State Fair—but the idea of taking this political-themed show to the nation's capital appealed to her. The engagement was also a historic milestone: the National was reopening after having been shut down for four years over the heated issue of audience segregation. Before and during World War II, theater audiences in many U.S. cities had had to face segregation as a way of life: too often blacks simply were not permitted to sit with whites—or, in some cases, even attend the same performances. In Texas blacks might even be forced to sit upstairs for *Porgy and Bess*. Such practices were hardly confined to the South: during the war the great contralto Marian Anderson, on concert tours of cities in the Northwest, often had to stay at a YMCA, because no first-class hotel would accept her. After the war audience segregation became a hot-button issue, but certain theater managers, such as the National's Marcus Heiman, refused to back down and integrate. The performers' union, Actors' Equity, issued a ruling refusing to let any of its members play before a segregated audience in America's capital. Heiman fought back, with the result that on July 31, 1948, the National ceased to be used for live performances and was converted to a movie house. Now it was being reborn as a legit, integrated theater, and on May 5 *Call Me Madam* finally visited the town that it had lampooned on Broadway for nearly two years.

The National, fresh from a $75,000 renovation, looked magnificent. In the audience were Irving Berlin, Howard Lindsay and Dorothy Stickney, Buck and Anna Crouse, Ina Claire, Ray Middleton, Washington socialites Mr. and Mrs. Morris Cafritz and Mr. and Mrs. Arthur Gardner, and a large contingent of senators from Capitol Hill. Possibly the only audience member who didn't enjoy the show was the wife of Senator Robert A. Taft; with her husband off stumping for votes for the Republican presidential nomination, Mrs. Taft seemed a bit uncomfortable during the performance of "They Like Ike."

The show came off splendidly, and afterward Bob Six threw an elegant black-tie party for 150 guests at the Chinese Room of the Mayflower Hotel. The Asian motif was temporarily redone so that the room resembled a chic French nightclub, with tiny tables, flowers, and hurricane lamps, and a sumptuous buffet. Ethel, as trim as she'd ever been, looked smashing in a ballerina-length silver-and-brocade gown. The affair lasted until past four in the morning, and even the most casual observers could see, from the way Ethel beamed at Six throughout the night, that she was a woman passionately in love. Over the next few days, photos of the smiling couple turned up in newspaper spreads across the country. To be given this kind of treatment in Washington thrilled Ethel, and she regarded the event as one of the highest points of her professional life. Best of all, she had embarked on what seemed to be another great romance.

Call Me Madam played a four-week limited run at the National, with Richard Eastham taking over for Paul Lukas as Cosmo. Audiences were enthusiastic and even Perle Mesta made a special trip from her post in Luxembourg to attend one of the last performances.

Ethel then turned her attention to the final details of securing her divorce from Bob Levitt. She grew extremely nervous recalling the complicated circumstances of her first two divorces, and she prayed that there would be no legal hitches that might come to the attention of some enterprising newspaper reporter. She needn't have worried. On June 7, 1952, she flew to Mexico City, where her lawyer, Paul O'Dwyer, was already waiting. Because of her own stable financial condition and because she wanted no trouble from Levitt, who knew the truth about the validity of her divorce from Bill Smith, it was arranged that he would have to make no alimony payments. Ethel received custody of both Ethel Jr. and Bobby, with Levitt reserving the customary visiting rights.

Ethel's greatest grief over the failure of her marriage to Bob Levitt would not come until years later. At the time it seemed the only sensible thing for her to do. She and Bob had become incompatible, his career was in decline, his drinking was apparently uncontrollable. All these were facts that Ethel used as validation for her decision. But privately the grounded, upright daughter of Edward and Agnes Zimmermann was deeply disappointed that she had not been able to make either of her marriages work.

But she had great consolation, she told all her closest friends, in Bob Six. For a woman at forty-four, Six was a gift that gave her inexpressible joy. He seemed to her the most gallant of men: his hosting of the Washington party was all the proof she needed. It was best, then, that she did not know that the evening had value to Six for another reason. He would list it as a tax deduction: with the presence of so much press, including camera crews from NBC-TV, it had enormous value as a public-relations boon for Continental Airlines.

Before the closing of *Call Me Madam*, Ethel received the best news she'd ever had from Hollywood: 20th Century Fox had agreed to let her reprise her role in the film version the studio was preparing for 1953 release. In the past neither Ethel nor her agents had expended much energy to secure the film versions of her Broadway successes, and perhaps on some level she even understood why MGM had felt she was too old and not sexy enough to play Annie Oakley on the screen. But Sally Adams was not a role that depended on youth or sensuality, and Irving Berlin, no doubt feeling that he owed Ethel a great deal because she had kept *Annie* and *Call Me Madam* running for so long, lobbied hard with Fox's studio chief, Darryl Zanuck, to get Ethel the part. He pointed out that her earlier films for the studio had not shown her off to great advantage and that if she were presented as she was, not in a diluted version of herself, she would click with a movie audience, just as she had captivated Broadway. Although Zanuck might have more predictably gone with an established film star like Rosalind Russell or the studio's own Betty Grable, he listened and pondered, and eventually he came around to Berlin's way of thinking.

The screenplay had been in development for much of the year, and at a script conference on April 2, 1952, Zanuck seemed pleased with the progress being made, though he had some reservations about the satirical element. "I am desperately afraid of too much emphasis on the tongue-in-cheek attitude," he noted, and pushed screenwriter Arthur Sheekman to put greater depth of feeling into the scenes between Cosmo and Sally, to make them "not quite so flip and musical comedy." With characteristic perceptiveness he also felt that the picture should not be stylized. "This is a *personality* piece," he dictated in a memo. "It is not a *spectacle* piece. . . . Nothing on a grand scale, or we will lose the personality story." Revisions took place over the summer of 1952, and slowly a script emerged that was more focused and streamlined than the Broadway original. There were the usual interferences from the Breen office: Sally's line to Pemberton, "I'm the Madam, and you're just one of the girls," had to be softened to "I'm the Madam and you're just one of the . . . boys." By September 5 the final shooting script had been approved, and Ethel was on her way to Hollywood, where she had booked a suite at the Beverly Hills Hotel.

Ethel arrived on the 20th Century Fox lot amid much ballyhoo, as several of her biggest fans in the press, including Louella O. Parsons and Radie Harris, had gone out of their way to publicize her work on *Call Me Madam*. The film's producer, Sol Siegel, took the studio party line that the picture would have been unthinkable without Ethel. She was given one of Fox's top directors of musicals, Walter Lang, and Betty Grable, just coming off a ten-year run as the studio's number-one box-office attraction, insisted that Ethel be given her dressing room. A top-flight cast was assembled: George Sanders, who possessed a surprisingly good, mellow baritone, was ideal for Cosmo. The gifted Donald O'Connor, who had just had a big hit at MGM in *Singin' in the Rain,* was a wonderful foil as Kenneth (leaving Russell Nype out in the cold), and the lovely dancer Vera-Ellen, who had once backed Ethel up in *Panama Hattie*, was an excellent choice for Princess Maria.

From the start, Ethel was delighted with her director, the genial, workmanlike Lang. Born in Memphis, Lang had begun his creative life as a painter. He'd arrived in Hollywood in the 1920s and become a busy director during the silent era. After taking a break to concentrate on his painting, he returned to Hollywood and signed with Fox in the mid-1930s. He went on to turn out some of the studio's greatest successes, from the Betty Grable vehicles *Moon Over Miami* (1941) and *Mother Wore Tights* (1947) to Rodgers and Hammerstein's original screen musical *State Fair* (1945) to the Clifton Webb comedy *Sitting Pretty* (1948). He directed comedy with verve rather than style or sophistication, and his efficient work habits—his films consistently came in on schedule and on budget—made him a great favorite with studio bosses. Actors also liked working for him, because he seldom lost his temper. Barbara Hale, who starred opposite James Stewart in Lang's 1950 comedy *The Jackpot*, remembered the director as "a gentle genius."

Ethel seemed unusually edgy throughout the first few days of production. During filming of the picture's opening number, "The Hostess with the Mostes'," she repeatedly fumbled a phrase. Shaken, she turned to Lang and said, "Guess I've got to feel that I'm reaching through to the audience, and I can't seem to get even a glint out of the camera lens." The woman who claimed not to have a nerve in her body throughout twenty years of Broadway opening nights now seemed quite apprehensive. In the first few days, she studied the rushes obsessively, trying to learn how to build a performance for film. Lang was delighted with her work, but Ethel didn't relax her vigilance and continued to examine the rushes during the entire shooting schedule.

Filming progressed smoothly; Ethel even got along well with the notoriously difficult George Sanders. And despite her disappointment that Russell Nype was not signed to re-create the part of Kenneth Gibson, she adored working with the brilliant Donald O'Connor. They were wonderful in their scenes together, particularly the big comedy duet "You're Just in Love." Ethel responded to O'Connor's natural buoyancy and charm with a performance of great wit and color. O'Connor, for his part, returned the compliment. He'd often had occasion to observe that the great show-business personalities tended to remain the same on screen and in life; it was difficult to tell where the public persona of Bob Hope, for example, left off and where the private one began. It was nice for paying audience members, thought O'Connor, to see someone off-screen who appeared exactly as she did on— that way they could never be disillusioned. But O'Connor was delighted to discover that the private Ethel was entirely different from her showbiz persona. At big Hollywood parties, she seemed almost shy. O'Connor found her genuine, real, and all too human.

Since Denver was comparatively close to Los Angeles, Bob Six was a frequent visitor throughout the shooting, which wrapped shortly after Thanksgiving. Rosemary Clooney threw Ethel a grand farewell party at Romanoff's, where the guests included Joan Crawford, Jack Benny, Barbara Stanwyck, Ann Sothern, Joan Fontaine and Collier Young, and Humphrey Bogart and Lauren Bacall.

After spending the Christmas season in New York, Ethel, ever the staunch Republican, attended the inauguration of the thirty-fourth president, Dwight D. Eisenhower. ("They Like Ike" had proved prophetic.) When she returned to California on business, Six was with her as often as possible, still as solicitous as ever. Sometime earlier he had begun to press her for a more serious commitment. Ethel was enjoying her exciting life on the town with Six and saw no reason to rush into marriage, but as the months clicked by, there was no way to disguise, either to the world or to herself, how deeply in love she had fallen. Six appeared to have a bright future, and as far as Ethel could tell, he was completely attentive to Ethel Jr. and Bobby. He looked like a solid bet, and when he kept asking her to marry him, she eventually consented. While they were both in California, they traveled to Mexicali, a Mexican border town where they could get a quick, no-frills marriage without being bombarded by an avalanche of publicity. They were wed there on March 9. Six, concerned that the announcement of their union might hurt the film's chances at the box office, thought it best to keep the whole matter a secret for the time being. Also, he said, he had numerous business affairs that were going to occupy him intensely for the next few months. Better to wait until the summertime, which was the prime season for weddings anyway, before broadcasting the news.

His pragmatic, businesslike approach to the matter of marriage might have sent off some alarm signals for Ethel had she not been so blindly in love. In her professional life, Ethel's vulnerability might never reveal itself, buried as it was under the thick armor of genuine self-confidence she possessed. Men were another matter: Ethel in love was Ethel at her softest, most pliable, and eager to please. Never before had she seemed as starry-eyed about a man as she did about Six, and without thinking twice about it she happily agreed to keep the marriage under wraps.

Why Ethel was not present for the world premiere of the screen version of *Call Me Madam*, at Los Angeles's Fox Ritz Theatre on March 4, is not clear. Perhaps for all her studying of the rushes and her guarded optimism about the end result, she was simply terrified of failure. The premiere was a Hollywood opening night in the grand old style. Five thousand fans were jammed along both sides of Wilshire Boulevard's Miracle Mile, and celebrity guests included Joan Crawford, Jane Powell, Tony Curtis and Janet Leigh, Clifton Webb, Dorothy Lamour, and Decca Records' usurper of the role of Sally Adams, Dinah Shore. The only star from the film present was Donald O'Connor. The Hollywood press raved about *Call Me Madam*. "If anything," wrote Louella Parsons, "Ethel is better than behind the footlights, slimmer, prettier, funnier, and a one-woman riot. . . ." With such a reaction, Ethel felt confident enough to show up for the film's New York premiere at the Roxy, where the critical reaction was overwhelming. The *New York Times*'s Bosley Crowther found her "better than ever—in spades! . . . There should really be no need for 3-D pictures when there are people like Miss Merman still around." "Miss Merman has appeared in previous movies, of course," observed the *New Yorker*'s John McCarten, "but as I recall them, they didn't give her much elbow room. I hope the boys in Hollywood are now aware that she can fill all the room they can provide."

While some critics made note of the film's occasional longueurs in the second half, *Call Me Madam* was generally branded an enormous success as a movie musical. In later years Ethel took great pains to portray the movie as a smash, but although it did well, playing to great business in the metropolitan centers, it underperformed in smaller towns and rural areas.

(Again Ethel's refusal to tour in her Broadway shows may have been a factor.) In the end, *Call Me Madam* was 20th Century Fox's fourth-biggest grosser for 1953, with a take of $2.85 million (though that figure is less impressive when one takes into account the production cost of $2.46 million).

By June, Bob Six at last was ready to announce that he and Ethel were married. It was all but an open secret by this time, as Six had been closing in on a deal to purchase a large house on a vast estate in Cherry Hills Village, a posh suburb of Denver, and the press naturally concluded that he was buying it as a home for his new family. As soon as the Sixes had come clean, Broadway insiders were buzzing about the possibility that Ethel might leave her beloved New York for a life out west, but for the moment she remained silent on the subject. Only to her closest friends did she confess that the thought of being a proper married lady in Colorado held great appeal for her. She thought that bucolic Cherry Hills would be a wonderful place to raise the children, especially Ethel Jr., who, after years of spending family holidays in Glenwood Springs, loved the outdoors and had a great tenderness for all kinds of animals. Ethel also admitted that the long runs of *Annie Get Your Gun* and *Call Me Madam*, with only minimal time off, had left her exhausted. She'd worked hard and pulled her weight and made her producers and composers a great deal of money. Why should she have to apologize to anyone for wanting to leave Broadway behind?

While the Sixes were still negotiating for the property, however, a singing offer came up that she could hardly turn down. It came from Leland Hayward, who had just been engaged to produce a television special commemorating the fiftieth anniversary of the Ford Motor Company. Conceived as a panoramic view of American life through the first half of the twentieth century, it promised to be the most ambitious undertaking that the still-young medium had attempted. Hayward designed it as a bountiful mixture of drama, song, dance, history, and fashion; underlining the show's bigger-is-better approach was the fact that it would be telecast simultaneously on two networks, CBS and NBC, all of it live. The talent that Hayward had lined up included pop singer Eddie Fisher; famed contralto Marian Anderson; Kukla, Fran, and Ollie; crooner Rudy Vallee; rising young comic Wally Cox; CBS commentator Edward R. Murrow; and Broadway's Mary Martin. Hayward was intrigued by the notion of Mary and Ethel performing together, and as the showstopper for the entire telecast he wanted a special duet consisting of songs they'd both made famous. While some discouraged Hayward from the notion, predicting that Broadway's two biggest musical stars would never consent to appear together on the same program, he knew that Mary and Ethel had admired each other for years. (It is part of theater lore that Ethel reportedly once said of Mary, "She's okay . . . if you like talent.") After secretly promising each one final approval of the project, Hayward got them both to sign on.

The cost of the Ford show was staggering for the time—$500,000—but the corporation's chief executive, Henry Ford II, believed that such an important anniversary warranted the expenditure. In the end, Mary and Ethel each got separate assignments as well: Ethel was to sing a Dixieland arrangement of Irving Berlin's perennial "Alexander's Ragtime Band" and also to appear in a sketch as a World War I doughboy, in which she sang "Mademoiselle from Armentières," while Mary acted in a touching scene from Thornton Wilder's *Our Town* and performed "The Shape," a hilarious solo spot that surveyed changes in women's fashion over the past fifty years. The stars were to appear together twice: in a rather routine and pointless pantomime of "Your Folks and My Folks," an old vaudeville routine, and the big medley that Hayward had dreamed up. After some discussion it was decided not to limit the duet to their Broadway hits; in fact, very few of the numbers that each singer had made famous wound up in the finished product. Instead, Ethel's "I Got Rhythm," "I Get a Kick Out of You," and "There's No Business Like Show Business" and Mary's "A Wonderful Guy" and "My Heart Belongs to Daddy" were dropped in and around a cornucopia of popular chestnuts such as "The Sheik of Araby," "When the Red, Red Robin Comes Bob, Bob, Bobbin' Along," and "Melancholy Baby." One segment of the duet featured, at Ethel's suggestion, a collection of "I" songs: "I've Got You Under My Skin," "I'd Climb the Highest Mountain," "I Love a Parade," and so on.

Rehearsals were hectic, as the duet was extremely complex and had to be timed with absolute precision. Ethel took extensive notes during rehearsals, then went home and cheerfully typed up a neat, clean copy for herself and Mary. The segment's director, Jerome Robbins, hatched the brilliant idea of having Mary and Ethel positioned on two nightclub stools: no distracting backup singers, no choreography, just a simple setting that would allow the audience to concentrate on the singers and their songs.

Mary Martin was a more jittery performer than Ethel—most performers were—and she came close to falling apart when, hours before the telecast, Hayward reported that the conductor, Jay Blackton (a favorite of Ethel's, and creator of the brilliant duet for the two women), and the pianist, Johnny Lesko (a favorite of Mary's), would not be able to perform on the show, since it had just been discovered that neither one belonged to the television union.

Mary was panicked and wanted to withdraw; while Ethel was upset, she re-
solved to do her best under trying conditions, though the disastrous final
dress rehearsal, with two substitutes for Blackton and Lesko, only confirmed
her worst fears. Just before airtime Hayward informed Ethel and Mary that
a financial arrangement had been worked out with the union that would
permit Blackton and Lesko to go on.

The duet was destined to become show-business legend on its first
hearing. Millions of homes across America were suddenly converted into
nightclubs as Ethel and Mary pulled off an amazing musical challenge: a
thirteen-minute medley that never faltered, going consistently from one peak
to another. The adrenaline kept pumping at higher and higher levels; it is
difficult to imagine that many people watching were able to remain in their
seats for long. Among the high points: Ethel's captivating and highly original
rendition of "You Made Me Love You," Mary's charming "Mississippi Mud,"
the stunning "I" songs, and a counterpoint duet of "Tea for Two" and "Stormy
Weather." Both women were in superb voice, and the medley was all the
more successful for having two such distinctive talents playing off each other.
But in the end the greater triumph was Ethel's; Mary, good as she was,
couldn't help but pale a bit next to such an electric presence. The duet also
revealed to a wide audience the habit that Bert Lahr and several of Ethel's
other costars had complained about over the years—namely, her dislike of
looking at her stage partners. While Mary reacted naturally to everything
Ethel did, Ethel was mostly a laser beam of straight-ahead concentration,
directed squarely at the television audience and no one else.

The reaction was an astonishing eye-opener for both stars. The Ford
show was variously reported as drawing between 47 million and 60 million
viewers. Never had either Mary or Ethel dreamed of reaching such a vast
audience. The reviewers had nothing but superlatives for them. The *Washington Evening Star*'s notice was typical: "It is unbelievable, right now, at
any rate, that anything could come along to top the Martin-Merman duet."

The rest of the summer was occupied with preparations for the move to
Colorado. It was not an easy thing for Ethel to pack up twenty years' worth
of belongings at the Century and contemplate saying good-bye to Mom and
Pop Zimmermann, whom she had seen on almost a daily basis for her entire
life. It was difficult for Mom and Pop, too, but they believed Six to be a worthy husband and knew in their hearts that they couldn't stand in their
daughter's way. Ultimately Ethel's possessions filled four huge moving vans.
In September the Sixes moved into their new Cherry Hills home at 26 Sunset

Ethel the stenographer: at the Bragg-Kliesrath Corporation, mid-1920s

LEFT: Ethel as Broadway first discovered her: singing "Sam and Delilah" in the Gershwins' *Girl Crazy*, with pianist Al Siegel

Ethel as a medicine show performer in *Roaming*, one of her early short films

Stopping the show with "Eadie Was a Lady" in *Take a Chance*

With William Gaxton and Victor Moore in *Anything Goes*, her first Cole Porter show—and one of the big hits of 1934

Ethel in Hollywood: with Eddie
Cantor in 1934's *Kid Millions*

As Reno Sweeney in Paramount's
1936 film of *Anything Goes*

Ethel singing the execrable
"Shanghai-Dee-Ho" in the middling
film version of *Anything Goes*, with
Bing Crosby

Midthirties portrait of Ethel

Ethel, at 20th Century Fox for *Happy Landing,* answering fan mail. Throughout her career, she never employed a secretary.

"Down the rabbit hole": Ethel and Richard Carlson in *Stars in Your Eyes,* her 1939 near flop

Ethel and Bert Lahr, uneasy costars in the Porter hit *Du Barry Was a Lady*

OPPOSITE: Ethel's first time as solo star, in *Panama Hattie* (1940), with her comic trio of sailors, Rags Ragland, Frank Hyers, and Pat Harrington

RIGHT: With the Stork Club's Sherman Billingsley: Ethel desperately hoped that he would leave his wife for her.

LEFT: Ethel's first fling at marriage, to agent William Smith in 1940

Ethel with Paula Laurence and Allen Jenkins in her final Porter show, *Something for the Boys*

Ethel rushing to a performance, 1940s

Ethel turns ballad singer in the greatest hit of her career, Irving Berlin's *Annie Get Your Gun.*

The *Annie Get Your Gun* team: director Joshua Logan, composer Irving Berlin, producers Richard Rodgers and Oscar Hammerstein, book writers Dorothy and Herbert Fields; in front: stars Ray Middleton and Ethel

With husband no. 2, Robert D. Levitt: after their divorce and his death, Ethel always called him the great love of her life.

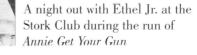

A night out with Ethel Jr. at the Stork Club during the run of *Annie Get Your Gun*

Call Me Madam's showstopper, "You're Just in Love": with Russell Nype

ABOVE: With Tallulah Bankhead and Meredith Willson rehearsing Bankhead's radio hit *The Big Show*

Ethel's disastrous third marriage was to Continental Airlines' Robert Six, here with Bobby and Ethel Jr.

Happy Hunting, with Virginia Gibson (second from left), Ethel, and Fernando Lamas (far right), whom she found the most troublesome costar of her career

Ethel goes dramatic as a hapless
horseplayer in *The U. S. Steel Hour*'s
"Honest in the Rain."

With teenaged Ethel Jr.

Ethel crowns her career as the domineering stage mother Rose in Jule Styne and Stephen Sondheim's *Gypsy*, with Mort Marshall, Karen Moore, and Jacqueline Mayro.

During *Gypsy*, Ethel got along beautifully with leading man Jack Klugman, but not so well with Sandra Church, who played Louise.

Ethel and Benay Venuta had a long, complicated friendship punctuated by many rifts. Here they are just before sharing a European vacation in 1960, during a break from *Gypsy*.

ABOVE: Ethel's first movie in nine years: the all-star comedy *It's a Mad, Mad, Mad, Mad World*, with Jonathan Winters

Ethel's new love, Ernest Borgnine, escorts her to the premiere of the movie *The Chalk Garden* in 1964.

With her grandchildren, Barbara Jean and Michael

The two people who never disappointed Ethel: her beloved parents, Edward and Agnes Zimmermann

Back where she belongs: Ethel's 1970 return to Broadway in *Hello, Dolly!* brought one ovation after another.

LEFT: Ethel launched a new phase of her career—as a concert singer—when she appeared with Arthur Fiedler and the Boston Pops in 1975.

The two queens of Broadway, Mary Martin and Ethel, reunited: at the Broadway Theatre, May 15, 1977

Ethel in her apartment at the Surrey Hotel, 1978

ABOVE: A new generation discovered Ethel with her hilarious cameo in the 1980 movie *Airplane!*

With her close friend Tony Cointreau at the Broadway revival of *My Fair Lady,* just two years before she fell ill

A seldom seen photograph from the 1960s, when her reputation as the queen of Broadway was cemented

Drive, which they dubbed "Six Acres." It had cost $79,000, and Ethel had put up the $10,000 down payment; Six claimed that with Continental's growing pains his cash flow was a bit shaky, but he assured her there was nothing to worry about and handed her a promissory note for $5,000.

From the beginning, Ethel loved the twenty-eight-room Graystone Tudor, whose interiors were dominated by carved oak walls. The previous owners had favored beige and other neutral tones for the walls, but Ethel, with her great love of color, had most of the interior repainted in turquoise and several of the rooms papered in bright chintz. In a rare display of posturing, she had the library outfitted with shelves of handsome leather-bound books, although she seldom took any of them down to read.

The children were placed in schools and got settled into their new environs. Ethel Jr. particularly delighted in her new home, whose grounds were overrun with chipmunks, black squirrels, and lots of other wildlife. Big Ethel seemed to make the transition to Rocky Mountain suburban matron with surprising ease. For years she had been developing a certain impatience with the demands of her Broadway audiences, and at last she felt she had given them their due; they could ask no more of her. She said often that she didn't miss live performing; all she wanted to do now was make the occasional television appearance and one or two movies a year. Fox was preparing another vehicle for her, and there were also some rumblings of interest from Columbia Pictures, which owned the rights to Rodgers and Hart's *Pal Joey* and was mulling over the possibility of having Ethel play the older-woman part of Vera Simpson. Everything seemed to be just as Ethel wanted it, and to interviewers she presented the confident picture of a woman who was mistress of her own fate. She told reporters that she had no intention of returning to Broadway. She was going to have a conventional, happy life at last.

Having made this bold public declaration about being through with live audiences, Ethel lost no time in accepting two performing engagements. The first, in August, was an outdoor appearance with the Denver Symphony Orchestra in the huge amphitheater at Red Rocks. It seemed an effective way of establishing good-neighbor relations in her new home, and locally her stock went skyrocketing. In October she introduced a brand-new show at the Dallas State Fair. Presented by Charles Meeker Jr., it was a revival of the big, old-time vaudeville program. Included on the bill were the ace tumbling team Los Gatos, the Wiere Brothers slapstick comedy act, veteran hoofer George Murphy of movie fame, and Ethel's good friend Russell Nype, who joined her for "You're Just in Love" and got a solo spot of his own.

On very little notice, she had paged her old friend from the pit of *Girl Crazy,* Roger Edens (who had since been busy writing and arranging for MGM musicals), to whip up an opening number for her. Called "A Lady with a Song," it was a bold statement of her down-to-earth performing style, for an audience that might not know a great deal about her.

Edens had also written "You're in Texas," a comic number in which she sang of her trepidation in bringing her own show to an area that had its own ideas about "culcher." Then she lit into a selection of songs from her Broadway shows ("I Get a Kick Out of You," "There's No Business Like Show Business"), as well as a few associated with Judy Garland ("Over the Rainbow," "Zing! Went the Strings of My Heart"). Clad in a form-fitting pink gown for the afternoon shows and basic black for evening, she knocked out her audiences and the critics, too. *Dallas Morning News* critic John Rosenfield felt that "only one other artist has been able to duplicate the Merman excitement in performance. And this was the late Italian tenor, Enrico Caruso, whose plenitudinous splendor of voice and exuberant directness of style could always set an audience on fire. Miss Merman does the same thing by almost the same means. Her voice is phenomenally big, rich, rangy and steady. She, too, can abandon herself to the mood of a tune and still seem to be holding equally much in reserve."

At first it seemed that Ethel's master plan to become a television and movie star was going to work out beautifully. In January and February of 1954, for a pair of appearances on NBC's splashy variety show *The Colgate Comedy Hour,* she was paid $50,000—the kind of money that she could have made on Broadway only by doing the eight-a-week grind for several weeks. One of these was the result of Leland Hayward's paging her to reprise her Reno Sweeney in a cut-down presentation of *Anything Goes.* Joining her were Frank Sinatra as Billy Crocker and Bert Lahr as Moonface Martin. In order to fit the one-hour time slot, the book scenes were trimmed to nothing, with some characters, like the ingenue Hope Harcourt, eliminated. With its interpolations from other Porter shows, such as "You Do Something to Me" and "Just One of Those Things," this was hardly textbook *Anything Goes.* Still, Ethel got to slam across "I Get a Kick Out of You," "Anything Goes," and "Blow, Gabriel, Blow" in her trademark style, and the segment was well received.

All of this was really just marking time while Ethel awaited the project she was banking on most. By the summer of 1954, her new film for 20th Century Fox, *There's No Business Like Show Business,* was finally ready to begin shooting. Ethel was delighted when she learned that the producer was to be Sol Siegel and the director Walter Lang, with whom she had worked so harmoniously on *Call Me Madam.*

Like *Alexander's Ragtime Band,* the new picture was conceived as a cavalcade of Irving Berlin songs, from the early days of his career to the present. What Darryl Zanuck wanted was a story about a kind of "royal family" of show business, whose triumphs and trials are viewed over a period of several decades; as with the earlier film, Zanuck hoped the format would make an effective prism through which the songs could shine. While he wanted the story to reflect a degree of seriousness, above all he stressed that it was to be "a showmanship venture; it is not a solo picture for anyone. Like *Call Me Madam,* it will have five or six roles of almost equal importance, where each star will have an opportunity to do what he or she does best."

By now the movie musical was facing hard times; fewer and fewer were being produced, and the spectacular production numbers that had prevailed in the 1940s were being scaled back. While *There's No Business Like Show Business* was to be an important, high-budget film in DeLuxe Color and using the studio's new widescreen process, CinemaScope, Zanuck's memos reflected the changing times. "I think we should avoid so-called elaborate production numbers," he wrote, "mainly because they have worn out their usefulness and audiences are becoming sick of them. . . . Our main aim in our music should be to strive for realism and personality effect rather than scope and size."

The screenplay had been begun by Lamar Trotti, who died suddenly in 1952. The project was then turned over to the studio's husband-and-wife screenwriting team of Henry and Phoebe Ephron. In a memo to the writers, Sol Siegel cautioned, "We have much more story than we need." For the part Ethel was to play, Molly Donahue, mother of the clan of performing Donahues, Siegel suggested borrowing elements from the character of the Marx Brothers' mother, Minnie, as "she was the business agent and the brains of the combination." Although they were not enthusiastic about the assignment, the Ephrons did their best to give the story focus and point. When the finished screenplay was sent to Ethel in Denver, she thought it was wonderful but worried that the role of Molly might be, in terms of dramatic scope, beyond her. Siegel did his best to reassure her, but he later recalled that once again she didn't fully calm down until after she viewed the first few days' rushes.

Fox had assembled a top-line cast to play the Five Donahues. Dan Dailey was Terry, the bighearted father of the brood. Donald O'Connor was reunited with Ethel to play Tim, the oldest son, while pop singer Johnnie Ray, who had recently had a hit single with his wailing performance of "Cry," was to play the younger son, Steve, who becomes a priest. Cast as daughter Katy was the studio's popular young singer/dancer Mitzi Gaynor. Zanuck was particularly high on having signed Ray, whose screen test he judged "simply tremendous," but Walter Lang was less enthusiastic. In November 1953 the director wrote to Ethel in Denver, "I am secretly hoping that something happens where we won't have to use [Ray] at all."

Also cast in the film was the studio's most valuable property, Marilyn Monroe. Early in 1954 she had married baseball star Joe DiMaggio, gone on suspension for several weeks, and subsequently signed a new, seven-year contract with Fox. In 1953 three of her films were among the studio's top five grossers in the United States, and two of them, *How to Marry a Millionaire* and *Gentlemen Prefer Blondes*, had easily outdistanced *Call Me Madam*. Monroe meant the future to the studio, and although she was not happy about being cast in *There's No Business Like Show Business*, she eventually came around and agreed to play the part of Vicky, the ambitious nightclub singer who breaks up the Donahues' act by stealing Tim and Katy to support her in her splashy New York show.

Ethel was suspicious of Monroe from the start, and she was not surprised when Monroe proved unreliable once filming had gotten under way. Frequently she would be late to arrive once a shot had been set up, and many hours were spent waiting for her to appear. On the positive side, Ethel became extremely close to Gaynor, who called her "Mom" both on and off the set.

During filming, Ethel remained hopeful that *There's No Business Like Show Business* would cement her new position in Hollywood. Certainly the part of Molly, in which she aged from energetic young vaudevillian to anxious mother of two sons overseas in World War II, offered her a more varied dramatic opportunity than anything she had yet attempted on either stage or screen.

Toward the end of shooting, Ethel suffered an attack of appendicitis. She was clearly in discomfort, and Sol Siegel asked her if there was anything he could do. "Don't worry," said Ethel, "I'll make it. I've met these before." Siegel insisted on calling a doctor, but Ethel was equally insistent that if she could just finish her afternoon's work and relax for a few days, the company would be able to stay on schedule. Siegel was astonished. Particularly in the face of Monroe's scattiness, Ethel's professionalism made a profound impression on him.

The production wrapped on August 27, 1954, and Ethel returned to Denver to wait for the film to be edited into what she hoped would be a colossal hit. That fall she agreed to appear in an abridged version of *Panama Hattie,* to be broadcast on CBS. As with the telecast of *Anything Goes,* there were interpolations—"Ridin' High," from *Red, Hot and Blue!* and "I Love You," from *Mexican Hayride*—but this time around, Ethel didn't come off well. Her performance seemed forced and awkward, and despite her matchless rendition of "Make It Another Old-Fashioned, Please," it was hard to argue with the *New York Times*'s Jack Gould, who thought "the show dragged badly and never achieved anything like the lilt or pep of last season's TV appearance of Miss Merman in *Anything Goes.*"

There's No Business Like Show Business was unveiled to the trade press in early December. Harry Brand, publicity chief for 20th Century Fox, sent a telegram to Ethel in Denver: DEAR ETHEL: WE HAD TRADE PAPER SHOWING OF THERE'S NO BUSINESS LIKE SHOW BUSINESS YESTERDAY AND IT WAS A SENSATIONAL SUCCESS. WITHOUT EXCEPTION ALL THE BOYS SAID IT WAS GREAT AND THEY ALL LOVED YOUR PERFORMANCE. The initial reviews confirmed Brand's report. DUST OFF ALL THE SUPERLATIVES FOR THIS ONE, headlined the *Film Daily* review, which predicted that the film would "undoubtedly roll up enormous grosses during the months ahead." *Motion Picture Daily* thought it "an excellent show" that was sure "to attract a huge crowd."

But when the film went into general release, the more discriminating reviewers took exception to the story's diffuse focus and the film's overproduction—exactly what Zanuck had cautioned against. The *New Yorker* criticized the "seedy plot" and Johnnie Ray's "caterwauling," which was one of the picture's overwhelming weaknesses; in his big religious number, "If You Believe," Ray contorted his face and torso to the degree that people in the theater could hardly have been blamed for thinking he was having some kind of seizure.

Mitzi Gaynor and Marilyn Monroe received the most critical attention, although many reviewers praised Ethel for her warm, nicely modulated performance as Molly. She was completely believable as the mother of three and always seemed to be listening to her fellow actors. In the end it might have been better if the story had concentrated on her and Dan Dailey, with side trips to the three children. It wasn't, as Siegel had judged, so much a case of too much story as one of too many characters, and audiences seemed to have difficulty caring about them. Adding to the trouble was the fact that the two new Berlin songs, Donald O'Connor's "A Man Chases a Girl Until She Catches Him" and "A Sailor's Not a Sailor Till He's Been Tattooed," the latter a labored, unfunny hornpipe with Ethel and Gaynor in sailors' uniforms and sideburns, were in no way memorable.

There's No Business Like Show Business was the kind of homespun Americana that 20th Century Fox had churned out a few too many times. While it grossed a respectable $4.5 million, such profits didn't mean much when measured against the huge production cost of $4.34 million. In her autobiography Ethel remarked flatly, "Somehow, *There's No Business Like Show Business* didn't turn out as well as *Madam*." Fox canceled plans for a third Merman vehicle, and before long Ethel knew that her dreams of a starring career in Hollywood were not to be fulfilled. By 1957 the screen musical had mostly faded from view, and it wouldn't be until the 1960s that it showed any genuine signs of life again.

After the release of *There's No Business Like Show Business*, Ethel returned to Denver, where the following months passed quietly. While working hard at being a model 1950s wife and mother, she guested on CBS's *The Shower of Stars* and *The Toast of the Town*. Apart from them, her principal project for 1954–55 was working with Pete Martin, an editor at the *Saturday Evening Post*, on a series of articles about her life that was soon to be published by Doubleday as a full-length autobiography. The book's eventual title, *Who Could Ask for Anything More?*, seemed to be a kind of summing-up. But Martin, an astute writer and editor, discerned immediately that Ethel was a study in conflict, both personally and professionally. Those closest to her, from her good chum Alice Welch to her father and mother, insisted to Martin that she was happier than she'd ever been. But while Martin found Ethel pleasant, she also seemed strangely remote. He had collaborated with both Bing Crosby and Bob Hope on their memoirs and found them delightful, but Ethel seemed to have little perspective on her spectacular career. When he probed for revealing anecdotes about the shows in which she had appeared or the many brilliant artists she had worked with, she had surprisingly little to say. Throughout much of 1955, Martin was in a state of mild panic, wondering if he was going to be able to turn in a manuscript that was in any way acceptable to his editors. In the end, *Who Could Ask for Anything More?* did a good job of capturing Ethel's voice and covering the basic facts of her career, but it failed to plumb any aspect of her life in depth. Overall, the book put forth a relentlessly shoot-from-the-hip attitude. Typical was Ethel's observation, "The way I get it, people make their own luck by putting out everything they've got, and the more they put out, the more luck they have."

When *Who Could Ask for Anything More?* was published in the summer of 1955, reviews were generally quite respectful. "Ethel on paper is as brash, brassy and breezy as Ethel onstage," wrote the *Pittsburgh Press*. A few critics were more on target. *Best Sellers* observed, "Ethel Merman's [book] exposes the reader to such a pitiless blaze of sunshine that he begins to think of mad dogs and Englishmen and long for just a bit of shade, if only for variety."

In September 1955, Ethel continued her pursuit of the mass media by agreeing to appear on CBS's highly rated *Person to Person,* hosted by Edward R. Murrow. *Person to Person* was a popular series that caught celebrities at home in their "natural" surroundings; the trouble was that given the series' rather starchy format, the celebrities usually seemed anything but natural. Ethel's segment was no exception. She greeted Murrow on the balcony of the house at Six Acres. The camera then followed her into the library, where she interacted rather formally with Six. ("How are you?" Six asked, and Ethel curtly responded, "Fine.") The children also seemed uncomfortable. Bobby, appearing quite cowed, repeatedly referred to Six as "Mr. Robert," while Ethel Jr., when asked by Murrow what she wanted to do when she grew up, seemed to be giving a pint-size press conference: "Well, Mr. Murrow, I like acting, but I don't sing. I like writing, and I've thought about being an airline stewardess. I think that would be fun." During her interview Ethel continued to hew to her own party line regarding her decision to turn her back on the stage.

"I gather," said Murrow, "you've given up Broadway and the bright lights to live in the shadows of the Rockies. How do you like it?"

"I just love it here," said Ethel. As if to complete the carefully prepared picture of domestic bliss, Rocky Mountain style, Six was observed grilling steaks marinated in garlic, soy sauce, and fresh ginger.

To the casual observer, it was all remarkably convincing. Ethel seemed to relish going to bed early, getting up in time to see the children off to school, shopping at the supermarket, heading up the local Easter Seals drive, participating in events sponsored by the Denver Chamber of Commerce, and dashing off in her new four-seater Thunderbird to meet her girlfriends for lunch. Many reporters beat a path to the door of Six Acres, always armed with the same question: would she ever return to Broadway? Always the answer was the same: an unequivocal no. "Broadway has been good to me," she was fond of saying, "but I've been good to it, too."

To her best friends, she confided that she missed her parents terribly, and occasionally she let it slip that Denver was not all it might be for a woman accustomed to Manhattan's stores and restaurants. "We've got maybe one really good store out there," she said in mid–1955, "but nothing up to the Bonwit, Bergdorf Goodman standard."

In fact, the genuine happiness of the early years of her relationship with Six was beginning to harden into a carefully constructed façade. Inactivity never agreed with Ethel; she habitually became restless and disgruntled when too much time elapsed between professional engagements. Continental Airlines was beginning to take off in a big way; all Six's hopes for the company looked to be on the brink of coming true. The result was that he was often in New York on business, leaving Ethel virtually alone in the big house. Six had a driving concern for his business interests. "Bob was a brilliant businessman," said his future sister-in-law, Jayne Meadows, "and he was *all* business." But having given up her own lucrative stage career to devote time to him and the children, Ethel was beginning to tire of his single-minded pursuit of financial success. Often when he was in New York, she would arrange to speak with him by telephone at an appointed time, but more often than not the scheduled conversation never took place. She began to try tracking him down, usually for the purpose of confronting him. He in turn began to resent being disturbed at the Ritz Towers or any of the other places he favored in Manhattan. Brutal quarrels, via telephone, frequently ensued. Ethel's worst fears began to surface: her history with Bob Levitt suddenly seemed to be repeating itself.

As always when faced with a personal dilemma, she sought to lose herself in work. In November 1955 she made her London debut, performing "There's No Business Like Show Business" at the Victoria Palace's royal variety show, with the queen, the Duke of Edinburgh, the Queen Mother, and Princess Margaret in attendance. In March 1956 she made her first attempt at a nonsinging role when she appeared in a half-hour condensation of George Kelly's *Reflected Glory* on the popular CBS anthology series *GE Theatre.* Perhaps it was the subject that struck a chord with her: *Reflected Glory* deals with a successful actress forced to choose between career and family. The kinescope of this telecast appears not to have survived, and Ethel refers to it rather dismissively in her autobiography, indicating that she did not feel her performance made the grade. But clearly her appetite to play serious parts had been whetted, because shortly afterward she made another dramatic appearance, on an episode of another anthology series, *The U.S. Steel Hour.* This time she was cast in an original teleplay by Mort Thaw called "Honest in the Rain," in which she played Libby, an aging spinster who tries desperately to conceal from her drab, middle-aged fiancé the fact that she is a compulsive gambler who has lost their entire joint savings account by playing the horses. The hourlong live telecast traced Libby's efforts to win back her losses, which only sends her further into debt. Ultimately she is picked up in a police raid and has to tell her shocked fiancé the truth.

It is tempting to see certain parallels between Libby's life and Ethel's own. Libby's closest relationship has been with her mother and father, and she began gambling as a way of filling the hours after they died. The fiancé, Henry, also seems to be primarily a source of anxiety: "Does he love me or does he only need me?" Libby wonders. "I need. But Henry isn't ready—he isn't ready to be needed."

Ethel was badly photographed in the segment, looking haggard and far older than the character's supposed age. Although she performed with heart and conviction, the reviews seemed designed to discourage her from any further dramatic outings. *Variety* found that the drama was "overboard on corny sentimentality" and that Ethel gave "a superficial walk-through of a poorly conceived part."

No films of interest presented themselves—*Pal Joey* would eventually go to Rita Hayworth—and Ethel began to grow more and more restless. In the late winter of 1956, she gave an interview to the *New York Times* in which she casually mentioned, "I may be back on Broadway in a musical next season." By April it was official: Ethel would return to Broadway the following fall. To the press she maintained that all was well at home in Denver. "This is strictly a one-show deal," she insisted.

The name of the new show was *Happy Hunting*. Her old friends Howard Lindsay and Russel Crouse had signed on to write the libretto. The score was to be written by newcomers Harold Karr (music) and Matt Dubey (lyrics), and she told reporters that she was looking forward to it very much.

Happy Hunting was a musical brought to life for all the wrong reasons. The wellspring of the show was Robert Six's greed and ambition. He had already grown dissatisfied with his marriage to Ethel Merman, Retired Broadway Star. To his way of thinking, if he had gone to the trouble of marrying Ethel Merman, she should remain in the limelight; there was much greater dollar-for-dollar value to Continental in having her in the full glare of the public eye. Now that Hollywood had once again turned its back on her, Six began prodding her to think about returning to Broadway. With that, her lovely dream of domestic quietude began to crumble.

Many songwriters had tried to lure Ethel back to the stage by sending her their scores, in either complete or partial form. Even Irving Berlin had tried to cajole her into doing a show he had partially written called *The Last Resorts*. Always the answer was no. Harold Karr and Matt Dubey, then, were extremely lucky to find her in a receptive mood when they flew out to Denver and auditioned their songs for the show that would become *Happy Hunting*. Ethel was not overly impressed, but in the face of Six's enthusiasm she agreed to consider the project. Six hammered away at her, telling her that he thought the score, even in its incomplete form, sounded like the basis for a tremendous hit.

Other pressures were brought to bear, too: Jo Mielziner, who had designed *Stars in Your Eyes* and *Annie Get Your Gun*, wanted to produce as well as design the show, and he worked overtime trying to persuade her that she should commit to it. So did Abe Burrows, one of Broadway's hottest directors since his success with *Guys and Dolls* and *Can-Can*. Six began canvassing several of his business associates to put up money for the show, and when Howard Lindsay and Russel Crouse expressed interest in writing the book, Ethel found herself outnumbered. Since it was so important to Six that she sign on, she decided to be a good wife and gave in.

Her own motives weren't entirely innocent. Like Six, she was driven partly by avarice. Anna Crouse felt that her decision to do *Happy Hunting* showed "one of her weaknesses. She said, 'I don't like these big composers getting all this money.' " Ethel reasoned that taking a chance on an unknown team might work to her advantage financially; it would be easy enough to refuse to do the show unless she gained leverage over the songwriters on the percentage of the show's profits. She was also beginning to worry a bit about her finances. Although she was well fixed for the moment, a great deal of money was going out, and not much was coming in. When they married, she and Six had agreed to split all expenses fifty-fifty, but in recent months she felt that she had been burdened with more than her fair share. Whenever the family flew anywhere on Continental, the airlines billed Ethel for three-quarters of the fares—for herself, Ethel Jr., and Bobby. There were many other bookkeeping habits of Six's that she was beginning to question, and she thought the best solution for the time being might be to return to work.

Harold Karr and Matt Dubey had a small reputation as special-material writers for nightclub performers, but neither one could remotely be called an exceptional talent. What they had was the particular brand of enthusiasm specific to amateurs; Karr, in fact, was a dentist who had long dreamed of writing a Broadway hit. (That same season Betty Comden and Adolph Green reportedly used him as the basis for their comic character Dr. Kitchell, the sad-sack dentist who longs to be a composer, in their hit show *Bells Are Ringing*.)

Lindsay and Crouse came up with a topical-themed plot based on Grace Kelly's much-publicized wedding to Prince Rainier of Monaco; clearly, they were hoping that lightning would strike a second time, as it had when they based *Call Me Madam* on current headlines. The end result in this case was a dead-end variation on the by-now-crusty-with-age formula of Ethel Merman musicals: brassy American dame remains true to her own code and comes out on top in the end. Lindsay and Crouse threw together a story about Liz Livingston, a rich, boisterous American widow from Philadelphia who desperately wants to get her pretty young daughter, Beth, into society but has consistently been snubbed by Philly's Main Line crowd. Mother and daughter show up in Monaco expecting to be invited to the big wedding, only to find out that once again they have been excluded. The mother meets the handsome heir to the Spanish throne and determines to win him for her daughter, thus guaranteeing their entry into the aristocracy, but winds up falling for him herself.

Abe Burrows felt that the most important part of directing a show was to cast it properly. Finding a leading man for *Happy Hunting* proved tricky:

Burrows needed an actor with sex appeal and charisma, yet someone who was willing to take a backseat to Ethel. For a time Georges Guétary, the French performer who had sung "I'll Build a Stairway to Paradise" in MGM's 1951 Oscar-winning film *An American in Paris*, was considered. But Six and his fellow backers felt that a bigger name was needed, and eventually, ex-MGM contract star Fernando Lamas was signed for the part.

Ethel had casting approval, and a number of girls read for the part of her daughter, Beth. Several were highly sophisticated, which, unfortunately, was not the point: the role of Beth wasn't supposed to be a Grace Kelly, but more on the order of Debbie Reynolds. One of those who tried out was Virginia Gibson, a promising, fresh newcomer with a few Hollywood films to her credit, among them *Seven Brides for Seven Brothers*. At Gibson's final audition, Ethel was sitting out front, and the creative team wanted to know if she needed to see Gibson dance. "I don't know anything about dancing," Ethel responded. "You say she can dance, that's fine with me."

Gibson won the role, but she was carefully instructed by her agent on how to behave. "When I went to rehearsal," Gibson recalled, "the agent said, 'Don't talk with her. Just say good morning and then sit down.' So I would say, 'Good morning,' and I would sit on one side, and she was on the other side. And one day she came over to me and said, 'Why don't you come over and sit with me?' They all acted so afraid of her. That's what I don't understand." Although Gibson allowed that Ethel could no doubt be difficult, she felt that "there was no BS with her. Everything was straight out— just honest and straightforward."

Ethel was to pay a high price for her desire to exert financial leverage over her composing team, since the score was unquestionably the weakest of any show she had ever accepted. Her ballads never really paid off. One waited in vain for her first-act closer, "This Is What I Call Love," to hit home, and the same was true of her second-act solo, "The Game of Love." She struggled to make them work by the sheer force of her personality. The Merman magic was there, but it was diminished, because the material wasn't on the level to which she had become accustomed.

Rehearsals for *Happy Hunting* got off to a bumpy start thanks to a tactless remark by composer Harold Karr. Reportedly, while Ethel was singing one of her numbers on the first day of rehearsal, Karr delivered a chilling verdict: "If I'd wanted it sung that way, I would have written it that way." After a terrifying silence, Ethel turned to Burrows and, pointing at Karr, said, "That man is never to speak to me again." None of the surviving cast members interviewed for this book recalls the incident, but Virginia Gibson remembers that Ethel was unhappy with the score from the start. Karr and Dubey had a way of growing quite defensive if one song or another didn't meet with Ethel's satisfaction, and although they would go off to try to polish their work, they didn't have the ability to come up with great showstoppers under pressure. Ethel was especially displeased with her opening number, and she complained until it was replaced with the rousing "Gee, But It's Good to Be Here."

The show's one good piece was a duet for Ethel and Gibson called "Mutual Admiration Society," and of all the tunes in the score it seemed to be the one most likely destined for hit status, but even it had a difficult time. Burrows had staged the number to be sung by the two women in profile, face-to-face, until Dubey objected, "Oh, Miss Merman—your voice is going to go into the wings." Another terrifying silence. Then Ethel, in a cold fury, responded, "My voice will *never* go into the wings." The staging remained as it was.

Rehearsals limped along, hampered by the quality of the music. "Happy Hunting," a lavish ensemble number for the second act, refused to be pulled into focus. Ethel grew increasingly uncomfortable with the material. Mark Zeller, a member of the ensemble, recalled that the new songwriting team "didn't give the impression of being conscious of other writers. They seemed very self-aggrandized in a way, confident about who they were, almost like someone who writes a great song in college. I would say stuff was asked of them that they couldn't deliver. They would come in [after being asked for rewrites] and look a little funny, and there was nothing fixed. It was a real puzzle."

As the out-of-town premiere in Philadelphia loomed, Ethel began to panic. She was at a crucial age for an actress—forty-eight—and she knew that starring parts on Broadway would not continue forever. Because Six and so many of his business cronies had invested in *Happy Hunting*, she felt more responsible than ever for delivering a big, big hit. Always the best judge of her material, she knew instinctively that she was saddled with a potential flop. The book that Lindsay and Crouse had come up with, entirely dependent on rather crude and obvious joke setups, was no more distinguished than the Dubey and Karr score. Asked by the Duke of Granada whether she knows the difference between Bourbon and Hapsburg, Liz Livingston replies, "Sure. One's whiskey and one's beer." When the duke mentions that one day he will be King Jaime, Liz observes, "You'll be the first Hymie that ever was a king." The musical numbers did not grow naturally out of the script; they were dropped in, with a resounding thud.

Initially Ethel seemed pleased that her new show had attracted the presence of a big, handsome movie star like Fernando Lamas. He was a stunning, sexy Argentine leading man with a strong voice, and he had shown off both qualities in films such as *The Merry Widow* (1952) and *Rose Marie* (1954). His MGM contract had expired in 1954, the same year he married Arlene Dahl, one of Hollywood's most beautiful actresses. With his peak Hollywood years behind him, he was looking for a worthy Broadway vehicle, and *Happy Hunting* seemed just the ticket.

While some company members thought Lamas pompous and humorless, others found him pleasant and companionable. As Virginia Gibson recalled, "Well, I just thought *movie star*. And his wife, Arlene Dahl, was always around and dressed to the nines. Merman was a big star, but she never had that movie-star thing that they had." Lamas's professionalism, however, remained in question. Early on, he loudly objected, in front of the entire company, to Ethel's familiar habit of throwing her lines out front rather than directly to him. On another occasion, when the show was being tried out in Philadelphia, supporting player Seth Riggs and several of the other actors were reporting to work when suddenly a ravishing blonde pulled up in a convertible and called out to Lamas. The actor turned to his fellow company members and said, "Tell them I'll be an hour late for rehearsal." According to Riggs, "He jumped over the side, didn't even open the door, and they went off." Lamas was also bored by the ritual of the stage manager's sharing his notes at the end of each day's work. One day in his dressing room, he was stark naked, washing off his stage makeup, and looking, Riggs recalled, "like a monster from the deep." The stage manager, Robert Downing, appeared in the doorway with a sheet of notes, and Lamas suddenly exploded, "SHUT THE FUCK UP!" Then he flung himself out of his chair and, still buck naked, chased Downing out onto the stage, screaming, "I'M GOING TO KILL YOU, YOU SON OF A BITCH!"

Unfortunately for Lamas his reception at the Philadelphia opening put Ethel on the defensive and gave credence to the by-now-widespread rumors that she could be tough on other players who tried to steal the spotlight. Incredibly, the trouble seems to have stemmed from the white suit that Irene Sharaff had designed for Lamas to wear in the show. Lamas's penis size was already the stuff of Hollywood legend, and he had requested that Sharaff design his costume to be as tight as possible, so he could show off his endowment. The result didn't satisfy him, and he ordered the pants to be recut for maximum effect. His ploy worked. On opening night in Philadelphia, he stepped out onstage in the dazzling white suit, with a matching California coat tossed around his shoulders. A chorus of gasps, from both women and men, swept over the theater. "Nobody looked at Merman," said Riggs, "and she was furious."

Bob Ullman, then working as a publicist for Karr and Dubey, also recalled Ethel's pique. "Lamas was no big talent," said Ullman. "He wore no underwear, and he was hung like a horse." Several of the company members heard Ethel scream at the stage manager in the wings, "I had people out front! I know what's going on! You tell him to wear a goddamn jockstrap!" But Lamas, whose movie-star status made him a costar with more clout than usual in a Merman show, refused to alter a thing. At the time, Arlene Dahl was in New York with her husband; Dahl remembered that "Fernando used to call Ethel 'the Mack Truck.' He'd say, 'She's run all over her leading men, but not me.' "

Ethel did a slow, deep burn while the reviews came in. Given the rickety condition of the show, the critics were surprisingly kind: the *Philadelphia Inquirer* complained that the show had "too much plot," but the *Philadelphia Daily News* said that "Miss Merman brings a formidable zest to everything she does." *Variety* admitted that the show had its "sodden spots" but felt that over the course of the six-week tryout it would shape up to be box-office gold once it reached Broadway. The best news was already coming from the cashier's windows: the Philadelphia run was sold out from the start, and during the show's second week there the box-office take was $60,280—a new house record for the Shubert.

The Boston notices also indicated a hit in the making. "Boisterous and hilarious," wrote the *Boston Advertiser*, adding that Ethel was "never better in her life." But the quality of the show was not improving significantly, and Ethel knew it. So did Lindsay and Crouse, who frantically reworked scene after scene, to little effect. An atmosphere of desperation prevailed, perhaps best personified by the ever-anxious, ever-perspiring Abe Burrows, who stood in the wings with a stopwatch; if a certain number of seconds elapsed without a laugh, he insisted that the authors insert one.

By the time *Happy Hunting* got to New York, the advance sale amounted to $1.5 million, but word had reached Broadway gossipmongers from the road that *Happy Hunting* was several notches below the Merman standard. During rehearsals at the Majestic Theatre, Arlene Dahl was frequently present backstage, and her stunning green-eyed, red-haired beauty seemed to rankle Ethel. One day Dahl was decorating Lamas's dressing room in his favorite color scheme of black and white, with shades of red. Ethel passed by the open door, stopped, surveyed the nearly finished result, and said to

Dahl, "It looks like a bordello. Well, he'll be right at home!" Later, Dahl, remembered, her renovation of Lamas's dressing room met with favorable comments and even wound up being photographed for a couple of magazine layouts. "Ethel called in a designer," said Dahl, "and had him redo her dressing room a couple of times. Not once, but twice. So childish."

But on opening night, when Ethel made her entrance, all the backstage tensions and the show's mediocre quality suddenly seemed unimportant. The ovation was deafening. This was more than an opening; it was a homecoming, a warm and ecstatic welcome back from the queen's self-imposed exile out west. When she finished "Gee, But It's Good to Be Here," the song's title seemed to take on a double meaning.

This was Broadway, expressing its love for one of its own. The screams and cheers reached a fantastic pitch, and for a while there seemed to be few worries. "Mutual Admiration Society" was warmly received, and the first act bounced along at a reasonably merry pace. But the faults of the leaden second act could not be hidden, even before an audience of well-wishers in the mood to welcome Ethel back to her rightful home. The new musical had worn out its appeal long before the final curtain descended. Standing at the back of the Majestic, Anna Crouse was in tears, "because you could tell that they were sitting there hating it."

The critics, delighted to have Ethel back, were generally kind. After allowing that the score was "hardly more than adequate," the *New York Times*'s Brooks Atkinson wrote that Ethel was "as brassy as ever, glowing like a neon light whenever she steps on the stage, full of self-confidence and band concert music. . . . Welcome home, Miss Merman. The neighborhood is always a little more jaunty when you are here." John McCain, writing in the *New York Journal-American*, called Ethel "ageless and individual; she can still sell a song better than anybody in the business. This new Russel Crouse–Howard Lindsay is by no means the happiest material she has ever dealt with, neither is the score by Matt Dubey and Harold Karr, but it doesn't matter. Big Merm just simply gets out there and takes charge. She swaggers and struts. Her numbers can be heard comfortably in Hohokus, NJ, and when she delivers a joke line, she will come down in the audience and hit you with the juvenile if you don't laugh. She is plainly the greatest."

Although she was disappointed in the way the show had turned out—forever after she would refer to it as "a jeep among limousines"—Ethel was determined to make it a hit, as much for Six and their fellow investors as for the sake of her own theatrical reputation. "If you watched her," recalled Mark Zeller, "she did the same thing exactly every night. She did her work in such a way that she needed to depend on things being the same. She couldn't deal with distractions, because it threw her. When someone was out front who was important to her, there was an extra charge, and it seemed like a different performance, but if you looked at it, she did exactly the same thing. It could be her cousin—not necessarily someone famous. But there was an emotional charge."

Jack Dabdoub, a member of the ensemble, remembered the impact that Ethel's voice could have on audience members. One night a little suntanned man was sitting at the front of the orchestra section, smiling and smiling as the show began. "He looked like he was anticipating Ethel coming onstage," said Dabdoub. "And then she sang 'Gee, But It's Good to Be Here,' and of course that high note on 'Here' was a money note for her. And I looked out in the audience, and this nice little man's face crumbled, and he reached in his pocket, and I realized he had a hearing aid. And the rest of the show, he had his hand inside his coat whenever she was onstage."

Six was frequently on the scene during the run of the show, and whatever was happening privately, it seemed to the members of the company that she was still very much a woman in love. She called him "Big Bear" and still acted downright girlish in his presence. To Helene Whitney, now appearing in her third consecutive Merman show, Ethel seemed more relaxed with the company than ever. Frequently during the big ensemble numbers, she would turn her back to the audience and try her best to break up the girls in the chorus. Much of the time she was making a dig at Fernando Lamas, whom she had not forgiven for the business of the tight white suit. She was as generous as ever, throwing lots of parties for the cast. At one of these, Virginia Gibson recalled, "Some of the kids were saying that they had seen Mary Martin in *Annie Get Your Gun*. And they were saying, 'Oh, but she is not as good as *you*,' and carrying on. So I said, after one glass of wine, 'Well, I love Mary Martin.' And there's a deathly silence. And she looks at me and says, 'I agree with Virginia. I love Mary Martin, too.' She didn't like to be BS'd."

Several months into the run, Ethel decided that something had to be done to spruce up Karr and Dubey's listless score. In particular, she'd had it with "This Is What I Call Love" and "The Game of Love." She saw to it that they were replaced with two fresh numbers, respectively, "Just a Moment Ago" and "I'm Old Enough to Know Better," but neither one came from the workshop of Karr and Dubey. They were written, at Ethel's request, by her old pal Roger Edens, who, because of his exclusive contract with MGM, didn't take credit but used his good friend Kay Thompson as his "front." Although the new songs were not outstanding, they were far better than what they replaced, and they gave the show a much-needed lift. Still, going back for another look at the show with its new material, *Variety* warned its readers that "not even the new songs or a top-form Ethel Merman can hide the fact that *Happy Hunting* is uninspired musical comedy."

Despite the fact that she received a Tony nomination for Best Actress in a Musical (losing to Judy Holliday in *Bells Are Ringing*), *Happy Hunting* brought Ethel little pleasure. And an incident with Gene Wesson, a member of the supporting cast, brought her a dose of frustration and anxiety. Wesson was being screen-tested for the role of John Barrymore in a forthcoming biopic, *Too Much, Too Soon*. In order to look convincing as the aging Barrymore, Wesson dyed his brown hair with touches of gray. Ethel noticed and objected immediately, and the show's management ordered Wesson to restore his hair to its original color. With such an important film opportunity hanging in the balance, Wesson refused, and suddenly he found himself fired. (To compound his problems, Errol Flynn got the part of John Barrymore.) In an interview with Sheilah Graham for her popular syndicated column, Wesson pointed to Ethel as the one responsible for his dismissal from the company, and Ethel lost no time in filing charges against him with Actors' Equity, under the rule that forbade any union member to take action detrimental to another union member. When Equity sided with her, issuing an apology to her on Wesson's behalf, the actor filed a $100,000 damages suit against the union on the grounds that it had "improperly censured" him as a result of Ethel's complaint and that he faced professional ostracism. Eventually Ethel was subpoenaed for an appearance in New York State Supreme Court in connection with the case, but her lawyer, again Paul O'Dwyer, argued that since she was not a party to the suit, she could not be subpoenaed in the matter. The case dragged on before it was finally resolved in Equity's favor. Wesson never again appeared in a Broadway show.

The run ground on, and the troubles with Lamas never really dissipated. He and Ethel were still not on speaking terms, although for the most part they kept their differences out of view of the rest of the company, until one night an onstage spat brought matters to a rather bizarre and inexplicable head. The end of the show had been blocked with both Ethel and Lamas downstage; he was to turn her around and walk her upstage while she delivered an aside to the audience over her shoulder. At this particular performance, Ethel's tight-fitting dress suddenly split all the way down her back. The rest of the company stood in the wings wondering what was going to happen. Lamas saved the situation by deftly pulling off his polo coat and draping it over Ethel's shoulders so they could finish the scene. "It was the most gentlemanly, wonderful thing," recalled Mark Zeller, "and a perfect opportunity for her to say thank you, to end this silly business." Instead, once they were offstage, she turned on Lamas with the full-voltage Merman fury, accusing him of spoiling her exit. Eventually Equity reprimanded Lamas—surely at Ethel's prodding—for various alleged offenses, including stepping on her lines, obstructing her curtain call, and ignoring notes from stage manager Robert Downing.

But if Ethel's never-forgive-and-never-forget position caused a major breach with her costar, she could be quite kind to the members of the company she liked and trusted. Very late in the run of *Happy Hunting*, Virginia Gibson received a tempting offer to appear as a regular on television's *Your Hit Parade*. Knowing that the show was soon to close and that stars were famous for not wanting to break in replacements, Gibson nervously approached Ethel with her dilemma. Ethel listened and after a moment said, "Do you think it will be better for you?" Gibson again said yes. "Well, are you going to get more money?" asked Ethel. Gibson again said yes. "Okay," said Ethel. "You can go."

On November 30, 1957, *Happy Hunting* closed after 412 performances. The show had become nothing more than a dreary obligation to Ethel, and she was relieved to see it come to an end. At the same time, she was concerned that such an inferior vehicle not be her theatrical swan song. "I'd like to do one more big show," she told a reporter shortly before *Happy Hunting* closed, "and then call it finis, as far as Broadway is concerned." Soon it was announced that she would return for the fall season in a new musical, *The Lady from Colorado*, about Katie Lauder, the Centennial State's first titled lady. The show never materialized, and it was probably a good thing, for it sounded like a retread of the old Merman formula. With the continued move toward ever-more-sophisticated shows such as *My Fair Lady* (1956) and groundbreaking ones such as *West Side Story* (1957), the prototypical Merman vehicle was looking even more like a dinosaur. Ethel was becoming a bit edgy about her professional status. She knew she could not afford to waste her talents on another turkey like *Happy Hunting*; she needed a change of pace, something with greater dramatic heft. But such a show might not be easy to find: she was now fifty, and the Merman legend seemed carved in marble. On top of that, she had no guarantees that her voice would hold up through her postmenopausal years. The rise of rock and roll had also dramatically altered the musical landscape, and she knew that there was every chance she might not be able to hang on to her audience in this time of rapidly changing tastes.

On Broadway, more was changing than the audience's taste in shows. The question of exactly when amplification arrived on Broadway is much debated among theater historians. Various forms of amplification had existed as far back as *Billy Rose's Jumbo* in 1935 and Earl Carroll's *Vanities* in 1940. By the early 1960s, the process of installing "foot mikes"—microphones positioned along the footlight troughs—was firmly in place. This period marked the beginning of what would become the steady rise of amplification on Broadway. In the 1961 musical *Carnival!*, Anna Maria Alberghetti wore a body mike, fastened to her lapel; when she turned suddenly from side to side, the sound could vary considerably, and the device gave her no end of trouble. (*Carnival*'s director, Gower Champion, was, as historian Mark N. Grant points out, an early proponent of sound enhancement.) This period also marked the beginning of the end of singers like Ethel, who could reach the last row in the balcony without the assistance of a microphone. A new generation was in the making, one that had grown up never hearing unamplified sound in the musical theater.

Despite reports that its producers had taken a $30,000 loss, *Happy Hunting* had made money. Still, it had not been the bonanza that Six had hoped for, and he made no secret of his disappointment. Nothing wounded Ethel more deeply than the feeling that she had been used, and that feeling was being driven home on a daily basis. Quarrels between the Sixes broke out with greater and greater frequency. Ethel tried her best to concentrate on raising the children, who were doing their best to cope with the growing atmosphere of hostility between their mother and Six. It was particularly hard for Ethel Jr., by now a sweet and rather shy teenager who was very conscious of dividing her time fairly between her parents. During the run of *Happy Hunting*, Virginia Gibson had taken Ethel Jr. ice-skating at Rockefeller Center. Afterward, as they sipped hot chocolate, the girl suddenly became anxious and asked, "What time is it?" "She didn't want to be late for meeting her father," observed Gibson. "She was very concerned with everybody."

The children's relations with Bob Levitt became even more emotionally charged in light of the fact that Six was rapidly revealing himself to be something of an ogre as a stepfather. He was especially mean-spirited and belittling where Bobby was concerned, and although Ethel often fought with him over the issue, she was hopeful that peace would eventually reign; the last thing she wanted was for Ethel Jr. and Bobby to suffer the fallout of yet another broken home.

In the intervening years, the intense pain of Ethel's divorce from Bob Levitt had been ameliorated to the extent that the two of them were once again on reasonably friendly terms. There was seldom any trouble about visiting rights—he usually had Ethel Jr. and Bobby every summer at his home in East Hampton, Long Island—and he and Ethel relaxed into something closer to the old, joking relationship they had enjoyed in the early days of their courtship and marriage. But Bob was also a continued source of sadness for Ethel. His career had seesawed dramatically. At the time of his divorce from Ethel, he had still been with the Hearst Corporation, as associate publisher of the *American Weekly* and the comic weekly *Puck*. In mid-1953 he became publisher of both publications and was given a vice presidency, but by 1955 he had been fired from the company. He took a job with Screen Gems, the television subsidiary of Columbia Pictures, but lasted there only a short time before being named president of California National Productions, an NBC subsidiary that produced television films. He managed to hang on there until December 1957, when he once again found himself unemployed. To Ethel, Bob "just seemed to go haywire," but the real trouble was that his problems with depression and alcohol had never received proper attention.

On top of everything else, he had bad luck with women. For a time he dated the beautiful movie actress Linda Darnell, but she had her own battles with alcoholism, and the relationship soon ended. In 1952 he married Sherry Shadburne, but their life together was a rocky one. To some of Ethel's friends and colleagues, Sherry seemed rather flashy and cheap. She had a habit of dolling up Little Ethel in gaudy clothes, including rhinestone shoes, that her mother deemed inappropriate. In 1956, Levitt divorced Sherry, and late the following year he married Barbara Kazanjian. Ethel hoped that he might at last find the happiness that had so far eluded him, but, conversely, she had begun to have serious regrets about the fact that their own marriage had not endured. Ethel worried about Levitt, and she may have made some of her concerns known to Six, who was far from a sympathetic audience. More and more she began to wonder whether Levitt might have been better off if she had stayed married to him.

On January 28, 1958, Ethel's worst fears for Levitt were realized when he was found dead in his Long Island home. The Suffolk County district attorney's office announced that the cause of death was an overdose of barbiturates, and there was no confusion whatsoever about whether it was an accident. Nearly twenty bottles of drugs and sleeping pills were found around the house, which made it appear that Bob had long been planning his suicide, accumulating a store of drugs until he had enough to do himself in. (Bob had been relying heavily on barbiturates for some time; following a lengthy investigation into his death, a New York pharmacist named Joseph Sachs had his license suspended for six months and was fined $2,000 for selling "habit-forming, dangerous, and new drugs without prescriptions.") Levitt left a note stipulating that his estate was to be split between Ethel Jr. and Bobby, except for a house in Sag Harbor that he'd bought a number of years earlier; in an unusual bequest, this was left to Lulu Wyche, a maid who had cared for the family. No bequest whatsoever was made to his third wife.

Ethel was devastated. Again her black-and-white view of the world had left her completely unequipped to deal with anything as complex as Bob's death. She simply could not and would not permit herself to fathom the conflicting, tormenting forces that had led him to such a sad end. Her grief was tinged with anger; in her autobiography she refers to Bob's suicide as "this horrible thing." Mostly what she felt was bottomless sorrow and guilt; she could not help but wonder if the tragedy would have occurred had their marriage survived.

The bitter arguments with Bob, the drinking, the suspected infidelities— all of his failings were now not forgotten but simply put aside. Bob had been a wonderful man, she insisted, and a great love of her life; in time he would graduate to *the* great love. In order to give her feelings a tangible weight, Ethel always carried around two mementos of him. After Bob's estate was probated, she was informed that his personal jewelry was to go to her. Years earlier she had given him a stunning set of cuff links and studs, made of crystal, diamonds, and onyx. She took them to her favorite jeweler and had them made into a bracelet, which she wore frequently. There was also a handsome Omega watch, engraved with Bob's initials; Ethel had it refitted with a solid gold band and wore it every day.

This low point in her life was only made worse by Six's callous and insensitive behavior. If Ethel had had serious doubts about her third marriage before, they were confirmed by Six's actions on the day Bob Levitt's body was discovered. Trying to control herself as best she could, Ethel gathered Ethel Jr. and Bobby together and broke the news that their father was dead. Bobby burst into tears and ran into his bedroom. When Ethel got up to console him, Six took her firmly by the arm and told her that if she made any move to comfort the boy, he would walk out the door and never return.

Chapter Sixteen

O ne morning in 1958, several months after *Happy Hunting* had closed,
Mark Zeller ran into Ethel while crossing Fifth Avenue. She was
carrying a script under her arm, and she looked jubilant. "Mark,"
she crowed, grabbing Zeller's hand excitedly, "I have the greatest script—
finally!"

It was Arthur Laurents's book for a new show called *Gypsy*, and it was
the most unusual and substantial project Ethel had yet been offered. After
Happy Hunting she had finally tired of playing blowsy, diamond-in-the-rough
musical-comedy parts, and she was eager to show that she could do something of a serious nature—hoping, no doubt, that she would be able to blot
out people's memories of *Happy Hunting*. *Gypsy* came along just when she
needed it most.

The show had begun with *Gypsy*, a memoir by America's striptease
queen, Gypsy Rose Lee. Much of the book was taken up with the very funny
(if heavily embroidered) account of Gypsy's early years, when, as Louise
Hovick, she traversed the country with her sister, June (who grew up to be
the actress June Havoc) and their mother, Rose, trying to break into big-
time vaudeville. Shortly after it was published in 1957, the book came to the
attention of David Merrick, who had in recent years become one of the most
powerful producers on Broadway. Merrick glimpsed its possibilities as a
stage musical and wasted no time in buying the theatrical rights.

On Broadway, Merrick was a law unto himself, a relentlessly brutal,
tough, yet undeniably imaginative producer who would go to any lengths to
guarantee that his shows succeeded. With the 1954 Harold Rome musical
Fanny, he helped to revolutionize the way in which Broadway shows were
promoted. He went into overdrive to sell it on radio and television, and he
even had stickers slapped up in public restrooms posing the question "Have
you seen *Fanny*?" Purists were shocked, but Merrick's strategy worked: despite middling notices, *Fanny* became a hit. In 1957, when his production
of John Osborne's *Look Back in Anger* was slipping at the box office, Merrick

paid a woman $250 to get out of her seat, climb up onstage, and slap actor
Kenneth Haigh, playing the troubled hero, across the face. The story was
picked up by newspapers everywhere, and *Look Back in Anger* played to full
houses for months. Merrick could be insulting to the show's creators if there
was trouble during out-of-town tryouts. He was particularly hard on actors,
whom he generally regarded as dirt under his feet. He considered himself a
bold and creative producer but was not an enthusiastic member of the theatrical community as a whole, in part because he felt that few of his colleagues could match him for brains and talent. "There's a horse's ass for
every light on Broadway," he once said dismissively.

For *Gypsy*, Merrick had joined forces with a coproducer, Leland Hayward, who had Jerome Robbins under contract. Robbins was the man Merrick wanted to direct and choreograph *Gypsy*. Robbins and Arthur Laurents
had recently collaborated on *West Side Story*, a show that had enlarged the
scope of what had been deemed possible in musical theater. They'd fought
bitterly during rehearsals, and Laurents was not keen to collaborate with
Robbins again, especially after he read Gypsy Rose Lee's book and found
little to interest him. It was only after a chance meeting with Selma Lynch, a
woman who claimed to have had an affair with Gypsy's hard-driving stage
mother, Rose Hovick, that he became interested in the story's possibilities.
Robbins had conceived of *Gypsy* as a kind of colorful, affectionate tribute to
the long-gone world of burlesque, and had even signed up a string of novelty
and animal acts. Laurents had other ideas: to him the truly compelling story
was not so much Gypsy as Rose, a willful, resourceful woman who would
stop at nothing to see that her two young daughters met with show-business
success. (While they toured the vaudeville circuit, staying in a series of flea-
bag hotels, Rose would frequently lift various items, justifying her actions by
snapping, "What they charge us for this room—they *owe* us that ashtray.")
Rose did in fact have a great deal in common with David Merrick.

Laurents set to work with a fire in his head, and though Robbins clung
to the idea that *Gypsy* should unfold as a parade of vaudeville and burlesque
routines, Laurents insisted that that part of the story was incidental. He
stressed that *Gypsy* was really about "the need for recognition, a need everyone has in one way or another." In a short time, a powerful story line emerged
about Rose, a domineering stage mother who dreams of stardom for her talented daughter June. Although she succeeds in building June into a popular
headliner on the prestigious Orpheum Circuit, the girl rebels and runs off to
get married. Rose's response is to focus all her energies on her older daughter, Louise. No matter that the girl lacks June's singing and dancing abilities:

Rose will not give up until her baby becomes a star. And Louise does just that, though not exactly in the way Rose had hoped. Quite by accident she steps into a strip number in a seedy Kansas City burlesque house and in time transforms herself into Gypsy Rose Lee, the wittiest and most elegant stripper in America.

Of all Broadway musical books, *Gypsy*'s may very well be the best crafted, the leanest, the sharpest, the funniest, the most disturbing and revealing. Much of its swift pace and strong point of view no doubt stem from the fact that Laurents knew exactly where he was going along the way, because he had the sense to write the ending first. What he devised was quite unlike any other musical finale: Gypsy has finally had enough of her mother's interference and, in an angry confrontation scene in her dressing room, tells Rose that she has to let go and let her live her own life. Yet for Rose this seems all but impossible. After a lifetime of scheming and sacrifice, how can she simply step into the background now? If she is to be cast aside, what has her entire life been about, up to this point? Rose's armor begins to melt: for the first time, she examines her own youthful dreams of fame and applause and the life she has spent enslaved to her own desperate, gnawing need to be noticed. It would be a scene and, eventually, a song, that would serve as both emotional breakdown and moment of truth, giving *Gypsy* the final piece of weight that Laurents had sensed the show needed.

The immediate problem was finding the right composer to do justice to the story. Irving Berlin was approached and refused: his shows revolved around sunnier themes, and *Gypsy* was too dark and disturbing for him. Cole Porter, ill and defeated—his right leg had recently been amputated, and it seemed to drain the last bit of spirit out of him—also passed on the project. Stephen Sondheim was Laurents's idea. Somewhat hurt that his lyrics for *West Side Story* had been largely overlooked in the shower of praise for Leonard Bernstein and Jerome Robbins, Sondheim was not eager to accept another lyric-writing job; he wanted to branch out as both composer and lyricist, and Laurents thought that the bittersweet flavor of *Gypsy*'s story would be ideally suited to his highly individual talents. Sondheim agreed, but Ethel didn't. She admitted that Sondheim was clever, but having rolled the dice with Harold Karr and Matt Dubey on *Happy Hunting*, she wasn't in the mood to be generous twice in a row. In the end the job went to Jule Styne, an unusual choice in the sense that he had penned a lot of big, romantic hits with Sammy Cahn, such as "Three Coins in the Fountain" and "Time After Time." True, he was a proven commodity on Broadway, with successes like *Gentlemen Prefer Blondes* and *Bells Are Ringing* to his credit, but these were

lighter, comedic shows. Could he really capture the deeper, darker tones of
Gypsy? Robbins wanted him, and after he swallowed his pride and auditioned for the job, so did Laurents. Sondheim was angry and disappointed,
and for a time it looked as if he would withdraw from the project altogether.
But the sage counsel of his mentor, Oscar Hammerstein, prevailed, and
Sondheim signed on as lyricist only. Styne, Sondheim, and Laurents worked
closely together, and the entire book and score were finished in an astonishing four months.

One of the reasons Ethel had been against Sondheim's composing the music was that she didn't think he would know how to write for her voice. Styne
assuredly did. He thought of her voice as a trumpet, and he wrote for it as he
would for an instrument. What he came up with was an exhilarating score that
felt as if it had been shot from a cannon. It played to all of Ethel's strengths.
With the exception of "Small World," the tender siren song that Rose uses to
snare the nebbishy candy salesman Herbie, all her numbers have a pulsating,
relentless drive. In her Berlin and Porter shows, Ethel had usually had a smattering of ballads to balance the big uptempo showstoppers, but the majority of
her pieces in *Gypsy* were written in a way that required them to be hurled at
the audience. Ethel loved the songs; she wept when she first heard them. It
was to be the most taxing, demanding score she would ever perform, for reasons that, at least initially, she probably didn't truly appreciate.

Laurents and Sondheim, by now close friends, provided their work with
a subtext that was rare in musicals of the period. Ethel's opening number,
the rousing "Some People," might seem at first glance to be a standard
establishing number—a bossy woman who knows what she wants, baldly
stating her philosophy on how to get ahead. To Laurents and Sondheim,
however, the song was really about Rose's desire to get her hands on a plaque
that hangs on the wall of her father's house—a plaque that she will sell to
help finance her dreams for June. Similarly, taken out of context, "Everything's Coming Up Roses" seemed a big, brassy paean to the power of positive thinking—just wait and see, tomorrow will be better—done in the old,
electric Merman style. But it was placed in a crucial spot in the show: the
railway scene, after June has deserted the act and run off to get married and
Rose has decided to concentrate all her hopes on the shy, awkward Louise.
Here the song becomes a chilling illustration of blind ambition mixed with
megalomania, as Herbie and Louise look on in horror.

Then there was "Rose's Turn," the number that Styne and Sondheim
had devised for Laurents's big moment of self-revelation at the end of the
show. More of an operatic scena than the standard eleven-o'clock number, it

was an explosive point in which Rose confronted her own thwarted ambitions, for her daughters but most of all for herself. It was a scorching expression of Laurents's belief that the play was really about the crying out for recognition. All her life Rose has demanded that people pay attention to her. Now, all alone on the empty stage of the theater where Gypsy is a headliner, she realizes that no one is left to listen.

There is a remarkable moment midway through "Rose's Turn," as the character's brash self-confidence begins to crumble. She starts out full bore, full of the old bravado and pizzazz, as she bitterly parodies one of Gypsy's strip routines:

> *Mama's talkin' loud*
> *Mama's doin' fine*
> *Mama's gettin' hot*
> *Mama's goin' strong*
> *Mama's movin' on*
> *Mama's all alone*
> *Mama doesn't care*
> *Mama's lettin' loose*
> *Mama's got the stuff*
> *Mama's lettin' go*

Suddenly she begins to unravel, sputtering out, "Mmmmm-mmm-Mama," then starting up again, trying to regain her momentum before breaking down entirely as she at last stops moving full speed ahead and takes stock of what is left of her life:

> *Why did I do it?*
> *What did it get me?*
> *Scrapbooks full of me in the background*
> *Give 'em love and what does it get you?*
> *What does it get you?*
> *One quick look as each of them leaves you*
> *All your life and what does it get you?*
> *Thanks a lot and out with the garbage*
> *They take bows and you're battin' zero!*

It would be the most emotionally naked moment that the Broadway musical had yet experienced; Handel could not have written a more searing-rage aria. The germ of the idea for Sondheim's lyrics stretched back to 1947, when Jessica Tandy had played the final scene of *A Streetcar Named Desire*, in which Blanche DuBois completes her mental disintegration before our eyes. By having Rose stammer "Mmmmm-mmm-Mama"—the thought of finally letting go of Louise is so terrifying that she can barely speak of it— Sondheim was providing her with a Blanche-like collapse. He explained all of this to Ethel, who listened to him at a steady emotional distance. Finally she interrupted him. There was just one thing she wanted to know: did "Mmmmm-mmm-Mama" come in on an upbeat or a downbeat?

It was a story that became part of Broadway legend, and it also set the tone for her relationship with Sondheim and Laurents as the show evolved. Sondheim, still smarting because she had vetoed him as composer, thought that she had learned her material like "a talking dog." Jerry Robbins, whom Ethel affectionately called "Teacher," would act out a scene or a song for her, and she would follow, mirroring him. While some actresses would have balked at learning material this way, preferring to discover the dramatic meaning for themselves, Ethel was a willing and pliable pupil; her trust in Robbins was absolute. Years later Sondheim complained that "Rose's Turn" suffered from Ethel's inability to approach it as a trained dramatic actress would. That said, he grudgingly gave her her due. "I thought in the first act," he observed, "which required her comic skills, she was nonpareil. In the second, where it required dramatic skills, it needed someone who had more experience playing drama. There was something less fulfilled in the second act than there was in the first. The reason that I wrote 'Everything's Coming Up Roses' the way I did was that I doubted that she could handle that scene as an actress. So I wrote a song of the type that she had sung all her life, like 'Blow, Gabriel, Blow,' which only requires a trumpet-voiced affirmation. I thought that we would let Herbie and Louise, in their reactions, give the scene the drama. But the intensity that Ethel put into it came as a surprise."

In all the years that have passed since *Gypsy* was born, both Laurents and Sondheim have frequently criticized Ethel for what they considered her lack of intellect. "Brains was not her forte," said Sondheim. Nor, for that matter, was coddling Sondheim, trying to win him over and make him her friend after she had nixed him for the show's music. Mary Martin might have operated that way; Ethel had no time for the theater's version of office poli-tics. She worked as hard on Rose as she had ever worked on anything in her life, certain that she had the juiciest role of her career.

"Ethel was dumb," agreed Laurents. But, like Sondheim, he recognized her native shrewdness. "I said when I met her, are you aware that Rose is a monster? She said she was, and she would do anything I wanted her to do. And she did. She was no fool *that* way. When it came to the tough part, 'Rose's Turn,' Jerry did it for her. Counted it out—five, six, seven, eight— and she followed him. She didn't think good mother, bad mother. She thought the way most stars thought, and, I think, the way many stars *still* think: 'I want the audience to like me.' "

As usual Ethel had cast approval. There were two neck-and-neck contenders for the part of Louise: Suzanne Pleshette and Sandra Church. At the last of Church's five auditions, Ethel sat in, and when she heard Church sing her plaintive solo, "Little Lamb," she burst into tears. Church got the job, but having heard of Ethel's reputation for being tough on actors, she told her agent that "Little Lamb" would no doubt be the first song to go. The other principal part was Herbie, Rose's put-upon boyfriend, who gives up his candy-selling business to go on the road as the manager of June's act. A number of top character actors were considered, but Robbins was intrigued by the idea of putting Jack Klugman in the part. A talented actor who had earned a small name for himself in the theater and on live television dramas, Klugman had no singing voice whatsoever and had never imagined he would be considered for a musical.

"I had to sing at the final audition," Klugman remembered. "Jule Styne didn't want me at all. He used to say, 'Jack, is this a talkathon?' But Ethel wanted me, and she made me get up with her and sing 'Small World.' And she sang the first part so quietly that her voice cracked. I was mesmerized; there was so much love in it when she sang. And I picked up the second chorus, and I sounded like Pinza." That night Robbins telephoned Klugman at home and said, "You got it! And it was the way you sang that did it."

Rehearsals got under way on February 11, 1959. Gypsy Rose Lee was an occasional visitor, recording the show's progress with her movie camera and feeling, as she later admitted, "like a ghost at a banquet." She hoped the show would be a hit, since her contract specified that she owned a piece of it. Ethel, too, had arranged a sweet deal, under which she would pull in 5 percent of the gross before the payoff to investors, and 7 percent thereafter. Also, her contract stipulated that Merrick and Hayward pay her board, lodging, and miscellaneous living expenses, since she had taken a furnished apartment at the Park Lane Hotel on Park Avenue for the run of the show and was still claiming Colorado as her primary residence. (This was later the source of a dispute, in which the Internal Revenue Service unsuccessfully tried to deny her claim for her travel expenses in New York.) Signing on for *Gypsy* had meant leaving Ethel Jr. and Bobby behind in Colorado, under the

supervision of a governess and Six—on the increasingly rare occasions
when he was home. It was a difficult decision on Ethel's part, but she knew
that *Gypsy* presented too good an opportunity to pass up, even if it meant
enduring the longest separation from her children she had known.

Robbins, Laurents, Merrick, and Hayward all smelled a substantial hit
in the making. Everyone was happy—everyone except Sondheim, a rather
withdrawn, melancholy presence during rehearsals, and June Havoc, who
objected to the way her family was portrayed in Laurents's script and refused
for months to sign the release allowing her name to be used in the show.
(Havoc later relented, but her feelings about *Gypsy* were always confused and
complicated; in particular she was not fond of Ethel's no-holds-barred interpretation of Rose. The real Rose, she pointed out, had been a charmer and a
seductress. Or, as she memorably put it, "Ethel was a calliope. Mother was a
clarinet.")

With so many temperamental talents on board for *Gypsy*, there was
bound to be friction. Robbins was as much of a monster as ever, taking out
his frustrations on those least able to defend themselves. One of Robbins's
prime targets was Lane Bradbury, who played June. Robbins had favored
Carol D'Andrea, the original June, who had worked with him in *West Side
Story*. But when Merrick fired her, her replacement, Bradbury, suddenly
found herself Robbins's special victim. As ever, Ethel was exempt from
Robbins's tirades. She proceeded as she always had, leading the company
in her usual brisk, businesslike way and maintaining a healthy distance
from most in the cast.

One person she decided was worthy of her time was Jack Klugman.
Their friendship, however, almost didn't get off the ground. Like Virginia
Gibson in *Happy Hunting*, Klugman initially thought it best to keep apart
from Ethel. "So for the first several days when we rehearsed, I didn't talk to
her," Klugman recalled. "I would never say hello unless she said it first.
And finally one day, she said to me, 'You're a moody son of a bitch, aren't
you?' So I said, 'Well, you're a star.' And she said, 'Have I been a star with
you?' And I said, 'No.' So she said, 'Well, then. Cut the shit.' "

Klugman, coming from a serious theater background, also had difficulty
adjusting to Ethel's peculiar way of rehearsing—namely, her habit of throwing her lines out front. "She would never look at you onstage. And as an
actor, of course, this bothered me. So I went to Jerry Robbins and said,
'Jerry, I can't play this way. You've gotta have some control over her.' And
one day we were going through a scene, and she said her line out front, and
I purposely didn't say anything. And after a couple of moments, she turned

and looked at me, and then I gave her my cue. And she looked at me for a long time—the longest five minutes in the world—and she doesn't say anything. And I thought, 'Well, she's going to kill me right here.' She knew exactly what I was doing. But then she went on, and from then on she always looked at me when she gave me the lines."

After all the sets and costumes had been packed off to Philadelphia for the out-of-town tryout, *Gypsy* had its first hearing in front of an audience: this was the time-honored "gypsy run-through" for people in the theater community before a show went out of town. Comedienne Carole Cook was in the audience that day and watched, amazed and exhilarated, as the cast, clad mostly in capri pants and blue jeans, gave a thrilling performance of the show. Robbins was on hand to narrate scene changes and stage directions, which the actors would mime. "I swear it was the best performance I saw of *Gypsy*," said Cook. "It was so *raw*." When Paul Wallace, as Tulsa, the chorus boy June runs off with, came out and performed his dazzling song-and-dance solo, "All I Need Is the Girl," many in the audience were sure that Ethel would see to it that the song was dropped. "Everyone always said that about her, going way back to the beginning of her career," said Cook. "But anytime I saw her, other people had great numbers."

When *Gypsy* opened in Philadelphia at the Shubert Theatre on April 18, it was too long and received mixed reviews. Far more troubling, though, was the tension in the company. Jerry Robbins's heinous treatment of Lane Bradbury reached its peak in Philadelphia, when he got mad at her for forgetting a piece of stage business and intentionally hid the batons she was to use in the "Dainty June and Her Farmboys" number. Bradbury was forced to mime the action of twirling the batons, with tears streaming down her face for all in the audience to see. Ethel, who had also taken a dislike to Bradbury for the simple reason that she didn't think she was very good in the part, made no move to intercede. Besides, she was having her own troubles with Sandra Church, who by now was romantically involved with the much older Jule Styne, a relationship that unnerved Ethel. "She didn't care for anyone who she thought was competing with her," said Klugman. "Sandra was going with Jule Styne, and Ethel didn't like it, because that meant that Sandra had a little clout."

Church's big strip solo near the end of the show, "Let Me Entertain You," also gave rise to tension between the two women. According to Church, Robbins was at a loss for the right way to stage the number. "He kept trying different things," recalled Church, "and he was going to have Ethel walk behind me in back of this see-through curtain. I didn't want that, so I did it poorly. When I got her out from behind me, I went back to doing it well." For her part, Ethel objected to one element of the staging of "Rose's Turn," in which Church came wandering onto the stage just as the number was reaching its climax. Although the idea was Robbins's, Ethel got it into her head that Church was trying to upstage her and protested so violently that the number was sensibly reworked with Ethel alone throughout.

Though Laurents and Sondheim longed for Ethel to dig deeper into the material, she was unquestionably giving the most powerful and heartfelt performance of her life. She was particularly moving in the scene in which Herbie, shocked and disgusted by the fact that Rose has pushed Louise into a burlesque show, walks out. For Rose's denunciation of Herbie—"You can go to hell!"—Ethel worked up genuine tears as her voice broke with emotion, providing the show with one of its emotional peaks. Certainly no other singer could have handled the role's daunting vocal demands with the aplomb that Ethel did, but the real key to her fine performance was that she refused to see Rose as an out-and-out bitch. "Ethel played her as a heroine," said Klugman. "Someone who sacrificed everything for her daughters. That's how Ethel saw her." It is tempting to interpret this as an instance of Ethel's projecting her own life onto the character she was playing: her blind reverence for her own parents may have affected how she brought Rose to life, without her realizing it.

Laurents dismissed this interpretation as "revisionism": "She didn't think of Rose as a heroine—all of that came later. She did exactly what she was asked to do at the time. She didn't question any of that. Because, you see, Rose is dumb. Like Ethel. She doesn't calculate. She doesn't weigh things. She just blunders right ahead. She doesn't think about right or wrong. I didn't like Ethel. She wasn't really my kind of person. But I didn't dislike her either. She was just . . . Ethel. When we were in Philly, Ethel was looking through the keyhole in Jule's room to see if he was fucking Sandra Church. She didn't think about things like that. She just did and said whatever came to mind with no thought of the consequences. In Philly we all had duty nights to take Ethel Jr. out. And Ethel would say terrible things in front of the girl. We were at the Variety Club, and the kid was eating ice cream while Ethel is tossing back the booze, and she's saying, 'SO! IS JULE FUCKING SANDRA? IS HE?' Right in front of the girl."

After the overlong show was pruned in Philadelphia—one entire number, "Mama's Talkin' Soft," for Baby June and Louise, was cut—preparations were made for the New York opening. It was Ethel's first time doing a show in the cavernous Broadway Theatre, which was too big a space for a show that really focused on the problems of three individuals, but she approached rehearsals with gusto and frequently dropped hints in interviews that Broadway was going to see an entirely new side of her—the side that knew how to act. "I've had people come backstage and say, 'Gee, I didn't know you could act that well,' " she told one reporter. "Gypsy Rose Lee herself came backstage one night and said, 'You made me cry.' I've never been given the opportunity to do this before."

Tempers continued to flare right up to the New York opening night. Jule Styne had taken great care with *Gypsy*'s overture—it was a brilliant job, played largely by musicians from swing bands rather than Broadway's usual orchestral suspects—and Styne was justly proud of it. But close to opening night, it was clear that the theater's big velvet stage curtain was going to soak up all the sound coming from the pit. Styne asked Robbins to have the pit raised a little, and Robbins dismissed the request, saying, "We'll get to it next week." Styne exploded. "He got up onstage with Jerry," recalled the composer's widow, Margaret Styne, "and told him, 'You've got to do this right now, and if you don't, I'm going to throw you into the pit and they won't hear *you* either.' "

Gypsy's opening night, May 21, 1959, finally arrived. Among the avalanche of congratulatory telegrams was one that Ethel would have reason to remember. It was from producer Frederick Brisson, husband of Rosalind Russell, and it read: DEAREST ETHEL GLAD YOU ARE BACK AND IF YOU NEED AN UNDERSTUDY I KNOW WHERE YOU CAN GET ONE GREAT GOOD LUCK FOR THE BIGGEST HIT EVER LOVE FREDDIE BRISSON.

From the first downbeat, everything on *Gypsy*'s opening night went magnificently. Laurents had devised a stunning entrance for Ethel, one that took the audience by surprise, signaled in an instant that *Gypsy* was something daring and unusual, and quickly assumed its place in theatrical history. As Baby Jane and Baby Louise are onstage, rehearsing for Uncle Jocko's amateur kiddie show, Rose comes marching down the center aisle of the theater shouting instructions while the girls go through their routine: "SING OUT, LOUISE: YOU'RE BEHIND, HONEY, CATCH UP, CATCH UP!" Gone were the glamorous outfits of Mainbocher and Irene Sharaff: since Rose was down on her luck, Ethel entered wearing a ratty coat and carrying a big, vulgar purse and a little dog named Chowsie, so named because, like Rose, he loved Chinese food.

One number after another was ecstatically received, and Ethel remembered every detail and nuance that Jerome Robbins had spent hours drumming into her. At the end of the first act, "Everything's Coming Up

Roses" sent the audience out into the lobby both shaken and elated. They couldn't imagine what this monster stage mother was going to try next; as for the song, it already sounded like a classic Merman anthem, right up there with "There's No Business Like Show Business."

The triumph wasn't entirely Ethel's. The numbers for the other characters also went over, especially Paul Wallace's showstopping "All I Need Is the Girl," Sandra Church's striptease to "Let Me Entertain You," and "You've Gotta Get a Gimmick," the hilarious comedy song for the trio of strippers (Faith Dane, Chotzi Foley, and Maria Karnilova) that no star in her right mind would have had cut. But tension built backstage as the night neared its end. "Rose's Turn" had to surpass everything else that had come before it; otherwise the whole point of the show would be lost. Could Ethel sustain her energy and concentration and pull off this diabolically difficult number?

The instant she opened her mouth—"HERE SHE IS, BOYS! HERE SHE IS, WORLD! HERE'S *ROSE!*"—there was never any doubt. "She wasn't tired at all," remembered Marie Wallace, who was making her Broadway debut as one of the showgirls. "She just stood up there and sang out." During the early part of "Rose's Turn," Ethel, imitating Gypsy's bumps and grinds, shimmied back and forth, showing off her fabulous legs as she wrapped the stage curtain around herself in time to the music. She might be poking fun at Gypsy's silly strip numbers, but Rose's emotional pain came through with raw power. It was counterpoint, just as Robbins had hoped, and it was so beautiful, so mesmerizing, that several of the showgirls, banded together in the wings watching, suddenly began to cry. At the end, the applause for "Rose's Turn" was shattering.

And so were the next day's notices. Writing in the *New York Herald Tribune*, Walter Kerr called *Gypsy* "the best damn musical I've seen in years," a quote that Merrick instantly slapped across the show's newspaper ads. The reviewer for the *New York Mirror* wrote that "Stephen Sondheim has set revealing lyrics to a zestful score by Jule Styne, and Jerome Robbins has worked the wordage and music into a nostalgic saga of heartbreak and triumph." But the real heroine of the hour was Ethel. Richard Watts in the *New York Post* wrote that "her incomparable ability to belt out a song has long been one of the joys of the theater, but she is likewise a brilliant actress, as *Gypsy* proves. By playing the ruthless mother mercilessly but adding her own quality of humanity, she makes the dreadful lady terrifying but somehow gallant and even pathetic." In the *New York Times*, Brooks Atkinson wrote, "Since she acts the part of an indomitable personality, she gives an

indomitable performance, both as actress and singer." But the most percep-
tive comments came from the *New Yorker*'s Kenneth Tynan. He had two
minor quibbles: first, the lack of a strong male vocal presence, and second,
that the second act revisited some of the territory of the first, as we watch
Rose try to make a star of Louise just as she did of June. About Ethel's performance, however, he had no reservations: "Miss Merman not only sings,
she acts," wrote Tynan. "I would not say that she acts very subtly; Rose,
after all, with her dreams of glory, her kleptomania, her savage parsimony,
and her passion for exotic animals and Chinese breakfasts, is scarcely a
subtle character. Someone in the show describes her as 'a pioneer woman
without a frontier,' and that is what Miss Merman magnificently plays." (In-
terestingly, Tynan objected to "Rose's Turn," with its intensely introspective
section, since he felt, "Once Miss Merman has started to sing, nothing short
of an air-raid warning should be allowed to interrupt her.")

Ethel was elated by the success of *Gypsy*. She loved receiving the parade of celebrities—Bob Hope, Bing Crosby, Judy Garland, Robert Young,
Katharine Hepburn—who beat a path to her dressing room after the show to
pay her homage. Her success also provided a wonderful distraction from the
problems with Six, who was now spending most of his time in Colorado anyway. On June 3, 1959, Ethel arranged to get the night off from *Gypsy* to catch
a night flight to Denver so she could attend Ethel Jr.'s graduation from
Cherry Creek High School.

Ethel returned to the cast and continued with the run. Her relationship
with Jack Klugman remained as congenial as ever, but she was growing
more and more displeased with Sandra Church. A misunderstanding at an
Actors' Fund benefit performance of *Gypsy* led to a major breach between
the two actresses. Church was irritated by a bit-part player's drawing out all
her lines for maximum attention, and she complained to the stage manager
about it. Somehow it got back to Ethel that Church had leveled the criticism
at her. Merrick and Hayward both called Church aside, demanding to know
how she could have done such an insensitive thing to a great star and insisting that she apologize. Although Church felt she had done nothing wrong,
she reported to Ethel's dressing room to discuss the matter and was refused
admittance by the dresser. There followed a chill between the two women
that took months to thaw.

Then, in August, real trouble came. Ethel's throat doctor, Stuart Craig,
had warned her early on in *Gypsy*'s rehearsal period that he feared the songs
were keyed a bit too high for her and that she might possibly suffer vocal

distress as a result. Ethel insisted she could perform the score with no difficulty and ignored Craig's advice. Then, at a Saturday-night performance in August, a blood vessel in her throat hemorrhaged. Craig put her on a sustained period of vocal rest, and her standby, Jane Romano, took over. Insiders predicted huge losses, but *Gypsy* did well enough during Ethel's brief absence, in part because Romano's salary was a fraction of her own. The critics came back to review the show and gave Romano warm notices. Unfortunately, she believed her own press and hit Merrick and Hayward with demands for a salary increase. This kind of behavior didn't sit well with Ethel, and Romano was quietly dropped from the show.

By the time *Gypsy* reached its 176th performance in October, it had grossed a record sum of $1.7 million. One week in January 1960 brought a box-office take of $86,400, believed to be a single-week record at the time. As the run continued, the inevitable accusations that Ethel was walking through her performance began to surface. Again ticket buyers were warned not to attend matinee performances, because the star noticeably took down the voltage. (The matinees in *Gypsy* were especially tricky, because the mothers in the audience tended to take a dim view of the character of Rose and withhold applause.) Opinions vary on whether Ethel's performance did lose some of its bite as the run went on. For Sandra Church the answer is yes. "Jerry made her act as no one did," said Church, "until slowly and surely, she stopped and slipped back into what was not acting." Jack Klugman disagrees: "People said she walked through the show. She *never* did. I was there."

With Ethel's success in *Gypsy,* NBC decided to build an entire television spectacular around her. She had done plenty of guest shots on all manner of variety shows, but *Ethel Merman on Broadway* would place her in the center ring. The program was to be sponsored by Ford Startime, and she was given three popular leading men: Fess Parker (television's Davy Crockett), comedian Tom Poston, and blond movie heartthrob Tab Hunter. One sketch featured Ethel as a pistol-packin' mama in pursuit of Parker, while another presented her as a garrulous American tourist confronting a member of Her Majesty's guard (Poston) at Buckingham Palace. Finally she played a patient of psychiatrist Hunter who decides to try some role reversal. (They wind up singing "You're Just in Love.") Unfortunately, the sketches were of execrable quality—forced and unfunny. The only high point came at the end of the hourlong telecast, when Ethel sang her big medley of showstoppers. The program did yield one memorable anecdote. Ethel was quite taken with Hunter and began a casual flirtation with him that met with a chilly response. She began to get frustrated, until one night during *Gypsy* she asked Jack Klugman if Tab Hunter was gay.

"Is the pope Catholic?" Klugman shot back.

Ethel thought for a moment, looked puzzled, and said, "Yes."

By the fall of 1959, it was clear to Ethel that her marriage to Six had deteriorated beyond repair. During the Christmas holidays, she had a brief vacation scheduled, and she and Six had promised Ethel Jr. and Bobby that they would spend it in Montego Bay, Jamaica, getting some sun, swimming, and snorkeling. For the sake of the children, Ethel and Six managed to maintain a truce during the trip, but the tension between them was excruciating. For some time Ethel had known about Six's infidelities while he was on the road; soon she would discover that he was having a serious relationship with television actress Audrey Meadows, famous as Alice Kramden on *The Honeymooners*. When news of Six's romantic exploits began making the gossip columns, Ethel felt deeply hurt and humiliated. In a heated exchange of letters, she and Six decided to go their separate ways.

Six was out of her life, but not with a Fing! When someone merited a Fing!, it meant that Ethel had placed that person in Coventry and she was not about to revisit the matter. With Six, her sense of betrayal cut too deeply for her to be able to dismiss him so decisively. Following her marriage to Six, she had boasted both privately and publicly that she no longer needed Broadway; to paraphrase *All About Eve*'s Margo Channing, she now had something better to do with her nights. Now she realized, bitterly, that the Broadway audience was the one constant in her life, the one anchor that had never failed her. She was a fifty-two-year-old woman with three failed marriages behind her, and she knew that the odds of finding another great love were slim. She kept up her brisk, no-nonsense front. Privately she felt a welling up of anger and sadness that would only intensify in the years to come.

Accompanied once again by her lawyer, Paul O'Dwyer, Ethel obtained a quickie divorce in Juarez, Mexico—the very scene of her split with Bob Levitt.

A wave of disappointment swept over the company with the presentation of the 1960 Tony Awards. *Gypsy* was nominated in eight major categories, including Best Musical, Best Actress in a Musical (Ethel), Best Featured Actor and Actress in a Musical (Klugman and Church), though not, inexplicably, for Laurents's brilliant script. But *Gypsy* failed to take home a single Tony.

The night's big winners were Jerry Bock's *Fiorello!* and Rodgers and Hammerstein's *Sound of Music*, whose star, Mary Martin, was given the Best Actress prize that many had automatically assumed would go to Ethel. *The Sound of Music* probably owed its multiple wins to the sentimental vote, since Oscar Hammerstein was ill and died in August of that year. Because Martin was a friend as well as a performer she admired, Ethel said very little about losing the Tony, other than the often-quoted "How are you going to buck a nun?"

After *Gypsy* had played about eighteen months, Sandra Church left the cast. She and Ethel had long since patched up their difficulties, and a civil atmosphere prevailed once again, but everyone in the company knew that Ethel was much happier with Church's replacement, Julianne Marie.

Another replacement, Alice Playten, who succeeded Karen Moore as Baby Louise, remembered a telling incident when she was introduced to Ethel at her first run-through. "She took my hand and she said, 'Do you know about the laugh line?' " Playten recalled. "It was this line: Louise asks, 'Mama, how come I have three fathers?' and Rose would say, 'Because you're lucky.' It got a laugh every night. I saw the Broadway revival with Tyne Daly, and I thought, 'They don't know about the laugh lines.' I think Miss Merman's humor and delivery of comedy lines was perfection. She could trust material. Everybody else digs into these lines like they're something to be mined."

Apart from *Gypsy*, Ethel's only other activities at this time were appearances during Richard M. Nixon's presidential campaign. When he lost in November 1960 to John F. Kennedy, Ethel was asked to perform at the January 20, 1961, inaugural and happily agreed. Even though she was a staunch Republican, she was first and foremost a patriot and regarded it as her duty to show up.

In July 1960, Ethel had a monthlong vacation, and she spent it taking her first grand tour of Europe, accompanied by Bobby, as well as Benay Venuta. The trio traveled in style in a chauffeur-driven car with a separate station wagon carrying all their luggage. Bobby had been dreaming of seeing the great European cathedrals and art treasures, and he went out every day in pursuit of them. He was joined by Benay, who, being a talented painter herself, had a passionate interest in visiting all the museums. Ethel, for the most part, regarded Europe as a place to shop and go to nightclubs. She even passed on seeing the Sistine Chapel, despite Bobby's pleas for her to join him.

The same year, 1960, brought great changes to Ethel Jr.'s life. After her graduation from Cherry Creek High School, Ethel Jr. had entered Colorado

College in Colorado Springs. She was only seventeen and not at all sure what she wanted to do with her future. At times she expressed a strong desire to be an actress, and she did participate in college stage productions, including *Brigadoon* and *Summer and Smoke*, in which she played the love-starved spinster Alma Winemiller. At other times she talked of pursuing a degree in veterinary medicine. Ethel showed little concern that her daughter seemed pulled in several directions simultaneously. Aimless enthusiasm, she reasoned, was part of being young.

During her freshman year at Colorado College, Ethel Jr. met an attractive fellow student, a senior from Wayne, Pennsylvania, named William Geary. They fell in love, and by the end of the school year Ethel Jr. discovered that she was pregnant. She informed her mother of the news. It would have been a golden opportunity for Ethel to explode in moral indignation, as many other mothers of the period might well have done. But she had not forgotten her own past; this was exactly how she had come to marry Bob Levitt. Instead of assigning blame to her daughter, Ethel provided her with loving support and had good things to say about William Geary, whom she found an amiable and responsible young man. In the interest of keeping the press temporarily at bay, news of the marriage was not made public until September 1960.

On February 20, 1961, Ethel Jr., now residing with Geary in Colorado Springs, gave birth to a seven-pound, five-ounce daughter, Barbara Jean. Big Ethel delighted in being a grandmother, and as soon as she could arrange a brief time away from *Gypsy*, she flew to Colorado to be with her daughter and granddaughter. Prior to the arrival of the baby, Ethel Jr. had seemed the happiest of housewives. Big Ethel had spent the Christmas holidays of 1960 with the Gearys and marveled at her daughter's ability to turn out a sumptuous, multicourse Christmas dinner. As a new mother, though, Ethel Jr. seemed less able to cope. She was barely eighteen, with no staff to help her, and initially she seemed overwhelmed by the responsibilities of caring for an infant. Again Ethel assumed that all would be remedied once Ethel Jr. got used to the routine.

Around this time, Ethel's principal professional concern was whether or not she would get to play Rose in the screen version of *Gypsy* that Warner Bros. would eventually produce. That question had been on her mind from the moment the show opened. Jacqueline Mayro, who played Baby June, remembered one night when she was running a 104-degree fever and was kept out of the show by her mother. It happened to be a night that Mervyn LeRoy, the director assigned to the picture, and several Warners executives were going to be in the audience. Soon a call came from assistant stage manager Ruth Mitchell: "Miss Merman doesn't care how sick your daughter is. She wants the full original cast on tonight."

Had Ethel really wanted to hedge her bets, it might have been best for her corporation, MerSix, to purchase the rights. But she had good reason to believe that she had the film in the bag. Mervyn LeRoy came to see her backstage time after time, always assuring her that she didn't need to worry: no one else would be playing Rose on-screen.

Just to be safe, however, she agreed to do something she had never done before: she would head up the national company in a nine-month cross-country tour. Those who were aware of her aversion to taking a show on the road were astonished. But Ethel knew that *Gypsy* was the high point of her career, and she wanted to share it with a wider audience—especially since she thought such a move might help her when she starred in the film version. People across the nation would buy tickets to see her onstage, then line up again at the box office when the movie was released.

And then, while the show was nearing the end of its Broadway run, the news was announced: Rosalind Russell would play Rose in the Warners film. It was the most stunning shock of Ethel's career; she had naïvely thought Mervyn LeRoy to be a man of his word. Jack Klugman recalled that Ethel was heartbroken: "Mervyn LeRoy came to see the play nine times and said, 'Ethel, I would never do this picture without you. This is your legacy.' All that stuff. I was there. He was an SOB."

The casting took place in an under-the-table way. A few years earlier, Frederick Brisson, producer of *The Pajama Game, Damn Yankees*, and other stage hits, had purchased the screen rights to the Broadway comedy *A Majority of One*, starring Gertrude Berg. Brisson was the husband of Rosalind Russell, and he sold the rights to Warners with Russell attached. There was one further condition: since Warners had the rights to *Gypsy*, the studio would have to use her in that film as well—otherwise no deal. As a box-office name, four-time Academy Award nominee Russell looked like a better bet than Ethel, and the studio agreed to Brisson's terms.

Ethel was now hardly in the proper frame of mind to undertake the national tour, but a commitment was a commitment, and she refused to back out. As time went on, the idea of playing across the country became a very specific kind of challenge: she would show those fools in Hollywood exactly how Rose *should* be played, and the movie would suffer as a result. She railed about the Warners executives as "those son of a bitches" and prepared to leave New York.

Julianne Marie played Gypsy on tour, and Alfred Sander was to play Herbie, as Jack Klugman preferred not to go on the road. But Ethel was used to Klugman's way of playing the part and very soon lost patience with his replacement, to the extent that Sander started having trouble retaining his lines. The upshot was that she pressured Merrick to get Klugman, at least for the start of the tour.

Gypsy closed at the Imperial on March 25, 1961, after 702 performances. (Merrick, among others, always thought that the run was shorter than it should have been, considering the show's quality, but Sondheim may have been right when he said that *Gypsy* told the audience things it didn't necessarily want to hear.) The national tour opened in Rochester, New York, on March 29. Ethel put on her best public-relations face in a way that was somewhat unusual for her, gushing to a reporter from the *Rochester Times-Union*, "I'm really excited about coming to Rochester." Klugman played Herbie in Rochester only, then left and was replaced by Sander, who finally proved acceptable to Ethel. The company moved on to Toronto, where the show was dwarfed in the enormous, three-thousand-seat O'Keefe Center. The cast was surprised to find the reviews mixed to downbeat, but the tour's company manager, Richard Grayson, observed, "The quality of our notices was almost uniformly in direct reverse proportion to the size of the theater. *Gypsy* is really a musical play about five or six people. It's not about big production numbers. So we got our best notices when we played real theaters."

But not always. When the show came to Boston's lovely Colonial Theatre, the *Christian Science Monitor* dismissed it as "a moderately weak musical with an immoderately starry star," handicapped by a book that "sputters into second-act vulgarity." But audiences everywhere loved it. On opening night at Detroit's Riviera Theatre, the applause on Ethel's entrance was so deafening that she had to break character and bow before the show could continue. (This moved even Ethel, who exclaimed to a reporter, "Touring! I'm sold!") The show continued on through Cleveland and Chicago before heading to San Francisco for an August 7 opening at the Curran Theatre, where the box office had taken in $60,000 on the first day it was open. In San Francisco the audience reaction to the show was overwhelming, and the run continued until late September.

While the show was playing to packed houses in San Francisco, Ethel injured her back severely: two of her vertebrae locked while she was bending over to put something in a bureau drawer. Richard Grayson picked her up at her hotel every morning at ten and drove her to the doctor. She was in agony for much of the San Francisco run, but she didn't miss a single performance, and was feeling somewhat better by the time the company moved on to Los Angeles for the October 2 opening at the Biltmore Theatre. This engagement presented a problem for Ethel: the star dressing room was below stage level, down a long staircase, with the rest of the dressing rooms a flight below that. Since she was still suffering some residual pain, Ethel asked Grayson to order a portable dressing room from one of the movie studios that could be placed directly on the side of the stage. Grayson explained that there was no room for such an accommodation—as it was, the crew was going to be lucky to be able to load the production into the tiny theater. "You've got to promise me you'll do that," she said to Grayson in a threatening tone. Grayson promised to do everything he could, but the best he could come up with was a makeshift arrangement with ropes and pulleys and curtains, a long mirror and a dressing table and a clothes tree. Ethel was not happy; Grayson had failed to carry out her wishes. "She never felt the same way about me after that," he recalled. "She played every performance with this arrangement, but she felt that I was turning her down."

The Los Angeles run was not a happy one for other reasons. Here Ethel had been especially determined to show "those son of a bitches" a thing or two about playing Rose. When the company arrived in town, the duplicitous Mervyn LeRoy resurfaced. He came to see her and requested as many house seats as he could possibly obtain for his friends and colleagues. He told Ethel that although it had not been announced, Rosalind Russell was seriously ill and was almost surely not going to be able to play Rose in the movie. "I think you're going to end up getting this part," he confided to Ethel, whose dream of recording her performance on film was suddenly given new life. She decided to follow LeRoy's advice and play Hollywood politics, down to ordering a full bar and cocktail glasses so she could properly entertain the studio brass after the show. All too soon she found out that LeRoy had misled her yet again. She was furious with herself for being taken in a second time, and she finished *Gypsy*'s run in a foul humor. After that the tour closed in St. Louis, and she retreated to New York to spend Christmas with the two people who had never let her down: her beloved Mom and Pop.

● ●

During *Gypsy*'s run, Ethel made the acquaintance of an attractive young man named Tony Cointreau. His surname was both exotic and familiar-sounding, and she soon found out why: Tony's father, Jacques Mercier-Cointreau, was chairman of Cointreau, Ltd., the company that manufactured the famous orange-flavored liqueur. Tony was charming, with impeccable manners. He wanted to become a pop singer, and from the time Ethel met him backstage at *Gypsy*, she offered him her steady encouragement. She was delighted by his graciousness and gentle wit, and she promptly introduced him to Ethel Jr., who dated him briefly before she went off to Colorado College. Tony had the quality that Ethel prized above all else: trustworthiness. As their surrogate mother-son relationship developed, Ethel realized that this was one person who was not out to use her, who wanted nothing from her but friendship.

The same could hardly be said of another person she met around this time, a husky-voiced, flashy brunette named Jacqueline Susann. The daughter of the prominent Philadelphia portrait artist Robert Susann, Jackie had been in New York since the late thirties, when she landed a bit part in, and was promptly bounced from, Clare Boothe Luce's hit *The Women*. Jackie had struggled and failed as both an actress and a playwright. For years she had floated around the fringes of B-level New York show business, as a television hostess and a commercial spokeswoman, and she showed up frequently in Broadway nightspots such as Toots Shor's and Danny's Hide-a-Way, because her husband, Irving Mansfield, was a Broadway press agent and a radio and TV producer. She was a shameless sycophant and a desperately devoted fan of Ethel's. Jackie saw *Gypsy* again and again and was overwhelmed by Ethel's performance, but she was not content to admire from afar. She had become friends with Benay Venuta, still Ethel's closest professional friend, and through Benay managed to get herself introduced to Ethel. Soon Jackie was dogging Ethel's every step.

Initially Ethel liked her well enough: Jackie was bright and irreverent and showbizzy, with a sharp, bawdy wit. Since the troubles with Six had worsened, Ethel had started to relax her strict rules about drinking too much after a performance, and once the final curtain fell on *Gypsy*, she and Jackie and Benay were seen out together in various after-hours spots.

To several of Ethel's friends, Jackie's motives seemed transparent. "Jackie had a terrible mouth," said Tony Cointreau. "She became friends with all these stars—Judy Garland, Ethel—through her husband, and then she would go to the 'little people' and say the most horrible things about them. That's when I first met Jackie. She was talking to the 'little people' and saying these horrific things about Judy and Ethel, and she didn't know that I knew Ethel."

All too soon Ethel grew uncomfortable with Jackie's obsessive behavior and began trying to put some distance between them. Jackie's reaction was to come on stronger than ever. Too late Ethel realized that she had become the object of a crazed star crush. It all built to a frenzy one night after a performance of *Gypsy*. Jackie and Irving were out at a restaurant with Ethel and Benay when Jackie, having had far too much to drink, exploded in a rage at Irving and turned a table over on top of him. Ethel, mortified, got up and left, shouting at Jackie that she never wanted to see her again. Jackie, undeterred, followed Ethel to the Park Lane and stood in the hallway outside her apartment in the early-morning hours, hammering on her door and screaming, "Ethel, I love you!" until Ethel was forced to have the Park Lane's security team remove her.

Ethel ended the short-lived friendship with Jackie, but Jackie's intense fixation on Ethel had become well known, and some Broadway insiders speculated that the two women really might have had a brief sexual relationship. This appears to have been nothing but speculation: there is no hard evidence that Ethel was ever sexually involved with another woman. Although she tossed around the terms "fag" and "dyke" casually, she had no deep-seated issues with either male or female homosexuality; this was simply her coarse way of expressing herself. Over the years she enjoyed friendships with many prominent gay women in the business, including actresses Mary McCarty and Fannie Flagg, among others, but as she once told Tony Cointreau, "I just never could go that route. I always liked a man's most desirable part."

Where was Ethel to go after *Gypsy*? It had provided her with the pinnacle of her career, and she knew that she would have to choose her next move carefully. Plans were afoot for her to make her London debut as Rose, but the production never materialized. Ethel always claimed that she didn't do a London run of the show because Jack Klugman and Julianne Marie were not available, but it is more likely that she simply did not care enough about taking *Gypsy* abroad.

The loss of the *Gypsy* movie to Rosalind Russell continued to be an open wound, exacerbated when Warner Bros. released the film in the fall of 1962 to middling reviews. Although Russell had a few effective moments as Rose, her performance too often seemed like a broad stand-up comedy routine, and the decision to alternate her own gravelly singing with the dubbed vocals of Lisa Kirk made Rose sound like a case of musical split personality. The *New Yorker* dismissed it as "thoroughly repellent." In his *New York Times* notice, Bosley Crowther devoted most of his space to praising Ethel's performance in the original. "That tornado of a stage mother that Ethel Merman portrayed on Broadway . . . comes out little more than a big wind in the portrayal that Rosalind Russell gives her."

Such reviews were cold comfort to Ethel, who would continue to look on losing Rose on film as the greatest professional disappointment of her life. But she did receive consolation in the form of another movie job. Stanley Kramer, who had made a considerable name for himself in Hollywood as the producer/director of serious pictures that dealt with controversial themes such as nuclear attack (*On the Beach*) and the Holocaust (*Judgment at Nuremberg*), was eager for a change of pace. He was assembling a big, expensive picture called *It's a Mad, Mad, Mad, Mad World,* which would be a tribute to the days of the great slapstick filmmaker Mack Sennett. The plot was really just an excuse for a series of screen-filling sight gags: while traveling through the California desert, a random collection of motorists witnesses a fatal car accident. In his final minutes, the driver of the car (played by Ethel's old pal Jimmy Durante) lets it slip that he was on his way to collect a fortune—"350,000 big ones"—buried at a site in Santa Rosita State Park that he refers to only as "the Big W." The witnesses all take off in search of the money, stopping at nothing to sabotage one another along the way.

It's a Mad, Mad, Mad, Mad World was an enormous, $9.5 million production with a top-line cast. The principal scavengers were played by Mickey Rooney, Buddy Hackett, Sid Caesar, Edie Adams, Jonathan Winters, Terry-Thomas, Phil Silvers, Milton Berle, and Dorothy Provine, with Ethel rounding out the cast as Berle's overbearing, loudmouthed mother-in-law, Mrs. Marcus. Spencer Tracy was the police chief who keeps the whole crowd under surveillance, and there were cameo appearances by a host of famous comics, including Jack Benny, Jerry Lewis, Eddie "Rochester" Anderson, ZaSu Pitts, Buster Keaton, Ben Blue, and Andy Devine.

The various slapstick routines were extremely tricky to stage and shoot, and the filming, much of which took place in the extreme heat of Southern California, stretched on for months. Having so many big comedic talents gathered for one project proved a challenge for Kramer. Ethel was indulgent of the rampant egos surrounding her on the set and got to be friendly with Edie Adams, with whom she often rode back to her hotel at the end of the day's work. "I used to do a take-off on her in my act," said Adams. "I would hold a note, and the trumpeter would hold the note with me, and I'd pull out a gun and shoot the trumpeter. Fortunately, she thought it was very funny." Occasionally, as they were piling into the car to leave the location, Ethel would mutter to Adams, "I think I've had enough of comics for one day."

Still, she liked the part of Mrs. Marcus, and the rushes looked promising. There was one particularly funny scene in which she berated both Berle and Provine from the backseat of a car; on-screen she had never displayed such breathtaking comic timing. She was also delighted when her costars threw a party for her at the Beverly Hills Hotel. Around 150 Hollywoodites were invited to the formal dinner, and Ethel was asked, as she so often was at affairs in her honor, to sing. She obliged with "I Get a Kick Out of You" and "There's No Business Like Show Business." The *Los Angeles Times* observed, "For filmdom functions, it wasn't such a mad, mad, mad, mad party. Very sedate." But Ethel seemed pleased as she gasped, upon making her entrance, "Nobody ever did anything like this for me before!"

No other movie offers were immediately forthcoming, and she still had no interest in returning to Broadway, so she decided to go where the big money was—Las Vegas. In October she opened at the famous Flamingo Hotel, home to such topflight Vegas entertainers as Dean Martin, Sammy Davis Jr., and Lena Horne. The hotel had opened in 1946—at a total building cost of around $6 million—most of it contributed by Bugsy Siegel, Lucky Luciano, and other prominent New York mobsters. It boasted elegant gardens and spectacular swimming pools, and by the 1950s it dominated Vegas's strip, an enormous attraction for both tourists and celebrities. The Flamingo was memorably described by Dean Martin's biographer, Nick Tosches, as "the pleasure dome of the new prefab promised land: a land of chrome, not gold; of Armstrong linoleum, not Carrara marble; of heptalk, not epos or prophecy." It was to be Ethel's first club date since her appearance at Casino in the Park in the early 1930s, and with a whopping salary of $40,000 weekly (before taxes), she was eager to make a success of it.

She didn't, quite. Her opening was attended by a number of celebrity friends, including Judy Garland, Patricia Kennedy Lawford, and Mitzi

Gaynor, as well as Mom and Pop Zimmermann. She had the expert support of Russ Black and his orchestra, plus pianists Morty Jacobs and Marty Harris; with the exception of one number new to her, "A Lotta Livin' to Do" from Broadway's *Bye Bye Birdie*, she sang the old songs from her old shows. But attendance soon fell off, for the simple reason that Ethel was not a club performer. It was thrilling when she hurled her great songs through the expanses of a Broadway theater, but in a club setting she couldn't quite establish the right rapport with the audience. Performers such as Frank Sinatra and Lena Horne could sell big, uptempo numbers, but they also knew how to banter, to give the impression to every single customer that they were performing for him and him alone. Ethel couldn't manage that. Her performing style was inflexible, and she wasn't able to alter it for a roomful of half-soused gamblers who, she suspected, weren't giving her their full attention anyway.

On top of that, Ethel developed a case of "Vegas throat" during her Flamingo engagement. This was a common ailment for singers new to the desert climate: their voices suddenly became dry and raspy. On a live recording of the engagement issued by Reprise (which later had to be partially rerecorded), both Ethel's speaking and singing voices sound desiccated and hoarse; by now she had also developed a habit of finishing off the final consonant in her lyrics in a way that sounded almost like she was doing a comic Italian accent ("The Hostess with the Mostes' on the Ballllll-a").

For the paying customers, she put up a good front and indicated that her club debut was a career highlight. "Up until last year," she said as part of the carefully scripted banter from which she never deviated, "when I toured with *Gypsy*, my professional life was sort of confined to Broadway and Hollywood. I didn't tour and I didn't play clubs. My friends always used to say, 'Ethel, you don't know what you're missing.' Well, tonight I learned what they're talking about."

It was a good try, but the truth was that Ethel loathed Vegas. She missed New York and returned there as soon as her run at the Flamingo ended. She did, over the next few months, trot out her act at such tony spots as the Deauville in Miami Beach and Harrah's South Shore Room at Lake Tahoe, but as Phyllis Diller, by now a veteran of the club circuit, put it bluntly, "Ethel's act simply did not fly." There was still television, however, and on April 8, 1963, Ethel wowed the small-screen audience with an appearance on the Academy Awards telecast, performing a medley of Irving Berlin tunes while charging down into the audience (and perilously close to the cameras).

It was one of the few times anyone had performed at the Oscars while mingling with the crowd, and her stunt picked up a lot of favorable notices.

On June 4, Ethel hit the road in a six-week theater-concert tour, appearing mostly in tent shows and other summer-theater venues. She opened at the Melody Fair Theatre in Buffalo, New York, and continued through the Northeast. In Boston, critic Elliott Norton put his finger on the problem: many of the songs in her shows needed context, he observed, and added, "Although Ethel is a wonder, she is human. To entertain at the top of her bent, she needs a show."

Actually, a show had been offered. David Merrick was producing a new musical based on Thornton Wilder's hit comedy *The Matchmaker.* It was called *Hello, Dolly!*, and Jerry Herman, the talented young composer of *Milk and Honey,* had, with Merrick's encouragement, written it expressly for Ethel. Herman had made a careful study of all her recordings, and the part of Dolly was perfectly tailored to her talents. With Merrick at the helm, Herman dared to dream that Ethel would sign on.

Herman was in Merrick's office the day the producer made the call pitching the show to Ethel. "He said that he would like to set up a time to audition it. And he went absolutely ashen. Here the great moment came, and he just turned sort of a pale gray and said, 'Are you sure, Ethel? Are you really sure? This is so right for you.'" When Merrick hung up, he told Herman, "She says she will never do another Broadway show because she has spent her life in dressing rooms." At that point, said Herman, "I turned the same color that he did!"

Ethel had legitimate reasons for saying no to *Dolly!* Number one, she was tired of long Broadway runs and wanted to concentrate on films and TV. Number two, while she had originated every role she had played onstage, Ruth Gordon had made a brilliant success of *The Matchmaker* less than a decade earlier; the memory of Gordon's triumph was still fresh, and Ethel didn't want to risk comparison. If Merrick thought he might be able to persuade her, he was wrong. And while *Hello, Dolly!* would turn out to be a history-making success, it did not have the spark and originality of *Gypsy.* Ethel never regretted her decision.

She continued to keep closer tabs on both her children. Ethel Jr. had had a second child, Michael, born on November 10, 1962. Having one child at such an early age had been a challenge that taxed Ethel Jr. to her limits, and the pressures of having two were overwhelming. "My grandmother was a very powerful personality," recalled Barbara Geary. "My mom was extremely intelligent and fairly emotionally vulnerable. I think she inherited some of the depression stuff from her father. Gram didn't really have time for that. Not to say that she didn't love her, but that sensitivity and anguish she didn't understand, and therefore she gave it no time. Her attitude was, 'Get over it! Get better!' "

Bobby, for his part, had shown a marked interest in going into the theater—not, to Ethel's relief, as a performer but as a director. After she finished her summer tour, Ethel joined him in Europe, where he was making the rounds of major theaters, informally studying various up-to-date production techniques before enrolling that fall as a directing major at the Carnegie Institute of Technology's College of Fine Arts. Soon he had been appointed assistant stage manager for a school production of *As You Like It,* and he seemed eager to complete his education and get his career rolling.

Now that her children had embarked on new phases of their lives, Ethel began searching for new vistas herself. For years she had been a frequent guest on the top variety shows of Dinah Shore, Frank Sinatra, Perry Como, and others. But what she wanted now, more than anything, was a series of her own. Not a variety series—those she considered a dime a dozen—but a sitcom that would allow her to show off a side of her talents that many television viewers might not know about. Her current agent, the notoriously tough and belligerent Milton Pickman, began casting around for the right project and received an agreement from a longtime Merman admirer, Lucille Ball, to film a series pilot for her production company, Desilu. The result was *Maggie Brown,* a sort of second cousin to *Panama Hattie.* Ethel played Maggie, the goodhearted owner of a nightclub in the South Pacific during World War II, who operates an illegal beer machine in her basement and tries to keep her beautiful young daughter from falling prey to the crowd of sailors who frequent the bar.

Susan Watson, who played Ethel's daughter in the pilot, remembered that Ethel had a great deal riding on its success. "I felt that she really wanted this to happen," said Watson. "It was a thin plot, but she was good in it. She knew where the jokes were. And yet there was a kind of—I don't want to call it innocence, but she was so wound up in what she was doing that it was sort of like she had blinders on. I could feel that. You could see that she was eager to make it work—'How about this? *This* would be better!'—that sort of thing." Despite enthusiastic endorsement by Lucille Ball, CBS did not pick up *Maggie Brown.* Ethel was bitterly disappointed and frequently asked her friends and managers, "What do I have to do to get hot?"

That fall, Ethel brought her nightclub act to New York with an engagement at the Plaza Hotel's elegant Persian Room. Comedienne Kaye Ballard recalled an incident that underlined just how alien the nightclub milieu was to Ethel. As she led up to her big show-hits medley, she told the audience, just as she always did, about Vinton Freedley casting her in *Girl Crazy*. As it happened, Freedley himself was sitting at one of the front tables. By now he was an elderly and somewhat frail man, all but forgotten, and rather desperate for recognition. When he heard his name mentioned, Freedley called out, "Ethel! I'm here!" Ethel, thinking there was a heckler in the audience, turned her gaze on his table.

"Ethel! It's me—Vinton!"

Ethel's smile remained fixed on her face. "HI!" she bellowed, and went right on with her patter.

In November, *It's a Mad, Mad, Mad, Mad World* was launched with a massive four-day press junket in Hollywood, attended by some 250 journalists from every major U.S. city, as well as from Europe, Latin America, and Asia. Like all the principals, Ethel made herself available for interviews. The total cost of the junket was estimated at around $280,000, but it was considered worth it by Kramer and United Artists, which anticipated getting $3 million worth of free TV exposure. The studio couldn't control the reviews, of course, which were mixed. The *New York Times* found it "wild and hilarious all the way" and praised Ethel's "brass-lunged, bargain-basement champion mother-in-law," but *Newsweek* found it "redundant, ridiculous, and too insistent" and thought that the slapstick scenes revealing Ethel in her bloomers approached "outright disgust." In the end even the worst notices didn't matter: with so much star power and heavy promotion, the film was practically a guaranteed hit, and Ethel delighted in its success, especially as it came on the heels of *Gypsy*'s cinema failure.

Soon after, Ethel returned to television for a series of guest shots: *The Red Skelton Hour, The Lucy Show,* and a pair of appearances on *The Judy Garland Show,* one of which turned out to be history-making: she shared the stage with both Garland and the red-hot rising star Barbra Streisand, who had just made a big hit on Broadway in *I Can Get It for You Wholesale* and was about to star in the new Jule Styne–Bob Merrill show *Funny Girl*. Those who knew Streisand in the early days of her career maintain that she was a true diva from the beginning, and her behavior on this occasion clinched it. She appeared quite chilly toward Ethel, who in turn nearly steamrollered her. When she asked Streisand what was next for her and Streisand mentioned *Funny Girl,* Ethel spoke over the top of her: "WONDUHFUL! WONDUHFUL! WHO'S THE COMPOSAH?" When Streisand mentioned Jule Styne's name, Ethel exploded with, "HE WROTE *GYPSY*! YOU'RE IN GOOD HANDS, GIRL!" The three women then joined forces for "There's

No Business Like Show Business." Streisand barely knew the lyrics, and Ethel sailed right past her. Even so, Ethel recognized a brilliant talent when she heard one, and in years to come she would be generous in her praise of Streisand.

Ethel also had nothing but kind words for Garland. The problems of getting the deeply troubled star to submit to the rigors of a weekly television show were chronicled in Mel Tormé's memoir *The Other Side of the Rainbow,* and certainly there were many guest stars who resented the chaotic conditions of appearing on Garland's show. But Ethel always defended her, often saying, "You can't speak against that girl. She's a great talent, and she's very, very sick, and she needs our understanding."

One of Ethel's close friends around this time was Temple Texas, a six-foot-two blond beauty and onetime actress who was now a successful publicity agent. Temple was Ethel's kind of woman: bawdy, boozing, and fun-loving, and Ethel delighted in her company. On November 20, 1963, at the home of Temple and her husband, agent Joseph Shribman, Ethel met Ernest Borgnine.

No glamorous leading man, Borgnine was a hefty forty-six-year-old character actor who had come up the hard way, playing small parts on Broadway before being typecast as a heavy in Hollywood films. He'd startled audiences with his convincing portrayal of Fatso Judson, the sadistic sergeant who beats Frank Sinatra's Angelo Maggio to a bloody pulp in *From Here to Eternity,* and two years later he had his breakthrough role in *Marty,* a quiet drama about a lonely Bronx butcher for which Borgnine received the 1955 Best Actor Oscar.

Winning the award hadn't brought him all he might have expected. With his offbeat looks and persona, he was difficult to cast, and his starring career in Hollywood was spotty. His reputation as a screen heavy had also spilled over into his private life. His first marriage, to Rhoda Kemins, ended in divorce in 1958, with his wife charging that he'd beaten her. On the set of the film *Badlanders,* he met Mexican actress Katy Jurado, and they were married a year later, but their relationship was stormy; in 1961 the press reported that they'd gotten into an argument in a nightclub that culminated in his slapping her. He and Jurado were divorced in 1963—the same year he met Ethel.

From the start, Borgnine courted Ethel with the fervor of a lovestruck teenager, and she succumbed. She paid no attention to friends' warnings of his marital past or to the nine-year age difference between them. She knew that for a woman in her mid-fifties, there weren't going to be many more chances, and she decided that at last she had found the ideal man. "I can see where she fell hook, line, and sinker," says Tony Cointreau. "Borgnine was so charming—a million watts. I thought, 'This is the most perfect couple God ever put together.' They even looked right together." Although Borgnine was starring in a hit television series, *McHale's Navy,* he flew from California to New York to be with Ethel as often as possible. On one of his visits, during the week between Christmas 1963 and the New Year, he popped the question, and Ethel said yes. To reporters she laid it on thick: "I've never been in love, really in love, before. For the first time in my life, I feel protected." As she had with Bob Six, she attempted to play the devoted wife who was willing to take a backseat to her husband: "Wherever Ernie is working is where I'll be."

Their relationship continued at a peak of intensity throughout the first half of 1964. To Eric Knight, a pianist in some of her club appearances (and later, her principal conductor), she seemed the picture of the radiant bride-to-be. Knight recalled one evening when he and his wife invited Ethel and Borgnine to dinner at their Manhattan apartment: "We're sitting on two chairs, and they're on the sofa, and Borgnine starts his Italian wooing: he takes her shoe off and starts kissing her toes! She ate it up. He gave her the treatment."

In February 1964, Ethel took time out from her new romance to make her official London debut, at the famed cabaret Talk of the Town. The night-club, a rebuilt version of the old variety theater the Hippodrome, had opened in 1958 and quickly became one of London's hottest spots. Ethel was in magnificent vocal shape, her notices in the British press were glowing, and audiences flocked to the show, delirious at their first opportunity to hear her live. Again one of the high points was Ethel's blazing rendition of "Blow, Gabriel, Blow."

Upon her return from London, Ethel and Borgnine set a date for their wedding: June 26, 1964. Ethel busied herself with the immense chore of shipping her furniture and paintings out to California, where the couple planned to live in Borgnine's spacious Beverly Hills home. Ethel was still very much the secretary: she monitored the packing herself, taking precise inventory of each of the boxes and affixing labels to them that described their contents. To friends she bubbled with excitement about her impending marriage; later she would claim that privately she was beginning to have doubts.

On June 26, wearing a flowing chiffon dress in three shades of yellow, Ethel married Ernest Borgnine in the garden of his house. Five hundred friends were in attendance, including Jack Benny, Milton Berle, Bob Hope, Gypsy Rose Lee, Lucille Ball and Gary Morton, and Vivian Vance. There were already storm warnings before the ceremony began. Granddaughter Barbara Jean, now three and a half years old, innocently pulled a carnation off the trellis that had been set up in the garden, causing Borgnine to lose his temper and scream at her. It was a tense moment, and there was more to follow: In midceremony Bobby, who was tossing Barbara Jean up in the air, misjudged his strength, and the child accidentally dislocated her shoulder. Immediately after the vows were spoken, Ethel accompanied the little girl to the emergency room of a local hospital.

The Borgnines had long planned to spend their honeymoon on a three-week tour of Japan, Hong Kong, and Honolulu. Only at the last minute did Ethel discover that Borgnine had not financed the trip—it had come his way in the form of a paid publicity junket. With her enormous sense of pride and fair play, Ethel was outraged, feeling that her groom had deceived her. The bickering began on the plane trip to Tokyo and gradually intensified. Exactly what happened once the couple arrived in Tokyo is not known, since Ethel would remain reticent about the details of her honeymoon for the rest of her life. But several of her friends over the years indicated that some sort of violent episode may have taken place. "He had hit her," said Eric Knight. "She told me this."

All that is really known is that Ethel spent only a day or so in Tokyo before flying back to California. There, in the house in Beverly Hills, she faced yet another humiliation—the maid. Ethel later told reporters that she had "objected strenuously to that woman." She may have had her reasons. Many years later, Barbara Jean Geary was working on a film set in Portland, Oregon, where she met a man who had been an assistant director on *McHale's Navy*. "He told me that the real story was that Ernest had a script girl from *McHale* that he was having an affair with the whole time he was courting my grandmother," recalled Barbara. "He installed her in the house as a maid, and she discovered that, and that was why she left."

Largely to avoid bad press, Ethel and Borgnine kept up appearances until August 3, when Ethel moved out of the house and into a hotel. Eventually she had her belongings repacked and returned to the apartment at the Park Lane. On November 18, Ethel won an interlocutory divorce decree in Santa Monica Superior Court. Deeply embarrassed and hurt by the abrupt failure of this marriage, Ethel barely discussed it with anyone in the years to come. When she did, she briskly dismissed it, in true Greatest Generation fashion, by saying, "It all came down to dollars and cents."

The collapse of her fourth marriage brought Ethel an avalanche of un-wanted publicity and carved a major chasm right through the middle of her life. It quickly became part of show-business lore, providing Middle America with all the evidence it wanted that performers were volatile, self-centered people who had no business being married in the first place. In Hollywood and theater circles, the thirty-eight-day marriage became a running joke, as legendary as a ballyhooed Broadway musical that winds up running for one night. "Over with faster than the Borgnine-Merman marriage" became a shorthand way of defining failure.

For Ethel it seemed that an irreplaceable part of her life was over. To admit this to herself was unbearably painful and sad, for she was a woman who needed to love and be loved; her Broadway success, staggering as it was, would never be enough to satisfy her. Always she had before her the example of what she considered the ideal marriage, and it sickened her to think that the daughter of Edward and Agnes Zimmermann was a four-time loser. She felt betrayed, angry, and afraid, but not completely without hope. "She never stopped wishing," said Tony Cointreau, "that she would find another person to love. She told me it was something she prayed to God for every day."

T he mid-1960s marked the beginning of the most bitterly unhappy period of Ethel's life. After the cataclysmic marriage to Borgnine, one disappointment seemed to follow another. To her closest friends, she was beginning to reveal a sadness and loneliness she had not exhibited before. There were also numerous professional setbacks. More than anything she continued to want movie roles and a TV series of her own. But by 1965 she was fifty-seven, and looked very much a middle-aged lady—never the most marketable commodity in Hollywood. One of the properties she pursued was *A House Is Not a Home,* in which she would have played the notorious madam Polly Adler, but eventually the role went to Shelley Winters. Ethel did receive an offer from producer Ross Hunter for another madam role, this time in a comedy he was preparing for Universal, *The Art of Love.* For years Hunter had been making a great deal of money producing lavishly upholstered films such as *Imitation of Life* (1959) and *Midnight Lace* (1960), and Ethel was pleased to be asked to appear in one of his pictures. Her role as Madame Coco was definitely a supporting part, but since the leads were being played by Dick Van Dyke and Carl Reiner, then very hot names in television, the film seemed a good bet. Decked out in a variety of wigs in shades ranging from orange to pistachio, Ethel stole what there was to steal of the film. At one point she was called upon to sing a French song. "I can't even say 'Oui,' " Ethel told a reporter, "so I had to learn the song phonetically." It was released in mid-1965 to thumbs-down reviews and very little box office.

Not long after her split from Borgnine, Ethel received an invitation to take her club act to the Hilton in Sydney, Australia. Roger Edens was available and enthusiastically agreed to be her pianist (along with Eric Knight), even going so far as to waive his fee. For Ethel the two-week engagement was a delightful reunion with Edens, and she was further cheered when audiences turned up in big numbers and the Australian press gave her warm notices. As she returned home through the Far East, Ethel pondered the fact that for a rich and successful woman she had really seen very little of the world; her travels abroad had basically been confined to her 1955 appearance at the Royal Variety show and her 1960 grand tour of Europe with Bobby and Benay. As it happened, Bobby was experiencing a case of wanderlust himself. Since Ethel had been cheated out of seeing the Far East on her honeymoon with Borgnine, she agreed to finance a trip for the two of them. They flew out of Los Angeles in mid-August 1965 and landed in Tokyo, where Bobby took in a performance of the Grand Kabuki. Ethel insisted, as she had in Europe, on having a chauffeur and an English-speaking guide to take them from place to place. Once they'd spent a few days in Tokyo, mother and son headed for Kyoto, then Osaka, Hong Kong, Agra, Jaipur, Bombay, and Moscow—where they saw Laurence Olivier perform *Othello* in Russian with the Moscow Art Theater—then Leningrad and Helsinki. In her memoirs Ethel makes little of this trip. The few anecdotes she recorded are show-business-related: about a performance of *My Fair Lady* in Russian and running into celebrity photographer Jerry Zerbe on the flight from Moscow to Leningrad. The trip seems to have been primarily a chance for Bobby to expand and deepen his knowledge of foreign production styles and techniques. Bobby was eager to get on with his career, and after their return he took a job at the American Shakespeare Festival in Stratford, Connecticut.

As far back as the mid-1950s, Ethel had made a discovery that may have surprised her as much as it did her closest friends: she liked opera. At the recommendation of those in the know, she began attending performances by the great Croatian soprano Zinka Milanov at the Metropolitan Opera's old location on Thirty-ninth Street and Broadway. Her interest in opera would continue into the 1970s, and she could be seen from time to time sitting in a box for Milanov's performances. On one of these occasions, she told her escort, stage director Michael Manuel, "She's like me—been around forever and knows what the hell she's doing." Ethel tended to enjoy performances by big-voiced sopranos like Milanov and Joan Sutherland: no-frills, stand-and-sing divas with amazing instruments. In the spring of 1966, when the Variety Club International was planning a New York tribute to Britain's Prince Philip, then touring the United States, Ethel urged the event's producer, Jule Styne, to include Milanov, whom she considered "one of the great ladies of the Met." Milanov wanted to sing "O mio babbino caro," but she was unceremoniously dropped from the show at the last minute, and never got to be part of a chorus line of stars, including Lillian Gish, Arlene Francis, Kitty Carlisle, and Ethel, decked out in costumes from *Hello, Dolly!* singing "Hello, Philip!"

Ethel was less enamored of Maria Callas. When the quixotic soprano returned to the Met for performances of one of her great roles, Puccini's *Tosca*, in 1965, Ethel was present but was shocked to learn that Callas had skipped a supper-dance in her own honor at the chic restaurant the Four Seasons. Ethel registered her disappointment with a reporter from the *New York Post:* "Imagine that broad not showing up."

On February 10, 1966, an event occurred that would have significant and enduring impact on Ethel's professional reputation: Bernard Geis Associates, a small but enterprising Manhattan publishing firm, brought out Jacqueline Susann's novel, *Valley of the Dolls*.

Having faced the fact that her acting career was dead and not likely to be resurrected, Susann had turned to writing some years earlier and in 1963 had published her first book, *Every Night, Josephine!*, a gently amusing memoir of her pet poodle. But *Valley of the Dolls* was quite a different matter from *Josephine!* It was a cliché-ridden and salacious yet undeniably fast-moving and engrossing novel about three young women who enter show business and gradually lose their way in a maze of pills, alcohol, and abusive men. Nothing quite like it had ever appeared before: there were sexual encounters every few pages, and Susann made liberal use of "screwed," "balled," "humped," "tits," and various other four-letter words then unheard of in a book released by a mainstream publisher. *Valley of the Dolls* also boasted scenes of drug addiction, anal penetration, abortion, and sex in a swimming pool, all set against a glittering show-business background in a story that spanned twenty years.

Valley of the Dolls was a pure roman à clef, and not remotely a subtle one. Neely O'Hara, the singer/dancer who becomes a pill-addicted star, was clearly based on Judy Garland; Jennifer North, the body beautiful with no talent, was a composite of such ill-fated sex goddesses as Marilyn Monroe and Carole Landis; and Anne Welles, the prim New Englander who becomes a famous model and television personality, was Jackie's cleaned-up version of herself.

If Ethel had been any kind of reader at all, *Valley of the Dolls* was the kind of book she might have picked up, and it probably wouldn't have taken her much more than a paragraph to realize that Helen Lawson, the aging, hard-as-nails Broadway star, was a character all too obviously based on The Merm.

The resemblance of Helen to Ethel could not possibly have been coincidental. Helen is a foul-mouthed, tough-talking dame who is the reigning queen of Broadway musicals. When we first encounter her, she is rehearsing a new show called *Hit the Sky,* and she gives her withering opinion of one of its songs: "It stinks! It doesn't say anything. . . . The tune's okay, but you'd better tell Lou to come up with a better set of lyrics." Like Ethel, Helen drinks champagne on the rocks and has a Renoir in her apartment. Like Ethel, she has a collection of leather-bound classic books that her attorney has provided as set dressing, but she insists, "You'll never convince me people actually read that shit. I tried a few pages once. . . . Christ!" Like Ethel, Helen has great vulnerability where men are concerned; she is always looking for love and threatening to quit the stage as soon as she finds it.

But the characteristic of Helen's that seemed to strike the strongest chord with readers was her professional toughness. Early in the novel, we see her cruelly arrange the firing of an attractive ingenue who she has decided is getting too much attention. Readers, especially those in the theater community, jumped on this episode as a perfect chance to connect the dots from Helen to Ethel, and as *Valley of the Dolls* steadily climbed the bestseller list—it was number one on the *New York Times* list for a record-shattering twenty-eight weeks—it became common knowledge that Helen was Ethel scarcely disguised. Even the rhythm of the names—Helen Lawson / Ethel Merman—was the same. To her closest friends, Jackie delighted in the unflattering portrait of Ethel, and several industry insiders wondered if Ethel would take the catfight to the next level by suing Jackie, but Donald Preston, the novel's editor at Bernard Geis, wasn't worried. "Really, people don't do that," he said. "It's a very difficult thing to prove. Bernie Geis wished that Merman would have sued. He thought that would have made the book!"

Ethel didn't pursue any legal action, and on the rare occasions when an interviewer cautiously inquired about the resemblance between herself and Helen Lawson, she responded briskly that she hadn't read the book—that she didn't read trash. The following year, when the movie version of *Valley of the Dolls* was released, Susan Hayward played Helen, complete with a Brooklyn accent that seemed perilously close to Ethel's Queens one.

The rest of Ethel's career would be a look back, not ahead. On January 16, 1966, she turned fifty-eight. She had been a star in the theater for thirty-six years, a record all the more remarkable when measured against the careers of most of her contemporaries in Hollywood, who had managed to stay at the very top for only a few years. In the movies, to be forty was for most women a time of quiet desperation, of taking stock and reshaping their careers, swallowing their pride and accepting mother and character roles. Because her vehicles had been so carefully tailored to her talents, and because most of them featured such top-quality musical material, Ethel had been able to put off dealing with the age bridge—which was much less considerable on Broadway than in Hollywood. But now it seemed unlikely that she could ever again play a genuine romantic lead. Even her diehard fans began to believe her when she told the press, over and over, that she was finished with Broadway.

There wasn't much more she wanted to do in any case. By the mid-1960s, the quality of Broadway musicals had dropped off markedly. Cole Porter had died in 1964. Jule Styne was to reach another peak in his career with *Funny Girl*, then do a slow fade. Irving Berlin's *Mr. President* in 1962 was a dismal, old-fashioned flop, and while Richard Rodgers kept trying until his death in 1979, his career really did not survive the loss of Oscar Hammerstein.

The 1960s was a decade littered with expensive failures: *Greenwillow, Tenderloin, Donnybrook!, Sail Away, Subways Are for Sleeping, All American.* Of course there were still flashes of brilliance, such as Jerry Bock and Sheldon Harnick's score for *Fiddler on the Roof* or John Kander and Fred Ebb's for *Cabaret*. But in general a decline had set in. Attending a Broadway musical had not yet become an outrageously expensive proposition—the ticket prices were still generally under $10—but events had been set in motion that would eventually make going to the theater an elitist rather than a popular pastime. In the 1960s Broadway theater owners acquiesced to the demands of Local One, the stagehands' union, agreeing to set minimum quotas of stagehands, whether or not they were needed—a move that would in future years help to send the cost of Broadway shows skyrocketing.

Another developing trend that affected sixties musicals was the casting of big movie and television names, regardless of their singing ability or significant stage experience: Robert Horton in *110 in the Shade*, Maureen O'Hara in *Christine*, Vivien Leigh in *Tovarich*, Anthony Perkins in *Greenwillow*—all were inferior shows that didn't survive despite their star wattage. Big- and small-screen names were also unaccustomed to the physical demands of an eight-a-week run: witness Lucille Ball's collapse from exhaustion that necessitated the closing of the potentially lucrative *Wildcat*.

Ethel couldn't understand this turn of events. To her way of thinking, if they couldn't sing, they had no business doing a musical. For those who could sing—Mary Martin in *Jennie*, for example—if they couldn't get the right material, what was the point? They were only damaging the reputations they had so carefully built up. Ethel's standards remained high, and as she said repeatedly, Broadway had been good to her, but she'd been good to Broadway. If this was the new Broadway, they could do without each other.

And then she received a call from Irving Berlin. Still smarting from the failure of *Mr. President,* Berlin had hit on the idea of reviving his biggest smash, *Annie Get Your Gun*—but only if Ethel agreed to do it. Despite the fact that she was pushing sixty, the idea of bringing *Annie* to a younger theatergoing generation appealed to her. And to give the project true nostalgic weight, it would be produced by half of the original producing team, Richard Rodgers, by now the head of musical theater projects at Lincoln Center. The revival was set to open at the New York State Theater, the new home of New York City Opera, in May, at the end of the 1965–66 season.

Although Ray Middleton was still capable of reprising Frank Butler, the role eventually went to Bruce Yarnell, a virile, good-looking actor with a terrific singing voice. Both Rodgers and Ethel had wanted someone young and sexy, and Yarnell certainly filled the bill: he was ten years old when Ethel had opened in the original *Annie*. Yarnell was known as a western hero, having appeared on NBC's *The Outlaws*, but his own typecasting amused him. "I can't ride," he once said. "I can't draw. I can't shoot. I can't lasso. The only thing I can do is sing." Ethel persuaded Benay Venuta to play the second female lead of Dolly Tate. Jerry Orbach, who had scored great successes in *The Fantasticks* and *Carnival!*, was luxury casting for the part of Charlie Davenport. Apart from Ethel, the only holdover from the original *Annie* was Harry Bellaver, repeating his role as Chief Sitting Bull.

Berlin and Dorothy Fields sat down to work on the show and reshaped it considerably. Some numbers and a couple of secondary characters were dropped altogether. More than anything else, Berlin wanted another hit song to come out of this revival. One day he turned up with "An Old-Fashioned Wedding," a comedy duet in which Annie and Frank disagree about how they'll be married: Frank wants a simple ceremony, but Annie holds out for something grand. "An Old-Fashioned Wedding" was written in the contrapuntal style that had worked so brilliantly with "You're Just in Love." Ethel was sure from the moment she heard the new song that it would land with the audience.

The production, with designs by Paul McGuire and costumes by Frank Thompson, was on a much grander scale than the original *Annie*. Berlin was in a state of elation during rehearsals, watching the action as he sat at a table, bouncing his hands up and down. There were a few bumps in the road, of course, particularly when Bruce Yarnell's wife, Frances, alienated

Ethel by telling her, "I'm so glad that you're Bruce's *leading lady*." Franz Allers, the conductor, likewise rubbed her the wrong way with his autocratic style; often during rehearsals they clashed in a war of tempos.

Annie had its out-of-town tryout at Toronto's massive O'Keefe Center. There one of the local critics wrote a sharp review attacking Ethel for attempting to revive the show at her age. Ethel was deeply wounded by the writer's comments, but her age had definitely been a point of some discussion as the show was being assembled. There'd been some talk of her wearing a chin strap in order to pass as a younger Annie, but Ethel rejected the idea out of hand. "Jesus, they know what I look like!" she informed Rodgers. "They wanna come and see Merman. If they don't, they don't! I'm not worried."

Overall, though, it was a happy company. Often Ethel invited Jerry Orbach, Ronn Carroll, and several other cast members to her hotel room, where they would play word games well into the night. On one particular night, Yarnell tossed back one drink too many and passed out on the daybed in Ethel's suite. To the delight of the other company members, Ethel bent over him, unzipped his pants, and pulled down his trousers so that when he woke up, he would wonder what had happened during the night.

Jerry Orbach was particularly impressed by Ethel's eye for detail. "She would dumbfound people by saying, 'The third light on the second balcony rail should be pink, and it's amber,' " he recalled. "She had all-around expertise." Even more important, her voice was in excellent condition. After thirty-six years in the theater, it had naturally darkened slightly, from a trumpet to a trombone, but its power was undiminished and the pitch was as true as ever.

Annie was by now part of show-business legend, and when it opened in New York on May 31, 1966, both the audience and the press welcomed Ethel back ecstatically. Although there were moments in the first act when she seemed to be pacing herself slightly, every solo of Ethel's was cheered at length, but the real showstopper was the new song. As "An Old-Fashioned Wedding" was encored again and again, Ethel pulled out all the stops by beating on Yarnell's chest to try to make him listen. In fact, the song was reprised so many times that some of the critics had to exit before the final scene to file their reviews by deadline.

The next day Vincent Canby's notice in the *New York Times* set the tone for all the others. "Little Sure Shot is older," he wrote, "but she also is more mellow. Most important, the pipes sound as true, if not quite so loud, as they ever did. And that implacable, straightforward thrust towards a comic situation can't be stopped by anything—neither by time nor by a first-night audience whose love threatened to turn the show into a noisy devotional service." *Newsday* thought that the revival seemed "a lot better than most of the current musicals that assail our ears and dull our other senses."

Despite the sniping of some Broadway veterans who called the show *Granny Get Your Gun*, the box-office response was tremendous. After the professional disappointments of recent years Ethel was pleased to be back in New York with a hit, and she was in gleeful, wicked humor throughout the run. One of her favorite targets was Benay. One night Benay reported to work at the theater and told Ethel how she'd been getting crank telephone calls from someone who breathed into the receiver and hung up.

"Benay, this sounds terrible," said Ethel. "I would get yourself a car service. It sounds like you've got a real crazy there."

That night Ethel pulled Ronn Carroll aside and urged him to telephone Benay late at night. "I don't care what you say to her," she whispered, "but end the conversation with, 'Go fuck yourself!' " Then she laughed uproariously.

Despite the advances Jerome Robbins had made in her acting technique in *Gypsy*, Ethel now fell back on her old habit of facing front and selling her lines directly to the audience. One evening she noticed Jerry Orbach doing some piece of business on one of her joke lines. She went to the stage manager, Bill Ross, and complained. Ross watched carefully at the next performance, and when Ethel came offstage, he said, "Ethel, he's just reacting, punching up your joke." "You tell Jerry and EVERYBODY ELSE," Ethel demanded, "I don't react to *their* jokes, and they don't have to react to *mine*."

The show was supposed to fold after its five-week engagement at the State Theater, but it was extended by another eight weeks; then Rodgers decided that a road tour was called for. For the most part, Ethel enjoyed the tour although, as always, there were moments when she had to assert herself. The Philadelphia run coincided with an extreme heat wave. On the first day at the Forrest Theatre, Ethel found the temperature stifling and called for the house manager. "Miss Merman," the officious manager informed her, "I come in here every day at four-thirty and turn on the air-conditioning. It will be fine." Ethel stared him down and said nothing. The following day the theater was again uncomfortably stuffy, and again Ethel summoned the house manager. "It's hotter than hell," she snapped. "Miss Merman," he said, in a tone even more glacial than the one he'd used the day before, "I come in here at four-thirty and turn on the system. Everything will be all right."

"Oh, yeah?" said Ethel. "Well, I was here at four-thirty today, and *no one* was here. You throw another log on the air conditioner or you can get yourself another girl singer!"

During the Philadelphia run, Ethel caught a bad cold that soon developed into pneumonia. One night, the other actors arrived at the theater and discovered her lying backstage on a cot, seemingly unable to speak. Her understudy assumed that she would be going on, retired to her dressing room, and emerged in her Annie Oakley costume. Ethel looked up at her. "Forget it, kid," she said, and got up and sang the entire show in what Ronn Carroll remembered as "this terribly sweet, non-Merman voice."

Frequently while the show was on the road, Ethel and some of the other cast members were invited to postperformance parties at the homes of local theater patrons. At one of these affairs in Detroit, the hostess approached her and said, "I hope you don't mind. I have a piano player. I hope you'll sing."

"Sure, honey," said Ethel. "My fee is ten thousand dollars. I'd be happy to sing for you."

The resultant publicity from the tour was so intense that Rodgers decided to bring *Annie Get Your Gun* back to New York, where it settled in for several months at the Broadway Theatre, playing to overflow houses. In March 1967, NBC aired an abridgement of the show, filmed in color, of which only the audio section appears to have survived. Annie or Granny, Ethel had once again shown everyone who was the Queen of Broadway.

Ethel might have returned to New York in glory, but her happiness was undercut by her concern for her daughter. Casting a shadow over the past several years was her knowledge that Ethel Jr.'s life was slowly unraveling. Being both a mother and wife had simply pushed the young woman to the breaking point, and her marriage to Bill Geary had broken up in 1965, with great sadness and regret on both sides. Ethel Jr. moved to a small rental house in West Hollywood just off Melrose Place, trying to find work wherever she could get it. It was all too much for her, and her mood swings, so reminiscent of her father's, were becoming more and more dramatic. At some point she suffered a complete nervous collapse. Very little headway had yet been made in medical treatment for the condition—the field of psychopharmacology hardly existed, and the development of antidepressants was a long way off—so Ethel Jr. was put on various cycles of tranquilizers. Once she confided to Tony Cointreau that all the heavy medication "really scares me."

She continued to flail about, looking for some kind of career. When she first moved to Los Angeles, Ethel Jr. had had vague thoughts of supporting herself by acting in television commercials, but she quickly found that world too tough and competitive. She complained to her close friends that as long as she remained in show business, she was destined to be known as Ethel Merman's daughter, and she began wishing that she had explored some other career route. Then she began working with a small experimental theater collective and seemed quite happy doing so. She also became romantically involved with an actor named Monty Pike, a colorful figure on Los Angeles's fringe theatrical scene. Ethel Jr. began to think that perhaps she had found herself in the world of alternative arts and culture that Monty represented.

For Big Ethel, America in the mid-1960s seemed like alien territory. She could not understand the spirit of revolt, of questioning authority, of tearing down icons and trying to find a new path. She had lived her life in the musical theater, and she really knew very little about the world outside it. She helped her daughter financially as much as possible, paying her psychiatrist's bills and trying to be as supportive as she could. At other times she responded to Ethel Jr.'s rapidly changing lifestyle with her usual knee-jerk abruptness, and Ethel Jr. always threw it right back at her with equal vehemence. Bobby, too, seemed to be losing his career momentum as he began to drift into the counterculture in San Francisco, where he was now living and where he eventually went to work teaching at the famed American Conservatory Theater. Ethel visited him there and was stunned by the creative acting methods that the students were encouraged to pursue. "If I had to do all of these things," she told Mark Zeller, "I'd never get onstage."

Bobby did win Ethel's approval, however, when he became romantically involved with Barbara Colby, a talented brunette actress who was one of the founding members of the American Conservatory Theater. Barbara had made her Broadway debut in 1965 in *The Devils*, with Jason Robards and Anne Bancroft, and had amassed an impressive list of regional theater credits, later returning to Broadway as Kristine in *A Doll's House* with Liv Ullmann. She had a warm, no-nonsense personality, and Ethel considered her a good, stabilizing influence for her son.

By the summer of 1967, Ethel Jr. seemed to be responding fairly well to her latest round of medication. She had grown tired of the chaotic pace of Los Angeles and longed to return to Colorado College and complete her education. At last she seemed to have hit on something she wanted to pursue professionally: teaching theater to small children. It was something that would take her out of her mother's shadow, and she was delighted to be back in the more tranquil environment of Colorado. She talked of buying a horse and settling into the outdoor life she had long since come to love.

Her health by now was relatively stable, and once she got established in Green Mountain Falls, a little resort town near Colorado Springs, she telephoned Bill Geary to ask if he might allow the children to visit for a short while. The arrangements were made, and Barbara Jean, now six, and Michael, five, joined her at her cabin. The children slept in her bedroom at night, and Ethel Jr. took the sofa.

It was there, lying in her nightgown, that Barbara Jean found her on the morning of August 23. When Barbara Jean spoke to her mother, there was no answer. Her face had a strange bluish cast, and when Barbara Jean touched her, her skin felt cold. The child ran out to summon help from a tourist who was staying nearby, but it was too late. Her mother was dead.

In a chilling replay of Bob Levitt's death, the police found several pill bottles scattered about, along with a couple of empty vodka bottles. The combination had been lethal, and the coroner estimated that Ethel had died around midnight. His official report, however, stated his belief that the overdose had been an accident rather than suicide, and the details of the case—the presence of her children, the fact that her life was on the upswing—seemed to bear out his verdict.

For Barbara Geary, looking back nearly forty years later, the tragedy seemed shrouded in ambiguity. "I think that it was kind of unintentional suicide, if that makes sense," she said. "She had had a nervous breakdown, she was getting her life together, and then here come her two children to visit her. I can see how she might have been overwhelmed. Here they are, they need to be taken care of. 'Am I a person who really wants to take care of them?' Not that she didn't love us. I think she might have been overwhelmed by her old life. We represented the stuff that dragged her down. Who knows? Only she knows."

Her daughter's death drained Ethel of all hope, sense, and reason. Upon hearing the news, she broke down completely. Benay Venuta agreed to accompany her on the trip west, but by the time they flew to San Francisco, where they were to meet Bobby before going on to Colorado Springs, Ethel was in a state of hysteria. A doctor contacted by Bobby gave her a strong sedative that calmed her to the point where she was at least able to think rationally. She went along with Bill Geary's decision that the children should not learn the truth immediately. They were whisked away to the home of Bill's sister and told that their mother was sick and in the hospital. They were not informed of her death until a week later, after the cremation and funeral had taken place. Her ashes were interred at the Evergreen Shrine of Rest, where Ethel purchased a special room that she hoped would one day be the final resting place for the entire family.

On her return to New York, Ethel barricaded herself in her apartment, spending night after night crying herself to sleep. Despite her erratic attendance record at St. Bartholomew's, she had always been a devout believer in God, and she now began to look for ways of adding new dimensions to her spiritual life. Eventually she discovered the *Daily Word*, the monthly publication of Unity Village, which had a different reading for each day of the week. The Unity movement had been founded in 1889 and had always stressed embracing God as a way of maximizing each individual's potential for joy and ultimate fulfillment. (This was not always as pure in motive as it sounded; during the second half of the twentieth century, Unity, with its message of positive thinking, would be sought out by many as a tool for achieving prosperity.) Ethel cared little about Unity's spiritual teachings on a broader canvas; she only knew that the simple, heartfelt messages in the *Daily Word* brought her greater comfort than anything else had, and her grief gradually subsided to the point where she could manage it. She was especially moved by a passage that read, "The light of God surrounds me / The love of God enfolds me / The power of God protects me / The presence of God watches over me / Wherever I am, God is." She began to feel that she was no longer alone, and the *Daily Word* would help her to find her way spiritually for the rest of her life.

Chapter Nineteen

● ●

E thel's period of solitary mourning continued. On September 15,
1967, she appeared on *The Ed Sullivan Show*, singing a song not
associated with her: Gordon Jenkins's "This Is All I Ask." It was one
of the most tender, emotionally connected performances she had ever given.
For those who knew that Ethel Jr. had died only weeks earlier, "This Is All
I Ask" was a study in heartbreak.

By now she had left the Park Lane and moved to the Berkshire Hotel at
21 East Fifty-second Street. Carleton Varney, an imaginative decorator employed by the brilliant interior design leader Dorothy Draper, was assigned
to give her apartment a makeover. "Ethel was not a person who didn't like
what she had," observed Varney, and the new apartment featured many of
her favorite pieces from the Park Lane, including her big brass bed, her
enormous faux-Tiffany chandelier, the beautiful bar she'd had with her for
years, a set of large marble urns, an imposing Victorian chest of drawers, a
handsome rocking chair where Pop Zimmermann always sat, and her collection of paintings, including Edseid's *Ladies at the Footlights,* which always
hung over her mantelpiece. The first thing she did at the Berkshire was to
have the stove removed from the kitchen. Since she didn't cook, she considered it a waste of space; a hot plate would do for boiling water for tea. She
instructed Varney to outfit the bedrooms with great walls of storage space,
since she liked to slide back the doors and see all of her sequinned gowns
and fur coats lined up neatly in a row. She also had a little artificial Christmas tree sitting year-round on a table by the front door. She plugged the tree
in every night and told her friends that looking at it gave her comfort, just as
reading the *Daily Word* did. But no spiritual discipline could fully erase the
terrifying emptiness that she felt in the wake of Ethel Jr.'s death.

Once again work proved to be her salvation. According to Tom Korman,
who had succeeded Milton Pickman as her agent, she wanted to work as
often as possible, so long as the terms were good. Korman lined up a string
of guest appearances for her on a number of high-profile series: the popular

sitcom *That Girl*, starring Marlo Thomas; the smash-hit action spoof *Batman*, in which she played Lola Lasagne, the loudmouthed girlfriend of the arch-villain the Penguin (Burgess Meredith); and, most curiously, on *Tarzan*, in which she did a two-part stint as a missionary.

There were still offers of Broadway shows, but always she said no—especially to ideas as unappealing as a musical version of Fellini's *La Dolce Vita*. The world of popular music was no longer dominated by the solidly tuneful, reliable standards of Cole Porter, Jule Styne, Richard Rodgers, and Irving Berlin, as the perpetual evolution of rock and roll had completely reconfigured its landscape. Ethel thought all of this was a fad that couldn't possibly last—but she was wrong. Step by step the new sound was shaping much of what was being done on Broadway. In 1968, Burt Bacharach and Hal David would open *Promises, Promises*, a show written entirely in the style of their Top 40 pop hits. Later in 1968, *Hair*, the first rock musical, became an era-defining Broadway hit. (Ethel was less disturbed by *Hair*'s use of four-letter words than she was by what she considered the cast's sloppy comedy technique. "They don't know how to sell a gag," she complained. "You gotta face front and throw it right out there!") Purists were shocked by it, but the effect of *Hair* was widespread. More and more musicals began reflecting the new pop culture, and heavily amplified sound became standard practice on Broadway. In the future, more and more Broadway shows, from *How Now, Dow Jones* to *The Grass Harp*, would forsake traditional musical theater for the jangly, contemporary sound of music heard on television theme songs and commercials.

Ethel reacted to this movement by turning her back on it. Since the revival of *Annie Get Your Gun* had ended up being such a smash, she decided to defy the new era by resurrecting another of her old hits. Early in 1968 she received an offer to star in *Call Me Madam* on the winter-stock circuit. By now the heyday of stock was past, having been undermined by changing audiences and the success of television, but it still proved to be a viable avenue for many old-time stars, particularly those whose film careers had faded. Audiences flocked to see how their favorites were holding up—whether it was Joan Fontaine in *Private Lives* or Sylvia Sidney in *Arsenic and Old Lace* or *Brigadoon* with Ann Blyth or *Auntie Mame* with Gypsy Rose Lee. Since Ethel loathed touring and demanded top production values, the prospect of appearing in stock had never appealed to her, and initially she said no to the idea. (Tom Korman recalled that her first response was always no.) But when nothing else of interest had presented itself and she knew she needed a distraction from brooding about Ethel Jr.'s death, she eventually agreed.

Call Me Madam opened for a two-week run at the Parker Playhouse in Fort Lauderdale, Florida, on March 25, then moved on to Miami's Coconut Grove Playhouse. After a hiatus it returned that summer to the St. Louis Municipal Opera and Kansas City's Starlight Theatre. Then she took the show on the circuit run by John Kenley, a highly regarded producer whose company, the Kenley Players, was generally thought of as the Tiffany's of summer-theater companies.

Kenley was one of the producers for whom actors loved to work, because he paid his stars enormous salaries and did his best to guarantee the public quality productions—sometimes he even managed to get his hands on the sets from the Broadway original. Over the years he had honed a formula that had proved consistently successful: he would book huge theaters, keep the ticket prices low, and wind up filling every seat in the house.

Since Kenley's production of *Call Me Madam* would have minimal rehearsal time, as was the custom in summer stock, Ethel called on two actors who had played the show with her on Broadway: Russell Nype and Richard Eastham. While her relationship with Nype was as warm as ever, she clashed with Eastham immediately when the actor went behind her back to request above-the-title billing with her. "She cut him dead," recalled Arthur Bartow, who played Pemberton Maxwell on the tour. "She would not talk to him. She would not ride in the same car with him."

John DeMain, the conductor for the Ohio run, remembered a conference with the Kenley choreographer over "Something to Dance About." The decision was made that the Kenley dancers simply weren't up to the elaborate choreography required for the number, so certain cuts were made. In rehearsal Ethel was supposed to come back in for the final chorus, but she missed her cue. "So we did it again," said DeMain, "and again she didn't come in. She had a sense of how long she waited offstage, and she hadn't waited long enough. She wasn't listening to the music! So she got rather testy. And we played it uncut, and she was fine. I told the choreographer he would have to stay up all night and think up choreography to cover the cut, because she couldn't learn it *with* the cut."

Cast in the role of the princess was Donna McKechnie, who got off on the wrong foot with Ethel immediately. She had two numbers, "It's a Lovely Day Today" and "The Ocarina," in which the princess's dance role had been expanded. One day as she was rehearsing "The Ocarina," Ethel and Russell Nype strolled in and sat down front. McKechnie decided to show off a bit but was deflated instantly when Ethel suddenly boomed, "WHO DID SHE FUCK TO GET TWO DANCE NUMBERS?"

Only a few years later, McKechnie would achieve Broadway stardom in *A Chorus Line*. At the time of *Call Me Madam*, however, she was just a struggling dancer—specifically, a dancer who perspired a lot. McKechnie played *Call Me Madam* during a typically hot midwestern summer, suffocating underneath a heavy wig and makeup. Ethel didn't spare her as much as a hello on the way from dressing room to stage. One night the stage manager knocked at McKechnie's dressing room and handed her a note. It was from Ethel, asking that she stop sweating so much onstage; the star found it very distracting.

McKechnie's Merman experience did have a happy ending. Toward the end of the run, she got a job on Broadway and gave her notice. On her last night with the *Call Me Madam* company, McKechnie noticed that when Ethel was onstage with her, she was making a little clucking noise with her throat and crossing her eyes. McKechnie thought for a moment that she was having a stroke. She ran offstage and told the stage manager of her concern. It was Ethel, honoring an old vaudeville custom: when a performer left the company, his fellow actors paid tribute to him by trying to break him up onstage.

Still deeply depressed by her daughter's death, Ethel kept the company members at an even greater distance than she normally did. But she occasionally indulged in lighter moments, especially when she and John Kenley sat up late at night talking after the show. "It was drinky-poo, drinky-poo," said Kenley. "And she did love her men. We used to have these amazing, graphic conversations about her men. And years later when I saw her and we were talking about something of a personal nature, I said, 'Oh, now, Ethel, you and I never did get personal.' And she said, 'What in the hell are you talking about? What was all that stuff we used to talk about if it wasn't personal?' And I said, 'No, Ethel. That wasn't personal. Clinical. Clinical, darling.' "

In 1969 it was announced that Ethel would return to the Kenley circuit in *Gypsy*, again with DeMain conducting. Unfortunately, she found out that John Kenley was planning to economize by cutting a couple of scenes, including one of her favorites, the one in the Chinese restaurant when Rose steals the silverware. Ethel declared that she would deliver the original *Gypsy* in all its glory or she wouldn't deliver it at all; she was not going to let Kenley palm off a bargain-basement version. She nixed the tour and was replaced by Jane Kean. Later, Ethel complained to DeMain that Kenley "wanted to do some kind of high-school production" of her favorite show. Perhaps she simply didn't feel up to returning to such a demanding part ten years after she had created it. And surely, the dressing room scene with

Gypsy, to say nothing of "Rose's Turn," would have been all the more grueling for her in the wake of her daughter's death.

In late 1968 and 1969, Ethel concentrated on television appearances, with guest shots on *Hollywood Palace, The Carol Burnett Show,* and several of the then-popular talk shows. One week in the midwinter of 1969, while serving as cohost of *The Mike Douglas Show* in Philadelphia, she received a surprise on-air visit from Barbara Jean and Michael and burst into tears in front of the television audience. She stood back and beamed with pride as Douglas brought Michael forward and egged him on to do a rain dance he'd learned in WEBELOS.

Try as she might to persuade the press and public that she'd "had it" with Broadway, Ethel's level of activity in the late 1960s was not sufficient to keep her fully engaged; she had too much vitality, too much drive, and she needed a more demanding outlet than the occasional guest spot on television. This period of professional restlessness in her life coincided with an offer from David Merrick: it wasn't a new show but one that had been running for six years and one she'd initially turned down—*Hello, Dolly!*

Ethel's original concern about not wanting to be compared with Ruth Gordon, creator of the role of Dolly in Thornton Wilder's *The Matchmaker,* now seemed a moot point. Carol Channing had created the musical Dolly back in 1964 and, an inspired clown, had made the part her own. When she left the show in August 1965, a long parade of actresses had come in as replacements: Ginger Rogers, Martha Raye, Betty Grable, Pearl Bailey, and Phyllis Diller. (The touring Dollys included Mary Martin, Eve Arden, Yvonne De Carlo, and Dorothy Lamour.) All had something individual to bring to the part, and Merrick reveled in the publicity value that came from announcing the next star to assume the role. (This was the beginning of a trend that would one day transform Broadway yet again, when a show became not so much a vehicle designed for a particular performer as something any viable star could be plugged in to; it was the show, not the star, that endured.)

Ethel's interest in *Dolly!* was piqued when she learned that Jerry Herman had originally written two songs for her that had never been used. They had been tailored to her voice, but since Channing was no vocalist, they had to be dropped. Once Ethel heard and liked the new/old songs—"World, Take Me Back" and her favorite, "Love, Look in My Window"—she agreed to become the seventh Broadway Dolly. The press announced that it was to be for a limited run only: from April through June 1970.

Before she went into *Dolly!,* Ethel dropped by the St. James Theatre one night to see Phyllis Diller in the show, which had been playing to rather sparse houses. Afterward Diller asked her if she was going to wear a chest mike—now a fixture on Broadway—when she took over the part. "No," answered Ethel, "we just want to keep it in the theater." (In fact, she did wear a body mike in *Dolly!* because it was part of the sound design: since the rest of the cast was being miked, Ethel would have sounded conspicuous without one.)

The show's original director, Gower Champion, had rehearsed all the other replacement Dollys, but when Merrick persuaded Ethel to take over, Champion bowed out, saying he couldn't bear putting one more star through her paces. He passed on his directing chores to the stage manager, Lucia Victor, and his wife, Marge Champion, who worked with Ethel for two weeks prior to the opening. When Marge arrived at rehearsal, she found that certain problems had already arisen. Victor complained that Ethel was taking her opening number, "I Put My Hand In," at a deadly slow pace. Marge agreed but wisely chose not to confront Ethel on the matter. It was clear to her from the outset that Ethel was exceptionally nervous about taking over a part that had been a Broadway hit with six other actresses.

"I tried, in every way, to be supportive of her anxiety," recalled Marge, "and to assure her how really perfect she was for that show." In two weeks' time, Ethel's confidence had grown, and her performance gained in rhythm, color, and bite. To Marge, she caught something that eluded a number of the other Dollys: she could play not only Dolly Levi but Dolly Gallagher, the Irish colleen who had married a Jewish man.

"This steamroller suddenly happened to the show," recalled Marcia Lewis, who played Ernestina Money. "We went from the littlest audiences you could imagine in the St. James Theatre to absolute pandemonium around the block. Ethel taught me how to plant. I used to watch her so closely, and she would find where she wanted to stand—which of course was dead center down front—and you could almost feel her roots being put down through the floor. She looked to the left and the right and the balcony, but that spot man had her there, and that's where she stayed."

When Ethel unveiled her Dolly at the St. James Theatre on March 30, 1970, the audience was in a frenzy of anticipation. The moment she made her entrance, pulling down the newspaper she is reading as the trolley car chugs onstage, the entire crowd jumped to its feet for a prolonged ovation. They were all standing again when, in Dolly's famous red gown and plumed hat, she appeared at the top of the Harmonia Gardens staircase just before launching into "Hello, Dolly!" John Montgomery and David Evans were the two actors positioned at the bottom of the staircase as she descended, singing the number. "She came down the steps, and they just wouldn't stop,"

Montgomery remembered. "David Evans was across from me, and we were looking at each other. I was trembling, and David started crying. As the number got going, they screamed and applauded all through it."

The title number, in fact, played beautifully into the sentiment attached to the occasion; many of the lines were weighted with double meaning. When Ethel sang "IT'S SO NICE TO BE BACK HOME WHERE I BE-LONG!" the audience erupted in cheers for more than a minute. They had the same response to similar lines, such as "DOLLY WILL NEVER GO AWAY AGAIN!" and "TOMORROW WILL BE BRIGHTER THAN THE GOOD OLD DAYS!" at which the orchestra had to come to a full stop, waiting for the applause to subside.

There was a third standing ovation for her at the finale, one that went on and on. In between, all her numbers were greeted with such ecstatic cheers that some of the opening-night critics complained that they couldn't make out all the words. Both of the new numbers, especially "Love, Look in My Window," were enormous hits with the audience; they would have the distinction of being the last songs Ethel would introduce. Taking Lucia Victor's advice, Ethel smiled while she sang "Love, Look in My Window," so as to ease the tear-jerking nature of the song. But anyone, friend or fan, who knew of the heartbreak Ethel had experienced in the last decade could hardly have helped being moved to tears when she sang:

> *Love, look in my window,*
> *Love, knock on my door,*
> *It's years since you called on me.*
> *How I would love hearing your laughter once more*
> *So if you should ever be in the neighborhood . . .*

The *New York Times* responded to Ethel's return by writing her a series of love letters. Walter Kerr called her voice "exactly as trumpet-clean, exactly as pennywhistle-piercing, exactly as Wurlitzer-wonderful as it always was. Right from the first notes, the first words . . . you know it's all still there, dustproof, rustproof, off and aloft and ringing."

Ethel's presence in *Dolly!* was like a transfusion for the sagging show. In a season where the other big musical hits were the decidedly second-rate *Applause* and *Coco*, starring, respectively, Lauren Bacall and Katharine Hepburn, two of the most unmusical stars ever to have crossed a Broadway stage, *Dolly!* rode high. Even in the midst of such a triumph, Ethel Jr. was ever present in her mother's thoughts. Helene Whitney recalled going backstage to see Ethel on *Dolly!*'s opening night. The first thing Ethel did was clasp her hand and say, "Helene—she didn't commit suicide." To Whitney, Ethel offstage had none of the drive and fire that she remembered from the three shows they'd done together. Now she seemed tired, defeated, and overwhelmingly sad.

Yet professionally Ethel had not mellowed at all. She still insisted that everyone around her give 100 percent to the show, and she flew into a rage if she felt that someone was slacking off. "She was playing a matinee one day," said Biff Liff, then an associate in the Merrick office, "and she was pissed off at something, which she was usually. She told me to get my ass down to the theater and fire the stage manager. She was unhappy about something. She said the guy up in the booth was drunk, because he didn't know how to put a spotlight on her. She said, 'Fire everybody! They don't know what they're doing!' I thought to myself, 'That will be a day in heaven, if I could ever fire a stagehand.' But she was a pro from beginning to end. She gave every night and was just terrific."

With such a success, Merrick wasn't about to let her off the hook after three months. More than anything he wanted her to beat the record-breaking run of 2,717 performances established by *My Fair Lady* some years earlier. Although the hot, humid summer in New York had sapped her energy, Ethel agreed to extend the run, and *Dolly!* did not close until its 2,844th performance, on December 27. Broadway had a new all-time champion show, and Ethel could be proud that it was she who'd helped make it so. Since Merrick had backed out of throwing a closing-night party, Ethel hosted one herself, at the Grenadier, near the United Nations. At the end of the evening, feeling no pain, she got up and sang "I'll Pay the Check" from *Stars in Your Eyes*, which moved the entire cast to tears.

Dolly didn't keep her promise about never going away again. The last performance of *Hello, Dolly!* marked the end of Ethel Merman's forty-year conquest of Broadway. Hers was a record that no other star would ever come close to matching, but it was something even larger than that: Ethel's departure was nothing less than the end of the kind of Broadway she had helped create. Over the next decade, the great old-fashioned star vehicles would not disappear, and musical comedy would certainly continue to indulge in nostalgia: witness the huge success of *No, No, Nanette* in 1971 and *Irene* in 1973. But however profitable these shows were, they took a decided backseat to the musicals being created by Stephen Sondheim. Beginning with *Company* in 1970, Sondheim devised a new kind of show, one with a brittle sophistication and intellectual content that far surpassed anything that had been attempted in the past. The critics, for the most part, gave him their seal of approval, and the 1970s became the Age of Sondheim. In *Company, Follies, A Little Night Music,* and *Pacific Overtures,* a big, well-trained, traditional musical-theater voice was not nearly as important as the ability to communicate the tensions, anxieties, and quirks with which the songs were really concerned. As a result, "character" voices became more important than ever; merely passable singers such as Alexis Smith, Glynis Johns, and Hermione Gingold were elevated to belated Broadway stardom, while such vocal powerhouses as Karen Morrow, Nancy Dussault, Eydie Gormé, and Mimi Hines fell by the wayside as the shows, not the singers, became of paramount importance. The directors of musicals gained ever more importance, too, none more so than Harold Prince, who staged the Sondheim shows, and the extraordinary Michael Bennett, who would revolutionize the Broadway musical with *A Chorus Line,* a kind of ensemble docudrama about the struggles of Broadway gypsies. If *A Chorus Line* was the way of the future, it looked as if stars would no longer be absolutely necessary.

Ethel's response to the new Broadway was outwardly one of cool detachment. She didn't exhibit much interest in following most of the new shows or in gossiping about people she knew in the theater. The steady distance she kept from Broadway surprised even some of the friends who'd known her for a long time. Whenever she appeared on television talk shows, the big question, "Will you ever do another Broadway show?" was inevitably asked and just as inevitably answered: "Broadway's been pretty good to me, but then I've been pretty good to Broadway."

Still, it is difficult to believe that the shift in Ethel's behavior around this time didn't have something to do with the fact that the biggest part of her career was behind her. She had always been quick to drop those she suspected were disloyal or trying to manipulate her, but now her temper grew worse. Part of her trouble was alcohol. For years she had been drinking Almaden on the rocks, but now she'd switched to vodka, which she drank straight, and she could become quite belligerent after she'd had a few. Unfortunately for her, she enjoyed keeping company with others who drank and encouraged her to do so. Chief among these was Goldie Hawkins, proprietor of Goldie's New York, a popular piano bar at 232 East Fifty-third Street frequented by the Broadway crowd. Goldie had elevated sycophancy from a hobby to a vocation: like Sherman Billingsley, he made sure that celebrities kept beating a path to his door by always giving them the royal treatment. Ethel became the joint's leading regular, and fans often popped in hoping that she might even be persuaded to get up and sing a few of her famous songs. Often when she was at Goldie's, however, Ethel was in no condition to be singing at all. On these occasions she could become loud and argumentative, and if an eligible man was present, she had a way of becoming disconcertingly coquettish in an attempt to seduce him. Goldie Hawkins set the pattern for many of the gay men who became hangers-on in the years that followed by urging her consumption of alcohol. A heavy boozer himself, he seemed to delight in the belligerent, tough-talking side of Ethel that inevitably appeared—as if he were conjuring up the legend he so desperately wanted to believe in.

In contrast, over the next few years, Ethel continued to enjoy a great warmth and closeness with many friends, both old (Josie Traeger, Martha Neubert, Alice Welch) and young (Tony Cointreau and his partner, James Russo). But to others she seemed increasingly irritable, more and more given to angry, violent outbursts and confrontations. As the decade rolled on, some would find that her deep sadness, her unquenchable anger, her growing sense of isolation, all rendered her more like Helen Lawson than even Jackie Susann might have imagined.

Chapter Twenty

B y the mid-1970s, New York would reach its all-time nadir of livabil-
ity. Burglaries and muggings were rampant, Harlem was a squalid
and frightening place that had lost practically every shred of its former glory, prostitutes and junkies had taken over much of Times Square,
and many ordinary New Yorkers were afraid to use the parks, which had
become havens for criminals and drug dealers. The city's sad decline was
reflected in many of the period's plays and films—everything from Jules
Feiffer's *Little Murders* and Neil Simon's *The Prisoner of Second Avenue* to
Alan J. Pakula's *Klute* and Martin Scorsese's *Mean Streets*.

Ethel was angered at and resentful of the changes in her beloved city,
which were causing her to feel increasingly alienated from the mainstream
of life. On January 16, 1971, she turned sixty-three, and she continued to
suffer setbacks that made her feel ever more vulnerable. Her apartment had
been hit during a burglary at the Berkshire, and she'd been robbed of many
of her cherished possessions, including much of her jewelry collection.

Then, early that year, Mom Zimmermann, who had been growing increasingly frail over the past months, suffered a severe heart attack. Ethel
was devastated. Her connection with her parents had never lessened in
intensity; as one relationship after another had failed her, it had only
become closer. Barbara Geary felt that Ethel's involvement with Mom and
Pop Zimmermann was so overpowering that there was really no room for
anyone else to get close to any of them. During Mom Zimmermann's recu-
peration at Roosevelt Hospital on West Sixtieth Street, Ethel was a dutiful
daily visitor. Pop Zimmermann was also succumbing to old age, as his eyesight had deteriorated to the point where it was hard for him to navigate on
his own. Still, his memory was keen and his wit as sharp as ever, and Ethel
maintained her long-held habit of joining him for a drink before dinner,
whether she was staying in or going out. Pop loved scotch, and he looked
forward all day to the early evening, when they would spend an hour talking
together over a cocktail.

All these changes, both in the world at large and close to home, served to sour Ethel's general outlook. It was now more than ever the case that her lack of inner resources proved detrimental to her. True, she had proved that she could forge through the collapse of her marriages and the tragedy of losing her daughter by marching straight ahead and absorbing herself in work. But apart from reading her devotions in the *Daily Word*, she had little ability to process the transitions in her life on any deeper level. Her reactions were too strong, too instantaneous, too briefly considered, and, in most cases, too irreversible to bring her any genuine level of inner peace and understanding. As people age, their lives generally grow either larger or smaller. Ethel's had begun to shrink.

One source of genuine pleasure that remained was her grandchildren. In her worst moments, she denigrated her grandmother status. "Grandmother— what does that mean?" she asked Mary Henderson, curator at the Museum of the City of New York. "It's nothing—just a word." Still, she felt a great sense of responsibility to her grandchildren, and it did not diminish when Bill Geary remarried. Wherever she was, she telephoned Barbara Jean and Michael every week, keeping close tabs on them. In the spring of 1971, the children showed up on a segment of Ralph Edwards's long-running television program *This Is Your Life*, which surprised celebrities with a half-hour "live" biography in which friends, family members, and coworkers turned up to pay the subject tribute, all secretly arranged in advance with Edwards. The trap was set for Ethel on the set of *The Merv Griffin Show*, where she was appearing singing "World, Take Me Back" and "Love, Look in My Window." When Edwards made his trademark move—ripping the cover off a photo album—and proclaimed, "ETHEL MERMAN—*THIS* IS YOUR LIFE!," Ethel dissolved in tears. She was so overcome with emotion that the taping of the program had to be delayed for several minutes while she got herself under control and the location changed from Griffin's set to Edwards's. Among the surprise guests were Josie Traeger, Goldie Hawkins, and Benay Venuta. All gave touching and heartfelt tributes, with the exception of Benay, who came off as a relentless self-promoter. Ethel was joyously tearful throughout, but when Barbara Jean and Michael came out, she collapsed altogether. It was a rare moment for the public to see the warmhearted, unabashedly sentimental side of Ethel.

She also took the two children on lengthy vacations in the summertime. In 1971 they all went to the newly opened Walt Disney World in Orlando, Florida. The marathon amusement park, which hadn't yet unveiled many of what would become its most famous attractions, was tremendously exciting for Barbara Jean and Michael. Ethel accompanied them on some of the more sedate rides—she loved It's a Small World and the Country Bear Jamboree—but she passed on the fast ones, such as Space Mountain. Generally she preferred summer holidays with a water setting, and took the children several times to Seaview, a charming and picturesque enclave of Fire Island. Ethel rented a spacious house there, watching as Barbara Jean and Michael spent day after day paddling in the surf and collecting shells on the beach. One summer was spent in Kennebunkport, Maine, and another on Saint Martin, where they stayed at Mary's Fancy, an old plantation house that had been transformed into an elegant hotel. One day during the Saint Martin vacation, Barbara was running around on a hillside chasing butterflies, when Ethel suddenly started to weep uncontrollably. As Barbara recalled, "She said, 'That's just like your mother.' She was doing that all the time. I think Mom became more golden in death than she was in life. All the difficulties were forgotten." The family trips would come to an end by around 1974, as the children got older, but Ethel cherished them as long as they lasted.

During the early 1970s, Ethel continued making frequent appearances on the television talk shows. One topic that came up often was the fact that she had missed winning the Tony Award for her greatest role, Rose. One night while chatting with Johnny Carson on the *Tonight Show,* she stated that she had never won a Tony Award. Unbeknownst to her, the executive committee of the Tonys had already convened and agreed to present her with a special award for lifetime achievement in the theater. Soon after it was announced that Ethel would be honored at that year's ceremony, Tony Cointreau received a telephone call from her. "Oh, my God," she said, "I am so embarrassed. I just found my Tony Award for *Call Me Madam.* I was using it as a paperweight in my desk." When she accepted her lifetime Tony at the show's telecast ceremony on April 23, 1972, Ethel tactfully refrained from mentioning her earlier award.

When Ethel was unhappy about something, she was never unhappy alone. Over the years those who most consistently bore the brunt of her wrath were her managers. Her attitude toward them generally ran to various shades of contempt. Most of them she regarded as either parasites or incompetents—or both—and she treated them accordingly. *They* weren't the talent, she reasoned; they were simply there to find her work and make her money, and she held them to the same high standard to which she held the other actors in her shows. Her feelings in this regard had probably been colored by her loss of the film version of *Gypsy*—forever after, she blamed that on her agents, who were summarily dismissed when Rosalind Russell's casting was announced. Those who followed formed a kind of revolving door of go-getters and yes-men, most of whom were on the receiving end of Ethel's fury in a very short time.

"I found her one of the most difficult people I've ever represented," said Tom Korman. "She had such crazy idiosyncrasies. She wore blinders. When she had something in her mind, that was it, and you couldn't change her mind. But she was so great as a performer that the minute she got onstage, I forgave her for everything she did." Her working relationship with Korman ended when he came up with an offer for her to make a guest appearance on the popular sitcom *The Odd Couple,* playing Jack Klugman's aunt. Ethel was incensed that her own agent would even *consider* that she would play the aunt of her onetime leading man, and very soon Korman was replaced by a refined and witty Englishman, Lionel Larner, who in recent years had become one of the top agents in the theater world.

A long honeymoon period marked Ethel and Larner's professional relationship, but soon they, too, had their rocky moments. One night Larner escorted her to the opening of *Sherlock Holmes*, starring John Wood and Tim Pigott-Smith. After the curtain came down, he took her back to meet Wood. At Sardi's after the show, Ethel turned the girlish charm on high voltage— too high—for Wood. They all had a drink together, and Wood suddenly said, "You know, Miss Merman, I've loved every minute of this, but I must make an appearance at a party upstairs."

As Wood left their table, Ethel turned to Larner and snapped, "Faggot!"

"No, Ethel, he's not a faggot," said Larner calmly. "(A) he's married, (B) he's had an affair with one girl in the company, and (C) I think he's having an affair with another."

"He's a *faggot*," said Ethel.

"Ethel," said Larner, "if King Kong walked in here and didn't want to fuck you, you'd call him a faggot." Ethel laughed, and the incident blew over, but there were many similar situations. Once, at a party celebrating one of his exhibits, Carleton Varney seated her next to a fellow interior decorator at a dinner; Ethel called Varney aside, yelling, "You've seated me next to a fag!" before getting up and storming out. Such behavior was shocking and misleading: in her rational moments, Ethel outwardly indicated no significant degree of homophobia. But if she had to attend a social gathering, she was often hoping to find romantic male companionship. She had gay friends galore; what she craved was a lover, possibly even another husband. And as is the case for many other gay icons in show business then and now, there was a part of her that resented the homosexuals who held her in such high esteem.

One business associate who was able to stay in her good graces was Gus Schirmer, whom she described as "more my personal manager than an agent." The scion of the famous music-publishing family, Gus had begun his career working in summer stock; after working in Los Angeles, where he represented a number of top film stars, he returned to New York as head of his own agency. He was noted for the compassion he showed his clients and for the imagination and drive with which he managed their careers. Ethel signed with him in the mid-1970s and quickly came to admire his scrupulous honesty and good humor, and Gus remained one of the few business associates about whom she had nothing nasty to say.

In the spring of 1973, Agnes Zimmermann suffered a devastating stroke that robbed her of the power of speech and left her completely paralyzed on her left side. Unable to feed or bathe herself, she remained at Roosevelt Hospital for more than eight months, and when Ethel wasn't performing out of town, she joined Pop at his daily visits. She was deeply impressed with the care given Mom by her physician, Dr. Albert Attia, and the Roosevelt Hospital nursing staff. (Dr. Attia would soon become Ethel's personal physician.) When Mom was finally scheduled to be released from the hospital, Ethel decided that she would need to keep even closer tabs on her parents' situation than she had before. She arranged for the Zimmermanns to move into an apartment at the Berkshire, just a few floors below her own. The apartment was set up as a mini-hospital, with all the necessary medical machinery and a round-the-clock nursing staff, whose praises Ethel continually sang. Mom continued to suffer from expressive aphasia: she could understand what was being said to her, but, having lost the power of speech, she was unable to respond. She could write a bit, but only in a practically illegible scrawl. Through it all, Ethel remained a study in devotion and never lost patience with her mother. "Although everybody told me that Ethel was kind of tough and loud," said Dr. Attia, "I didn't see that part of her. I saw the concern for her parents. She had the characteristic of that sort of caring individual." She even saw to it that the furniture in the new apartment was arranged exactly as it had been at the Century, so that Pop, with his bad eyes, could navigate easily.

When Ethel entertained at the Berkshire, she liked to have friends in for drinks and then take them all out to a restaurant in the neighborhood.

"She would invite a group of us to dinner," recalled Kay Armen, the noted pop contralto who was a good friend of Ethel's. "First she would invite us to the hotel, and everybody would have their drinks, and Mom and Dad would be part of the party. We would go to the restaurant afterward, and Mom and Dad didn't come. But they felt like part of the group, and everybody treated them with such respect." One evening at the Berkshire, Armen leaned down over Agnes's bed and clutched her hand. "Mama," she said, "I want you to get well, so you can be up and around again, because we all love you so much." Agnes squeezed her hand in response, and the tears began to flow down her face.

That Christmas, Ethel had a small party at the Berkshire for a few of her friends. She decided that everyone should sing a few carols around Pop's piano. Agnes began, with great difficulty, to try to sing along, and Ethel visibly fought back tears. One of her guests, musical director Hal Hastings, remembered thinking, "Ethel was a tough, tough broad—and a little girl with her parents."

Ethel's sense of loyalty, like her sense of outrage, had deep roots. Her gratitude toward the staff at Roosevelt Hospital was so great that she decided to become a volunteer there. Once a week she reported to work as a saleslady—"Pink Ladies," they were called, because of the smocks they wore—in the hospital's gift shop, and she delighted in waiting on the relatives and friends of patients, selling them a book or a box of chocolates or a plant, ringing up the sale, and counting out the change. She approached this work with the same command of accuracy and organization she brought to her own correspondence and bill paying. It wasn't long before word got out that one day a week Ethel could be glimpsed at the gift shop, and many fans beat a path to the hospital door just to gawk. Ethel had no patience with such sycophancy: she was there to do a job, plain and simple.

On January 13, 1974, Mom Zimmermann's long struggle came to an end, as she slipped away quietly in her room at Roosevelt, where she had returned sometime earlier. The fact that her mother's suffering had ended was of little consolation to Ethel. Mom and Pop had always been there for her, through all the betrayals, real or imagined, of so many other people in her life. She had never suffered the slightest schism with Mom, never felt the need to escape from her loving devotion, and the sense of loss that swept over her now was overwhelming.

Agnes Zimmermann's funeral was not particularly well attended. Among the mourners were Lionel Larner and Benay Venuta, who was appalled by the small turnout.

"Lionel, look at this place," said Benay. "It's empty. It's a disgrace."

"Well," said Larner, "you can't go through life telling your best friends to go fuck themselves and expect them to turn up at your mother's funeral."

Agnes Zimmermann was cremated and her ashes sent to rest with Ethel Jr.'s at the Evergreen Shrine of Rest in Colorado Springs. To friends Ethel often commented that one day the entire family would all be there, together for all time. It was a thought that seemed to provide her with some degree of solace.

In the mid-1970s, Ethel's highest-profile engagements were confined to television: *What's My Line?*, *The Tonight Show* with Johnny Carson, and a ninety-minute CBS special, *'S Wonderful, 'S Marvelous, 'S Gershwin*, hosted by Jack Lemmon. By now, she had entered a period of vocal decline. Perhaps it was partly a slackening of her musculature because she was no longer singing eight performances a week. Perhaps, too, it was because after years of singing the same material, she was no longer emotionally connected to it, and the result showed in the voice. The climactic notes that had once seemed so effortless now sounded aggressively pushed out. At this point, it was no longer inaccurate to refer to her as a "belter."

In June 1974 she toured Maryland with Carroll O'Connor, star of television's most popular comedy series, *All in the Family*. Ethel was delighted to have O'Connor sharing the bill with her; *All in the Family* was one of her favorite shows, and secretly she may have hoped to be invited to make a guest appearance. She and O'Connor played the Painters Mill Music Fair, the Shady Grove, and the Melody Fair before O'Connor had to return to California to begin shooting the new season of *All in the Family*. Ethel's guest shot on the show never materialized, but she did maintain a friendship with O'Connor and his wife, Nancy, one that had its rocky moments.

One night when the O'Connors were in Manhattan, they took Ethel to the Café Carlyle, one of New York's most elegant supper clubs, to hear the brilliant cabaret singer Bobby Short perform. The evening was a disaster: Ethel horrified the O'Connors by gargling with wine while Short was singing. The next day, when she called the O'Connors to thank them for the evening, Nancy O'Connor lit into her. "Ethel," she said, "you are the first lady of the American musical theater, and that behavior is just not acceptable. How would you like it if someone did that to you?"

In fact, odd, inexplicable incidents such as the one at the Carlyle had been cropping up for some time. When Ethel was invited to a cocktail or dinner party at someone's house, she often seemed shy and reserved.

Whenever she was accompanied by Tony Cointreau and James Russo, she insisted that they sit on either side of her, so she wouldn't have to make conversation with any of the other guests. At other times she exhibited behavior that seemed incongruous for the carefully brought-up daughter of Edward and Agnes Zimmermann. One night, Ethel was having dinner at Dorothy Fields's apartment. Also present were Mr. and Mrs. Harold Rome, Burton and Lynn Lane, and the actress Shirley Booth. Dinners at Dorothy's were elegant affairs, with the best food and wine served. After the meal Dorothy always liked to have her guests gather around the piano and perform. On this particular evening, Shirley Booth got up to sing "Love Is the Reason," which she had introduced in Dorothy's 1951 show with Arthur Schwartz, *A Tree Grows in Brooklyn*. It was a charming number, and although Booth was no singer, she delivered it with the same quirky comic verve that had delighted the show's audiences. Everyone applauded. Then came Ethel's turn. She got up and in clarion tones launched into her own version of the same song. Lynn Lane remembered all of the guests being horrified. No one knew what to say; no one would even attempt to fathom why Ethel had pulled such an ungracious stunt in the home of one of her dearest friends.

In September 1974 Ethel played a two-week engagement at London's Palladium. Ticket sales were spotty, but her disappointment in the public reception was offset by the fact that Bobby had come along as her stage manager. By now Bobby was living in Bolinas, California, a tiny town just north of San Francisco. If Bobby had been seeking a place to drop out of sight, he could not have done much better than Bolinas, which had long been famous for the antisocial nature of the people who lived there; repeatedly over time, road signs on Highway 1 directing motorists to Bolinas had been pulled up by the locals. To close friends Ethel worried about the reclusive life Bobby was leading, and she longed for him to rejoin the mainstream, but as time went on, he became more and more isolated, living very simply and working at odd pickup jobs.

She was also somewhat disturbed by a recent professional turn of events. On September 23, 1974, *Gypsy* had returned to Broadway in a major revival at the Winter Garden Theatre. This time around, Arthur Laurents directed the show himself, but Ethel did not reprise her triumph as Rose. Instead the part went to Angela Lansbury, who in 1966 had capped her career with her delightful performance in Jerry Herman's *Mame*. Her stage career since then had foundered, with the flops *Prettybelle* and *Dear World*, and she was looking for a way to spruce up her stature on Broadway. The part of Rose seemed just the ticket. In a round of press interviews, Laurents was quite vocal about the fact that Lansbury's conception of Rose was much closer to the one he had always envisioned, in large part because, unlike Ethel, she was a trained actress who would be able to delve deeper into the role's darker dimensions. In particular he was proud of the impact that "Rose's Turn" had in Lansbury's hands, and he came up with a chilling device for the end of the number: as the audience applauds, Rose, dazed by the thought of being the center of attention at long last, keeps bowing and bowing, even after the ovation has died away. "With Angie it was really a marvelous ending," said Laurents, "which you needed an actress to do. You couldn't have done it with just a singer." Ethel was wounded by these sentiments, and it came as no surprise that she did not deign to attend the revival. Nor can one imagine her being pleased when, a few months after the show closed in January 1975, Lansbury won the Tony Award for Best Actress in a Musical.

Ethel continued appearing on television, which brought in good money for minimal effort on her part, but in the end she didn't find the work especially fulfilling. Despite her protestations to the contrary over the years, she was a star of the theater; like Mary Martin and Carol Channing, she gave her live audiences a charge that could not be fully captured on film or tape. There was another problem with on-screen appearances: Ethel was beginning to look her age. She had put on weight, and her face had developed a distinct jowliness that she'd inherited from Mom Zimmermann. Gus Schirmer urged her to get a face lift, but the thought of cosmetic surgery frightened her, and she demurred, insisting, "I don't want to look like a Ubangi!" Instead she tried to update her image by getting a new haircut, with bangs. James Russo laughingly called it her Toni Tennille look, and it was not particularly flattering.

A new musical remained out of the question, but there was another possibility that she had only occasionally tapped into: performing as a soloist with symphony orchestras. It was to be her next major career move, and her last. The project began with Eric Knight, Ethel's nightclub pianist, who had for some years been writing arrangements for the acclaimed Boston Pops Orchestra, led by its popular music director, Arthur Fiedler. Bill Cattell, the interlocutor between Boston radio station WGBH and the Boston Symphony Association, asked whether Merman might ever be interested in appearing with the Pops. After thinking it over, Ethel decided she liked the idea, and Knight quickly found himself pressed into rescoring her nightclub act (five saxes, three trumpets, three trombones, guitar, bass, drums, and piano) into a string-heavy symphonic setting. At their first meeting, Merman and Fiedler kept their distance from each other, but as they began working together, they warmed up. At the Boston Pops concert in May 1975, Ethel's performance consisted of the medley of her old hits she'd been doing for years, and despite the fact that she was now backed up by a symphony orchestra, not one element in her performance had changed. Everything was still in place; audience members who had seen her do this act for years could practically move their lips along with her when she told the story of having been cast in *Girl Crazy*, finishing with, "And you know, ladies and gentlemen, you never change a note in a Gershwin tune." As encores she did "They Say It's Wonderful" and "There's No Business Like Show Business." Despite the fact that a distracting wobble had crept into her voice and she had to reach a bit more for the climactic notes, slightly distorting the vowels, she was in thrilling form, her intonation remarkably solid. The only thing that was new was her gown, in her new favorite color, lavender. She had admired the Chinese red gown in the same style that Kay Armen had worn in a concert; when Armen told her that she'd gotten it from a Lebanese wholesaler in New York, Ethel paid him a visit and ordered half a dozen copies in various colors.

It didn't matter that the Pops concert was a retread of old material. The program, taped and later telecast in the summer of 1976 as part of the American Bicentennial celebration, was an enormous success for Ethel. As she slammed out the last note of "Everything's Coming Up Roses," the final song in the medley, the audience at Boston's Symphony Hall was on its feet instantly. Ethel said, her voice nearly breaking with what seemed to be genuine emotion, "Thank you, ladies and gentlemen, for one of the most wonderful nights of my career. I really mean that, from the bottom of my heart."

In no time Ethel decided that she wanted to seek more work on the symphony circuit. After a particularly successful engagement with the Pittsburgh Symphony, in which she sang her hits medley and narrated Prokofiev's *Peter and the Wolf*, conducted by film critic and TV personality Gene Shalit, she engaged agent Robert Gardiner to handle concert bookings exclusively. Gardiner, unfortunately, was another agent who was on the receiving end of Ethel's contemptuous treatment. In Gardiner's case it was a matter of personal dislike: she simply found him too obsequious. "Gardiner was crazy about Merman, and Merman couldn't stand anyone who was crazy about her," observed Eric Knight. "She looked upon them as the pure personification of 'sycophant.'" Nevertheless, she was happy with the bookings Gardiner arranged for her, beginning with the Indianapolis Symphony in 1976 and continuing, over the next several years, with the Wichita, Nashville, Detroit,

Pittsburgh, Seattle, Oklahoma City, and Dallas symphonies, among many others. She commanded a good salary—$15,000 per performance—and despite the fact that she was forced to wear a body mike to carry over the huge orchestras in the cavernous halls, she much preferred concert work to nightclubs: no talking in the audience, no cigarettes, no clinking of glasses, no dishes being rattled. Even though the material was almost always the same, Ethel did insist on having ample rehearsal time in her contract: as she went from one new town to another, one new concert hall to another, her sense of perfectionism allowed no room for hitches or surprises.

Just as she was embarking on this new phase of her career, however, she was engulfed by another tragedy in her personal life, this one even more senseless than the one that had taken Ethel Jr. from her. For some time Bobby had been separated from Barbara Colby, a fact that distressed Ethel. She had been tremendously fond of Barbara, and she partly blamed their marital woes on the aimless lifestyle that Bobby was leading in Bolinas. Barbara, however, had been flourishing professionally. In the mid-1970s she had made a couple of high-profile guest appearances on CBS's popular comedy series *The Mary Tyler Moore Show*, as a hooker whom the character Mary Richards befriends while she's temporarily jailed for refusing to reveal a news source. With her shrewd comic timing and a voice as husky as Suzanne Pleshette's, Barbara got a favorable reaction from both the critics and audiences. The result was that she had been cast in a recurring part on *Phyllis*, a new comedy series starring Cloris Leachman, created by MTM, Mary Tyler Moore's production company. It was the dream of many actresses, Ethel included, to land a regular role on a series, and Barbara seemed to be entering a golden period of her life.

In July 1975, Ethel flew to Los Angeles to sing a concert. On the night of July 24, she and Rose Marie went to the Dorothy Chandler Pavilion to see Nanette Fabray in a revival of *Wonderful Town*. Afterward the three women went out and ate two hot fudge sundaes apiece and had a good time laughing and getting caught up with one another. The moon was shining that night, and when they went out on the street, Ethel looked up at the sky and gasped, "Look at that fuckin' moon!" Fabray made her promise to telephone when she reached the Beverly Hills Hotel, where she was staying. No phone call came, so Fabray called the hotel, where eventually she got through to Ethel's room. Ethel then told her the horrible news: Barbara Colby was dead. She and a friend, actor James Kiernan, had been fatally gunned down in a drive-by shooting in West Los Angeles while they were leaving a yoga class they were teaching. The senseless murder—which was to remain unsolved—

shattered the acting community in Los Angeles. "If there was a kinder, nicer lady," said MTM president Grant Tinker of Colby, "I have never met her."

Ethel was inconsolable. She wept bitterly, railing to Fabray and Rose Marie about the unfairness of life, and how she did not understand what the world had become.

Like Bobby, Barbara had been drawn to Eastern religions and philosophies. At the memorial service for her, which was held in Santa Monica, various people spoke of the importance of not mourning her loss; she had, it was explained, simply passed on to a higher plane of existence, and it was important for those who survived her to keep peace and joy in their hearts. Ethel was as appalled by the sentiments expressed as she was by the overpowering smell of incense and the fact that the guests were all asked to remove their shoes. In the case of Barbara's death, as in so many other instances in her life, Ethel could respond only with anger and bewilderment. After the service she wept in Rose Marie's arms. Apart from her grief over Barbara, she was deeply concerned about her son. "I don't know what to do about Bobby," she said over and over again. "He's just lost." Her anxiety over Bobby's lifestyle would intensify in the years to come; some of Ethel's friends claim that Bobby lived on a raft in Hawaii for a time in the 1970s.

Perhaps it was this string of personal catastrophes, amplified by Ethel's inability to process them on any transcendant level, that led to an increase both in her drinking and in the intensity of her temperamental outbursts. Ethel remained most comfortable with her old, nonprofessional friends—the ones from her Astoria days—partly because she believed that they accepted her completely for who she was; the question that they might use her or manipulate her for their own benefit was a moot one. She didn't see Josie Traeger as much, because Josie had moved to Florida, but she kept up with Josie's sister, Anna Freund. Frequently she spent the weekend with Anna at her modest, neat-as-a-pin home in Islip, Long Island, and at one point she even talked about taking a little apartment there so they could spend even more time together. But several of her professional friends found themselves all but banished.

Her relationship with Benay Venuta was a particularly complicated one. While she relied on Benay for company, it is likely that part of the reason Ethel felt comfortable around her was that Benay posed no real threat to her professionally—in the world of Broadway, Benay was a respected working performer but something of an also-ran. For her part, Benay later admitted to Barbara Seaman, Jackie Susann's biographer, that she had loved Ethel as one might love a difficult relative but had found her coarse, bigoted, and narrow-minded. In Benay's own words, she felt that many would not have been so enamored of Ethel had they known what "a sad, dull, middle-class lady" she really was. The two women had had minor altercations over the years, but none as cataclysmic as the one that occurred in the 1970s during a party Benay was throwing for jewelry designer Donald Stannard. Earl Wilson, the well-known syndicated columnist, and his wife, Rosemary, were among the invited guests. Ethel had been drinking during the evening and at one point she cornered Benay in the foyer.

"I've got something to tell you, and you're not going to like it," she said.

"Then, Ethel, don't tell me," said Benay. "Everybody's having a good time."

But Ethel had opened the door, and nothing would prevent her from charging through it.

"You'd have never gotten Earl Wilson here if you hadn't told him it was a party for me," she snarled at Benay. Then she turned to Stannard. "Nothing against you, Donald," she said, "but he wouldn't come to a party for you." She saved her exit line for Benay: "I'm sick of you using me," she hissed, then grabbed her coat and walked out.

What followed between the two women was a silence that ended only a couple of years later when, out of the blue, Ethel called Benay and invited her over for cocktails. Benay showed up, intending to ask her what the scene at the Stannard party had been all about. When she saw Ethel, however, she thought better of it, certain that Ethel had been drunk and wouldn't even recollect the incident.

Despite the fact that these chaotic episodes were multiplying, Ethel's life remained for the most part precise and orderly. Thanks to wise investments and good counsel from her financial adviser, Irving Katz, she had plenty of money. She had always handled her own correspondence—she'd recently graduated to an electric typewriter that had cursive script—and paid her bills the minute she got them. At the time of her marriage to Bob Six, she had created a corporation, American Entertainment Enterprises; the bulk of her salary was funneled into it, and AEE paid most of her bills. Although Ethel was always insistent about picking up the check when she joined friends for drinks or dinner, she'd never been in the habit of throwing her money around. While she was touring, her needs were relatively simple.

Over and over she stated, "All I want is to travel first class and have my own bathroom."

Her taste in entertainment was relatively simple and straightforward, too. She enjoyed going to club acts performed by her friends, and as she still knew nothing about cooking, she loved going out for dinner. But her favorite places were anything but high end. Maxwell's Plum on Manhattan's East Side was a spot she frequented, but she could most often be seen at Goldie's New York or at Mayfair, a little restaurant on Fifty-third Street and First Avenue that served simple fare: chicken, burgers, roast beef. She almost always had roast chicken, accompanied by several glasses of Almaden on the rocks. At King Dragon, her favorite Chinese restaurant ("Let's go to the Chinks," she would say to Tony Cointreau and James Russo), she would have chicken chow mein, which she declined to share with any of her guests. While dining out, she was treated like royalty, and at Mayfair, frequented largely by gay men, she was always the center of attention. At King Dragon the owners cooed over her: "Missy Merman!" they would say. "We just love Missy Merman!" They also concocted a drink for her called the Merman Stinger: one part brandy, two parts Galliano, one part fresh lime juice, served straight up.

Ethel was still in demand on television, and during the mid-1970s she turned up most frequently as Johnny Carson's guest on *The Tonight Show*. Her most notable appearance on the show came in 1976, when she electrified the audience with a blazing rendition of "Blow, Gabriel, Blow," with Carson's brilliant bandleader, Doc Severinsen, performing the trumpet solo. Whenever she appeared on *The Tonight Show*, her routine was the same: no matter how tumultuous the audience reaction, she gave an almost casual bow, then strode over to the couch to sit with Carson and his sidekick, Ed McMahon, and chat. Usually, as she began talking, the applause was still swelling, and if it lasted long enough, she would occasionally make another simple bow. But she never milked the applause, never seemed desperate for the audience's attention.

The television appearance that may have meant the most to Ethel was her guest shot on *The Muppets*, the enormously popular syndicated series starring Jim Henson's worldly-wise puppets. When people asked her why she was going to do the show, Ethel replied with total ingenuousness, "It'll be good exposure!" At sixty-eight, she was keen to connect with the younger generation of television viewers, most of whom had never seen her in the theater. Ethel was quite effective on *The Muppets*, especially when she did something new for her—a soft, slow rendition of "There's No Business Like

Show Business," which she sang to Kermit the Frog. At the end of the episode, when she gently patted the Muppets on the head, she showed an almost childlike delight. After the taping the producers gave her a Kermit doll, a Miss Piggy doll, and a Fozzie Bear doll. Ethel was delighted with the gifts, and kept the dolls in a miniature brass bed by her own bed at the Berkshire.

She still hungered for a television series of her own, something that seems to have annoyed Benay Venuta over the years. "But you don't have to be Lucille Ball," Benay had always said. "Isn't it enough that you're number one on Broadway?" Perhaps it was to Benay, but not to Ethel, and Gus Schirmer finally wangled her a role on a pilot for a CBS comedy series, *You're Gonna Love It Here.* Ethel was to have a recurring role as a musical-comedy star who dumps her orphaned grandson on his bachelor uncle (played by Austin Pendleton). Ethel showed her usual flair for comedy, but the script was a poor one, and she wasn't surprised when CBS passed it over for the fall lineup of 1977.

By far her most spectacular performance of the mid-1970s came, unsurprisingly, in her natural habitat. Attorney Arnold Weissberger had hatched an idea for Ethel to appear with Mary Martin in a one-night-only concert to benefit the Theater and Music Collection of the Museum of the City of New York, a treasure trove of theatrical memorabilia housed on 104th Street and Fifth Avenue. Both stars were intrigued by the notion of reuniting twenty-four years after their history-making appearance on *The Ford Fiftieth Anniversary Show,* and soon all the contracts were signed, with the concert date set for May 15, 1977, at the Broadway Theatre. Eric Knight was Ethel's conductor, John Lesko was Martin's, and Jay Blackton served as music director. Ticket prices ran up to $150, and after an advertisement was placed in the *New York Times,* the entire theater sold out almost immediately.

Nostalgia, which had been a key component in the entertainment industry since the arrival of *No, No, Nanette, Follies,* and *Irene* earlier in the decade, was still a potent box-office draw in New York, as shown by Town Hall's Legendary Ladies of the Movies film-clip/personal-appearance series with Bette Davis, Joan Crawford, Myrna Loy, and other Golden Age movie queens. But even in this context, the Merman-Martin concert stood tall as the most eagerly anticipated theatrical event of the time.

Anna Sosenko, a seasoned pro at producing benefits, signed on to helm the project. Although Ethel tended to blow hot and cold with Sosenko—she didn't entirely trust her—the two women had a great deal in common. Sosenko was a tough, unyielding businesswoman who was accustomed to getting her

way and was not at all above riding roughshod over others. She had first come
to prominence as the impresario behind The Incomparable Hildegarde, the
elegant cabaret chanteuse whose trademark number was "Darling, Je Vous
Aime Beaucoup," which Sosenko had written for her. Sosenko had supervised Hildegarde's engagements, picked out her clothes, even designed her
lighting. This background gave her definite ideas on the subject of stars and
how they should be treated. "A big theatrical problem," she once said, "is
that there are too many producers who have money but don't know anything
about theater. Theater should be run like Bloomingdale's. The president
knows merchandising from A to Z. Therefore he is able to hire the right
people for the right departments."

Sosenko immediately tried to cut corners on the benefit, but Ethel wasn't
having any of it. Sosenko and the show's director, Donald Saddler, wanted
Ethel to make her entrance dressed as *Gypsy*'s Rose, with Mary coming on
at the same time, costumed as Nellie Forbush in *South Pacific*.

"With Chowsie?" said Ethel, remembering the little dog she'd carried
when she made her entrance in *Gypsy*.

"We don't have money for a dog," replied Sosenko.

"You don't get a dog, you don't get me," answered Ethel. She also demanded limousine service for both Martin and herself; Sosenko had hoped
to persuade both stars to travel to and from rehearsal by taxi. Mary had a few
demands of her own: for one thing, she insisted on a body mike, and, reluc-
tantly, Ethel went along with it.

Ethel and Mary were delighted to be working together after so much
time. Neither woman's sense of perfectionism had diminished, and for two
weeks before the performance, they rehearsed together in a small room in
Steinway Hall on Fifty-seventh Street. Mary, who hadn't performed for the
past eight years and whose husband and career architect, Richard Halliday,
had died a few years earlier, was exceptionally nervous, and Ethel had to
assure her repeatedly that everything would be fine once the night of the
concert arrived. Ethel, on the other hand, appeared not to have a nerve in
her body. As they rehearsed, she camped up the lyrics, in a tribute to her
many gay friends: "Don't know why / There's no action in this fly, / Stormy
leather!" "Merman, Merman," Mary gently remonstrated. But as the rehearsal period went on, Ethel became very serious about the task at hand.
One day as they were working, a gang of chorus gypsies who had finished
their rehearsal in a neighboring studio was standing outside the room where
Ethel and Mary were working, listening through the open transom. Ethel

heard a noise from the corridor and went to open the door. As she did, the gypsies, who were literally standing on one another's shoulders, fell into the room.

"HELLO!" said Ethel. "What are you doing here?"

"We're sorry," said one of the gypsies. "We got so excited listening to you."

"How much time do you have?" asked Ethel. When they told her they were through for the day, she invited them in, and she and Mary did the entire Ford duet for them.

To promote the show, Ethel and Mary gave a round of interviews, including one on the popular daytime talk show *Lifestyles with Beverly Sills*, chatting about their careers and, in particular, their appearance on the Ford show in 1953. "I was in the midst of my third mistake in life," Ethel said, referring to Bob Six, "my third marriage. They all go by numbers." She also added that when she sang, she was never "diaphragm-conscious. I take a breath when I need to. When they start talkin' to me 'bout head tones, I don't know what they're talkin' about."

One day after rehearsal, Ethel and Mary were riding to their respective homes in the limousine that Ethel had strong-armed Anna Sosenko into providing for them. As the limo made its way through the theater district, with its profusion of sex clubs and porn theaters, Ethel heaved a sigh and muttered, "Jesus. Just look how they've fucked up Times Square."

The weekend of the concert arrived. Mary was still nervous about her appearance and marked her way through nearly the entire dress rehearsal, singing full out only on her signature number, "My Heart Belongs to Daddy." Ethel, on the other hand, was as unperturbed as ever, singing full voice on every single song. One thing she insisted on was being positioned on stage right (which, from the audience's vantage point, is on the left) for their duets, which Donald Saddler felt had something to do with the fact that "when we look at the stage, because we read from left to right, our eyes automatically go left first."

On the night of May 15, the Broadway Theatre was a scene of pandemonium, overrun by both ticket holders and people on the street clamoring to get their hands on a ticket at any cost. Even though both women understood the level of expectation surrounding the concert, neither one was prepared for the reception that greeted them when they burst through matching paper hoops to the tune of Stephen Sondheim's "Send in the Clowns." As had been planned, Mary was in Nellie Forbush's sailor's outfit from the "Honey

Bun" number in *South Pacific*, and Ethel was in Rose's ratty coat from the first scene of *Gypsy*, carrying a 1977 stand-in for the original Chowsie. The audience could not contain its excitement; the applause and cheering went on for nearly four minutes. It was, Ethel later said, "the meaning of a love-in."

Cyril Ritchard, who had costarred with Mary in *Peter Pan*, was the evening's host. Ethel and Mary sang all their great hits, and Mary, sadly, ran into trouble whenever she tried to sing high notes: she popped into head voice, which emerged as a thin falsetto. (She did, however, sound terrific when she tore into "A Wonderful Guy.") It was Ethel's show nearly every step of the way: the climax of the first half was her stunning performance of "Blow, Gabriel, Blow." It was now done at a slower, jazzier tempo, with a scat section in the middle and a finish (with trumpeter Dick Perry) so thrilling that the audience members could not remain in their seats.

After the entr'acte both Ethel and Mary opened the second half in red Dolly Levi costumes and drew huge laughs with their opening lines. "Well! Hello, Ethel!" exclaimed Mary, and Ethel answered, "Well, hello, *Maaaaaaarry!*" An all-star chorus of "waiters" from the Harmonia Gardens, including Joel Grey, Yul Brynner, Burgess Meredith, and—Mary's son—Larry Hagman, lined the stage. Then came a reprise of the Ford show medley. Mary softened some of the notes that twenty years earlier had been full throttle, and at the end of the duet she couldn't sustain the final high note on "There's No Business Like Show Business." Ethel hung on to it until the double bar.

Reviewing the event in the *New York Times*, Walter Kerr left no doubt which star came out on top. "Ethel Merman is the bonfire and Mary Martin is the smoke," he wrote, going on to add that Ethel was "too hot for Fahrenheit to measure, too bright to be stared at without a pair of those goggles that riveters wear." In the *New York Post*, Martin Gottfried observed, "We've lost something and our theater has lost something. We've lost our capacity to adore and our theater has lost the impulse to make us adore." In the end the benefit cleared $145,000 for the museum.

Ethel had hoped that she and Mary could perform similar programs elsewhere, but Mary, still insecure about her vocal condition, declined.

Her performing schedule permitting, Ethel had continued her weekly stint at the Roosevelt Hospital gift shop. But by now she was eager to do something even more useful. She thought she might be of greater benefit if she had actual contact with the patients and soon she was assigned to visiting rounds in the morning. She would put on one of her best dresses and high heels and go from room to room, asking the patients if there was anything she could get them—a newspaper or a magazine—or if they just wanted to talk. Sometimes they would dictate a short note or postcard to her for her to mail to a relative. More than one patient was startled out of his postsurgical stupor when Ethel barreled into his room and announced, "HI! I'M ETHEL MERMAN!" "I was always afraid that she would give them cardiac arrest," said Tony Cointreau. "But she would come home and say, 'My hand to God, I feel so *good.*' "

By now Pop Zimmermann seldom left his apartment at the Berkshire. He could neither see nor hear very well, but Ethel told friends that however upsetting his physical decline was, she was grateful that his mental faculties were intact. After Pop had a lengthy stay at Roosevelt Hospital in the fall of 1977, however, Ethel knew that he couldn't last much longer. Dr. Attia permitted him to be moved back to the Berkshire with full-time nursing care, and Ethel remained more vigilant than ever. Bob Schear remembered paying a visit with her prior to the opening of the John Kander and Fred Ebb show *The Act*, starring Liza Minnelli. He first went to Ethel's apartment for drinks, and on the way to the theater, they stopped by Pop's apartment. The old man was lying in bed, and Ethel leaned over the railing to speak to him.

"HI, POP!" she said, speaking at the top of her lungs so he could hear her. "JUST CAME IN TO SAY GOOD NIGHT. WE'RE GOING TO SEE JUDY'S LITTLE GIRL." Then she added quietly to Schear, "Hold his hand. He's trying to talk to you."

Schear obeyed. Pop seemed unresponsive, until Ethel said, "WANT ME TO SING A LITTLE SOMETHING?"

The old man nodded, and Ethel sang one of his favorites, "Moonshine Lullaby."

On December 22, 1977, Edward Zimmermann died. As difficult as her mother's death had been for her, Pop's passing hit her even harder. She had always been, to a great extent, a daddy's girl, and friends and relatives believed that her brash and exuberant nature had its source in Edward's outgoing and confident personality. Bob Levitt, years after his divorce from Ethel, once commented that he had always felt that Edward was a cipher who had lived through Ethel and her success for his entire life. Perhaps there was a grain of truth in that observation, but mostly Edward had felt something that Levitt could probably never have fathomed: the undiluted, unconditional love of a father for his only child. As the decades rolled on and Pop remained the one man who never failed to love and protect her, Ethel had returned his devotion with an even greater intensity.

Edward Zimmermann's ashes were sent to rest alongside his wife's in Colorado Springs, and again Ethel repeatedly told her closest circle that someday she would join them. Over the next few years, there were those who felt that she seemed almost in a holding pattern of anticipation. Perhaps it was just a state of confusion, an overpowering feeling of emptiness that had descended on a woman whose long, long childhood had finally come to an end.

One night after attending the theater, Ethel and Bob Schear were on their way to Joe Allen's, the popular actors' hangout on West Forty-sixth Street. As they walked up Eighth Avenue, a marquee for one of the gay porn theaters was all lit up with the title of the current film: ANY-THING GOES.

"Would you get a fuckin' look at that marquee?" Ethel laughed. "This is what my life has come to."

What her life had really come to, professionally speaking, was an occasional television appearance stuck in between a steady round of symphony engagements. The wobble in her voice that had been noticeable a few years earlier had miraculously receded, and she consistently sounded in excellent voice. As Eric Knight succinctly put it, "She always produced." The heavy schedule of orchestra concerts also enhanced her ability to handle an audience. Once, at the Mann Center for the Performing Arts, the outdoor summer venue of the Philadelphia Orchestra, a violent storm erupted. Ethel turned around to see the orchestra's entire string section fleeing offstage, all the players clutching their expensive instruments. She turned back to the audience and said, "I thought the thunder was the timpani. Look what happens when I sing! Some people break glasses. I start a storm." After the wind died down, she returned to the stage and sang the entire program, to an ecstatic ovation. Much as the fans in the audience loved her, though, she had a rather ambivalent attitude toward them; after forty years of being at the top, she had naturally developed a certain cynicism toward her public. Often when it was time to sign autographs, she exited via the stage door carrying her purse and a shopping bag in one hand and holding her escort's hand with the other. "Sorry, can't sign anything!" she would say. "I've got both hands full!"

She went to the theater, though not as often as might have been expected, and she didn't care much for most of what she saw. Or heard. She was disgusted by the fact that amplification had completely changed the experience of the Broadway musical. Well into the 1970s, a "sound designer" was often credited in a show's *Playbill*, though the results were highly variable: it was often impossible to tell from what point onstage a particular sound was originating. Also, orchestrations were becoming ever thicker, louder, and less and less grateful to the singer. In Ethel's day, orchestrators had seen to it that certain sections of the music receded, giving the singer a chance to present the vocal line to maximum effect. From the late 1970s, many orchestrators would pour on a wall of sound without regard to the vocal line, assuming that the singer's amplification could be magnified until the words could be made out clearly.

Sitting through *The Act* with Liza Minnelli in 1977, she suddenly grabbed Bob Schear's arm and whispered, "She's fuckin' lip-synching!" At the curtain call, Minnelli took her bows bathed in sweat with a towel wrapped around her neck. "Boy, her mother wouldn't be pleased with her," muttered Ethel. "The whole trick is to look like you weren't working hard."

Ethel's most high-profile project during the late 1970s was not a TV show or a concert but a book. For some time people had been pressing her to write a second autobiography; *Who Could Ask for Anything More?* had, after all, come out in 1955 and had ended on a rather valedictory note indicating that The Merm was through with Broadway (and would remain happily married to Bob Six). So much had happened since then that Ethel was finally persuaded to give her life story another go. Simon & Schuster made the best offer, and George Eells, a show-business biographer who had written well-received books on Cole Porter and on the rivalry of Hedda Hopper and Louella Parsons, was assigned to be her credited collaborator.

Eells came to the Berkshire armed with a tape recorder and a notepad and worked with her in five-hour sessions. Whether Eells found her an easier subject than Pete Martin had is not documented, but he did have the benefit of spending many hours at the Museum of the City of New York, where Ethel had donated her many scrapbooks, tapes, and other career memorabilia.

Rather than pick up where Pete Martin had left off, Eells correctly assumed that the first book was ancient history and started from the beginning of Ethel's life. The result was a mixed bag. While the main events of Ethel's career were efficiently chronicled, the second book, titled *Merman—an Autobiography*, had little more depth than its predecessor, and it lacked some of the punch and personal flavor that Martin had added. When it was published in the spring of 1978, it received its biggest burst of attention from a chapter entitled "My Marriage to Ernest Borgnine"—which was followed by a blank page. It had been Ethel's idea, and though the executives at Simon & Schuster had been reluctant to approve it, she insisted it would be the one thing about the book that readers would never forget. Once again her career instincts were correct: to this day the blank page has given *Merman* a kind of immortality among show-business memoirs. The press was mostly positive—the *New York Times*'s review had the feeling of a teacher giving a passing grade to an average student, but it complained that "her straight-from-the-shoulder manner keeps some cool distance between her and the reader." The book was selling briskly: at the Chicago Marshall Field's alone, she signed 606 copies.

By mid-June 1978, *Merman* had sold over 39,000 copies and was in its third printing, giving her good cause to gloat. When she appeared in bookstores to sign copies, she was often approached by fans who wanted her to sign other memorabilia. Usually she refused: she was there to sign her book, and that was all. In Dallas one admirer brought an original pressing of the audio recording of her 1953 Ford show with Mary Martin. When he told her that it was a collector's item listed at $200, Ethel responded, "My book is number eight on the bestseller list in Chicago. That's what I care about."

By the early 1980s, many more of Ethel's show-business friends and contemporaries had passed away, and she was acutely aware that she was the possessor of much more past than future. Dorothy Fields and Betty Bruce had both died in 1974. Nearly all of her male costars—including Bert Lahr, Eddie Cantor, Paul Lukas, George Sanders, and William Gaxton— were long gone. Jack Haley passed away in 1979. Even Bruce Yarnell, her much-younger costar from the *Annie Get Your Gun* revival, had died in 1973. For Ethel the past was not bathed in the rosy glow of nostalgia; paradoxically, she seemed at times almost bitter about the fact that she had worked so hard, while insisting that it was the only honorable way for anyone to pursue her career.

She refused to indulge in sentimentality about most of the people she'd worked with, but, as always in the Merman Book of Rules, there were a few exceptions. In 1979, while in Los Angeles for a concert, Ethel paid a call on her old friend Jimmy Durante, who had suffered a debilitating stroke and was confined to a wheelchair. Temple Texas drove her out to see Durante, and Ethel was devastated when she saw him in such a frail condition. She maintained a good front, standing up and singing several of the songs from their two shows together, *Red, Hot and Blue!* and *Stars in Your Eyes.* But on the way back to Temple's house, Ethel broke down, crying so hard that Temple had to pull off to the side of the road. "Why Jimmy?" she said over and over. "Why such a wonderful guy? Why do some people have to go through that?"

Since she was still in exceptional voice, Ethel found herself becoming more and more concerned with the question of maintaining her name before a rapidly changing, youth-oriented public. She didn't want to settle for being a once-a-year guest on *The Merv Griffin Show*, reminiscing about her glorious past; she longed to do unusual projects that would permit her to connect with a new audience. In 1979, A&M Records came to her with a creatively bizarre idea. The disco craze had been going strong ever since the record-breaking box-office success of 1977's *Saturday Night Fever*, and its influence had even been reflected in performances by the older generation. On her syndicated talk show, Dinah Shore could be heard singing the occasional number to an updated, disco accompaniment. Even the old *I Love Lucy* theme song, by Harold Adamson and Elliott Daniel, had been given the treatment with a popular single, "Disco Lucy." A&M's vice president of artists and repertoire, Kip Cohen, wanted to know if Ethel would be willing to record an album of her old Broadway hits set to a disco beat. Ethel, always looking for "good exposure," discussed it with Gus Schirmer and quickly said yes.

The brilliant Peter Matz was assigned to arrange—or rearrange—several of Ethel's old songs. He immersed himself in the new sound by listening to about a hundred disco albums. He put together a bare rhythm track of "There's No Business Like Show Business," "Something for the Boys," "Alexander's Ragtime Band," "Everything's Coming Up Roses," and other pieces. Ethel studied the vocal lead sheets and rhythm tapes that Matz sent her, then came into the studio and recorded the vocals to the rhythm tracks. While she was working, she noticed what the A&M employees were wearing: T-shirts with ETHEL BOOGIES printed on the front in big block letters.

When *Disco Ethel* was released by A&M in the summer of 1979, Ethel gave a round of interviews to the press in which she proclaimed the album the greatest thing since 7-Up. She worked hard plugging *Disco Ethel* on television talk shows and in record stores, once again refusing to sign old *Playbill*s or LPs—just the new record, please—and sometimes she cut off her gushing fans with what the *Village Voice*'s Arthur Bell described as "the warmth of a fjord."

Unfortunately, by the time the album was released, the disco craze had faded, almost overnight. Radio stations, having decided that the future of rock music lay in New Wave and elsewhere, gave the album minimal air-play, and *Disco Ethel* bombed, very quickly becoming the biggest joke of Ethel's career since her quickie marriage to Ernest Borgnine.

By now, the Berkshire had gone co-op, and the new owners were in the process of removing all permanent guests from the building. Ethel, incensed at such treatment, declined to buy the apartment she'd lived in for so many years. Bobby had returned to New York to live—they were getting along better than they had in years—and Ethel had come to depend on him for many things. To her friends Frank Pescha and Bill Murdock, she wrote that "my son is here taking charge" of all arrangements for the move—wherever that might be.

In a short time, she had settled on her new home: the Hotel Surrey at 20 East Seventy-sixth Street. She rented 8D&E, an agreeable, spacious, two-bedroom, two-bathroom suite, decorated once again by Carleton Varney. She enjoyed exploring a new neighborhood and soon found two new favorite haunts, both coffee shops: the Skyline on Lexington Avenue and Three Guys on Madison.

Ethel continued to busy herself in television, filming episodes of popular series such as *Hee Haw* and *The Love Boat* (the first of several appearances). In 1979 she agreed to appear on a PBS special, *Musical Comedy Tonight!*, hosted by Sylvia Fine Kaye, which spotlighted milestone musicals by re-creating their best numbers in the original orchestrations. Ethel was the star attraction of the segment devoted to *Anything Goes* and was scheduled to sing the title number, "I Get a Kick Out of You," and, with Rock Hudson, "You're the Top." But in rehearsal it became evident to all concerned that something was worrying her; she insisted that she did not recognize the lyrics to "Anything Goes." When Sylvia Kaye questioned it, Ethel became belligerent and insisted that the words she'd been given weren't the right ones. The awkward moment passed, and Ethel retired to her dressing room. After she emerged, she sang the number with no trouble. But it was an odd, unsettling moment that cast something of a shadow over the taping.

This strange disturbance was echoed a few months later, at a party at Nanette Fabray's house in Los Angeles. Ethel came, escorted by Gus Schirmer, and sat with him for the entire evening, refusing to mingle at all. She seemed unnaturally quiet, and at one point in the evening Fabray came over to her and asked, "Ethel, are you all right?" Ethel bristled and became hotly defensive, insisting that she was fine. Fabray let the matter rest but was left with lingering and disquieting doubts about her friend's state of mind.

One night in a Chinese restaurant in Manhattan, Sandra Church saw her sitting in a booth and went over to say hello.

"It's me, Ethel," she said. "Sandra—your stage daughter."

Ethel looked at her for a long time. "You're not Sandra," she finally said. "You couldn't be Sandra Church. I don't know who you are."

Out of the blue came an offer for a movie. In 1977 the writing team of Jim Abrahams and David and Jerry Zucker had come up with the script for *Kentucky Fried Movie,* a wild spoof of the seventies pop culture that took potshots at popular TV shows and commercials. The jokes were anything but subtle, but the film found its audience and turned out to be a sleeper hit at the box office. Now Abrahams and Zucker had come up with another script, and this time they were handling the directing chores, too. This one was called *Airplane!,* and it lampooned the airborne disaster movies—*The High and the Mighty, Zero Hour!, Airport, Airport 1975*—that had become a tried-and-true moneymaking formula in Hollywood. The talented comedians Robert Hays and Julie Hagerty were the leads, but to add to the movie's tongue-in-cheek tone, a crazy-quilt supporting cast had been assembled, from Peter Graves, Leslie Nielsen, and Robert Stack, all old-time stars of action movies and TV shows, to Kareem Abdul-Jabbar to Barbara Billingsley, the mother on *Leave It to Beaver.*

Abrahams and the Zuckers belonged to the Mel Brooks school of comedy, piling up one genre-spoofing idea after another. They came up with a scene in the psychological ward of an army hospital, in which a shell-shocked officer named Lieutenant Hurwitz is suffering from the delusion that he was Ethel Merman. Abrahams and the Zuckers thought what would really make the joke land was for Ethel Merman herself to play Lieutenant Hurwitz. The offer was floated out to Gus Schirmer, and Ethel agreed to do it.

Shooting her brief scene in *Airplane!* required of Ethel only a single day's work, and she thought little more about it, but when the film was released in 1980, it was a huge box-office hit, and Ethel's scene turned out to be an audience favorite. Even college students who had only a vague idea of Ethel's career got the joke and laughed uproariously. Ethel was delighted with the attention generated by her cameo shot; again she thought it was an example of "good exposure," and this time she was right.

Barbara and Michael were by now college age, and it looked as if Barbara was going to be part of the third generation of Ethel's family to pursue work in the theater: in the late 1970s she became a pupil at the Dell'Arte International School of Musical Theater. Following that she spent some time at the Edinburgh Festival.

Ethel was guardedly supportive of her granddaughter's theatrical endeavors. Earlier, when Barbara had acted in high-school plays, Ethel had tried to be present whenever her schedule permitted. Barbara had played the part of the housekeeper, Frau Schmidt, in a school production of *The Sound of Music*, and when she was trying to raise a fake window onstage, it came off in her hands. She gamely recovered by saying, "Oh, stupid window," and instantly won her grandmother's approval for having such onstage savvy. Another time Barbara had played Martha, the repressed lesbian schoolteacher in Lillian Hellman's *The Children's Hour*. "It really wasn't her cup of tea," said Barbara Geary. "She sat in the front row. She had a giant charm bracelet, and you could hear the clink of it from the stage. I thought, okay . . . Gramma's not really into this one."

By the early 1980s, Barbara was living in New York. Apart from getting Barbara an interview with a friend who was a director of commercials, Ethel didn't go out of her way to forge professional connections for her granddaughter, and Barbara didn't expect her to. "I wasn't really into doing commercial theater at that point," Barbara said, "so I didn't really ask her for help. The kind of theater that I wanted to do was not what she liked or understood." Michael in the meantime had entered the Florida Institute of Technology as a photography major. Subsequently he moved to the Florida Keys, driving a tow truck for a time and picking up other miscellaneous jobs to support himself.

In the summer of 1980, Ethel flew to Hamilton, Ontario, to appear on the syndicated television series *The Palace*, starring Jack Jones. Eric Knight was along as her conductor, and their segment went well. At the curtain call, Ethel came out to take her bow and found herself standing onstage next to Marty Allen, the rotund, frizzy-haired comedian who was Jones's sidekick on the show. As a joke Allen began twisting garlands of roses around her feet. Suddenly Ethel tripped and hit the stage with a horrible thud. She lay perfectly still on the stage floor, and by the time Knight hurried down from his seat in the second balcony, she still had not moved. The cast and crew dithered over her, fearing the worst, as the show's doctors tried to revive her. After several minutes Ethel regained consciousness but refused to consider being hospitalized, screaming at the doctors, "GET AWAY FROM ME!" She seemed somewhat disoriented for several hours afterward, and by the next day, when she and Knight flew back to New York, her face was badly swollen and bruised. On the plane ride, she wore a kerchief and dark glasses and spoke barely a word to Knight.

Ethel refused to consider a lawsuit, but back in New York she did submit to a series of X-rays. Although no fractures were revealed and little more was said about the accident, her behavior became more erratic than ever. A few months later, she and Knight were scheduled to perform in Monte Carlo at Princess Grace's annual gala to benefit the International Red Cross. Knight's wife, Joan, came along, having paid her own way. Ethel seemed chilly and distant on the plane ride over, and once they were in Monte Carlo, she summoned Knight to her hotel room.

"How dare you bring your wife to this job on my coattails?" she demanded.

Knight was stunned that she would treat him this way after a sixteen-year working relationship. He took a moment to recover himself and then he let her have it.

"Ethel, I don't need you to bring my wife to Europe. My wife came with me for the International Red Cross when I was conducting Carol Lawrence, and Carol never said anything." Knight was so piqued that he considered resigning then and there, but in time Ethel withdrew and seemed to be try-ing to make up for her gaffe. They performed together with the Seattle Sym-phony, and she handed Knight a birthday present of fifty dollars, something she had never done before.

Deep down Ethel was beginning to have a gnawing feeling that Broadway had begun to forget about her, or at the very least to have taken her for granted. The year 1980 marked her fiftieth anniversary in the theater, and few in the Broadway community seemed to notice or care. One who did was Bob Schear, who took it upon himself, without telling her, to try to have a Broadway the-ater renamed for her. He went first to the owners of the Alvin, where he was turned down flat. (It was later rechristened the Neil Simon.) He also met with rejections from the owners of the Imperial, the St. James, and nearly every other theater in town. Finally he tried the owners of the Apollo, which had recently been remodeled. The owners were enthusiastic about the idea, and it seemed sentimentally fitting—the Apollo was the theater where Ethel had performed both *George White's Scandals* and *Take a Chance.* With the deal all but signed, Bob went to see Ethel to tell her the good news he thought was certain to please her.

Ethel was incensed; the idea flopped with her on every conceivable level. For one thing, she hated surprises of any kind. For another, the idea that someone would try to drum up support for her without her knowledge, as if she were a charity case, infuriated her. Finally, the fact that it would be the Apollo, and not one of the more prestigious theaters, that would be named after her was an insult.

"DID I EVER ASK YOU TO DO ANYTHING ABOUT NAMING A THEATER AFTER ME?" she railed at Bob. "WHO THE HELL GAVE YOU PERMISSION TO DO THAT—AND THE GODDAMN APOLLO? WHAT THE FUCK DOES THAT HAVE TO DO WITH ME? YOU THINK THAT THEATER'S GOING TO BE THERE IN TWENTY YEARS? MARK MY WORDS—*IT ISN'T GOING TO BE THERE!*"

As it happened, she was right: the Apollo closed only a few years later.

Schear wrote to her attempting to assuage her anger. In response Ethel wrote him a letter, typed on her own electric typewriter:

Dear Bob—

Thank you for your letter of September 28th. I appreciate you having my interests at heart and I think part of the success that I have been fortunate to achieve has been because I have had such nice friends.

All good wishes,
Ethel

She open-copied the letter to her financial adviser, Irving Katz, and did not speak to Schear again for nearly a year.

In the fall of 1980, Ethel was on hand at the New York State Theater for an all-star gala honoring Beverly Sills at her final operatic performance. The opera was New York City Opera's production of *Die Fledermaus,* and in the famous act 2 party scene a collection of Sills's show-business friends and colleagues each did a special turn. Before this, however, the audience had to endure the first part of *Fledermaus*'s act 2, which was given an extremely arch and unfunny performance, with Kitty Carlisle in the trouser role of Prince Orlovsky. In the dressing room she shared with Mary Martin and Eileen Farrell, Ethel sat with her hands folded across her stomach and her feet propped up, staring at the television monitor as the act dragged on. Finally she pronounced the whole performance "shit" and asked Farrell how long it was going to go on.

Things didn't get much better once the stars began parading across the stage, as there were too many opera stars offering up painfully labored versions of pop songs—notably Leontyne Price's "What I Did for Love." Walking off with the whole show were Mary, with a stunning rendition of "My Heart Belongs to Daddy," and Ethel, with "There's No Business Like

Show Business." At the party afterward, Ethel admitted to a reporter that she had never actually seen one of Sills's operas. (Her enthusiasm for the art form however, continued. Her current favorite was the magnetic American baritone Sherrill Milnes, whom she heard in his Met performances of *Rigoletto* and *Macbeth*. She had started to pick up some of the terminology associated with opera singers, and after one of her concerts jokingly asked Bob Gardiner, "What was better tonight—my head voice or my chest voice?")

In the early 1980s, Ethel and Knight were still keeping up a busy concert schedule, although Ethel had become something of a harder sell on the symphony-orchestra circuit. Almost always her concerts were attached to a subscription series, and how well she drew often depended on the venue itself. She was a smash at the Hollywood Bowl, but at a place like Red Rocks in Colorado ticket sales were sluggish. More and more, Bob Gardiner would have to spell her name to the orchestra booking managers who weren't entirely sure who she was. Gardiner recalled this period as "the beginning of the end" of the glory days of American symphony orchestras.

Ethel's encores now included, to piano accompaniment, "What I Did for Love" from *A Chorus Line* and a tender version of Gershwin's "Someone to Watch Over Me." Audience reaction was nearly always enthusiastic, but Gardiner had the impression that Ethel no longer derived any deep enjoyment or satisfaction from her concert appearances. Although she usually remembered to thank the audience "from the bottom of my heart," it was, according to Gardiner, part of the script, uttered by rote. "She always thanked Eric," recalled Gardiner, "and she always perfunctorily thanked the orchestra. You never got the impression that anything really came from the heart." For Ethel it was just her job—not an occasion for wearing her heart on her sleeve.

The tensions between Ethel and Eric Knight continued to build as they went from one engagement to another in the early 1980s. They performed "Everything's Coming Up Roses" at the presidential inauguration of Ronald Reagan, hosted by Frank Sinatra. Then came a booking with the Philadelphia Orchestra and, with the American Symphony Orchestra, another benefit for the Museum of the City of New York, held on May 10, 1982, at Carnegie Hall. It was Ethel's belated Carnegie debut, a landmark occasion that was further sweetened by the fact that onstage after the concert she was to receive the Pied Piper Award for Lifetime Achievement from the American Society of Composers and Publishers. Only three performers had received the honor previously: Frank Sinatra, Barbra Streisand, and Fred Astaire.

During the concert Ethel did something she'd never done before: she neglected to introduce Knight to the audience. Whether it was done out of spite or because she legitimately forgot is questionable. When ASCAP's president, Hal David, reminded her that she should introduce him, she immediately rectified the oversight, but in Knight's mind it had been an intentional slight, and it spelled the end of their eighteen-year working relationship.

The reviews of the Carnegie Hall concert were, as usual, superb. In the *New York Times*, John S. Wilson wrote, "Miss Merman's performance was, as it always has been, larger than life. The broad gestures may seem awkward, her phrasing may twist a tune to wind it up for the delivery of a wallop, and she may suddenly dance into little tripping fairy steps that nobody else could get away with. But with Miss Merman, this is all part of her blatant mystique." In the *New York Post*, Clive Barnes wrote his review as—literally—a love letter, ending it with "P.P.S.—Do you know—I heard and understood every damn word you sang."

Although Ethel was anything but a constant theatergoer, she dutifully went to see her close friends perform. It didn't matter to her whether the venue was Broadway, the straw-hat circuit, or a nightclub. When Carole Cook's husband, Tom Troupe, starred in *Same Time, Next Year* at the Westbury Music Fair, Ethel trekked out to Long Island twice to see the show. She showed up for all of Cointreau's club engagements, often bringing an entire table of friends along with her and always picking up the check at the end of the night. Occasionally she could be spotted at a Broadway opening night. On August 25, 1980, accompanied by Tony Cointreau and James Russo, she attended the Broadway opening of David Merrick's new musical, *42nd Street*. It was her kind of show—tuneful, rousing, fast-paced, and old-fashioned—and she enjoyed it immensely. At the curtain call, Merrick gravely stepped to the front of the stage and announced that the show's director, Gower Champion, had died earlier in the day. It was a moment of overwhelming shock both for Jerry Orbach and the actors gathered onstage and for the audience. Ethel was shattered by the news and immediately expressed her concern for Champion's girlfriend, *42nd Street* leading lady Wanda Richert.

Other shows inspired either indifference or outrage in her. When Andrew Lloyd Webber's *Cats* was opening on Broadway in 1982, she received an invitation to a cocktail party that Josh and Nedda Logan were hosting for Webber. She sent it along in the mail to Cointreau, scribbling on the card, "WANNA GO?" Then, having circled Webber's name, she wrote, "WHO

THE HELL IS HE?" When John Kander and Fred Ebb's *Woman of the Year*
reached Broadway in 1981, Ethel was in the first-night audience. Ethel's
opinion of Lauren Bacall's musical abilities had not changed since *Applause*
eleven years earlier. As Bacall barked out her first few lines, Ethel, seated in
the third row of the orchestra on the aisle, bellowed, "JEEZUS!" "People
onstage heard it," said the show's conductor, Donald Pippin. "*I* certainly
heard it." At intermission Ethel came breezing into Bacall's dressing room,
despite the doorman's attempts to prevent her from entering. As a dazed Bacall looked on helplessly, Ethel said, "Honey, I have to have a drink," and
went to the bar to fix herself one. After she tossed it back, she said, "Oh,
that's just what I needed. Okay—see you onstage, second act!" and barreled
out of the room without saying a word about the performance. According to
Pippin, "Bacall was, for the first time in her career, absolutely speechless."

In recent years Ethel had taken to brooding about the collapse of her
marriage to Bob Levitt, whose stature in her memory as the great love of
her life had only increased with the passage of time. It was not enough that
she wore his ring and gold watch; Ethel wanted to feel a greater degree of
closeness with her favorite husband. How she accomplished this was extreme: she arranged for his body to be exhumed and cremated, the ashes
deposited in an urn that she kept in her bedroom closet. To her friends she
insisted that it was a wonderful balm to be able to feel Bob's presence in her
apartment—so much so that she sold the chapel she had purchased in Colorado and had the remains of Ethel Jr. and Mom and Pop Zimmermann
shipped to her apartment. It was, as none of her friends needed to be told,
the act of a deeply lonely woman.

As always, Ethel could lash out with no warning if she felt that a friend
had betrayed or manipulated her. When Varney asked her to allow the Surrey apartment he'd decorated to be photographed for a story in *Architectural
Digest,* Ethel agreed. She had always liked Varney and had supported his
work through the years, dutifully attending his various showings and exhibi-
tions. Unfortunately, Varney did not show up to supervise the *Architectural
Digest* shoot, and as strangers marauded through her apartment, moving all
her furniture around to get the best possible shot, Ethel felt the welling up
of her least favorite feeling—that of having been used—and her friendship
with Varney subsequently went through a cooling period.

Relations with the Surrey were not as good as the ones she had enjoyed
with the Park Lane and the Berkshire. "In those days," recalled Surrey em-
ployee Paula Palma, "we did not have hospitality training like we did later.
She was used to top-grade service, and I'm sure it irritated her. She was a

little gruff, but still cordial." When Ethel's first lease came up for renewal, the hotel tried to triple her rent. Ethel insisted that the lease specified "reasonable increase"—she did not consider a threefold hike remotely reasonable. In October 1982, Manhattan Supreme Court Justice Louise Kaplan ruled that the Surrey had the right to evict her, but Ethel won in the end, when it came to light that the Surrey had neglected to sign the two-year renewal lease by the specified deadline of June 30. Still, the management of the Surrey had its ways of getting back at her through a variety of petty machinations, such as interrupting her house telephone service.

In time Ethel had chosen to overlook her differences with Benay and Bob Schear and picked up both friendships again. But not even family members were safe from her wrath, as Barbara Geary discovered during the 1982 Christmas season. Having majored in costume design and dance at Humboldt State University, she had returned to New York for the holidays, bringing her boyfriend (later husband), Jeff Sennerling, to her parents' house for dinner. Ethel was also present, her fondness for Bill Geary never having abated over the years. Barbara and Jeff were going through a delayed, quasi-hippie period of their own, and Jeff turned up at the table with long hair and no shoes. Ethel was outraged, and the next day she called Bill Geary's wife, Margaretta, and let her have it.

"How dare you allow them to sleep in the same bedroom?" she demanded. "He didn't even have shoes!" She unleashed such a torrent of verbal abuse that Margaretta collapsed in tears.

When she heard what had happened, Barbara fired off a sharp, angry letter to Ethel, telling her that she had no right to treat her stepmother in such a harsh manner. Ethel refused to back down from her position, and Barbara responded by borrowing one of Ethel's old tactics. She simply cut her grandmother out of her life. "We thought she was just being monstrous," said Barbara. "I couldn't just slough it off and let her have her way."

• •

Although she had never been anything resembling a hypochondriac, Ethel monitored her health very carefully. She knew that she'd been drinking too heavily in recent years, as she had switched between vodka and Almaden on the rocks, and by 1982 she had stopped drinking altogether, never touching anything stronger than a Tab. Much of her concern over her health reflected her staunch professionalism. If a concert date loomed and she suddenly felt a cold coming on, she instantly turned up in the office of Dr. Attia requesting that he do whatever he could to ensure that she didn't have to cancel her upcoming performance. Apart from a very mild case of hypertension, so insignificant that it didn't require medication, and some lower back pain, Ethel exhibited only one real health problem: she had recently been diagnosed with the optical condition known as macular degeneration. Both her peripheral vision and straight-on vision were beginning to be affected—in dimly lit restaurants she often failed to recognize old friends until they were practically on top of her—but so far her eyesight had not declined to the point that it was interfering with her life in any crippling way.

On January 14, 1983, just two days before her seventy-fifth birthday, Ethel was delighted to receive a congratulatory telegram from President Reagan: THERE'S NO DAY LIKE A BIRTHDAY / NANCY AND I HOPE THAT YOUR SPECIAL DAY COMES UP ROSES AND HAPPY MEMORIES / HAPPY BIRTHDAY AND MAY GOD BLESS AND KEEP YOU FOR MANY MORE.

There were many projects on the horizon, the most intriguing of which was a major feature film to be based on her life. Producer Lester Linsk had obtained her permission to pursue the idea, and Ethel looked forward to what he might come up with. She had also been scheduled to appear with Mary Martin on the Emmy Awards telecast in September 1982. But earlier that month, Mary, in San Francisco for her talk show, *Over Easy*, was badly injured when a drunk driver hit the taxi in when she was traveling with her manager, Ben Washer, and her close friend Janet Gaynor. (Washer was killed, and Gaynor never really recovered from her injuries, which led to her death in 1984.) "Millions of people will miss seeing us on the 'Emmys,' " Ethel wrote to Mary, "but *I* will miss us most of all—I was anxiously looking forward to our duet together. Get well, we'll do it again. Much love, Merman."

In the spring of 1983, Ethel was still maintaining the usual busy round of activities. In February she had sung a successful symphony engagement at the Peabody Auditorium in Daytona Beach, Florida. Her next major date was the April 11 Academy Awards telecast, in which she was to perform a medley of Irving Berlin songs. While in Los Angeles she was hoping to get down to Rancho Mirage to visit Mary Martin in her new home and see how she was doing postrecovery.

Two weeks before she was scheduled to leave, Ethel ran into *New York Post* gossip columnist Cindy Adams at Gallagher's Steak House on West Fifty-second Street.

"What are you doing, Ethel?" Adams asked her.

"Whaddya mean, 'What am I doing?' " snapped Ethel. "What the hell is it with you? You act like you don't expect me to be doing *anything*. I'm busier than I've ever been in my whole life. I'll tell you what I'm doing. I'm going to be on the Oscars. I'm also going to be on the Tonys. I'm set for both telecasts. How do you like that for doing?"

A few days prior to her trip, however, Ethel telephoned Dr. Attia, sounding much more distraught than he'd normally heard her sound. "I'm very anxious about this performance," she said. "I'm having difficulty writing." The following day she called the doctor again. "I'm having difficulty with my speech," she said, the concern in her voice almost palpable. "Words are not coming out."

This conversation took place on April 7, the day she was to leave for Los Angeles. She was in her apartment, having finished packing her trunks. As was her custom, everything had been carefully hung—including the gown that Bob Mackie had specially designed for her to wear on the Oscar show— and all the drawers were precisely labeled with their contents. When she was finished speaking with the doctor, she called Tony Cointreau and James Russo to tell them good-bye, then lifted the receiver of the house phone to request a bag pickup.

On the other end of the line, the concierge heard a muffled cry and then a loud thud. Fearful that something was wrong, the hotel staff sprang into action. When they rushed upstairs to Ethel's apartment, they found her lying in front of her door in a semiconscious state. She had managed to unlock the bolts on the door before she became powerless to do anything at all. Irving Katz, her financial adviser, was telephoned and came immediately to the Surrey. The decision was made not to summon an ambulance; instead Katz rushed her to St. Luke's–Roosevelt Hospital in a taxi.

Dr. Attia wasn't on duty when Ethel arrived at the hospital. The procedure that needed to be performed was the injection of dye into the cranium in order to track the circulation in the brain, but at the moment there was not a physician present who could supervise such a procedure. Instead Ethel was given a CAT scan without contrast. The initial diagnosis was a stroke, but when Dr. Attia finally appeared on the scene, he arranged for a second, proper CAT scan, performed by staff neurosurgeon Dr. Robert Schick. What the second test revealed was an enormous, stage-four tumor of the brain, much too large to be considered operable. The news came as a shock to all concerned, since Ethel had had none of the classic symptoms of a brain tumor: no headaches, no vision problems other than the normal ones associated with her macular degeneration. By now she had lost her ability to speak, and for all those close to the family it was like the rerun of a nightmare—she seemed to be going down the exact same path her mother had traveled.

Bobby, who by now was once again living in California, returned to New York immediately and impressed both friends and the hospital staff with his constant devotion to his mother. For some of the physicians, his attitude occasionally verged on interference, as when he discovered a doctor in Japan who was performing experimental treatments on patients with brain tumors. Bobby became insistent on flying Ethel to Japan, hopeful that she might revive under alternative methods of treatment, but Dr. Attia talked him out of it, certain that she would never survive the plane trip. The only hope for even partial recovery was a round of radiation, which the doctors were all but certain that so large a tumor was bound to resist.

For the next several weeks, Ethel was confined to the institution she had generously served for more than ten years. Gus Schirmer did not want the true nature of her condition to be revealed to the public, and every few days there appeared optimistic reports on her supposed progress. On April 26 the *New York Times* ran an item stating that she had been "delighting fellow patients at St. Luke's–Roosevelt Hospital with morning song sessions." It was also reported, incorrectly, that she had undergone surgery to remove the brain tumor and that her recovery had been "going smoothly."

The truth was that she was suffering from an aphasia similar to the type that had felled her mother. She could communicate only in guttural moans. When she tried to speak her name into a tape recorder as part of her physical therapy, it came out "Ethel Methyl." Her television was turned to Channel 5, with a note attached to it that said, "DON'T CHANGE THIS CHANNEL." One day *There's No Business Like Show Business* was shown as an afternoon movie selection, but the film scarcely seemed to register with Ethel.

Her hair had fallen out, and with her eyes clouded in sorrow, her bloated face a study in torment, she looked nothing like herself; it was almost impossible to tell whether the person lying in the bed was a man or a woman. Dropping by to visit her, some friends initially thought that they'd wandered into the wrong room. Certain visitors she recognized; others she met with a blank stare. Now recovered from her injuries, Mary Martin came to visit her and held her hand for a long time, offering warm encouragement—but Ethel was not persuaded that she would get better.

Perhaps out of the need to bestow some kind of poetic touch on the terrible fate that had wreaked havoc on a woman who was considered a titan in her industry, a number of her hospital visitors concocted fanciful stories about their bedside conversations with her. Ann Miller insisted that Ethel had said to her, "How could this happen to me? I've always been a nice person." In fact, she could not utter more than a word or two, and those only with staggering effort. One of the words she used in the presence of Tony Cointreau was "terrible." She said it over and over—"terrible, terrible"—staring off into the distance at nothing, her voice choked with agony.

She wanted more than anything to be at home, which was where Bobby wanted her, too. Eventually the doctors agreed that she would do just as well at the Surrey, provided she had twenty-four-hour nursing care, since she still was unable to bathe or feed herself. By midsummer she was back in her apartment; the doctors prescribed heavy doses of the steroid prednisone to try to keep the tumor in check. Bobby coordinated all the arrangements between the hospital and the Surrey, even joining her hospital bed with the big brass bed that she'd had for so long. He also did his best to sustain the illusion that Ethel was making a speedy recovery, writing to Mary Martin in San Francisco that Ethel was healing and slowly regaining her energy. In fact, the prednisone treatments did restore her power of speech.

But only for a brief time. At the Surrey, she became a virtual prisoner, at the mercy of the decrepitude that she had always feared would overtake her life. There were occasional outings in Central Park. She remained estranged from Barbara, who described herself at the time as "not mature enough to make the gesture to her."

Yet beyond the paralysis, the disfigurement, the alarming weight loss, Ethel was still, on occasion, recognizably herself. One day while she was in her wheelchair being pushed around Central Park by Goldie Hawkins and her nurse, she came face-to-face with Barbara, who, though currently living in New Orleans, where she operated a theatrical-mask shop, was in New York for a brief stay. Ethel immediately turned her face away from her granddaughter. They sat in silence for several minutes. "She couldn't speak," said Barbara. "It was very difficult. It was a terribly awkward thing."

To those who had written Bobby off as a self-indulgent free spirit, his vigilant care of his mother came as a pleasant surprise. He stayed with her at the Surrey, attending to her every need and running interference with the press, so the rest of the world would not find out how desperately ill Ethel really was. Dorothy Strelsin, Madeline Gaxton, Tony Cointreau, James Russo, and others in her close circle were frequent visitors. To Gus Schirmer, Ethel put up a brave front, insisting that he not book any engagements until December. But as the weeks went by, it became clear to one and all—and in time to Ethel herself—that she was not going to recover.

Soon 1983 gave way to 1984. One day Tony Cointreau came to the Surrey bearing a gift: a pillow, needlepointed with the song title "He's Me Pal," the number Ethel had sung as a child for Agnes and then for the soldiers at Camp Yaphank and Camp Mills. Singers who suffer from aphasia often can sing more easily than they can speak, and such proved to be the case with Ethel. She took the pillow from Tony, lifted it to her face, and began to cry softly. Then she sang "He's Me Pal" from beginning to end.

Ethel's seventy-sixth birthday came and went. Bobby was grateful that she was able to remain at home at the Surrey, but as she continued to decline, it was difficult to be grateful for much of anything.

Early in the morning on February 15, Ethel slipped away in her sleep. That night all the theaters along Broadway dimmed their lights in her memory.

Her death was marked in all the major newspapers and magazines, with the *New York Times* giving her obituary front-page placement with the headline ETHEL MERMAN, CLARION VOICE OF MUSICAL COMEDY FOR DECADES, IS DEAD AT 76. The author of the obituary, Murray Schumach, observed, "Beginning in 1930, and continuing for more than a quarter of a century thereafter, no Broadway season seemed really complete unless it had a musical with Ethel Merman." He went on to recall how "her delighted customers knew that when the 'belter' strode onstage, turned her round eyes on them, raised her quizzical eyebrows and opened her wide mouth, they would get full value wherever they sat. She needed no hidden microphones. Equally important, they knew that when they bought tickets for a Merman show—usually well in advance—she would be there, her face beaming, strong arms churning, regardless of snowfall or flu epidemic." It was a touching tribute, unfortunately marred when Schumach repeated the incorrect information that Ethel Jr. had committed suicide in 1967.

But Ethel might have been even more touched by the letters from readers that poured into the *Times* that week, particularly one from Sherry Terzian of Los Angeles, a graduate of William Cullen Bryant High School. After calling Ethel the school's "prize graduate," Terzian went on to say, "We were not only proud of her but we also tried to emulate her. Ethel Merman became a role model for many, and the rest of us fantasized about making the transition from Bryant to Broadway the way she did."

Bob Schear took out an ad in *Variety* that read "ETHEL MERMAN—YOU'RE THE TOP—NOW AND EVER." Oddly, no other paid tributes appeared in the publication—not from the American Theater Wing, not from her agency, not from any of the theater owners.

Within a week of her death, the *New York Times* reported that she had left an estate of roughly $800,000, most of which would be divided among Bobby, Barbara, and Michael. There were individual bequests to friends, totaling $26,000. A sum of $5,000 and four of her Norwegian marble urns were left to Bill Geary, with a gift of $1,000 going to the Actors Fund of America. The will, which had been dated November 18, 1980, also directed that her personal effects be sold.

The figure of $800,000 surprised many of her friends, who had assumed all along that she'd amassed a great deal more than that. They were right—the amount reported by the *Times* did not take into account the vast fortune that she had set aside, from *Gypsy* onward, in the American Entertainment Enterprises, an amount that ran into the millions.

Ethel's private service, organized by Bobby, was a quiet, low-key affair in the chapel at St. Bartholomew's. The Reverend Bruce Forbes officiated over a straightforward Episcopal service with no theatrical trappings whatsoever, apart from a framed photograph of her next to an enormous bouquet of red roses—seventy-six in all, one for each year of her life.

Broadway has a long history of honoring its departed giants with tributes that for sheer theatricality sometimes rival the shows in which the stars appeared. Normally they take place at one of the theaters associated with the actor. Several of Ethel's friends planned a proper, Broadway-style memorial tribute but were dissuaded from going ahead with it by Anna Sosenko, who boasted of plans to produce one of her own. Two memorials would cut into each other, Sosenko complained, assuring all concerned that she would give

Ethel an appropriate tribute sometime in the next six months. For whatever
reason the tribute never took place, though in 1985 Sosenko did finally produce a kind of valentine to Ethel. Once again it was a benefit for the Museum
of the City of New York, and the stars on the program included Elaine
Stritch, Carol Channing, Dorothy Stickney, Maria Karnilova, and Benay
Venuta, but it was not by any stretch of the imagination a genuine memorial
service.

On October 10, 1984, a public auction of Ethel's great store of possessions was held at Christie's East, including her collection of paintings, her
furniture, bric-a-brac, and theatrical memorabilia. The prop rifle from *Annie
Get Your Gun* by itself brought $1,500. The total amount derived from the
auction was in excess of $120,000.

For those who work in the theater, life assigns few crueler fates than the
passing of time. Throughout her career Ethel had been the embodiment of the
rambunctious, audacious spirit of New York as it was expressed in the music
of Gershwin and Porter and Berlin. But the wised-up, straight-shooting, and
sentimental musical heroine she represented was a type that had passed out
of fashion by the time of her death, supplanted by the creations of Sondheim
and his musical age of anxiety, and by the bland, cardboard figures of Andrew
Lloyd Webber, who exist only as pawns in a mammoth visual spectacle. The
great age of personalities had long since faded, and although Ethel's vocal
powers had miraculously never abandoned her until her final illness, she
came face-to-face with a different sort of march of time, one that ran parallel
to the actual passing of the years: the blazing genius she had given to the
world would have had difficulty maintaining a home for itself in modern
show business. A kind of stasis had crept over her professional life: as a
performer she was forever looking back. And although she cherished her
own glorious past and would never have wished to be born at any other time,
she would not have wanted to live to see her brilliant record fall into neglect,
the victim of the ignorance of new audiences and the very different concerns
of the new Broadway.

But the final victory was inarguably hers. The titanic talent and iron
discipline and fearsome work ethic she possessed all assured her a place in
theater history that is unassailable. As Donald Pippin remarked, "Merman
belonged to an era that is gone. We have no one near her skill and what she
represented in the business." Her retirement from Broadway created a void
that has never come close to being filled by the many talented, big-voiced
stars who came along in her wake. Her specter lingers over revivals of her

best shows, whether on Broadway or in regional theater. Others may succeed in investing the roles with something unique of their own. In the 1989 Broadway revival of *Gypsy*, staged by Arthur Laurents, Tyne Daly gave a rich, persuasive, multilayered performance as Rose. But no one has ever approached the vocal magic that Ethel brought to the score. An actress starring in a revival of *The Sound of Music* or *South Pacific* can easily escape comparison with Mary Martin; an actress taking on *Call Me Madam* or *Annie Get Your Gun* is doomed to confront the shadow of Merman.

The New Yorkers who loved Ethel could hardly be blamed for feeling that perhaps she stood for the best part of themselves—the most democratic of stars, born and bred in the most democratic of American cities, a woman who could bring an audience to its feet one night and be glimpsed the next day shopping at Lamston's or enjoying a bowl of split pea soup at the Skyline Coffee Shop. Those who had branded her temperamental had missed the point: her talent was so immense that she was incapable of playing the game any way but hers.

New York's own uniqueness, the brashness and brilliance and flouting of convention that was once such a source of pride, continues to do a slow fade. With banks, Starbucks coffeehouses, and chain stores rapidly replacing ethnic restaurants, secondhand bookshops, and other small businesses that were once such a vital part of Manhattan's character, New York seems increasingly to embrace the subdued, well-ordered blandness of other American cities. So it seems all the more heartening that this far-from-pretty girl from Astoria, this essence of the irregular weave, could once make the choices she made and lead the life she did. For in the end, the thing that many people appreciated most about Ethel was her honesty. She believed in the sentiments of her time, the honest sentiments expressed in her songs and her shows. And that raucous, outsize voice, which could be received with offense by the ears of non–New Yorkers, was the truest expression of the woman behind it.

The legend of Ethel Merman the tough broad will never die. Tough she certainly was. But it is important to remember Margaret Whiting's observation when she went to visit Ethel one day at the Berkshire.

"One look at that Christmas tree she kept on the hall table," said Whiting, "and I knew exactly who she was."

ACKNOWLEDGMENTS

B ooks are often born out of unexpected, almost casual comments or happenings. This one certainly was. As the features editor of *Opera News*, I was working on the magazine's second annual "Divas" issue, when I decided that it would be a good idea to include an article on one Broadway diva among all the operatic ones. Clearly the first choice was Ethel Merman, and to write the piece I called on a fine writer, Barbara Seaman, whose excellent biography of Jacqueline Susann, *Lovely Me*, I had admired very much. Barbara accepted the assignment, then withdrew; the publisher of the book she was then writing had moved up her deadline, and she could not fulfill her commitment to *Opera News*. Since not much time was left until the magazine's deadline, I decided to write the article myself. Barbara called to compliment me on the end result, and during our conversation I mentioned that someone should write a proper biography of Merman. "Why don't you do it?" said Barbara. I was momentarily stunned at the thought—then I was off and running. I am grateful to Barbara for setting me on the path toward writing this book.

My dear friend Helen Sheehy, the accomplished biographer of Eva Le Gallienne, Margo Jones, and Eleanora Duse, also prodded me to take on this project. Another fine biographer, Barry Paris, sent me mementos and other intriguing tidbits on Ethel, cheering me on every step of the way.

Others, too, offered encouragement. I spoke with two of our leading American musical-theater scholars: Robert Kimball provided welcome positive reinforcement, and Miles Kreuger gave me a fascinating glimpse of theatergoing in the age of Merman. Ron Bowers, former editor of *Films in Review*, gave me access to his vast personal library, no doubt saving me hundreds of dollars at Strand Book Store.

In 2004 I spent several days in New Orleans, carefully going through the exhaustive collection of Merman's video appearances owned by George Dansker. Over the next two years, George generously provided me with new video footage that came into his possession. Thank you, George.

Joel Blumberg, host of the WGBB radio series *Silver Screen Audio,* spent a wonderful day with me, giving me an insider's tour of Astoria, the New York neighborhood where Ethel was born and grew up. At her alma mater, William Cullen Bryant High School, I received assistance from principal Christopher Pellettieri and teacher and archivist Alyson Roach.

I received assistance from many of the most important performing-arts archives in the country. Ethel's career memorabilia was left to one of Manhattan's great institutions, the Museum of the City of New York. My thanks to Martin Jacobs, curator of the museum's theater collection, for his advice, answered questions, and many kindnesses. I would like to thank the staffs of the Lincoln Center Library for the Performing Arts, the New York Historical Society, the Queens Historical Society, the Harry Ransom Humanities Research Collection at the University of Texas at Austin, the Howard Gotlieb Archival Research Center at Boston University, the DeGolyer Library at Southern Methodist University, the Film and Television Archives at the University of California at Los Angeles, the Harvard Theater Collection, the American Musical Theatre Collection at Yale University's Music Library (special thanks to Richard Warren), and the Academy of Motion Picture Arts and Sciences. Both Rebecca Paller and Richard Holbrook at the Paley Center for Media guided me through the center's rich collection of Merman video appearances. One of my biggest finds came at the University of Southern California Cinema and Television Archive, where Ned Comstock turned up various treasures, including unpublished transcripts of interviews that Pete Martin had conducted for the 1955 memoir he wrote with Ethel, *Who Could Ask for Anything More?*

Many thanks to Bill Braun for his support during the formative stages of this project. Also helping out in a variety of ways were Clifford Capone, Erik Dahl, Elizabeth Diggans, *Opera News*'s tireless editor in chief F. Paul Driscoll, Lauren Flanigan, Craig Haladay, Al Koenig, Terry Marlowe, Arlo McKinnon, Eric Myers, Karen Kriendler Nelson, David Niedenthal, Patricia O'Connell, Robert Osborne, Fred Plotkin, Carl Raymond, Lisa Ryan, John J. D. Sheehan, Sam Staggs, Tracy Turner, Tom Viola, and Oussama Zahr. Special thanks to Louise T. Guinther and Maureen Sugden for their superb copyediting.

Most of all I am deeply indebted to the following people—a few of them, sadly, no longer living—who spoke with me about various aspects of the life and career of Ethel Merman. They include Edie Adams, Kay Armen, Dr. Albert Attia, Bobbi Baird, Kaye Ballard, Mary Ellin Barrett, Arthur Bartow, Warren Berlinger, Alex Birnbaum, Klea Blackhurst, Betsy Blair, Ken Bloom, Forrest Bonshire, Patricia Bruder, David Brunetti, Bruce

Burroughs, Marilyn Cantor, Ronn Carroll, Marge Champion, Vivian Cherry, Sandra Church, Steve Cole, Carole Cook, Marilyn Cooper, Anna Crouse, Leslie Cutler, Jack Dabdoub, Arlene Dahl, John DeMain, Phyllis Diller, Richard Dyer, Marta Eggerth, Harvey Evans, Nanette Fabray, the Reverend Bruce Forbes, Robert Gardiner, Betty Garrett, Virginia Gibson, Dody Goodman, Dolores Gray, Richard Grayson, Jess Gregg, Tony Gribin, Don Grody, Svetlana Grody, Barbara Hale, Sheldon Harnick, Kitty Carlisle Hart, Hal Hastings, June Havoc, Jerry Herman, George S. Irving, John Kander, Jane Kean, John Kenley, Jack Klugman, Eric Knight, Tom Korman, Rosemary Kuhlmann, Lynn Lane, Lionel Larner, Arthur Laurents, Jack Lee, Sondra Lee, Brenda Lewis, Marcia Lewis, Don Liberto, Biff Liff, Terry Lilly, Patti LuPone, Jacqueline Mayro, Donna McKechnie, Jayne Meadows, Dina Merrill, John Montgomery, Bruce Moore, Karen Morrow, Jerry Orbach, Paula Palma, Joan Patenaude-Yarnell, Donald Pippin, Alice Playten, Seymour "Red" Press, Donald Preston, Seth Riggs, Rose Marie, Donald Saddler, Bob Shaver, Jeannie Jones Snow, Stephen Sondheim, June Squibb, Richard Stack, Gloria Stuart, Margaret Styne, Carol Swarbrick, Tom Troupe, Lewis Turner, Bob Ullman, Carleton Varney, Marie Wallace, Susan Watson, William Weslow, Margaret Whiting, Helene Whitney (a.k.a. Helen Miles), Lou Wills Jr., Jane Wyatt, Gretchen Wyler, and Mark Zeller.

Of all those I interviewed, I am most deeply indebted to a select few. Bob Schear, whose friendship with Ethel stretched back to her days in *Gypsy*, was an invaluable resource, never too busy, night or day, to ponder my questions.

Barbara Geary, Ethel's granddaughter, supported this project from the start and was unfailingly helpful throughout the writing of the book.

Tony Cointreau and James Russo were the two people without whose cooperation I never could have written the book that I envisioned. They met with me many times at their home in New York and cheerfully fielded my long stream of phone calls when they probably wanted to sit back and let the machine pick up. Tony and Jim were of the greatest assistance in helping me separate fact from the Merman mythology, in weeding out many of the stories that, however funny, are also apocryphal.

For their ongoing personal support, thanks to my parents, Jack Kellow and Marjorie Kellow; my brother and sister-in-law, Barry and Kami Kellow; and my nephews, Trevin and Morgan Kellow. Also thanks to Omus and Jessica Hirshbein, for being there, always.

I want to express my deepest gratitude to those who sent my book out into the world. For my brilliant agent, Edward Hibbert, his colleague Tom

Eubanks, and the staff of Donadio & Olson, I have nothing but praise. Edward is a writer's best friend—a shrewd adviser, a tough editor, and an unfailing encourager.

At Viking, I have had the pleasure of working with Ann Day, Laura Tisdel, and Francesca Belanger. Their efforts have made me feel that this is "our" book rather than "my" book.

To my editor, Rick Kot, my profound appreciation for his keen perceptions, sound judgment, warm friendship, and unshakable integrity. Rick was behind this project from the beginning. To have him as my editor means more to me than I can possibly express.

Brian Kellow
New York City
December 2006

APPENDIX

Girl Crazy

Alvin Theatre
OPENED: October 14, 1930
CLOSED: June 6, 1931, after 272 performances
PRODUCERS: Alex A. Aarons and Vinton Freedley
DIRECTOR: Alexander Leftwich
MUSIC: George Gershwin
LYRICS: Ira Gershwin
BOOK: Guy Bolton and John McGowan
SET DESIGNER: Donald Oenslager
COSTUME DESIGNER: Kiviette
CHOREOGRAPHER: George Hale
CONDUCTOR: Earl Busby
CAST: Allen Kearns, Ginger Rogers, Willie Howard, Ethel Merman (as Kate
    Fothergill), William Kent, Peggy O'Connor, Eunice Healy, Lew Parker,
    Carlton Macy, Clyde Veaux, Olive Brady, Chief Rivers, Donald Foster
ETHEL MERMAN'S SONGS: "Sam and Delilah," "I Got Rhythm," "Boy! What Love
    Has Done to Me"
NOTES: George Gershwin conducted the opening-night performance of *Girl
    Crazy*.
    Ethel's pianist, Al Siegel, was taken ill on opening night and replaced
    by Roger Edens.

George White's Scandals (Eleventh Edition)

Apollo Theatre
OPENED: September 14, 1931

CLOSED: March 1932, after 202 performances
PRODUCER AND DIRECTOR: George White
MUSIC: Ray Henderson
LYRICS: Lew Brown
SKETCHES: George White, Lew Brown, Irving Caesar
SET DESIGNER: Joseph Urban
COSTUME DESIGNER: Charles LeMaire
CONDUCTOR: Al Goodman
CAST: Rudy Vallee, Willie and Eugene Howard, Ethel Merman, Everett Marshall, Ethel Barrymore Colt, Ray Bolger
ETHEL MERMAN'S SONGS: "Life Is Just a Bowl of Cherries," "Ladies and Gentlemen, That's Love," "My Song," "The Good Old Days"

Take a Chance

Apollo Theatre
OPENED: November 26, 1932
CLOSED: July 1, 1933, after 243 performances
PRODUCERS: Laurence Schwab, B. G. (Buddy) DeSylva
DIRECTOR: Edgar MacGregor
SONGS: Nacio Herb Brown, Richard Whiting, Vincent Youmans
BOOK: B. G. (Buddy) DeSylva and Laurence Schwab (additional dialogue by Sid Silvers)
SET DESIGNER: Cleon Throckmorton
COSTUME DESIGNER: Kiviette and Charles LeMaire
CHOREOGRAPHER: Bobby Connolly
CONDUCTOR: Max Meth
CAST: Jack Haley, Jack Whiting, Sid Silvers, Ethel Merman (as Wanda Brill), June Knight, Douglas Wood, Mitzi Mayfair, Robert Gleckler
ETHEL MERMAN'S SONGS: "I Got Religion," "Rise and Shine," "You're an Old Smoothie," "Eadie Was a Lady"
NOTE: *Take a Chance* began life as *Humpty Dumpty,* which opened at Pittsburgh's Nixon Theatre on September 26, 1932, and closed shortly thereafter. Following extensive revisions, it reopened with the new title.

Anything Goes

Alvin Theatre
OPENED: November 21, 1934

CLOSED: November 16, 1935, after 420 performances

PRODUCER: Vinton Freedley, Inc.

DIRECTOR: Howard Lindsay

MUSIC AND LYRICS: Cole Porter

BOOK: Howard Lindsay, Russel Crouse (based on a an original by P. G. Wode-house and Guy Bolton)

SET DESIGNER: Donald Oenslager

GOWNS: Jenkins

CHOREOGRAPHER: Robert Alton

MUSICAL DIRECTOR: Earl Busby

CAST: William Gaxton, Victor Moore, Ethel Merman (as Reno Sweeney), Leslie Barrie, Bettina Hall, Vera Dunn, Helen Raymond

ETHEL MERMAN'S SONGS: "I Get a Kick Out of You," "You're the Top," "Anything Goes," "Blow, Gabriel, Blow," "Buddy, Beware"

NOTES: Ethel Merman re-created the role of Reno Sweeney in Paramount's 1936 film version of *Anything Goes*, although "Blow, Gabriel, Blow" was lost in the transfer.

Featured in a small part was future television star Vivian Vance.

Although Ethel usually stayed with a show until it closed, she left *Anything Goes* in the summer of 1935. Benay Venuta succeeded her as Reno.

Red, Hot and Blue!

Alvin Theatre

OPENED: October 29, 1936

CLOSED: April 10, 1937, after 183 performances

PRODUCER: Vinton Freedley

DIRECTOR: Howard Lindsay

MUSIC AND LYRICS: Cole Porter

BOOK: Howard Lindsay, Russel Crouse

SET DESIGNER: Donald Oenslager

COSTUME DESIGNER: Constance Ripley

CHOREOGRAPHER: George Hale

CONDUCTOR: Frank Tours

CAST: Jimmy Durante, Ethel Merman (as "Nails" O'Reilly Duquesne), Bob Hope, Paul Hartman, Grace Hartman, Polly Walters, Prentiss Davis, Leo Shippers, Bernard Jannsen, Bill Benner

ETHEL MERMAN'S SONGS: "Down in the Depths," "You've Got Something," "It's De-Lovely," "Ridin' High," "You're a Bad Influence on Me," "Red, Hot and Blue"

NOTES: For the second Merman show in a row, Vivian Vance had a bit part.
Ethel took *Red, Hot and Blue!* on tour to Chicago, where it did not find an audience. This experience seems to have soured her on touring in general.

Stars in Your Eyes

Majestic Theatre
OPENED: February 9, 1939
CLOSED: May 27, 1939, after 127 performances
PRODUCER: Dwight Deere Wiman
DIRECTOR: Joshua Logan
MUSIC: Arthur Schwartz
LYRICS: Dorothy Fields
BOOK: J. P. McEvoy
SET DESIGNER: Jo Mielziner
COSTUME DESIGNER: John Hambleton
CHOREOGRAPHER: Carl Randall
CAST: Ethel Merman (as Jeanette Adair), Jimmy Durante, Richard Carlson, Mildred Natwick, Tamara Toumanova, Mary Wickes
ETHEL MERMAN'S SONGS: "This Is It," "A Lady Needs a Change," "Just a Little Bit More," "I'll Pay the Check," "It's All Yours"
NOTES: Appearing in small parts were Dan Dailey, who would become a major movie star at 20th Century Fox, and Walter Cassel, who would have a distinguished opera career highlighted by the world premiere of Douglas Moore's *The Ballad of Baby Doe.*
Appearing in the corps de ballet were Maria Karniloff (Karnilova) and future dance greats Alicia Alonso and Nora Kaye, as well as Jerome Robbins, who would go on to choreograph *Call Me Madam* and choreograph and direct *Gypsy.*

Du Barry Was a Lady

46th Street Theatre
OPENED: December 6, 1939
CLOSED: December 12, 1940, after 408 performances
PRODUCER: B. G. (Buddy) DeSylva
DIRECTOR: Edgar MacGregor
MUSIC AND LYRICS: Cole Porter

BOOK: Herbert Fields and B. G. DeSylva

SETS AND COSTUME DESIGNER: Raoul Pène DuBois

CHOREOGRAPHER: Robert Alton

CONDUCTOR: Gene Salzer

CAST: Ethel Merman (as May Daly), Bert Lahr, Betty Grable, Ronald Graham, Charles Walters, Benny Baker, Jean Moorehead

ETHEL MERMAN'S SONGS: "When Love Beckoned," "Come On In," "But in the Morning, No!," "Do I Love You," "Du Barry Was a Lady," "Give Him the Oo-La-La," "Katie Went to Haiti," "Friendship"

NOTES: Future Hollywood successes in the cast included Betty Grable, who became 20th Century Fox's number-one star, and Charles Walters, who became a fixture at MGM, first as choreographer and later as director.

Also achieving a measure of Hollywood fame were chorus girls Janis (here Janice) Carter and Adele Jergens.

Panama Hattie

46th Street Theatre

OPENED: October 30, 1940

CLOSED: January 3, 1942, after 501 performances

PRODUCER: B. G. (Buddy) DeSylva

DIRECTOR: Edgar MacGregor

MUSIC AND LYRICS: Cole Porter

BOOK: Herbert Fields, B. G. DeSylva

SET AND COSTUME DESIGNER: Raoul Pène DuBois

CHOREOGRAPHER: Robert Alton

CONDUCTOR: Gene Salzer

CAST: Ethel Merman (as Hattie Maloney), James Dunn, Joan Carroll, Betty Hutton, Arthur Treacher, Pat Harrington, Frank Hyers, Rags Ragland, Phyllis Brooks

ETHEL MERMAN'S SONGS: "Visit Panama," "My Mother Would Love You," "I've Still Got My Health," "Let's Be Buddies," "I'm Throwin' a Ball Tonight," "Conga," "Make It Another Old-Fashioned, Please," "You Said It"

NOTES: Following the success of *Panama Hattie*, B. G. DeSylva went to Hollywood to work for Paramount Pictures, taking with him Betty Hutton, who became one of the studio's top stars.

Hollywood success was also achieved by chorus girls June Allyson, Vera-Ellen, Lucille Bremer, Betsy Blair, and Doris Dowling.

Something for the Boys

Alvin Theatre
OPENED: January 7, 1943
CLOSED: January 8, 1944, after 422 performances
PRODUCER: Michael Todd
DIRECTOR: Hassard Short
MUSIC AND LYRICS: Cole Porter
BOOK: Herbert and Dorothy Fields
SET DESIGNER: Howard Bay
COSTUME DESIGNER: Billy Livingston
CHOREOGRAPHER: Jack Cole
CONDUCTOR: William Parson
CAST: Ethel Merman (as Blossom Hart), Bill Johnson, Allen Jenkins, Paula
Laurence, Jed Prouty, Betty Garrett, Betty Bruce, Stuart Langley
ETHEL MERMAN'S SONGS: "Something for the Boys," "When We're at Home on
the Range," "Hey, Good-Lookin'," "He's a Right Guy," "The Leader of a
Big Time Band," "There's a Happy Land in the Sky," "By the Miss-iss-
inewah"
NOTES: After Paula Laurence left the cast, the part of Chiquita Hart was
assumed by Betty Bruce, who became a lifelong friend of Ethel's.
When Ethel briefly fell ill during the run, Betty Garrett took over for
her and later went on to Broadway and Hollywood fame.

Annie Get Your Gun

Imperial Theatre
OPENED: May 16, 1946
CLOSED: February 12, 1949, after 1,147 performances
PRODUCERS: Richard Rodgers and Oscar Hammerstein
DIRECTOR: Joshua Logan
MUSIC AND LYRICS: Irving Berlin
BOOK: Herbert and Dorothy Fields
SET DESIGNER: Jo Mielziner
COSTUME DESIGNER: Lucinda Ballard
CHOREOGRAPHER: Helen Tamiris
CONDUCTOR: Jay Blackton
CAST: Ethel Merman (as Annie Oakley), Ray Middleton, William O'Neal, Marty
May, Harry Bellaver, Lea Penman, George Lipton, Betty Anne Nyman

ETHEL MERMAN'S SONGS: "Doin' What Comes Naturally," "You Can't Get a Man with a Gun," "There's No Business Like Show Business," "They Say It's Wonderful," "Moonshine Lullaby," "I'm an Indian Too," "I Got Lost in His Arms," "I Got the Sun in the Morning," "Anything You Can Do"

NOTES: Warren Berlinger, in a bit part, became a popular face in young adult parts on Broadway, in films, and on television.

With a nearly three-year run on Broadway, *Annie Get Your Gun* was the longest-running success of Ethel's career, but it was not enough to secure her the film version, which went to Betty Hutton.

Call Me Madam

Imperial Theatre
OPENED: October 12, 1950
CLOSED: May 3, 1952, after 644 performances
PRODUCER: Leland Hayward
DIRECTOR: George Abbott
MUSIC AND LYRICS: Irving Berlin
BOOK: Howard Lindsay, Russel Crouse
SET AND COSTUME DESIGNER: Raoul Pène DuBois
CHOREOGRAPHER: Jerome Robbins
CONDUCTOR: Jay Blackton
CAST: Ethel Merman (as Sally Adams), Paul Lukas, Russell Nype, Galina Talva, Alan Hewitt, Owen Coll, Lilia Skala
ETHEL MERMAN'S SONGS: "The Hostess with the Mostes' on the Ball," "Washington Square Dance," "Can You Use Any Money Today?," "Marrying for Love," "The Best Thing for You Would Be Me," "Something to Dance About," "You're Just in Love"
NOTES: Two of Ethel's songs, "Free" and "Mr. Monotony," were dropped while *Call Me Madam* was in its pre-Broadway tryout. "Mr. Monotony" finally made it to Broadway in the 1989 retrospective *Jerome Robbins' Broadway*.

In 1953, Ethel starred in the film version of *Call Me Madam*, making it the first time since *Anything Goes* that she had re-created her stage role on-screen.

Happy Hunting

Majestic Theatre
OPENED: December 6, 1956

CLOSED: November 30, 1957, after 412 performances

PRODUCER: Jo Mielziner

DIRECTOR: Abe Burrows

MUSIC: Harold Karr

LYRICS: Matt Dubey

BOOK: Howard Lindsay, Russel Crouse

SET DESIGNER: Jo Mielziner

COSTUME DESIGNER: Irene Sharaff

CHOREOGRAPHERS: Alex Romero and Bob Herget

CONDUCTOR: Jay Blackton

CAST: Ethel Merman (as Liz Livingstone), Fernando Lamas, Virginia Gibson, Gordon Polk, Olive Templeton

ETHEL MERMAN'S SONGS: "Gee, But It's Good to Be Here," "Mutual Admiration Society," "Mr. Livingstone," "This Is What I Call Love," "A New-Fangled Tango," "The Game of Love," "Happy Hunting," "I'm a Funny Dame," "Just Another Guy"

NOTES: "The Game of Love" and "This Is What I Call Love" were eventually dropped because of Ethel's dissatisfaction with them. They were replaced, respectively, by two new songs, "I'm Old Enough to Know Better" and "Just a Moment Ago." They were written by Roger Edens, although because of his contractual commitment to MGM, he chose not to take credit for them. Kay Thompson was listed as the composer of both numbers.

Cast as one of the newspaper reporters was future Academy Award winner Estelle Parsons.

Gypsy

Broadway Theatre

OPENED: May 21, 1959

CLOSED: March 25, 1961, after 702 performances

PRODUCERS: David Merrick, Leland Hayward

DIRECTOR AND CHOREOGRAPHER: Jerome Robbins

MUSIC: Jule Styne

LYRICS: Stephen Sondheim

BOOK: Arthur Laurents

SET DESIGNER: Jo Mielziner

COSTUME DESIGNER: Raoul Pène DuBois

CONDUCTOR: Milton Rosenstock

CAST: Ethel Merman (as Rose), Jack Klugman, Sandra Church, Lane Bradbury, Paul Wallace, Maria Karnilova, Faith Dane, Chotzi Foley, Mort Marshall, Erv Harmon, Peg Murray, Marilyn Cooper

ETHEL MERMAN'S SONGS: "Some People," "Small World," "Mr. Goldstone, I Love You," "You'll Never Get Away from Me," "Everything's Coming Up Roses," "Together, Wherever We Go," "Rose's Turn"

NOTES: While *Gypsy* was generally recognized by many (including Ethel herself) as the crowning achievement of the Merman career, it failed to win a single Tony Award, the honors that year being split by *Fiorello!* and *The Sound of Music.*

Ethel campaigned long and hard for Warner Bros.' film version of *Gypsy,* which in the end went to Rosalind Russell. Close friends called it the greatest professional disappointment of her life.

Although she went briefly on the road with *Red, Hot and Blue!,* *Something for the Boys,* and *Call Me Madam,* Ethel mostly kept to a no-touring rule. *Gypsy* was an exception: she starred as Rose in a nine-month cross-country tour.

Annie Get Your Gun

Revival at New York State Theater

OPENED: May 31, 1966

CLOSED: November 26, 1966 (having moved to the Broadway Theatre, where it played 78 performances)

PRODUCER: Music Theater of Lincoln Center (Richard Rodgers, director)

DIRECTOR: Jack Sydow

MUSIC AND LYRICS: Irving Berlin

SET DESIGNER: Paul McGuire

COSTUME DESIGNER: Frank Thompson

CHOREOGRAPHER: Danny Daniels

CONDUCTOR: Jonathan Anderson

CAST: Ethel Merman (as Annie Oakley), Bruce Yarnell, Rufus Smith, Jerry Orbach, Benay Venuta, Harry Bellaver, Jaime Rogers, Jack Dabdoub, Ronn Carroll

ETHEL MERMAN'S SONGS: the same as in 1946, with the addition of "An Old-Fashioned Wedding," which she performed with Bruce Yarnell.

NOTES: Ethel was fifty-eight when she revived *Annie,* prompting many to dub the show *Granny Get Your Gun.*

"An Old-Fashioned Wedding" was the last hit song of Irving Berlin's
career.

Hello, Dolly!

St. James Theatre

OPENED: January 16, 1964

ETHEL'S FIRST PERFORMANCE: March 28, 1970

CLOSED: December 27, 1970, after 2,844 performances (in 210 of which Ethel
Merman starred)

PRODUCER: David Merrick

DIRECTOR AND CHOREOGRAPHER: Gower Champion

MUSIC AND LYRICS: Jerry Herman

BOOK: Michael Stewart

SET DESIGNER: Oliver Smith

COSTUME DESIGNER: Freddy Wittop

CONDUCTOR: Saul Schechtman

CAST: Ethel Merman (as Dolly Levi), Jack Goode, Russell Nype, Danny
Lockin, June Helmers, Marcia Lewis, Georgia Engel, David Gary, Patricia
Cope

ETHEL MERMAN'S SONGS: "I Put My Hand In," "World, Take Me Back," "Put
on Your Sunday Clothes," "Motherhood," "Dancing," "Love, Look in My
Window," "Before the Parade Passes By," "Hello, Dolly!," "So Long,
Dearie"

NOTES: Ethel was the seventh actress to star on Broadway as Dolly Levi, the
others being the part's originator, Carol Channing, followed by Ginger
Rogers, Martha Raye, Betty Grable, Pearl Bailey, and Phyllis Diller.

Jerry Herman composed *Hello, Dolly!* with Ethel in mind. When she
turned it down and the part went to Channing, two songs, "World, Take Me
Back" and "Love, Look in My Window" were dropped, to be restored six
years later when Ethel assumed the part.

A Gala Tribute to Joshua Logan

Imperial Theatre

OPENED: March 9, 1975 (special one-night benefit)

PRODUCERS: Friends of the Theater and Music Collection of the Museum of the
City of New York

DIRECTOR: Anna Sosenko
CAST: Ethel Merman, Henry Fonda, James Stewart, Joshua Logan
CHOREOGRAPHER: Donald Saddler

Together on Broadway: Mary Martin & Ethel Merman

Broadway Theatre
OPENED: May 15, 1977 (special one-night benefit)
PRODUCERS: Friends of the Theater and Music Collection of the Museum of the City of New York, Anna Sosenko
DIRECTOR: Donald Saddler
COSTUME DESIGNERS: Morty Sussman, Jean-Louis
MUSICAL DIRECTOR: Jay Blackton
CONDUCTORS: Eric Knight, John Lesko

FILM APPEARANCES

In the early 1930s, Ethel Merman made a number of short films. For Warner Bros. Vitaphone: *The Cave Club* (1930). For Paramount: *Her Future* (1930), *The Devil Sea*, *Roaming* (both 1931), *Old Man Blues*, *Let Me Call You Sweetheart*, *Ireno*, *You Try Somebody Else*, *Time on My Hands* (all 1932), *Song Shopping*, *Be Like Me* (both 1933)

FEATURE FILMS

Follow the Leader (Paramount, 1930)
DIRECTOR: Norman Taurog
WRITERS: Gertrude Purcell, Sid Silvers
CAMERA: Larry Williams
CAST: Ed Wynn, Ginger Rogers, Ethel Merman (as Helen King)

We're Not Dressing (Paramount, 1934)
PRODUCER: Benjamin Glazer
DIRECTOR: Norman Taurog
WRITERS: Horace Jackson, Frances Marion and George Marion Jr., based on a story by Benjamin Glazer
CAMERA: Charles Lang

CAST: Bing Crosby, Carole Lombard, George Burns, Gracie Allen, Ethel Merman (as Edith), Leon Errol, Raymond Milland

Kid Millions (Goldwyn–United Artists, 1934)
PRODUCER: Samuel Goldwyn
DIRECTOR: Roy del Ruth
WRITERS: Arthur Sheekman, Nat Perrin, Nunnally Johnson
CAMERA: Ray June
CAST: Eddie Cantor, Ann Sothern, Ethel Merman (as Dot Clark), George Murphy

The Big Broadcast of 1936 (Paramount, 1935)
PRODUCER: Benjamin Glazer
DIRECTOR: Norman Taurog
WRITERS: Walter de Leon, Francis Martin, Ralph Spence
CAMERA: Leo Tover
CAST: Bing Crosby, George Burns, Gracie Allen, Charlie Ruggles, Jack Oakie, Wendy Barrie, Ethel Merman, Lyda Roberti, the Nicholas Brothers, Bill Robinson

Strike Me Pink (Goldwyn–United Artists, 1936)
PRODUCER: Samuel Goldwyn
DIRECTOR: Norman Taurog
WRITERS: Frank Butler, Walter de Leon, Francis Martin (additional dialogue by Philip Rapp), based on a story by Clarence Budington Kelland
CAMERA: Merritt B. Gerstad, Gregg Toland
CAST: Eddie Cantor, Ethel Merman (as Joyce Lennox), Sally Eilers, Harry Parke, William Frawley, Helen Lowell, Brian Donlevy, the Goldwyn Girls

Anything Goes (Paramount, 1936)
PRODUCER: Benjamin Glazer
DIRECTOR: Lewis Milestone
CAMERA: Karl Struss
CAST: Bing Crosby, Ethel Merman (as Reno Sweeney), Charles Ruggles, Ida Lupino, Arthur Treacher, Grace Bradley, Margaret Dumont

Happy Landing (20th Century Fox, 1938)
DIRECTOR: Roy del Ruth
WRITERS: Milton Sperling, Boris Ingster
CAMERA: John J. Mescall
CAST: Sonja Henie, Don Ameche, Ethel Merman (as Flo Kelly), Cesar Romero, Jean Hersholt, Billy Gilbert, the Raymond Scott Quintet

Alexander's Ragtime Band (20th Century Fox, 1938)
DIRECTOR: Henry King
WRITERS: Kathryn Scola, Lamar Trotti (adaptation, Richard Sherman)
CAMERA: J. Peverell Marley
CAST: Tyrone Power, Alice Faye, Don Ameche, Ethel Merman (as Gerry Allen), Jack Haley, Jean Hersholt, Helen Westley, Paul Hurst, Ruth Terry, John Carradine

Straight, Place and Show (20th Century Fox, 1939)
DIRECTOR: David Butler
WRITERS: M. H. Musselman, Allen Rivkin (additional dialogue, Lew Brown), based on a play by Damon Runyon and Irving Caesar
CAMERA: Ernest Palmer
CAST: The Ritz Brothers, Richard Arlen, Ethel Merman (as Linda Tyler), Phyllis Brooks

Stage Door Canteen (Sol Lesser–American Theater Wing–United Artists, 1943)
DIRECTOR: Frank Borzage
WRITER: Delmer Daves
CAMERA: Harry J. Wild
CAST: Cheryl Walker, William W. Terry, Marjorie Riordan, Lon MacAllister, Margaret Early, plus many guest stars, including Ethel Merman, Katharine Cornell, Katharine Hepburn, Helen Hayes, Ina Claire, Alfred Lunt, Lynn Fontanne, Judith Anderson, Edgar Bergen and Charlie McCarthy, Aline McMahon, Harpo Marx, George Raft, Tallulah Bankhead, Gertrude Lawrence, Gypsy Rose Lee, Virginia Grey

Call Me Madam (20th Century Fox, 1953)
PRODUCER: Sol C. Stegel
DIRECTOR: Walter Lang
WRITER: Arthur Sheekman
CAMERA: Leon Shamroy
CAST: Ethel Merman (as Sally Adams), George Sanders, Donald O'Connor, Vera-Ellen, Billy DeWolfe, Walter Slezak, Ludwig Stossel, Lilia Skala

There's No Business Like Show Business (20th Century Fox, 1954)
DIRECTOR: Walter Lang
WRITERS: Phoebe and Henry Ephron (Lamar Trotti, story)
CAMERA: Leon Shamroy

CAST: Ethel Merman (as Molly Donahue), Dan Dailey, Donald O'Connor, Mitzi Gaynor, Marilyn Monroe, Johnnie Ray, Hugh O'Brian, Richard Eastham, Frank McHugh, Rhys Williams, Lee Patrick

It's a Mad, Mad, Mad, Mad World (Stanley Kramer—United Artists, 1963)
PRODUCER/DIRECTOR: Stanley Kramer
WRITERS: William and Tania Rose
CAMERA: Ernest Laszlo
CAST: Spencer Tracy, Edie Adams, Milton Berle, Sid Caesar, Buddy Hackett, Ethel Merman (as Mrs. Marcus), Dorothy Provine, Mickey Rooney, Dick Shawn, Phil Silvers, Terry-Thomas, Jonathan Winters, plus many guest stars, including Jimmy Durante, Jerry Lewis, Don Knotts, Joe E. Brown, ZaSu Pitts, Ben Blue, Paul Ford

The Art of Love (Universal, 1965)
DIRECTOR: Norman Jewison
WRITER: Carl Reiner, from a story by Richard Alan Simmons and William Sackheim
CAMERA: Russell Metty
CAST: James Garner, Dick Van Dyke, Elke Sommer, Angie Dickinson, Ethel Merman (as Madame Coco la Fontaine), Carl Reiner

Won Ton Ton, the Dog Who Saved Hollywood (Columbia, 1976)
PRODUCER: David V. Picker
DIRECTOR: Michael Winner
WRITERS: Arnold Schulman, Cy Howard
CAMERA: Richard H. Kline
CAST: Bruce Dern, Madeline Kahn, Art Carney, Teri Garr, Phil Silvers, plus many guest stars, including Richard Arlen, Milton Berle, Janet Blair, Joan Blondell, Yvonne De Carlo, Alice Faye, Rhonda Fleming, Dick Haymes, Dorothy Lamour, Virginia Mayo, Ethel Merman (as Hedda Parsons), Ann Miller, Louis Nye, Walter Pidgeon, Aldo Ray, Ann Rutherford, Rudy Vallee, Henny Youngman

Airplane! (Paramount, 1980)
PRODUCER: Jon Davison, Howard W. Koch
EXECUTIVE PRODUCERS: Jim Abrahams, David Zucker, Jerry Zucker
DIRECTOR: Jim Abrahams, David Zucker, Jerry Zucker
WRITERS: Jim Abrahams, David Zucker, Jerry Zucker
CAMERA: Joseph F. Biroc

CAST: Robert Hays, Julie Hagerty, Peter Graves, Robert Stack, Leslie
Nielsen, Joyce Bulifant, plus many guest stars, including Howard Jarvis,
Kareem Abdul-Jabbar, Barbara Billingsley, Ethel Merman (as Lieutenant
Hurwitz)

TELEVISION APPEARANCES

Ethel Merman was a frequent guest on all manner of variety and comedy
series, talk shows, and game shows. What follows is a list of selected appearances only.

Thru the Crystal Ball, CBS, 1949
Texaco Star Theater, NBC, 1949
Toast of the Town, CBS, 1953
The Colgate Comedy Hour: The Ethel Merman Show, NBC, 1954
The Colgate Comedy Hour: Anything Goes, NBC, 1954
The Best of Broadway: Panama Hattie, CBS, 1954
The Shower of Stars: Show Stoppers, CBS, 1955
The Toast of the Town, CBS, 1955
Person to Person, CBS, 1955
The Chevy Show, NBC, 1955
GE Theatre, episode, "Reflected Glory," CBS, 1956
The U.S. Steel Hour, episode, "Honest in the Rain," CBS, 1956
The DuPont Show of the Month, NBC, 1957
The Perry Como Show, NBC, 1957
The Dinah Shore Chevy Show, NBC, 1958
The Frank Sinatra Show, ABC, 1958
The Eddie Fisher Show, NBC, 1958
The Ed Sullivan Show, CBS, 1959
Ford Startime: Ethel Merman on Broadway, NBC, 1959
The Bell Telephone Hour: The Four of Us, NBC, 1960
Perry Como's Kraft Music Hall, NBC, 1960
GE Theatre: The Gershwin Years, CBS, 1961
The Bob Hope Show, NBC, 1962
Vacation Playhouse: Maggie Brown (unsold pilot), CBS, 1963
Lincoln Center Day, CBS, 1963
The Red Skelton Hour, CBS, 1963

The Judy Garland Show, CBS, 1963, 1964

The Bell Telephone Hour: The Music of Cole Porter, NBC, 1964

The Lucy Show, episode, "Lucy Teaches Ethel Merman to Sing," CBS, 1964

The Lucy Show, episode, "Ethel Merman and the Boy Scout Show," CBS, 1964

Kraft Suspense Theatre, episode, " 'Twixt the Cup and the Lip," NBC, 1965

What's My Line?, CBS, 1965

The Mike Douglas Show, syndicated, 1965

The Dean Martin Show, NBC, 1965

I've Got a Secret, CBS, 1965

The Hollywood Palace, ABC, 1966

The Ed Sullivan Show, CBS, 1966

The Gypsy Rose Lee Show, syndicated, 1967

The Ed Sullivan Show, CBS, 1967

Annie Get Your Gun, NBC, 1967

That Girl, episode, "Pass the Potatoes, Ethel Merman," ABC, 1967

Batman, episode, "The Sport of Penguins," ABC, 1967

Batman, episode, "Horse of Another Color," ABC, 1967

Tarzan, episode, "Mountains of the Moon," NBC, 1967

The Hollywood Palace, ABC, 1967

That Girl, episode, "The Other Woman," ABC, 1968

The Ed Sullivan Show, CBS, 1968

The Dick Cavett Show, ABC, 1968

The Merv Griffin Show, syndicated, 1968

The Mike Douglas Show, syndicated, 1968

Around the World of Mike Todd, ABC, 1968

That's Life, episode, "Moving In," ABC, 1968

The Hollywood Palace, ABC, 1968

The Mike Douglas Show, syndicated, 1969

The Carol Burnett Show, CBS, 1969

The Tonight Show Starring Johnny Carson, NBC, 1970

This Is Your Life, syndicated, 1972

Bell System Family Theatre: 'S Wonderful, 'S Marvelous, 'S Gershwin, CBS, 1972

The Merv Griffin Show, syndicated, 1972

The Tonight Show Starring Johnny Carson, NBC, 1975

Dinah!, syndicated, 1975

Evening at Pops, PBS, 1976
The Big Event, NBC, 1976
The Bobby Vinton Show, syndicated, 1977
The Ted Knight Musical Comedy Variety Special Special, CBS, 1976
Steve Lawrence and Eydie Gormé Sing Cole Porter, ABC, 1977
The Muppet Show, syndicated, 1977
The Merv Griffin Show: The Belters, syndicated, 1977
Sha Na Na, syndicated, 1977
You're Gonna Love It Here (unsold pilot), CBS, 1977
The Love Boat, episode, "The Third Wheel," ABC, 1979
Musical Comedy Tonight!, PBS, 1979
Rudolph and Frosty, ABC, 1979
Hee Haw, syndicated, 1979
The Tonight Show Starring Johnny Carson, NBC, 1979
The Love Boat, episode, "Not So Fast, Gopher," ABC, 1980
Live from Lincoln Center: Beverly Sills Farewell Gala, PBS, 1981
The Love Boat, episode, "The Love Boat Musical," ABC, 1982
Night of 100 Stars, CBS, 1982
The Wonderful World of Musicals, BBC, 1982

MAJOR ACTING AWARDS AND NOMINATIONS

ANTOINETTE PERRY (TONY) AWARDS

1950: Best Actress in a Musical, *Call Me Madam*
1956: Nominee, Best Actress in a Musical, *Happy Hunting* (lost to Judy
   Holliday, *Bells Are Ringing*)
1959: Nominee, Best Actress in a Musical, *Gypsy* (lost to Mary Martin, *The
   Sound of Music*)
1972: Special Award for Lifetime Achievement

HOLLYWOOD FOREIGN PRESS (GOLDEN GLOBE) AWARDS

1953: Best Actress in a Musical or Comedy, *Call Me Madam*

DRAMA DESK AWARDS

1970: Outstanding Performance, *Hello, Dolly!*

NOTES

CHAPTER ONE

1 **"an infinitely romantic notion . . ."** Joan Didion, *Slouching Towards Bethlehem* (New York: Modern Library), p. 211

3 **"more like brother and sister than cousins,"** Ethel Merman and George Eells, *Merman* (New York: Simon & Schuster), p. 21

3 **"a beautiful fifth-floor walk-up,"** ibid., p. 21

4 **"Ethel always felt . . ."** author interview with Tony Cointreau, June 9, 2004

5 **"I'm not even sure . . ."** *Merman*, p. 21

7 **"intends to enter the business world,"** William Cullen Bryant High School yearbook, 1924

8 **"Wherever joy and laughter abound . . ."** ibid.

8 **"Boyce-Ite was an anti-freeze solution for automobiles,"** *Merman*, p. 26

CHAPTER TWO

9 **"you'd go right through the windshield,"** *Merman*, p. 28

10 **"ultra-chic,"** ibid., p. 27

12 **"a fascinating game,"** *New York Times*, n.d.

12 **"GEORGE WHITE'S SCANDALS PROVES . . ."** *Cosmopolitan*, October 1926

13 **"dog-faces,"** *New York Times*, October 11, 1963

16 **"Any time you're busted, kid,"** Gene Fowler, *Schnozzola* (New York: Viking, 1951), p. 73

16 **"I'm really a lucky guy . . ."** *Newsweek*, June 17, 1946

16 **"beat the air with his arms . . ."** ibid.

16 **"pronunciation of every word . . ."** *Brooklyn Citizen*, November 14, 1936

16 **"This girl was dynamite!"** ibid., p. 135

18 **"A big fat woman like that,"** Dody Goodman, interview with author, March 18, 2004

19 **"got to know the guys,"** *Merman,* p. 35

20 **"broke up the place,"** ibid., p. 36

CHAPTER THREE

24 **"unremitting battle against clichés,"** *New York Times Book Review,*
December 5, 1993

26 **"Miss Merman,"** *Merman,* p. 38

26 **"No, Mr. Gershwin,"** ibid., p. 38

26 **"a comely ballad singer,"** *New York Times,* September 15, 1930

26 **"promises well for her debut later in the season on the musical
comedy stage,"** ibid.

28 **"Roly-poly / Eating solely . . ."** Philip Furia, *Ira Gershwin: The Art
of the Lyricist* (New York: Oxford University Press, 1996), p. 79

28 **"all the big shots I'd sent notes and flowers to . . ."** *Merman,* p. 40

28 **"I thought my garter had snapped,"** ibid., p. 40

29 **"Ethel, do you know . . ."** ibid., p. 41

29 **"You've just been made a star!"** unpublished interview with Edward
and Agnes Zimmermann, housed at University of Southern California Cinema
Library

29 **"Did you ever see . . ."** ibid.

29 **"And never forget your shorthand,"** *Merman,* p. 41

CHAPTER FOUR

30 **"Your music does funny things to me,"** *New York Times,* September
26, 1973

30 **"One song, 'Sam and Delilah,' "** ibid., October 15, 1930

30 **"imitative of no one,"** *New Yorker,* n.d.

31 **"my favorite singer of songs,"** *Merman,* p. 48

31 **"I want you to be . . ."** ibid., p. 46

32 **"We all have that little policeman . . ."** Tony Cointreau, interview
with author, November 17, 2004

32 **"I'M TELLING YOU THE ONLY THING . . ."** *Merman,* p. 46

32 **"as close to a retraction . . ."** ibid.

33 **"Never before has Ethel Merman been more charming or stimulating. . . ."** *New York Evening Post,* April 25, 1931

36 **"finds himself the proprietor . . ."** *New York Herald Tribune,*
September 16, 1931

36 **"had no particular bearing on the song . . ."** *New York Sun,*
September 15, 1931

36 **"Ethel Merman has been called in . . ."** *New York American,* September 16, 1931

36 **"a gratifying moment,"** *Merman,* p. 56

37 **"no word has been invented to describe,"** ibid., p. 57

37 **"Ladies and gentlemen . . ."** Margaret Whiting, interview with author, November 11, 2003

38 **"My father told me . . ."** ibid.

38 **"I've never gone through . . ."** ibid.

38 **"I'm writing for pictures . . ."** ibid.

38 **"I've given you three or four good songs, . . ."** ibid.

39 **"just about walked away with the show,"** *Wilmington News,* November 17, 1932

39 **"fast on its feet . . ."** *New York Herald Tribune,* November 28, 1932

39 **"fast, loud and funny . . ."** *New York Times,* November 28, 1932

CHAPTER FIVE

41 **"I had a stupid contract,"** Jane Wyatt, interview with author, November 10, 1990

42 **"was like being in on a pass,"** *Merman,* p. 63

43 **"It was so extravagant and wonderful,"** Helen Hayes, interview with author, June 9, 1990

43 **"I was singing 'Eadie Was a Lady' . . ."** *Los Angeles Times,* December 24, 1933

44 **"all the tricks of the clever comedienne,"** *New York Daily News,* April 26, 1934

44 **"an unusual and very effective roughhouse comedienne,"** *New York Daily Mirror,* April 26, 1934

45 **"Why don't *you* tell him?"** Marilyn Cantor, interview with author, September 2, 2005

45 **"This woman is terrific . . ."** ibid.

46 **"Junior! Junior! It's Mama!"** ibid.

46 **"superior screen comedy,"** *New York Times,* November 10, 1934

46 **"The most important thing about the picture,"** *Vanity Fair,* December 1934

CHAPTER SIX

49 **"a beautiful story,"** *New York World-Telegram,* February 21, 1959

50 **"taken in three generations of theater historians,"** Ethan Mordden, *Sing for Your Supper: The Broadway Musical in the 1930s* (New York: Macmillan, 2005), p. 65

51 **"frantic flight from boredom,"** William McBrien, *Cole Porter: A Biography* (New York: Alfred A. Knopf, 1998), p. 150

51 **"like a band going by,"** ibid., p. 165

53 **"He would say . . ."** *The Stage,* December 1934

54 **"the best musical show in years,"** *Boston Evening American,* November 6, 1934

54 **"in liveliness and beauty . . ."** *Boston Post,* November 6, 1934

54 **"hers was a genuine triumph . . ."** *Boston Daily Record,* November 6, 1934

54 **"She could pick up anything . . ."** Anna Crouse, interview with author, March 18, 2005

54 **"He had the air of commander in chief,"** Nanette Fabray, interview with author, April 7, 2006

54 **"Oh, all right, I'll give you a check,"** Anna Crouse, interview with author, March 18, 2005

54 **"Vinton, I'd rather tell . . ."** ibid.

55 **"not suitable to the ears . . ."** *New York Herald Tribune,* November 22, 1934

55 **"She is vivacious and ingratiating . . ."** *New York Post,* November 22, 1934

55 **"I have a chance to show . . ."** *New York Herald Tribune,* December 2, 1934

CHAPTER SEVEN

59 **"The things that make life worth living . . ."** *New York Daily News,* October 23, 1935

59 **"My idea of real scenery . . ."** ibid.

59 **"dull and commonplace musical comedy,"** *New York Herald Tribune,* January 4, 1936

59 **"as well as possible,"** ibid.

61 **"What smells in here?"** *Omaha World-Herald,* June 21, 1936

61 **"Probably that part . . ."** ibid.

63 **"For Christ's sake,"** unpublished interview with Lew Kesler, housed at University of Southern California Cinema Library

65 **"the anatomical jokes . . ."** *New York Herald Tribune,* October 31, 1936

65 **"Broadway made vocal,"** John Mason Brown, *Two on the Aisle* (New York: W. W. Norton, 1938), p. 281

65 **"never to care about anything,"** *Brooklyn Eagle,* November 8, 1936

66 **"the public acted as if we were under quarantine,"** *Merman,* p. 83

CHAPTER EIGHT

68 **"beaming with fatuous good will,"** Pauline Kael, *5,001 Nights at the Movies* (New York: Henry Holt, 1982), p. 27

69 **"pace, humor, spectacle . . ."** *New York Times*, January 22, 1938

69 **"the Broadway torch singer . . ."** *Los Angeles Times*, January 27, 1938

70 **"a story of an imaginary character . . ."** Rudy Behlmer, *Memo from Darryl F. Zanuck* (New York: Grove Press, 1993), p. 13

71 **"demands recognition as the best musical show of the year,"** *New York Times*, August 5, 1938

71 **"a turning point of the industry . . ."** *Hollywood Reporter*, May 25, 1938

71 **"best acting part,"** *Los Angeles Examiner*, May 25, 1938

71 **"I think your performance . . ."** Ethel Merman to Sol Wurtzel, letter, May 25, 1938

71 **"I liked to be in control,"** *Merman*, p. 92

72 **"the red side,"** Joshua Logan, *Josh* (New York: Delacorte, 1976), p. 141

74 **"She took everything down in shorthand,"** Anna Crouse, interview with author, March 18, 2005

74 **"Ethel said she would try it in New Haven,"** ibid.

74 **"every indication of proving a big, popular success,"** *Boston Herald*, January 17, 1939

74 **"a field day,"** ibid.

75 **"As for Miss Merman,"** *New York Herald Tribune*, February 19, 1939

75 **"gives Merman a chance . . ."** *New York Daily News*, February 11, 1939

CHAPTER NINE

76 **"strictly carriage trade or nothing,"** *New York Journal-American*, June 15, 1959

77 **"I started giving things to people,"** *New York Herald Tribune*, January 12, 1950

79 **"The company for *Du Barry Was a Lady* was wacko,"** Lewis Turner, interview with author, March 29, 2006

79 **"When Cole got dirty,"** John Lahr, *Notes on a Cowardly Lion* (New York: Alfred A. Knopf, 1969), p. 205

80 **"She's an individual with a special way of working,"** ibid., p. 208

81 **"I saw this lady coming from one side of the stage . . ."** author interview with Don Liberto, April 5, 2006

81 **"Always give them the old fire,"** *Time*, February 27, 1984

81 **"She was screwing around all over the place,"** Lewis Turner, interview with author, March 29, 2006

81 **"It is scarcely an entertainment for children,"** *Boston Transcript*, November 20, 1939

81 **"to the accompaniment of raised eyebrows"** *Boston Globe*, November 14, 1939

82 **"comes a little short of expectations,"** *New York Times*, December 1939

82 **"Yeah. But what do I do next year?"** *Notes on a Cowardly Lion*, p. 207

82 **"Grable was happy to have a job,"** Lewis Turner, interview with author, March 29, 2006

82 **"How would you like to stick your cock up my ass and make some fudge?"** ibid.

83 **"After the curtain came down,"** ibid.

85 **"I'm not gonna be somebody's sweetheart,"** unpublished interview with Dorothy Fields, housed at University of Southern California Cinema Library

85 **"She was on the up-and-up every second,"** Lewis Turner, interview with author, March 29, 2006

86 **"a New York character in the best sense,"** Julian Myers, interview with author, February 11, 2004

87 **"I thought 'Make It Another Old-Fashioned, Please' . . ."** Betsy Blair, interview with author, December 12, 2005

87 **"HIYA, DOLLFACE!"** *Time*, April 24, 1950

87 **"perfectly democratic,"** Betsy Blair, interview with author, December 12, 2005

87 **"a weak sister,"** *Variety*, October 9, 1940

87 **"It isn't going to be easy to cut,"** *Boston Herald*, October 9, 1940

87 **"among the best in her long list of hits,"** *New York Journal*, October 31, 1940

87 **"her humor displays a new warmth,"** *Arts Monthly*, January 1941

87 **"Miss Hutton should be given one number,"** *New York Herald Tribune*, October 29, 1940

88 **"Tempers flared. Some ugly things were said,"** *Merman*, p. 116

CHAPTER TEN

90 **"June had that ambition,"** Betsy Blair, interview with author, December 12, 2005

91 **"made me feel like a star,"** June Allyson and Frances Spatz Leighton, *June Allyson* (New York: Berkeley Books, 1983), p. 16

91 **"Where the hell are all the people?"** unpublished interview with Robert Levitt, housed at University of Southern California Cinema Library

91 **"I'm terribly sorry I'm late,"** ibid.

91 **"Well, the party's over,"** ibid.

92 **"He was a very funny, acerbically funny man . . ."** David Brown, interview with author, December 8, 2005

93 **"confirmed reports of her marriage to Robert D. Levitt,"** *New York Times*, December 21, 1941

94 **"Get out of my way, Cuddles,"** *Merman*, p. 124

94 **"I never lose at this game,"** ibid.

96 **"I believe in giving customers . . ."** *Providence Sunday Journal*, May 10, 1953

96 **"I've never been poor . . ."** ibid.

97 **"an Oxford man posing as a mugg,"** ibid.

98 **"Undoubtedly the season's first smash musical hit,"** *Boston Herald*, December 19, 1942

98 **"Ethel Merman has never looked better,"** ibid.

99 **"Oh, just do whatever you want, darling,"** Betty Garrett, interview with author, June 12, 2004

99 **"One of the song and dance delights of the season,"** *New York Herald Tribune*, January 8, 1943

99 **"There is nobody quite like this Merman . . ."** *New Yorker*, January 12, 1943

99 **"because so many in the audience had men overseas,"** Lou Wills Jr., interview with author, March 18, 2005

99 **"I was so frightened,"** Betty Garrett, interview with author, June 12, 2004

100 **"Paula didn't stop doing it,"** Lou Wills Jr., interview with author, March 18, 2005

100 **"It was very traumatic for Paula,"** Betty Garrett, interview with author, June 12, 2004

101 **"a little china doll . . ."** *New York World-Telegram*, October 2, 1942

101 **"a sorry job of switching a show . . ."** *New York Herald Tribune*, October 2, 1942

102 **"bright, but it shares the structural weakness . . ."** *New York Herald Tribune*, January 24, 1943

CHAPTER ELEVEN

105 **"What the fuck is Malmaison?"** Dolores Gray, interview with author, October 31, 1990

105 **"The show would have been a perfect vehicle for Merman . . ."**
Howard Dietz, *Dancing in the Dark: Words by Howard Dietz* (New York: Quadrangle, 1974), p. 273

111 **"Ethel's sound was hers,"** Karen Morrow, interview with author, May 3, 2004.

111 **"Her mouth dropped open,"** Joshua Logan, *Josh* (New York: Delacorte Press, 1976), p. 225

111 **"Later, we dubbed it 'the goon look' . . ."** ibid.

112 **"Easy. You may think I'm playing the part . . ."** ibid., p. 227

112 **"The second act went roaringly,"** ibid.

112 **"burdened with a book . . ."** *New Yorker*, May 25, 1946

112 **"a great big, follow-the-formula . . ."** *Time*, May 27, 1946

112 **"routine,"** *New York Times*, September 29, 1946

112 **"By the time she is finished,"** *New York Times*, September 29, 1946

112 **"Miss Merman *is* Broadway,"** *Saturday Review*, June 15, 1946

113 **"If anybody asked . . ."** unpublished interview with Robert Levitt, housed at University of Southern California Cinema Library

113 **"Well, I guess that's right,"** ibid.

113 **"She did her job, she did it perfectly . . ."** Helene Whitney, interview with author, July 28, 2004

114 **"You march in that parade . . ."** William Weslow, interview with author, April 25, 2004

114 **"We never, ever do that,"** Warren Berlinger, interview with author, September 11, 2005

114 **"Get rid of her,"** ibid.

114 **"That story went right through the entire company,"** ibid.

115 **"He was full of himself,"** ibid.

115 **"The scuttlebutt was . . ."** Helene Whitney, interview with author, July 28, 2004

115 **"This was after she'd had two shows,"** Don Liberto, interview with author, April 5, 2006

115 **"What are you in here for?"** William Weslow, interview with author, April 25, 2004

116 **"I felt as if I had been freed,"** *Merman*, p. 149

117 **"when many people were on the town,"** David Brown, interview with author, December 8, 2005

117 **"Fine?"** ibid.

118 **"Because there was no air-conditioning . . ."** Nanette Fabray, interview with author, April 25, 2005

118 **"He never really amounted to a great deal,"** David Brown, interview with author, December 8, 2005

CHAPTER TWELVE

120 **"I didn't have a clue to what Ethel Merman really was,"** Marge Champion, interview with author, October 22, 2003

120 **"She seemed like the darling of the Bronx,"** ibid.

121 **"Who's Perle Mesta?"** Bob Thomas, *I Got Rhythm!: The Ethel Merman Story* (New York: G. P. Putnam's Sons, 1985), p. 105

123 **"common-law clients,"** *Esquire*, n.d.

123 **"You have to stage it with love,"** *New York Journal-American*, October 30, 1960

124 **"He was the cheapest man this side of the Mississippi,"** Helene Whitney, interview with author, July 28, 2004

124 **"poor famished faun,"** Gilbert Milstein, "Mainbocher Stands for a Fitting," *New York Times Magazine*, March 25, 1956

125 **"Next to Lee Shubert,"** ibid.

125 **"I believe in the exact opposite of realism on the stage . . ."** ibid.

127 **"In politics, I'm noncommital,"** *New York Times*, n.d.

127 **"Jerry said to me, 'This morning . . .' "** Donald Saddler, interview with author, March 23, 2004

128 **"When he gave her something she liked,"** ibid.

128 **"I hope this guy can sing and act,"** Ronald L. Davis interview with Russell Nype, DeGolyer Library, Southern Methodist University, August 22, 1983

129 **"A.S. (Academic Sexiness),"** *Mademoiselle*, n.d.

129 **"always looked as if she sniffed bicycle seats,"** Bob Ullman, interview with author, November 17, 2004

129 **"DEAR ETHEL: I KNOW YOU WILL BE BRILLIANT . . ."** telegram from Judy Garland to Ethel Merman, September 11, 1950, Museum of the City of New York

129 **"THEY MAY CALL YOU MADAME . . ."** telegram from Mary Martin to Ethel Merman, September 11, 1950, Museum of the City of New York

129 **"We gotta have something to lift the second act,"** Laurence Bergreen, *As Thousands Cheer: The Life of Irving Berlin* (New York: Viking, 1990), p. 502

129 **"Will probably not go down in the record . . ."** *Variety*, September 12, 1950

129 **"no *South Pacific*,"** *New Haven Evening Register*, September 12, 1950

130 **"What I'd like to do is a number with the kid,"** *Merman,* p. 164

130 **"We'll never get off the stage,"** *Merman,* p. 164

130 **"only an occasional flash of inspirational fire,"** *Boston Record,* September 21, 1950

130 **"Boys, as of right now I am Miss Birdseye of 1950,"** *Merman,* p. 164

131 **"the greatest musical comedy duet that's ever been written,"** Ronald L. Davis interview with Russell Nype, DeGolyer Library, Southern Methodist University, August 22, 1983

131 **"most enchanting scores . . ."** *New York Times,* October 13, 1950

131 **"indescribably soul-satisfying,"** *New York Post,* October 13, 1950

131 **"There hasn't been anything with more of a ballyhoo . . ."** *New York World-Telegram and Sun*, October 13, 1950

CHAPTER THIRTEEN

135 **"She opened her mouth and that trombone came out,"** Sheldon Harnick, interview with author, October 28, 2004

135 **"I've always suspected that Stritch's glands worked overtime,"** *Merman,* p. 180

135 **"A role is a very personal thing,"** ibid.

136 **"I gather you're well,"** ibid.

136 **"ATTA GIRL, ETHEL . . ."** *Elaine Stritch—at Liberty,* DRG CD, B000060P33, April 2002

136 **"Elaine wouldn't have known anyway . . ."** Dody Goodman, interview with author, March 18, 2004

137 **"In later years . . ."** Alex Birnbaum, interview with author, February 17, 2005

137 **"Life was so exciting and you were doing so many things,"** Ronald L. Davis interview with Russell Nype, DeGolyer Library, Southern Methodist University, August 22, 1983

139 **"shield, sounding-board, escort, and confidant,"** Christopher Wilson, *Dancing with the Devil: The Windsors and Jimmy Donahue* (New York: St. Martin's Press, 2000), p. 44

139 **"And to think I gave up a king for a queen!"** *Merman,* p. 173

139 **"epicene gigolo,"** *Dancing with the Devil,* p. 10

140 **"She loved tough, masculine guys,"** Bob Schear, interview with author, July 26, 2005

141 **"We all do it,"** Helene Whitney, interview with author, July 28, 2004

CHAPTER FOURTEEN

144 **"I am desperately afraid of too much emphasis . . ."** conference on writer's working script, April 2, 1952, 20th Century Fox files at University of Southern California Cinema Library

144 **"This is a *personality* piece,"** ibid.

144 **"I'm the Madam, and you're just one of the girls. . . ."** memo to Darryl F. Zanuck from Joseph I. Breen, April 30, 1952, University of Southern California Cinema Library

145 **"a gentle genius,"** Barbara Hale, interview with author, November 2, 2004

145 **"Guess I've got to feel that I'm reaching through to the audience,"** 20th Century Fox publicity handout, 1953, Margaret Herrick Library, Academy of Motion Picture Arts and Sciences

147 **"If anything, Ethel is better . . ."** *Los Angeles Examiner*, March 5, 1953

147 **"better than ever—in spades!"** *New York Times*, March 20, 1953

147 **"Miss Merman has appeared in previous movies,"** *New Yorker*, March 28, 1953

150 **"It is unbelievable, right now,"** *Washington Evening Star*, June 17, 1953

152 **"only one other artist has been able . . ."** *Dallas Morning News*, October 12, 1953

153 **"royal family,"** memo from Darryl F. Zanuck to Sol Siegel, December 17, 1952

153 **"a showmanship venture,"** ibid.

153 **"I think we should avoid so-called elaborate production numbers,"** memo from Darryl F. Zanuck to Sol Siegel, December 19, 1952, University of Southern California Cinema Library

153 **"We have much more story than we need,"** memo from Sol Siegel to Henry and Phoebe Ephron, February 2, 1953, housed at University of Southern California Cinema Library

153 **"she was the business agent . . ."** ibid.

154 **"simply tremendous,"** memo from Darryl F. Zanuck to Sol Siegel, December 19, 1952, University of Southern California Cinema Library

154 **"I am secretly hoping . . ."** Ethel Merman to Walter Lang, letter, November 12, 1953, Margaret Herrick Library, Academy of Motion Picture Arts and Sciences

154 **"Don't worry, I'll make it,"** 20th Century Fox publicity handout, 1954, University of Southern California Cinema Library

155 "DEAR ETHEL: WE HAD TRADE PAPER SHOWING . . ." telegram from Harry Brand to Ethel Merman, December 4, 1954, Margaret Herrick Library, Academy of Motion Picture Arts and Sciences

155 "DUST OFF ALL THE SUPERLATIVES . . ." *Film Daily*, December 8, 1954

155 "undoubtedly roll up enormous grosses . . ." ibid.

155 "an excellent show," *Motion Picture Daily*, December 8, 1954

155 "seedy plot," "caterwauling," *New Yorker*, December 25, 1954

156 "Somehow, *There's No Business Like Show Business* didn't turn out as well . . ." *Merman*, p. 192

156 "Ethel on paper is as brash . . ." *Pittsburgh Press*, July 3, 1955

157 "Ethel Merman's [book] . . ." *Best Sellers*, July 5, 1955

157 "Broadway has been good to me," *San Francisco News*, January 4, 1955

157 "We've got maybe one really good store out there," *Henderson (Kentucky) Gleaner*, August 30, 1955

158 "Bob was a brilliant businessman," Jayne Meadows, interview with author, February 16, 2005

159 "overboard on corny sentimentality," *Variety*, May 16, 1956

159 "I may be back on Broadway in a musical next season," *New York Times*, March 25, 1956

159 "This is strictly a one-show deal," *Denver Post*, April 3, 1956

CHAPTER FIFTEEN

161 "one of her weaknesses," Anna Crouse, interview with author, March 18, 2005

162 "I don't know anything about dancing," Virginia Gibson, interview with author, April 14, 2005

162 "When I went to rehearsal," ibid.

162 "If I'd wanted it sung that way," Klea Blackhurst, *Everything the Traffic Will Allow*, CD, Lunch Money Productions, B0002C72JU, 2001

162 "That man is never to speak to me again," ibid.

163 "Oh, Miss Merman—your voice is going to go into the wings," Virginia Gibson, interview with author, April 14, 2005

163 "didn't give the impression of being conscious of other writers," Mark Zeller, interview with author, June 17, 2005

164 "Well, I just thought *movie star*," Virginia Gibson, interview with author, April 14, 2005

164 "Tell them I'll be an hour late for rehearsal," Seth Riggs, interview with author, September 2, 2005

164 **"He jumped over the side . . ."** ibid.

164 **"like a monster from the deep,"** ibid.

164 **"SHUT THE FUCK UP!"** ibid.

164 **"I'M GOING TO KILL YOU, YOU SON OF A BITCH!,"** ibid.

165 **"Nobody looked at Merman, and she was furious,"** Seth Riggs, interview with author, September 2, 2005

165 **"Lamas was no big talent,"** Bob Ullman, interview with author, November 17, 2004

165 **"Fernando used to call Ethel 'the Mack Truck,'** Arlene Dahl, interview with author, July 8, 2005

165 **"too much plot,"** *Philadelphia Inquirer,* October 23, 1956

165 **"Miss Merman brings a formidable zest to everything she does,"** *Philadelphia Daily News,* October 23, 1956

165 **"Boisterous and hilarious,"** *Boston Advertiser,* November 18, 1956

166 **"It looks like a bordello,"** Arlene Dahl, interview with author, July 8, 2005

166 **"Ethel called in a designer,"** ibid.

166 **"because you could tell that they were sitting there hating it,"** Anna Crouse, interview with author, March 18, 2005

166 **"hardly more than adequate . . ."** *New York Times,* December 7, 1956

166 **"ageless and individual . . ."** *New York Journal-American,* December 7, 1956

166 **"a jeep among limousines,"** *Merman,* p. 197

166 **"If you watched her,"** Mark Zeller, interview with author, June 17, 2005

167 **"He looked like he was anticipating Ethel coming onstage,"** Jack Dabdoub, interview with author, September 12, 2005

167 **"Some of the kids were saying,"** Virginia Gibson, interview with author, April 14, 2005

168 **"not even the new songs . . ."** *Variety,* June 5, 1957

168 **"improperly censured,"** *New York Times,* April 8, 1958

168 **"It was the most gentlemanly, wonderful thing,"** Mark Zeller, interview with author, June 17, 2005

169 **"Do you think it will be better for you?"** Virginia Gibson, interview with author, April 14, 2005

169 **"I'd like to do one more big show,"** *Denver Post,* December 10, 1957

170 **"She didn't want to be late for meeting her father,"** Virginia Gibson, interview with author, April 14, 2005

170 **"just seemed to go haywire,"** *Merman,* p. 167

171 **"habit-forming, dangerous, and new drugs without prescriptions,"** *New York Times,* November 4, 1960

171 **"this horrible thing,"** *Merman,* p. 169

CHAPTER SIXTEEN

173 **"Mark, I have the greatest script—*finally!*"** Mark Zeller, interview with author, June 17, 2005

173 **"Have you seen *Fanny*?"** *New York Times,* n.d.

174 **"There's a horse's ass for every light on Broadway,"** ibid.

174 **"What they charge us for this room . . ."** television interview between Gypsy Rose Lee and Ethel Merman, *The Gypsy Rose Lee Show* (syndicated, 1967)

174 **"the need for recognition,"** Arthur Laurents, *Original Story by Arthur Laurents* (New York: Alfred A. Knopf, 2000), p. 382

178 **"a talking dog,"** ibid., p. 378

178 **"Teacher,"** *Merman,* p. 204

178 **"I thought in the first act,"** Stephen Sondheim, interview with author, July 8, 2005

178 **"Brains was not her forte,"** ibid.

179 **"I had to sing at the final audition,"** Jack Klugman, interview with author, August 5, 2003

180 **"Ethel was a calliope. Mother was a clarinet,"** June Havoc, interview with author, April 2, 2004

180 **"So for the first several days . . ."** Jack Klugman, interview with author, August 5, 2003

180 **"She would never look at you onstage,"** ibid.

181 **"I swear it was the best performance . . ."** Carole Cook, interview with author, July 31, 2005

181 **"Everyone always said that about her,"** ibid.

181 **"She didn't care for anyone who she thought was competing with her,"** Jack Klugman, interview with author, August 5, 2003

181 **"He kept trying different things,"** Sandra Church, interview with author, August 3, 2005

182 **"Ethel played her as a heroine,"** Jack Klugman, interview with author, August 5, 2003

183 **"I've had people come backstage . . ."** *Philadelphia Inquirer,* n.d.

183 **"We'll get to it next week,"** Margaret Styne, interview with author, September 14, 2005

183 **"He got up onstage with Jerry,"** ibid.

183 **"DEAREST ETHEL GLAD YOU ARE BACK . . ."** telegram from Frederick Brisson to Ethel Merman, May 21, 1959, Theater Collection, Museum of the City of New York

184 **"the best damn musical I've seen in years,"** *New York Times,* May 22, 1959

184 **"Stephen Sondheim has set revealing lyrics . . ."** *New York Mirror,* May 22, 1959

184 **"her incomparable ability to belt out a song . . ."** *New York Post,* May 31, 1959

185 **"Since she acts the part of an indomitable personality,"** *New York Times,* May 31, 1959

185 **"Miss Merman not only sings, she acts,"** *New Yorker,* May 30, 1959

185 **"Once Miss Merman has started to sing,"** ibid.

186 **"Jerry made her act as no one did,"** Sandra Church, interview with author, August 3, 2003

186 **"People said she walked through the show,"** Jack Klugman, interview with author, August 5, 2003

187 **"Is the pope Catholic?"** ibid.

188 **"How are you going to buck a nun?"** *Merman,* p. 206

188 **"She took my hand,"** Alice Playten, interview with author, July 14, 2003

190 **" 'Miss Merman doesn't care how sick your daughter is,' "** Jacqueline Mayro, interview with author, July 13, 2003

190 **"Mervyn LeRoy came to see the play nine times . . ."** Jack Klugman, interview with author, August 5, 2003

191 **"those son of a bitches,"** Richard Grayson, interview with author, March 28, 2005

191 **"I'm really excited about coming to Rochester,"** *Rochester Times-Union,* March 21, 1961

191 **"The quality of our notices . . ."** Richard Grayson, interview with author, March 28, 2005

191 **"a moderately weak musical . . ."** *Christian Science Monitor,* April 25, 1961

191 **"Touring! I'm sold!"** *Detroit News,* April 15, 1961

192 **"You've got to promise me you'll do that,"** Richard Grayson, interview with author, March 28, 2005

192 **"She never felt the same way about me after that,"** ibid.

CHAPTER SEVENTEEN

194 **"Jackie had a terrible mouth,"** Tony Cointreau, interview with author, February 16, 2005

194 **"Ethel, I love you!"** Barbara Seaman, *Lovely Me* (New York: William Morrow, 1987), p. 248

194 **"I just never could go that route,"** Tony Cointreau, interview with author, February 16, 2005

195 **"thoroughly repellent,"** *New Yorker*, November 17, 1962

196 **"I used to do a take-off on her,"** Edie Adams, interview with author, August 2, 2003

196 **"For filmdom functions . . ."** *Los Angeles Times*, September 23, 1962

196 **"the pleasure dome of the new prefab promised land,"** Nick Tosches, *Dino: Living High in the Dirty Business of Dreams* (New York: Delta, 1992), p. 203

197 **"Up until last year,"** *Merman in Vegas*, audio recording, Collectables COL-CD-6193

197 **"Ethel's act simply did not fly,"** Phyllis Diller, interview with author, November 18, 2003

198 **"Although Ethel is a wonder, she is human,"** *Boston Herald American*, June 11, 1963

198 **"He said that he would like to set up a time to audition it,"** Jerry Herman, interview with author, October 11, 2005

198 **"My grandmother was a very powerful personality,"** Barbara Geary, interview with author, January 15, 2004

199 **"I felt that she really wanted this to happen,"** Susan Watson, interview with author, February 4, 2005

199 **"What do I have to do to get hot,"** Tom Korman, interview with author, May 4, 2005

200 **"Ethel! I'm here!"** Kaye Ballard, interview with author, August 11, 2005

200 **"redundant, ridiculous, and too insistent,"** *Newsweek*, November 18, 1963

200 **"outright disgust,"** ibid.

201 **"You can't speak against that girl,"** Tony Cointreau, interview with author, February 16, 2005

202 **"I can see where she fell, hook, line, and sinker,"** Tony Cointreau, interview with author, November 17, 2004

202 **"We're sitting on two chairs,"** Eric Knight, interview with author, May 23, 2005

203 **"He had hit her,"** ibid.

203 **"objected strenuously to that woman,"** *Los Angeles Times*, November 19, 1964

203 **"He told me that the real story . . ."** Barbara Geary, interview with author, January 11, 2004

203 **"It all came down to dollars and cents,"** Tony Cointreau, interview with author, November 17, 2004

CHAPTER EIGHTEEN

206 **"She's like me,"** Bruce Burroughs, interview with author, December 7, 2004

207 **"Imagine that broad not showing up,"** *New York Post*, n.d.

208 **"It stinks!"** *Valley of the Dolls* (New York: Bernard Geis & Associates, 1966), p. 84

208 **"You'll never convince me people actually read that shit,"** ibid., p. 96

208 **"Really, people don't do that,"** Donald Preston, interview with author, September 9, 2005

210 **"I can't ride,"** *Life*, August 18, 1961

211 **"I'm so glad that you're Bruce's *leading lady*,"** Ronn Carroll, interview with author, July 8, 2003

211 **"Jesus, they know what I look like,"** ibid.

211 **"She would dumbfound people,"** Jerry Orbach, interview with author, July 20, 2004

211 **"Little Sure Shot is older,"** *New York Times*, June 1, 1966

212 **"Benay, this sounds terrible,"** Ronn Carroll, interview with author, July 8, 2003

212 **"I don't care what you say to her,"** ibid.

212 **"Ethel, he's just reacting,"** Jerry Orbach, interview with author, July 20, 2004

212 **"Miss Merman, I come in here every day at four-thirty,"** Ronn Carroll, interview with author, July 8, 2003

213 **"Oh, yeah?"** ibid.

213 **"Forget it, kid,"** ibid.

213 **"this terribly sweet . . ."** ibid.

213 **"I hope you don't mind,"** ibid.

213 **"Sure, honey,"** ibid.

213 **"really scares me,"** Tony Cointreau, interview with author, February 1, 2006

214 **"If I had to do all those things,"** Mark Zeller, interview with author, June 17, 2005

215 **"I think that it was kind of unintentional suicide,"** Barbara Geary, interview with author, September 8, 2005

CHAPTER NINETEEN

217 **"Ethel was not a person who didn't like what she had,"** Carleton Varney, interview with author, February 1, 2006

217 **"They don't know how to sell a gag,"** David Brunetti, interview with author, September 10, 2006

219 **"She cut him dead,"** Arthur Bartow, interview with author, March 29, 2005

219 **"So we did it again,"** John DeMain, interview with author, July 10, 2004

219 **"WHO DID SHE FUCK TO GET TWO DANCE NUMBERS?"** Donna McKechnie, interview with author, July 21, 2003

220 **"It was drinky-poo, drinky-poo,"** John Kenley, interview with author, May 4, 2005

220 **"wanted to do some kind of high-school production,"** John DeMain, interview with author, July 10, 2004

222 **"No, we just want to keep it in the theater,"** Phyllis Diller, interview with author, November 18, 2003

222 **"I tried, in every way,"** Marge Champion, interview with author, October 22, 2003

222 **"This steamroller suddenly happened to the show,"** Marcia Lewis, interview with author, April 30, 2004

222 **"She came down the steps, and they just wouldn't stop,"** John Montgomery, interview with author, September 10, 2005

223 **"exactly as trumpet-clean . . ."** *New York Times,* April 12, 1970

224 **"Helene—she didn't commit suicide,"** Helene Whitney, interview with author, July 28, 2004

224 **"She was playing a matinee one day, and she was pissed off at something,"** Biff Liff, interview with author, June 8, 2004

CHAPTER TWENTY

228 **"Grandmother—what does that mean?"** Mary Henderson, interview with author, November 3, 2006

229 **"That's just like your mother,"** Barbara Geary, interview with author, September 8, 2005

229 **"Oh, my God, I am so embarrassed,"** Tony Cointreau, interview with author, February 1, 2006

230 **"I found her one of the most difficult people I've ever represented,"** Tom Korman, interview with author, June 11, 2005

230 **"You know, Miss Merman,"** Lionel Larner, interview with author, April 25, 2005

230 **"Faggot!"** ibid.

230 **"You've seated me next to a fag!"** Carleton Varney, interview with author, February 1, 2006

231 **"more my personal manager than an agent,"** *Merman,* p. 254

231 **"Although everybody told me . . ."** Dr. Albert Attia, interview with author, September 28, 2005

232 **"She would invite a group of us to dinner,"** Kay Armen, interview with author, January 30, 2006

232 **"Mama, I want you to get well,"** ibid.

233 **"Lionel, look at this place,"** Lionel Larner, interview with author, April 25, 2005

233 **"Well, you can't . . ."** ibid.

233 **"Ethel, you are the first lady of the American musical theater,"** ibid.

235 **"With Angie it was really a marvelous ending,"** *Performing Arts,* n.d.

235 **"I don't want to look like a Ubangi!"** Lionel Larner, interview with author, April 25, 2005

236 **"Gardiner was crazy about Merman,"** Eric Knight, interview with author, May 23, 2005

237 **"Look at that fuckin' moon!"** Nanette Fabray, interview with author, April 25, 2005

238 **"If there was a kinder, nicer lady, I have never met her,"** *New York Post,* July 26, 1975

238 **"I don't know what to do about Bobby,"** Rose Marie, interview with author, May 3, 2004

239 **"a sad, dull, middle-class lady,"** Benay Venuta, interview with Barbara Seaman, April 17, 1984

239 **"I've got something to tell you,"** ibid.

240 **"All I want is to travel first class,"** Tony Cointreau, interview with author, February 1, 2006

240 **"Let's go to the Chinks,"** ibid.

240 **"Missy Merman!"** ibid.

240 **"It'll be good exposure,"** ibid.

241 **"But you don't have to be Lucille Ball,"** ibid.

242 **"A big theatrical problem . . ."** *West Side TV Shopper,* August 10, 1983

242 **"With Chowsie?"** Bob Schear, interview with author, July 26, 2005

242 **"Don't know why / There's no action in this fly,"** ibid.

243 **"HELLO! What are you doing here?"** ibid.

243 **"I was in the midst,"** *Lifestyles with Beverly Sills,* NBC-TV, May 1977

243 **"Jesus. Just look how they've fucked up Times Square,"** Bob Schear, interview with author, July 26, 2005

243 **"when we look at the stage,"** Donald Saddler, interview with author, March 23, 2004

244 **"the meaning of a love-in,"** *Merman,* p. 260

244 **"Ethel Merman is the bonfire,"** *New York Times,* May 13, 1977

244 **"We've lost something,"** *New York Post,* May May 21, 1977

245 **"HI! I'M ETHEL MERMAN!"** Tony Cointreau, interview with author, June 9, 2004

245 **"I was always afraid that she would give them cardiac arrest,"** ibid.

245 **"HI, POP!"** Bob Schear, interview with author, July 26, 2005

CHAPTER TWENTY-ONE

247 **"Would you get a fuckin' look at that marquee?"** Bob Schear, interview with author, July 26, 2005

247 **"She always produced,"** Eric Knight, interview with author, May 23, 2005

247 **"I thought the thunder was the timpani,"** ibid.

247 **"Sorry, can't sign anything!"** Scott Barnes, interview with author, June 10, 2004

248 **"She's fuckin' lip-synching!"** Bob Schear, interview with author, July 26, 2005

249 **"her straight-from-the shoulder manner . . ."** *New York Times,* June 16, 1978

249 **"My book is number eight . . ."** *Dallas Times-Herald,* June 22, 1978

249 **"Why Jimmy?"** Tony Cointreau, interview with author, February 1, 2006

250 **"the warmth of a fjord,"** *Village Voice,* August 27, 1979

251 **"Ethel, are you all right?"** Nanette Fabray, interview with author, April 7, 2006

251 **"It's me, Ethel,"** Sandra Church, interview with author, August 3, 2003

253 **"Oh, stupid window,"** Barbara Geary, interview with author, January 15, 2004

253 **"It wasn't really her cup of tea,"** ibid.

253 **"I wasn't really into doing commercial theater . . ."** ibid.

255 **"DID I EVER ASK YOU TO DO ANYTHING ABOUT NAMING A THEATER FOR ME?"** Bob Schear, interview with author, July 26, 2005

255 **"Dear Bob—,"** Bob Schear to Ethel Merman, letter, personal collection of Bob Schear

255 **"shit,"** Eileen Farrell, interview with author, April 16, 1997

256 **"What was better tonight—my head voice or my chest voice?"** Robert Gardiner, interview with author, March 21, 2005

256 **"the beginning of the end,"** ibid.

256 **"She always thanked Eric,"** ibid.

257 **"Miss Merman's performance was, as it always has been,"** *New York Times,* May 12, 1982

257 **"P.P.S—Do you know—I heard and understood every damn word you sang,"** *New York Post,* May 11, 1982

257 **"WANNA GO?"** Tony Cointreau, interview with author, November 17, 2004

258 **"JEEZUS!"** Donald Pippin, interview with author, February 22, 2005

258 **"Bacall was, for the first time . . ."** ibid.

258 **"In those days,"** Paula Palma, interview with author, February 1, 2006

259 **"How dare you allow them to sleep in the same bedroom?"** Barbara Geary, interview with author, September 8, 2005

259 **"We thought she was just being monstrous,"** Barbara Geary, interview with author, September 8, 2005

CHAPTER TWENTY-TWO

260 **"THERE'S NO DAY LIKE A BIRTHDAY,"** telegram from Ronald Reagan to Ethel Merman, January 14, 1983, personal collection of Bob Schear

261 **"Millions of people will miss seeing us on the 'Emmys,' "** Ethel Merman to Mary Martin, letter, September 7, 1982, personal collection of George Dansker

261 **"I'm very anxious about this performance,"** Dr. Albert Attia, interview with author, September 28, 2005

262 **"delighting fellow patients,"** *New York Times,* April 26, 1983

262 **"going smoothly,"** ibid.

263 **"How could this happen to me?"** Carole Cook, interview with author, July 31, 2005

263 **"terrible,"** Tony Cointreau, interview with author, February 1, 2006

263 **"not mature enough,"** Barbara Geary, interview with author, September 8, 2005

264 **"She couldn't speak,"** ibid.

264 **"ETHEL MERMAN, CLARION VOICE OF MUSICAL COMEDY FOR DECADES, IS DEAD AT 76,"** *New York Times,* February 16, 1984

264 **"Beginning in 1930, and continuing for more than a quarter-century thereafter,"** *New York Times,* February 16, 1984

264 **"her delighted customers . . ."** ibid.

265 **"prize graduate,"** *New York Times,* February 27, 1984

265 **"We were not only proud of her . . ."** ibid.

265 **"ETHEL MERMAN—YOU'RE THE TOP,"** Bob Schear, interview with author, December 2, 2006

266 **"Merman belonged to an era that is gone,"** Donald Pippin, interview with author, February 22, 2005

267 **"One look at that Christmas tree,"** Margaret Whiting, interview with author, November 11, 2003

BIBLIOGRAPHY

Abbott, George. *Mister Abbott*. New York: Random House, 1963.

Atkinson, Brooks. *Broadway*. New York: Macmillan, 1970.

Allyson, June (with Frances Spatz Leighton). *June Allyson*. New York: G. P. Putnam's Sons, 1982. New York: Berkley, 1983.

Barrett, Mary Ellin. *Irving Berlin: A Daughter's Memoir*. New York: Simon & Schuster, 1994.

Behlmer, Rudy. *Memo from Darryl F. Zanuck*. New York: Grove Press, 1993.

Berg, A. Scott. *Goldwyn: A Biography*. New York: Alfred A. Knopf, 1989.

Bergreen, Laurence. *As Thousands Cheer: The Life of Irving Berlin*. New York: Viking, 1990.

Berle, Milton (and Haskel Frankel). *Milton Berle: An Autobiography*. New York: Delacorte, 1974.

Brown, John Mason. *Two on the Aisle: Ten Years of the American Theatre in Performance*. New York: W. W. Norton, 1938.

Didion, Joan. *Slouching Towards Bethlehem*. New York: Modern Library, 2000 (originally published by Farrar, Straus, & Giroux).

Dietz, Howard. *Dancing in the Dark: Words by Howard Dietz*. New York: Quadrangle, 1974.

Eells, George. *The Life That Late He Led*. New York: G. P. Putnam's Sons, 1967.

Eliot, Marc. *Cary Grant: A Biography*. New York: Harmony, 2004.

Fordin, Hugh. *Getting to Know Him: A Biography of Oscar Hammerstein II*. New York: Random House, 1997.

Fowler, Gene. *Schnozzola: The Story of Jimmy Durante*. New York: Viking, 1951.

Furia, Philip. *Ira Gershwin: The Art of the Lyricist*. New York: Oxford University Press, 1996.

Gavin, James. *Intimate Nights: The Golden Age of New York Cabaret*. New York: Grove, Weidenfeld, 1991.

Grant, Mark N. *The Rise and Fall of the Broadway Musical*. Boston: Northeastern University Press, 2004.

Green, Stanley. *Broadway Musicals of the '30s*. New York: Da Capo Press, 1971.

Herman, Jerry (and Marilyn Stasio). *Showtune: A Memoir*. New York: Plume, 2005.

Hirsch, Foster. *Harold Prince and the American Musical Theater*. New York: Cambridge University Press, 1989.

Kael, Pauline. *5,001 Nights at the Movies*. New York: Holt, Rinehart, and Winston, 1982 (Henry Holt edition, 1991).

Kimball, Robert. *Cole*. New York: Holt, Rinehart, and Winston, 1971.

———. *The Complete Lyrics of Ira Gershwin*. New York: Alfred A. Knopf, 1993.

———, and Albert Simon. *The Gershwins*. New York: Atheneum, 1973.

Kissel, Howard. *David Merrick: The Abominable Showman*. New York: Applause Books, 1993.

Lahr, John. *Notes on a Cowardly Lion*. New York: Alfred A. Knopf, 1969.

Laufe, Abe. *Broadway's Greatest Musicals*. New York: Funk & Wagnalls, 1997.

Laurents, Arthur. *Original Story by Arthur Laurents: A Memoir of Broadway and Hollywood*. New York: Alfred A. Knopf, 2000.

Levy, Shawn. *Rat Pack Confidential*. New York: Doubleday, 1998.

Lobenthal, Joel. *Tallulah! The Life and Times of a Leading Lady*. New York: Regan Books, 2004.

Logan, Joshua. *Josh: My Up and Down, In and Out Life*. New York: Delacorte Press, 1976.

Martin, Mary. *My Heart Belongs*. New York: William Morrow and Company, 1976.

Marsolais, Ken, Rodger McFarlane, and Tom Viola. *Broadway Day & Night*. New York: Pocket Books, 1992.

McBrien, William. *Cole Porter*. New York: Alfred A. Knopf, 1998.

Merman, Ethel (and George Eells). *Merman*. New York: Simon & Schuster, 1978.

——— (and Pete Martin). *Who Could Ask for Anything More?* New York: Doubleday, 1955.

Mordden, Ethan. *One More Kiss: The Broadway Musical in the 1970s*. New York: Palgrave Macmillan, 2003.

———. *Sing for Your Supper: The Broadway Musical in the 1930s*. New York: Palgrave Macmillan, 2005.

Mosley, Leonard. *Zanuck: The Rise and Fall of Hollywood's Last Tycoon*. Boston: Little, Brown & Co., 1984.

Preminger, Erik Lee. *My G-String Mother*. Boston: Little, Brown & Co., 1984.

Reed, Rex. *People Are Crazy Here.* New York: Delacorte Press, 1974.

Rodgers, Richard. *Musical Stages.* New York: Random House, 1975.

Rogers, Ginger. *My Story.* New York: HarperCollins, 1991.

Rose Marie. *Hold the Roses.* Lexington: University Press of Kentucky, 2002.

Rosenberg, Deena. *Fascinating Rhythm: The Collaboration of George and Ira Gershwin.* New York: Dutton, 1991.

Russell, Rosalind (and Chris Chase). *Life Is a Banquet.* New York: Random House, 1977.

Seaman, Barbara. *Lovely Me: The Life of Jacqueline Susann.* New York: William Morrow, 1987.

Secrest, Meryle. *Stephen Sondheim: A Life.* New York: Alfred A. Knopf, 1998.

Shipman, David. *Judy Garland: The Secret Life of an American Legend.* New York: Hyperion, 1992.

Solomon, Aubrey. *Twentieth Century–Fox: A Corporate and Financial History.* Lanham, Maryland: Scarecrow Press, 1988.

Stevenson, Isabel, ed. *The Tony Award.* New York: Crown, 1987.

Taylor, Theodore. *Jule: The Story of Composer Jule Styne.* New York: Random House, 1979.

Thomas, Bob. *I Got Rhythm: The Ethel Merman Story.* New York: G. P. Putnam's Sons, 1985.

Tosches, Nick. *Dino: Living High in the Dirty Business of Dreams.* New York: Delta Books, 1992.

Trager, James. *The New York Chronology.* New York: HarperCollins, 2003.

Winer, Deborah Grace. *On the Sunny Side of the Street: The Life and Lyrics of Dorothy Fields.* New York: Simon & Schuster, 1997.

Zadan, Craig. *Sondheim & Co.* New York: Harper & Row, 1986.

INDEX